Building the Federal Schoolhouse

Building the Federal Schoolhouse

Localism and the American Education State

DOUGLAS S. REED

OXFORD

UNIVERSITY PRESS

Oxford University Press is a department of the University of Oxford.
It furthers the University's objective of excellence in research, scholarship,
and education by publishing worldwide.

Oxford   New York

Auckland   Cape Town   Dar es Salaam   Hong Kong   Karachi
Kuala Lumpur   Madrid   Melbourne   Mexico City   Nairobi
New Delhi   Shanghai   Taipei   Toronto

With offices in

Argentina   Austria   Brazil   Chile   Czech Republic   France   Greece
Guatemala   Hungary   Italy   Japan   Poland   Portugal   Singapore
South Korea   Switzerland   Thailand   Turkey   Ukraine   Vietnam

Oxford is a registered trademark of Oxford University Press
in the UK and certain other countries.

Published in the United States of America by
Oxford University Press
198 Madison Avenue, New York, NY 10016

© Douglas S. Reed 2014

Library of Congress Cataloging-in-Publication Data
Reed, Douglas S., 1964–
Building the federal schoolhouse : localism and the American education state / Douglas S. Reed.
pages cm
Summary: "Creating a truly national school system has, over the past fifty years, reconfigured local
expectations and practices in American public education. Through a 50-year examination of Alexandria,
Virginia, this book reveals how the 'education state' is nonetheless shaped by the commitments of local
political regimes and their leaders and constituents."—Provided by publisher.
ISBN 978–0–19–983848–6 (hardback)
1. Education and state—United States.   2. School improvement programs—United States.   I. Title.
LC89.R44 2014
379—dc23
2013047758

1 3 5 7 9 8 6 4 2
Printed in the United States of America
on acid-free paper

To my father, Donald James Reed, and to the memory of my mother, Caron Ann Reed.

The past is a great resource for the imagination;
it adds a new dimension to life, but on condition that
it be seen as the past of the present,
and not as another and disconnected world.
John Dewey, *Democracy and Education*

CONTENTS

Contents

LIST OF ILLUSTRATIONS

Figures

Tables

LIST OF ILLUSTRATIONS

Figures

Tables

PREFACE

In July 1963, President John Kennedy wrote a letter to a Mr. Gorman Ridgely, then chairman of the School Board in Alexandria, Virginia, about school dropouts. In the midst of that tumultuous summer of activism, President Kennedy sought the help of educators to solve "the grave civil rights problems faced by this Nation."[1] He specifically wanted help undertaking a "massive, nationwide effort ... to persuade our young people to return to school in September." According to the letter, the topic of school dropouts had surfaced during a meeting of educators at the White House, and President Kennedy took to the bully pulpit to ask personally for Ridgely's assistance in combating the problem. The request was a little complicated, however. Virginia had reluctantly given up its campaign of "Massive Resistance" against *Brown v. Board of Education* only four years earlier, and Alexandria's own record of compliance with *Brown* was, at best, paltry. Ridgely may have felt that Kennedy's letter was an indirect effort to pressure the school district to employ more active desegregation measures. Or he may have felt that the letter was simply another federal attempt to meddle in yet another local educational issue.

The President's letter, however, reassured him that "[i]t is the American tradition, which we all wish to preserve, that the responsibility for education remain at the State and local level." Nonetheless, Kennedy wanted Ridgely to document Alexandria's efforts—and gave him a deadline: "I ... suggest that you advise Commissioner [Francis] Keppel of the United States Office of Education of your progress—I would hope there could be an initial report by August fifteenth," with a follow-up report due at the end of September.[2] President Kennedy's request for Ridgely's assistance to help calm unrest in an era of demonstrations and protests was not remarkable. What *was* remarkable, however, was the president's inability, in 1963, to rely upon existing institutional and bureaucratic relationships between the federal government and a local school district to achieve his goals. The President of the United States had to *ask* a local school board president to report back to the

United States Commissioner of Education on an informational matter concerning civil rights and education.[3]

Within three short years, however, the "chain of command" for federal authority over education had grown so robust that mid-level Health, Education and Welfare Department officials were threatening to withdraw Alexandria's federal funding unless it redrew its school attendance zones to ensure better integrated schools. Forty-three years later federal authorities were more demanding, telling school officials that recent poor test scores in Alexandria's only high school meant that school officials had one of the four options: 1) close the school, 2) turn it into a charter school, 3) fire its principal and at least half of its teachers, or 4) fire its principal and implement a new system of evaluating teachers tied to student test scores (among other changes). Within two generations, the federal government had gone from an inability to gather even the simplest information about school district actions to requiring that particular individuals be fired for failing to meet federal criteria for student performance. This book seeks to tell the story of that change in educational governance. In short, it seeks to explain how what I call the "education state" came into being over the past fifty years as local, state, and federal authorities constructed a new template for the operation of schools in the United States.

In using the term "education state," I am explicitly leaning on the reader's familiarity with the term "welfare state," but I realize the phrasing may sound odd to readers accustomed to neatly assigning educational policies and practices to the proper category of local, state, and federal. By using the term the "education state" I seek to draw attention to the new forms of authority that exist in public education and how those forms of authority change our conceptions of both local politics and appropriate federal action in public education. This book contends that we can best understand public education in the United States not by viewing its constituent parts in isolation, but instead by understanding how they collectively operate as the education state. I define the education state as the set of resources and institutions—generally, but not exclusively, composed of local, state, and federal actors[4]—that organizes and conducts the public schooling of children in the United States. Within this education state, localities—cities, towns, school districts, counties—run the vast majority of this nation's schools, under the authority of state governments. They do so within a federal framework that has for the past fifty years aimed to expand educational opportunity and to make those opportunities more equitable. Together, these actors at multiple levels of governance and policymaking comprise the education state in the United States, both organizing schooling and expending resources within institutions. While many analysts, politicians, policymakers, and citizens alike assume that what happens in schools is simply the result of adding together local, state, and federal dictates, this book argues that schools are increasingly governed by an education state that is more than the sum of its parts. The process of building the education state over the past fifty years, replete with its tensions and contradictions, is the story of *Building the Federal Schoolhouse*.

Like other elements of the American state, the education state is complex and, at times, contradictory, generally because its constituent parts emerged at different times and have sought to achieve different goals. In short, education policy in the United States is split between two competing commitments: localism and equal educational opportunity. In turn, these rival commitments give a distinctive character to the education state in the United States. This book is an effort to understand how those values and their expression by different actors have, over the past fifty years, shaped the capacities and commitments of the education state.

Historically, the organization of schooling in the United States has been a local affair—funded primarily out of local property tax receipts, administered by a locally hired superintendent and governed, usually, by a local elected school board. The role of state governments in this activity was important but limited. The nineteenth century state constitutions that were adopted in the course of US westward expansion mandated the creation of public school systems, provided some general overview of their structure, and expended modest amounts of state money to support the enterprise, but they generally left the financing, operation, and conduct of the US public educational system to local authorities.

This localist version of the education state was lean, but it could also be fierce. The education state of the early twentieth century was a powerful actor: It compelled school attendance for all youngsters (sometimes against parental wishes); sorted students into categories of learning ability, while institutionalizing deaf, handicapped or blind students at centralized state-run facilities; and created and maintained systems of intentionally unequal schooling to ensure that African Americans would be subject to enduring disadvantage within American society. The authority of local and state-run institutions to engage in these activities was largely unquestioned. Local school districts—as agents of state-level, plenary police powers—could undertake a wide range of activities to promote their vision of the public good. If that locally articulated vision clashed with national norms or practices, the existing institutional framework did not provide much space to challenge local actors.

In the main, however, the growth of the public school system over the nineteenth and twentieth centuries in the United States was closely tied to the nation's self-understanding as a meritocratic society. In this system talent, work and ambition, combined with the opportunities that the educational system afforded, would yield individual success that would also generate benefits for society. Over time, public education became a cornerstone of America's self-conception: a democratic society that provided economic opportunity and social mobility to its citizens.

Yet because the educational system was highly localized, it was uneven and unequal. While national organizations of interest groups and teacher-training schools provided common templates of organizational forms (think of the comprehensive public high school or graded, age-leveled classrooms), the politics and administration of schools largely responded to local circumstances. Schooling was one of the most widespread governmental operations in the United States, and one in which authority was closely tied to local actors and local funders. Accountability for the outcomes of this enterprise—to the extent that accountability was expected—came through local school board elections and local decisions about property tax rates. Rarely did supporters of public schooling endorse the view that federal authorities ought to have more—or any—say in the organization and operations of schools.

That sentiment began a long process of change in 1954, when the United States Supreme Court declared in *Brown v. Board of Education* that public schools segregated by race violated the 14th Amendment of the US Constitution. Today, through such policies as No Child Left Behind and Race to the Top, the federal government is deeply involved in decisions about schools. Federal officials, judges, and Congress have undertaken these actions, for the most part, to promote the equity of schooling and to provide greater opportunities to students who have been excluded from quality education in the United States. These changes, however, have also reconfigured local politics and have confronted enormous implementation challenges because of the localist assumptions of American education.

This book seeks to understand how the construction of the "federal schoolhouse"—a federally defined, yet locally operated educational system—both responded to local circumstances and altered those local circumstances. Building the federal schoolhouse over the past fifty years has meant wresting away from local authorities exclusive control over public education in an effort to create new modes of public education within the same 'institutional skin.' This has required destructive as well as creative aspirations—seeking to limit the priorities and commitments of local regimes, but also forcing them to undertake new and transformative activities. This developmental process has produced a hybrid education state in which the traditional boundaries of intergovernmental relations (federal, state, and local) blur as multiple actors claim authority—and develop mutual interests—while engaging in the project of educating children. At the same time, it is localities—school districts, cities, and towns—that continue to operate schools. This fact—which I term "operational localism"—imposes responsibilities on local officials that constrain their ability and willingness to respond to federal directives. These obligations and responsibilities emerge from the political contexts of the community: operational localism is not merely the financing and administration of schooling but the construction and maintenance of political coalitions that endorse policies, generate local funds for schools, and legitimate administrative decisions.

Thus, the goals and priorities of local regimes and their sustaining coalitions—and whether they conflict or align with federal directives—help define the shape of the federal schoolhouse. In this way, locality matters to the construction of a federal schoolhouse because local regimes become the limiting condition of federal reform. At times, the federal government forces that limiting condition beyond the breaking point. At other times, the federal government tolerates the variability and incomplete implementation of federal reforms. The result is a localized federal education state, not uniform, not equal, but one in which federal ambitions rest uneasily with local governing realities.

The setting I use to tell this story of constructing the federal schoolhouse is Alexandria, Virginia, a small city of nearly 150,000 across the Potomac River from Washington, DC. Established in 1749, the city predates the creation of the District of Columbia, and it remains deeply committed to its colonial past, even as it courts suburban growth and urban redevelopment. Alexandria is not a large city—many regard it as a quaint mix of colonial village and established suburb—and it is by no means the bureaucratic labrynth of many large school systems. Unlike Boston, Chicago, Atlanta, Los Angeles, New York, and other major urban centers, Alexandria is the size of a city—and a school district—that is accessible to parents and civic activists. Its modest scale enables me to examine Alexandria's political regime and its ties to the education state without getting lost amid its educational bureaucracy. In many school districts of Alexandria's size across the country, the education state exerts much influence on the education of children, but it does so in ways not readily obvious. The presence of the federal government is not always noticeable at principals' breakfasts, school board sessions, or PTA meetings. Yet it is in those small- and medium-scale settings that state authority is frequently exercised, and by documenting those exercises of state authority, we can better understand how the federal schoolhouse has developed and how it currently operates. By locating this study in Alexandria, my aim is to understand the joint workings—or failings—of a system that is by no means a behemoth, but still reveals the features of the education state.

So Alexandria is the right size for an exploration of how local, state, and federal officials jointly created the distinctive structure called American public education. It is a story about urban politics, educational policymaking, and federalism, all told through the political and educational history of Alexandria—over a fifty-year period, from, roughly, 1960 through 2010. The changes in Alexandria—as well as in the Washington metropolitan area and, indeed, the nation as a whole—have been profound over this half-century and I do not pretend to provide either a complete narrative or a full accounting of all those changes. What I do aim to provide is an explanation of why the American education state is organized and functions the way it does.

The book is meant to contribute to both the study of educational policymaking and the study of American political development. Too often history is neglected in the design and implementation of policy, primarily because policymakers often do not see or feel the constraints of past decisions operating directly upon them. Old patterns just exist; they are normalized as the 'way things have been done around here' without a recognition that those patterns are the products of previous and continuing choices—as well as accidents of history.

Similarly, education has, for the most part, been left out of the study of American political development, which has largely been concerned with identifying the characteristics of a national American state and the ways that power has flowed through that state. Public education does not fit neatly into that research agenda because of its localist anchors. While recent efforts by scholars to bring the city into the orbit of American political development are welcome,[5] understanding public education from the perspective of political development requires a multi-layered investigation, not just a focus on cities alone or on federal programs. Both must be examined simultaneously.[6] Understanding how public education fits into the American state requires that we explore in close detail the complex and messy terrain of convoluted funding streams, clashing governmental mandates and conflicting governmental authority. This focus on the "bottom-up" dimensions of American state-building provides a new perspective on the structure and power of the American state. By examining how locals and federals have sometimes reluctantly created a joint enterprise to educate children in the United States, we can better see the complexity of the American state, as well as the profound challenges of education reform in the United States.

As complex and hybrid and imperfect as the education state may be, it nonetheless is a remarkable creation. Not without flaws, the American education state can nonetheless produce schools that, when run by creative and talented individuals equipped with sufficient resources, are vibrant sources of collective prosperity, community identity, and individual accomplishment. Far too many public schools are dropout factories or deadening zones of conformity, but when they are well-funded and well-run, public schools are cornerstone institutions of a legitimate democratic order. Historically, public schools in the United States have served multiple functions and provided multiple avenues of success for students. They have also been the sites of intense political contestation. As the governmental institution with which most Americans have the closest relationship, public schools play a vital mediating role in the balancing of public welfare and private interests. The ways public schools engage in that balancing have changed over the past fifty years, largely because a national citizenry and electorate have demanded that the federal government become increasingly involved in the means by which states and localities deliver education. These changes have had radiating effects throughout local governance, sometimes influencing the very ability of local governments and school boards to deliver the reforms sought by the federal government.

By the conclusion of this book, I hope the reader will be able to discern how federal authority works best in education, seeing ways that federal understanding of local dynamics and concerns—or lack thereof—shapes the nature of federal educational policymaking. In this regard, the book is also forward looking, as it thinks about the nature of possible regime transformations in Alexandria—and cities elsewhere—and how federal-level education reforms might hasten or thwart those changes in local governance.

Finally, but perhaps most importantly, this book is simply an accounting of how people within a specific place have fought over the things that are most important in their lives: their children. Despite all the federal policymaking, the local politicking, and the daily grind of reforming schools amidst real and challenging obstacles, this book is about the ways that parents, teachers, city officials, and school administrators—flawed as we all are—seek to make the schools their children need, and how the conflicts that ensue shape the nature of school reform. I offer no silver bullets in the book, only an effort to understand the complexity of how we govern schools and the connections that link the present complexity to our past commitments.

ACKNOWLEDGMENTS

Writing a book entails many surprises, frustrations, setbacks and satisfactions. In writing the acknowledgements, however, all that fades, and one is left with the unalloyed pleasure of thanking those that helped along the way. To write a note of thanks and appreciation and indebtedness to the many individuals and organizations who have supported, encouraged and improved this book is an honor, and one for which I am immensely grateful. First, this book began as a very different project under the Advanced Studies Fellowship, a three-year non-residential fellowship program directed by Carl Kaestle at Brown University and funded by the Spencer Foundation and the William and Flora Hewlett Foundation. Through that program I met a remarkable group of nine other scholars, many of whom are historians of education. The exchange and intellectual camaraderie of that program taught me a great deal about educational policy and historical perspectives on educational reform, but also about the value of smart, funny and gracious colleagues.

I would like particularly to thank Carl Kaestle for his wisdom, support, and encouragement of this project and Liz Hollander for invariably inviting us into their home with grace and warmth. My fellow ASFers, in alphabetical order, included Marguerite Clarke, Elizabeth DeBray, Kim Freeman, David Gamson, Nora Gordon, Chris Lubienski, Katie McDermott, Adam Nelson, and Beth Rose. Each read very early versions of this project and provided helpful feedback and encouragement as the project's initial focus—the politics of implementing No Child Left Behind—shifted into a historical examination of local reactions to federal educational education reforms. To the historians in the ASF program, thank you for providing, in effect, a three-year tutorial in the history of education.

I owe a significant debt to the Carnegie Corporation which provided a major grant in support of this project. The Carnegie Scholars program provided me with the freedom to explore the deep historical and local foundations of federal educational policies, for which I am very grateful. The project was also supported by a Senior Faculty Fellowship funded by the Graduate School of Georgetown University and I am thankful to Dean Gerry Mara and to the Government Department of Georgetown for encouraging this project. In particular, Mike Bailey, Jon Ladd, Hans Noel, and Dan Hopkins provided feedback on early versions of Chapter 4. The Woodrow Wilson International Center for Scholars, where I have the good fortune to be a Fellow in 2013–14, has been a very welcoming and productive academic home while I put the finishing touches on the manuscript. Philippa "Flip" Strum, William Pomeranz, Maria Cristina Garcia, Alison Brysk, Donny Meertens, Oksana Nesterenko, and Erica Marat provided helpful commentary on the first chapter.

In Alexandria, I am indebted to Valerie Meyer, records manager at the Alexandria City Public Schools Record Center, for her willingness to open the archives to me and for being so cheerful about my photocopying requests. Thank you also to the interviewees who generously gave of their time to help me better understand Alexandria: Vola Lawson, Connie Ring, Lonnie Rich, Herb Berg, Rodger Digilio, Bill Euille, Rob Krupicka, Suzanne Maxey, Lisa Staib, Jon Liss, Evelin Urrutia, Patrick Welsh, and Tammy Ignacio. The staff of the Local History collection at the Alexandria Public Library provided helpful assistance, and Anna Leider, Deputy Registrar of Voters, provided essential information on elected city officials and voting returns.

Others have listened to, read, and commented on various parts of the book, in various venues. At Georgetown, members of the Americas Initiative gave valuable feedback. In particular, John Tutino, Chandra Manning, Adam Lifshey, and Katie Benton-Holmes gave me very helpful suggestions. Chandra lent her expertise as both an Alexandria parent and an accomplished historian. My colleagues in the Program in Education, Inquiry, and Justice—Sabrina Wesley-Nero, Heather Voke, Heidi Elmendorf, Jennifer Woolard, Andria Wisler, and Tad Howard—all helped me think through many issues within the field of public education and social justice, and I greatly appreciate their insights.

Beyond Georgetown, Steve Teles was the first to see the broader implications of the local story I was telling and urged me to set the frame wider. Jeb Barnes, Jeff Henig, Clarence Stone, Marion Orr, James Patterson, Michael Paris, Gerry Rosenberg, and Tom Burke have all provided much-appreciated encouragement for the project. Various sections of the book have been presented at annual meetings of the American Educational Research Association, Law & Society Association, American Political Science Association, and at the Policy History Conference, and the discussants offered insightful comments: Alice O'Connor, Wayne Urban, Richard Harris, Christine Kelley, and Michael Paris. Thanks to the University Press of Kansas for permission to reprint portions of a chapter originally published in *To Educate a Nation: Federal and National Strategies of School Reform* (2007). Jeb Barnes and an anonymous reviewer wrote detailed and very helpful reviews of the project, and Dave McBride, Sarah Rosenthal, and Eswari Marudhu at Oxford University Press have been wonderful stewards of the book.

I have had the benefit of excellent research assistants. Patrick Carr aided my work in the archives immensely. Philip "J. R." Fujimoto and Mamie Voight (née Lynch) provided assistance with the GIS mapping, and Mamie also provided technical assistance with the regression analysis. Amaris Kinne and Karin Kitchens helped construct the enrollment and school budget databases from multiple sources. Charles Lee, Katie Suter, Danna Khabbaz, Trisha Tacke, Mary Beasley, Claire Tilton, and Andrew Whitacre all helped with secondary sources and the timeline. Victoria Edel, Jens Muenster, and Ambika Tripathi provided invaluable fact- and cite-checking. Andrea Mayer, graduate assistant extraordinaire, provided all-around assistance, as well as good humor (and dog-sitting).

Finally, my family and friends gave their encouragement and support. Marybeth McMahon was invariably upbeat about the project and for her enthusiasm and friendship, I am forever grateful. Charlotte Mooney-Jones, Christopher Jones, Edie Brashares, and Ben Simon provided excellent meals and good conversation. To the many parents at Key Elementary, Gunston Middle School, H.-B. Woodlawn Secondary Program, and Washington-Lee High School with whom I shared conversations about conditions and politics of schooling, I would like to say thank you for your passion and dedication to the cause of public education. In particular, a hearty thank you to Gerry and Pilar Sequeira, Lynn Ross, and Adrienne and Jim Connolly for their humor and friendship.

My wife, Denise Brennan, was always ready with support and counsel and I am very thankful for her love, care, and insight. My children, Emily and James, grew much during the writing of this book and I thank them for giving me the peace to write (mostly) and for the many times they insisted on doing other things. My mother, Caron Reed, passed away during the writing of this book and it is to her memory and to my father, Donald Reed, that I dedicate this book. Both were—in their own way—teachers and I hope this book honors their work and their lives.

LIST OF ABBREVIATIONS

AMO	Annual Measurable Objective
AYP	Adequate Yearly Progress
EAHCA	Education for All Handicapped Children Act
ELL	English Language Learner
ESEA	Elementary and Secondary Education Act
ESL	English as a Second Language
IAP	Individual Academic Plan
IDEA	Individuals with Disabilities Education Act
NCLB	No Child Left Behind
PLA	Persistently Lowest-Achieving School
PLP	Professional Learning Plan
SIG	School Improvement Grant
SOL	Standard of Learning

ALEXANDRIA CITY PUBLIC SCHOOL
SUPERINTENDENTS, 1933–2013

T.C. Williams, 1933–1963
John C. Albohm, 1963–1977
John Bristol, 1977–1980
Robert Peebles, 1980–1987
Paul Masem, 1987–1994
Herbert Berg, 1995–2001
Rebecca Perry, 2001–2008
Morton Sherman, 2008–2013
(*Note*: Interim superintendents omitted)

The Local Politics of Federal Education Reform

Introduction

The gurus of educational policymaking are perplexed. The puzzling persistence of educational underachievement continues to beset US schools, despite major changes in the role of the federal government in public education. Since 2002, the federal government has undertaken a broad and expansive intervention into public education, seeking to hold schools more accountable for the academic performance of students and close a stubborn achievement gap between minority and white students, as well as between poor and affluent students. The 2002 No Child Left Behind Act, as well as the Obama Administration's Race to the Top initiative, sought rapid and specific reforms in educational standards, accountability, and the measurement of student achievement, as well as reforms in hiring, training, and retention of teachers. Recently, federal officials have encouraged states to adopt an ambitious set of educational standards, the Common Core State Standards, hoping to create for the first time a true nationally comparable benchmark by which to evaluate students.

After over a decade of reforms, the question now to be asked is: what's changed? Where have these reforms been effective and why? On a national level, the conclusion is clear: No Child Left Behind has not changed student achievement in a dramatic fashion. The average eighth grade reading score for public school students on the National Assessment of Educational Progress, which assesses a sample of US students, was only three points higher in 2013 than it was in 2002, when NCLB was enacted. But that figure is misleading: for nine years after the enactment of NCLB, the average eighth grade reading score among public school students actually *declined* steadily until recovering to its pre-NCLB level in 2011. In fourth grade reading, the average score among public school students has been essentially unchanged for the past six years.[1] Math shows a more optimistic picture of growth, in both fourth and eighth grades, with a modest increase of seven points for both grades between 2003 and 2013. What is clear, however, is that the trend of improving math scores began long before NCLB, with the upward trend continuing, but not accelerating after NCLB took effect.[2] Based on NAEP test results, NCLB did not alter the general pattern of student achievement on fundamental skills such as math and reading in the United States: slowly and steadily improving math scores and generally flat reading scores. Similarly, NCLB's goal of closing the achievement gap has also not been fulfilled. Multiple studies show the continuing—and in some cases, growing—spread between white and minority students on NAEP math and reading assessments.[3]

On international comparisons, the story is similar for reading, worse for math. Between 2000 and 2012, the United States stayed roughly in the middle of the pack on reading literacy scores, based on the Program for International Student Assessment (PISA) test. In 2012, out of sixty-five countries, the United States scored measurably better than thirty-four countries, worse than nineteen and about the same as eleven countries. The 2012 US average score was not significantly different than the average of Organization for Economic Cooperation and Development (OECD) countries. For reading, these results are virtually identical to what they were in 2000.[4] For math, the news is significantly worse. In 2012, the US math average score was lower than the OECD average and higher than only six OECD nations. US fifteen-year-olds scored at roughly the same level as those in Spain, Portugal, and Italy and better than only Greece, Israel, Turkey, Cyprus, Chile, and Mexico, among OECD nations.[5] Despite the fact that NAEP has shown a consistent long-term increase in mathematics ability among eighth graders, the relative position of US fifteen-year-olds on the PISA test was roughly the same in 2012 and 2003, the two most comparable years during the implementation of NCLB.[6] This suggests that whatever improvement the United States has achieved in mathematics over the past fifteen years, other nations have met or surpassed that improvement.[7] And when you take into account other indicators of educational success—such as high school completion, college enrollment, and college completion—it is clear that the United States' former position as a global educational leader has been eclipsed by the rapid expansion of educational opportunities in other nations.[8] We are, increasingly, middle of the road in educational attainment, as well as in achievement. No Child Left Behind—and its expansive federal role in education—appears to have changed little in American public education, at least in terms of outcomes.

Yet when we look more closely at the institutions and practices of education in the United States much *has* changed over the past twenty years. New models and systems of delivering education—including voucher programs and charter schools—have proliferated in many parts of the country. The notion that a particular neighborhood is tied to a particular public school that educates all children within its attendance zone is increasingly an old-fashioned sentiment. Additionally, new pressures on teachers stemming in large part from the accountability movement, are not only changing curricula and classroom practices of teachers, but also forcing schools of education and teachers unions to improve the training of teachers and to enhance their skills. Principals and school district superintendents now are increasingly likely to emerge from business backgrounds, rather than rise through the ranks of teachers. Educational reform groups like Teach For America and New Leaders for New Schools are active in hundreds of school districts, placing in schools teachers and administrative personnel with scant traditional training, but with social movement zeal. Foundations like the Walton Family Foundation, the Bill and Melinda Gates Foundation, and the Broad Foundation seek to advance systemic reform through venture philanthropy, insisting on organizational or governance reforms to leverage their financial grantmaking. Finally, the federal government is playing a far more transformative role, searching for ways to alter existing practices—often in a misguided quest to reinvent the basic tasks of teaching children.

These contrasting perspectives—one of continuity and predictable levels of (under)achievement, the other of intense and persistent efforts at systemic change in public education—illuminate the reasons why our educational policy gurus are perplexed. Why has all this change produced little in educational improvement? Why do we see so little correlation between educational outcomes and educational reform? Our improvements in math do not seem to track the implementation of NCLB, or the adoption of charter or voucher programs. Student reading scores seem immune to innovations in teacher training. We have little systematic evidence that our new twenty-first century forms of educational delivery and governance are any better equipped to prepare children for the high-skill demands of globalization and increasing economic competition than the preceding forms.

Further complicating matters is the unevenness of educational reforms across the United States. In some states and in some communities, reforms seem to stick, to improve conditions of education, particularly for children in poverty. In other communities, however, a rapid policy churn produces wave after wave of reforms that often leave teachers, principals, parents, and even school district officials hunkered down, trying to wait out the current reform so they can get back to what they have done in the past.

These two aspects of contemporary US educational reform efforts—their unevenness across time and place and their seeming inability to significantly alter educational outcomes for millions of students—frame a central argument of this book: The construction of the education state in the United States has produced profound changes in educational governance, but state-building does not always improve how children learn, despite the fervent belief of many reformers. As a nation, the United States has witnessed over the past fifty years a remarkable transformation in how schools are governed. The perplexed state of the gurus of educational policymaking stems from a fundamental misapprehension about the relationship between educational improvement and educational governance within the United States. Change in the latter does not necessarily induce the former. While many advocates of federal reforms—from school integration to special education to

Race to the Top—argue that federal policies can incentivize educational improvement, the realities of educational localism in the United States mean that the task of
building the education state requires federal policy initiatives to dislocate and disrupt existing local arrangements, without assuming the responsibilities of actually
operating schools. And while many federal educational initiatives over the past fifty
years have greatly widened the educational opportunities of millions of children, the
localism that many reformers saw as the primary obstacle to greater equality in educational opportunity in the United States was, nonetheless, the primary means by
which these reforms gained political legitimacy—and were implemented—within
communities. Localism is a defining characteristic of the US educational system,
but it has largely been left out of the policy story of federal reform efforts. Without
an attention to the dynamics of localism, the stories of both federal efforts to reform
public education and the construction of the education state are incomplete.

The conflation of educational governance reform and boosting educational
achievement emerges, in no small part, from the complicated nature of US public education. Since its advent in the 1840s, public education in the United States
has been a primary responsibility of states and local governments. School districts
are the creation of state governments, and local funding—generally property tax
revenues—still accounts for over forty percent of all public educational revenues.[9] Beginning in the mid-twentieth century, however, the federal government
undertook its initial efforts to reshape American education, but not always with
educational goals in mind. The first wave of changes came about through school
desegregation and integration, while a second wave of federal involvement in schooling primarily focused on improving education to eliminate poverty. Later, special
education became a priority of federal educational policymakers. It was not until
the mid-1990s that the federal government undertook any effort to ensure that students achieved any particular level of educational performance. This effort to ensure
greater student proficiency in math and reading culminated in the 2002 enactment
of No Child Left Behind and has continued through the Obama Administration's
Race to the Top program.

Throughout this nearly sixty years of federal involvement in public education, federal authorities have continually stressed the importance of localism in
American education, all the while seeking to eliminate the worst consequences
of an excessive reliance on localism. The primary failing of excessive localism, of
course, is profound inequality among US schools—whether in Jim Crow schools in
the American South or due to great (and continuing) disparities in the money spent
on schools. As a result, much of federal education policy has, until recently, focused
on increasing the equality of educational opportunities among students. These
inequalities, both of educational opportunity and of educational outcomes, do not
occur, however, by happenstance. Schooling inequalities are often the byproduct
of economic disparities, racial segregation, and unequal access to power structures
within localities and within states. As a result, federal education officials have in

many instances struggled against local actors as they sought to implement reforms to equalize educational opportunities and to improve outcomes for children. This book seeks to understand how the political commitments and needs of local actors intersect with the priorities of federal education programs in ways that shape the effectiveness of federal educational policymaking and reconfigure local politics.

In the United States, the aspiration of building of a federal schoolhouse—the creation of a truly equal and national system of education—is sharply constrained and shaped by the ongoing commitments of those who have historically funded, designed, and operated schools in the United States: local school districts, shaped by state regulations. Because of this, local conditions, which vary considerably, affect the architecture of American schooling. As a result, an even, consistent application of federal educational policy will, perforce, result in an inconsistent realization of federal educational goals. The localist imperative to fund and operate schools— what I call operational localism—creates a localist politics of education in every community in the United States. That localist politics is tied in important ways to local power structures and a local regime that must balance educational needs with other municipal and regional demands, which, in turn, vary according to the local constellation of interests and political contexts. At the same time, however, new federal demands for changes in public education shape and, in some instances, dismantle local power structures, reconfiguring their constituencies, as well as their ability to deliver the services that the federal government is demanding from them. If all politics is local, changes in the federal role in public education will alter how local politics is structured and how it regards public education. This book explains how the education state is constructed through local regimes' accommodation, resistance to, and reconfiguration of, federal educational policy mandates, and, similarly, how that education state reconfigures local politics in the United States.

The construction of the education state generates a local politics of federal education reform by challenging or reinforcing the central dynamics of operational localism in public education. Through an examination of the patterns that emerge as a city responds to federal forays into educational policy, across time and across specific policy domains, the book offers a key to understanding both the efficacy of federal education reforms and the complex nature of educational governance and politics in the United States. The education state in the United States takes its distinctive shape, I argue, because it is the product of a patterned reconciliation between local regime demands and federal reform objectives in education.

This chapter lays out the central elements of the analysis, in five sections. "Operational Localism In Public Education" examines the nature of operational localism as well as the historical priorities of federal educational initiatives. "Local Regimes, Federal Reform, and the Politics of Public Education" turns to the nature of local regimes in American politics and how their relationship to both the institutions and policies of public education creates and sustains a particular kind of politics. "American Political Development and Education Policy" examines how the literature of American political development (APD) sheds light on education politics in the United States and how the central concerns of APD reveal important facets of contemporary educational policymaking. Part of the difficulty confronting analysts of education is coming to terms with the ways that that formal boundaries of institutions (state governments, school districts, the U.S. Department of Education) both simultaneously merge and remain distinctive as they develop and implement education policy. By conceiving of the American education state not as grouping of segmented entities arrayed in a federalist structure but more as partners, collaborators, enemies, and rivals struggling over how to reconcile federal demands with localist imperatives, I hope to contribute to a larger conversation within political science about the nature of the American state and how public education presents particular difficulties for both analysts and constructors of the American state. The final section, "Why Alexandria?" considers the historical and geographic contexts in which this argument will be made and the specifics of the research design for the book. By examining how Alexandria, Virginia has engaged four education policy issues over a fifty-year period, the book undertakes both a "within case" process tracing of specific policy initiatives and "cross-case" comparisons of particular federal policies. Doing so requires not only a narrative account of the political history of Alexandria in the second half of the twentieth century, but also an examination of particular pivot points in the implementation of federal education policies and how they intersected with (and partially changed) local regime imperatives within Alexandria.

Operational Localism in Public Education

Many educational policymakers—and politicians—may decry the complexity of our educational landscape, but it shapes the very ability of the federal government to achieve its objectives. Our current array of school, district, city, state, and federal educational structures emerged gradually over time, producing an enormously complex governmental entity—one much more complex (in an organizational sense) than the US military or the Social Security system, its only rivals in terms of total public expenditures.[10] To the extent that it still even exists, the iconic image of American public education—the little red schoolhouse, financially supported by local taxes and governed via direct democracy—now rests within a hybrid architecture of American schooling, designed and constructed in multiple sites by multiple actors. In principals' offices, in judges' chambers, in school board meetings, state capitols, Congressional offices, and the Department of Education, we have produced an education state that is an institutional bricolage, one in which the repeated efforts to reform or expand public schooling in the United States have created new layers of governing authority without the direct elimination of old forms of authority. As a result, multiple actors enjoy a legitimate ability to claim authority over public schools, ranging from federal judges to school board members, parents, state legislators, and federal bureaucrats. This section lays out the primary elements of that bricolage, focusing on the local and federal pieces of the puzzle.[11]

Formally, school districts are creations of state legislatures, corporate bodies formed to realize the state-level constitutional obligation to provide public education.[12] Indeed, state governments typically hold extensive statutory authority to determine the conditions of schooling. Whether they choose to exercise that authority (and which aspects of schooling they choose to regulate) is another matter altogether. The American states vary in their intensity of regulation of schooling, but since the mid-1980s a wide range of issues have been increasingly mandated by state governments: school curricula, the length of school days, the length of school years, teachers' job qualifications, student testing requirements, physical plant regulations, even permissible playground equipment. At the state level, these regulations are generally accomplished outright by legislative enactment, since school districts are the creation of state governments and exist, in a legal sense, to meet the state constitutional obligations to provide for a free public education. In short, as creations of state governments, school districts are directly regulable by them. As a matter of practice, however, the state governments traditionally have deferred to local districts and school boards: "in most states local school boards enjoy considerable power over the day-to-day operation and management of their schools …"[13]

As a result of this historical deference, the organization of public schooling in the United States is highly localized. While the term "local control" is certainly misleading in a formal sense, the ongoing fact that local authorities actually operate schools means that "operational localism" is the predominant form of public schooling in the United States. Its persistence and its appeal emerge from two important facets of American public education. First, geographically defined school districts (which retain the ability to exclude students who reside outside district boundaries) remain the predominant mode of organizing schools and, second, a large percentage of the money needed to operate these schools comes from local taxes on real estate within those district boundaries. The operational localism of public schooling—while increasingly challenged by vouchers and charter schools—rests upon a financial foundation of locally raised and utilized property taxes. Nationally, roughly forty percent of all public educational revenues come from local sources, making schools one of the most intensely localized of all governmental services, at least in terms of funding.[14] The localist nature of educational funding—shaky in some districts, robust in others—also legitimates the exclusion from local schools those students who do not live within school district boundaries, and, therefore, do not contribute to the local financial burden of operating schools. Indeed, with more state-level requirements and greater federal accountability requirements, a local district's ability to exclude students is, increasingly, the only vestige of pure local control remaining in the American school system.

The primacy of local funding and excludability of students from that funding highlight the central organizational fact of schooling in the United States: school districts operate public schools, not states or the federal government.[15] This fact has enormous consequences for the nature of education reform: The reform efforts of the state and federal governments (but particularly the federal) must land in particular localities, which possess particular, possibly unique, characteristics.[16] Because of the administrative reality of operational localism, local communities still have an enormous amount of moral authority to map out a vision of what they want in their public schools, as well as an ability to structure the implementation of reforms designed elsewhere. While school choice and charter schools have in some ways de-territorialized public schooling, the place-based model of public schooling nonetheless creates an expectation of local control that sustains much of the educational politics within communities, primarily because its jurisdictional geography determines both the enrollment and funding of schools. This book pays close attention to what happens to these ideas of local control—and localism more broadly—as other actors assert authority over public schooling, tracing the reactions of citizens and parents to the implementation of federal programs and mandates as they consider the task of schooling their children.

A Thumbnail Sketch of Federal Ambitions in Educational Policy and Politics

Given the historical primacy of state and local districts in educational governance, the most obvious fact about federal education policy is that there is no explicit constitutional role for the federal government to play in the provision and maintenance of public education. There is no national "education clause" of the US Constitution; in fact, any federal initiative in education must work around the explicit state-level constitutional requirements that the states build and support systems of public schooling.[17] Operational localism profoundly limits the federal government's ability to directly intervene in the ongoing conduct of education, absent a violation of some other federal constitutional principle. This lack of an explicit role for national educational policymakers forces the federal government to rely on its spending authority to induce policy change or innovation. That is, only by offering money to be spent on education in particular ways can the federal government affect how the states or school districts educate children.

Until comparatively recently, federal spending on public education was nonexistent; only within the past fifty years has it been used to regulate schools indirectly. Aside from a federal vocational aid bill enacted in 1918 and a 1950 "impact aid" bill for districts with a large federal presence (such as military bases or federal installations), no federal general aid bill providing money for elementary or secondary education passed out of Congress between 1870 and 1957.[18] Not until the 1957 Soviet launch of Sputnik challenged notions of US technological superiority did significant federal money provide for the operation of elementary and secondary educational programs. With the enactment of the 1958 National Defense Education Act, federal money began to flow to US classrooms for math and science education, but only with Congress's passage of the Elementary and Secondary Education Act of 1965 (ESEA) could one argue that a federal educational policy existed. Even then, the aim and purpose of that spending authority was, at least initially, focused on relieving the effects of poverty, not on changing how school districts delivered education.

The ESEA's focus on poverty emerged from a number of factors: the political demands of President Lyndon Baines Johnson's War on Poverty, the political appeal of equal educational opportunity, and the educational establishment's campaign for "compensatory education" to redress the educational harms that afflict poor children.[19] As a result, however, the nation's landmark education bill focused less on reforming education than on amelioration of the brutal effects of poverty on children. In this sense, ESEA's Title I (and indeed the entire project of "compensatory education") aimed to add additional resources to the existing localist structure, rather than revamp the local delivery of education. As Harvey Kantor writes, "Great Society policymakers were reluctant to mandate major change in local educational practices."[20] Similarly, Julie Jeffrey concludes that because education was not really the focus of the Elementary and Secondary Education Act, "little thought had gone into the whole problem of how education, formal or informal, related to the goals of the poverty program.... Policymakers and Congressmen just never looked at the evidence of what schools did."[21]

This is not to say, however, that the federal government was, at this time, unconcerned about the organization of schools and schooling. Indeed, the late 1950s saw the first major direct federal intervention in the administration of local schools, initially through desegregation court orders. Then, in the mid-1960s, Congress extended the Supreme Court's hopeful, but tentative, foray into equal educational opportunity through the 1964 Civil Rights Act and the 1965 Elementary and Secondary Education Act. Together, these two statutes increased the flow of federal money to states and school districts and required that this money not be spent in racially segregated schools. With the authority of these two landmark acts, the federal government built a modest bureaucracy to challenge the unequal distribution of educational opportunities between black and white Americans.[22] This effort to reorganize *de jure* segregated schools did not, however, directly concern itself with the reform of education per se, but rather with a local school district's ability to control who attended school with whom. What they did, or what they learned, after sitting down next to each other was still a matter for operational localism to determine.

Nonetheless, the conjunction of *Brown v. Board of Education*, Title VI of the Civil Rights Act of 1964, and the ESEA created a logic and a process of federal educational governance that was unprecedented in American history. For the first time, the federal government significantly disrupted local control, primarily because the federal courts and Congress set about to alter, powerfully and permanently, the racial policies of the South. Public education was caught up in that dual transformation of federalism and equality, but it was not, initially, the direct target of that transformation.

Later, federal efforts to desegregate public schools expanded into northern and midwestern cities that limited educational opportunities through de facto, rather than de jure racial segregation, but those efforts withered rather quickly in the mid-to-late 1970s. The experiences of cities like Boston and Detroit revealed little political will among whites to integrate fully the public schools in metropolitan areas with significant de facto school segregation. By the early 1990s, even the federal courts had tired of the task of desegregation and handed down a series of decisions establishing how school districts could emerge from court-ordered desegregation.[23] But the federal presence in school districts and states did not wane, even as enthusiasm for the desegregationist ideal faded. Partly inspired by the civil rights movement, activists demanded that children previously excluded from effective public education—children with special needs and children whose primary language was other than English—receive the protection of both federal courts and federal lawmakers. As a result, federal officials required localities to change practices in order to accommodate students with special emotional, physical, and linguistic needs. In 1975 the Education for All Handicapped Children Act—later dubbed the Individuals with Disabilities Education Act (IDEA)—imposed on states and local districts the obligation to ensure that all students received a "free and appropriate public education," limiting their ability to bar students with severe handicaps and disabilities from school. At roughly the same time, federal courts held that students who did not speak English were entitled to additional programs and services to ensure that they received an equitable education. These requirements were then soon incorporated into federal statutes.[24]

During the education reform movement of the 1980s and 1990s, political demands grew for broader reforms in public education, ranging from increased standards and heightened accountability to school choice and public charter schools. These demands, in turn, created political incentives for candidates and officeholders to champion the reform of public schooling. Most of these changes took place at the state level, but in 1994 the reauthorization of the federal Elementary and Secondary Education Act required, for the first time, that states create an accountability mechanism in order to receive federal educational money. This shift was a watershed moment in the history of ESEA. In 2002, No Child Left Behind expanded that modest system into a hybrid federal-state, standards-based accountability structure that required annual testing in grades three through eight and imposed sanctions on schools that failed to make adequate yearly progress toward state-defined targets of educational proficiency in reading and math among all students. NCLB, in historic fashion, placed the federal government in the position of demanding that states, districts, and schools engage in a process of continuous test score improvement or otherwise face federally mandated sanctions that would directly intrude on traditional prerogatives of local and state educational officials. More so than any other piece of federal educational policy (either judicially or legislatively imposed), NCLB cut into the traditional expectations that states and districts have held about how and what to teach. Court-ordered school desegregation may have altered who sits next to whom in a classroom, but it had little to say about what went on in a given classroom once those attendance patterns met federal standards of equality.

Supporters of NCLB argued that its federally imposed accountability mechanism promoted greater equity in education because it ensured that schools and school districts did not neglect any particular subgroup in their efforts to improve educational outcomes. Critics contended that its unrelenting focus on outputs simply forced schools and teachers to "teach to the test," and exacerbated a pernicious race-to-the-bottom dynamic among states as they established the lowest permissible standards to ensure the highest improvement rate. The literature supporting and denouncing NCLB is vast[25] and needs no full review here, but from the perspective of understanding who governs schools, one point needs to be stressed: Congress hoped NCLB would both compel states to define clearly what teachers should teach and how schools would determine which students had mastered those subjects. That effort to define federally the terms of classroom expectations and the measurement of teaching success was unprecedented in US educational history.

NCLB also represented, perhaps, the clearest manifestation of the American education state to date. As I indicated in the preface, the education state is not simply one central authority deciding all matters educational, but an assemblage of public entities that deploy resources within institutions to educate children collectively at public expense. Most political scientists who study education politics typically do not invoke the term the "state," undoubtedly because it seems like a reductionist or monolithic term that ignores the complexities of local, state, and federal elements of US educational politics and policymaking. But the notions of "state-building" and "state capacity" in many ways capture precisely the changes that federal involvement in public education has achieved over the past fifty years. The move from a mid-twentieth-century, predominantly localist vision of public education to NCLB's demand for explicit standards and explicit student performance targets is, from this perspective, part of the recent construction of the US education state. This expansion of the education state has not meant that the feds have centralized public educational offerings through NCLB, but rather that the federal government is using NCLB to standardize and regularize a particular form of educational accountability, across states and districts.

Desmond King and Marc Stears have argued that the American state is most visible precisely when it engages in "efforts to standardize key aspects of the American experience."[26] Moreover, they argue, if political scientists were to refocus "their attention on the dynamics to standardize, then key aspects of US state activity and policy [would be] revealed in a range of areas where they have previously been overlooked."[27] It is precisely that task of tracing the drive to standardize that I am undertaking in this book. Whether undertaken in conjunction with state and local authorities or in opposition to them, the major federal educational policy initiatives of the past fifty years—the federal government's efforts to integrate schools, to provide educational opportunities for special needs children, to meet the needs of English language learners, and to create a common accountability mechanism across states—all look very much like the emergence of an education state that seeks to standardize educational experiences across a variety of groups of students. By understanding the role of operational localism in this effort to standardize, we can see how it serves as a limiting condition on the aspirations of the education state to realize the "federal schoolhouse."

This book explores these four episodes of federal education policymaking by examining how this quest for standardization affected one rather small, but in many ways typical, community: Alexandria, Virginia. My aim is to examine how the federal efforts to reshape schools over the past fifty years have not only reconfigured schools, but affected the local politics of a place and reconfigured the local expectations and understandings of public education; the education state—as a hybrid entity—fuses federal ambitions to local realities. I do not claim that all cities and communities are like Alexandria, but I do claim that all American communities have had to contend—to a greater or lesser extent—with the issues created by rival claimants to authority that Alexandrians confronted within their schools and community. The story told in this book, then, is a story of the construction of the education state over time, viewed from the local perspective of one community. In this story, we can see how federal objectives in education clashed—or meshed—with the demands of operational localism and, in so doing, reconfigured the education goals and expectations of a community.

Local Regimes, Federal Reform, and the Politics of Public Education

Turning to the local to understand the politics of the federal may be counterintuitive, but, in the case of public education, it is essential because of the simple facts of operational localism. But operational localism is itself a complex dynamic, an organizational fact that goes beyond the administration of schools. The politics of the locality structure the nature of operational localism. While Progressive Era reformers may have sought to separate politics from the administration of schools, the politics of cities and towns remain strongly linked to the organization and delivery of public education.

Take for example the experiences of Washington, DC. In the early summer of 2007, Washington, DC Mayor Adrian Fenty appointed Michelle Rhee to be Chancellor of DC Public Schools. A former Teach for America teacher, and later an educational entrepreneur who founded the New Teacher Project (now TNTP), Rhee was the darling of the education reform movement. While she had never served as a high-ranking school administrator, she nonetheless brought with her both a zeal for reform and a nearly magnetic attraction to controversy. She railed against what she saw as the diminished expectations many held for DC's school-children, and she challenged, urged, and cajoled DC teachers to do more for the children in their care. She closed schools, fired teachers, and reorganized the admin-istrative structure of the DCPS central office. She sought to implement a radically different compensation structure that paid teachers six-figure salaries if they could boost student test scores. While many claimed that Rhee set the District on a path for meaningful educational improvement in its public schools, others—many oth-ers—contended that Rhee unnecessarily alienated both parents and teachers alike in her quest for reform.

Despite the disagreement over the success of Rhee's reforms, what is abun-dantly clear, however, is that a little over three years after her arrival, Michelle Rhee resigned. She resigned because her chief political backer and very public supporter, Mayor Adrian Fenty, lost in the September 2010 Democratic mayoral primary to DC City Councilman Vincent Gray, an ardent Rhee opponent. Fenty's public and unequivocal support for Rhee and her agenda of reform, combined with Rhee's penchant for controversy, knotted the political fates of the two securely together. As Rhee's unpopularity grew within the largely African American wards of the city, Fenty's reelection grew increasingly unlikely. Somewhat lost in the contro-versy over Rhee's departure and Fenty's defeat was Washington Teachers Union President George Parker's loss to Nathan Saunders, in a runoff election at the end of November, 2010. Rhee and Parker had negotiated IMPACT, the controversial program of value-added teacher evaluation that linked teacher performance reviews (and pay) to a demonstrated ability to increase student test scores. While Parker and Rhee did not always see eye to eye, DC teachers held him responsible for the union's inability to trim back Rhee's reforms. Newly elected President Saunders stated in an interview after his defeat of Parker, "what we've experienced in the last three years is a lot of blood on the floor, and it's been all teacher blood."[28]

Within six short weeks, three leading officials—the mayor of DC, the Chancellor of Schools, and the President of the Washington Teachers Union—were all drummed out of office. They were defeated largely because of the increasing unpopularity of their efforts to reform DC Public Schools—a school system widely regarded as one of the worst central city school systems in the nation. Why would this group of reformers be so handily cast out in a setting so desperate for a meaningful and effective restructuring of the system of public education? While Fenty, Rhee, and Parker all had their own political liabilities, one common element to their defeats was their efforts to restructure the existing regime of public education within the nation's capital. This regime, although it often provided inadequate education to children, proved quite adept at preserving its advantages and interests within the existing power structure of local Washington politics. The success of Vincent Gray's campaign highlights that resilience.

Theories of Urban Regimes and Schools

To better understand the dynamics of the relationships between school reform and urban politics, this book draws on two key concepts: Clarence Stone's regime theory and the notion of linked policy change over time. Articulated across several works, Stone's notion of "regime" reconceived the central political problem of cities. The key issue, for Stone, was not who controlled political outcomes in cities, but how do we account for patterned inequalities within cities, despite active and robust electoral participation of groups with divergent interests. In short, Stone conceptualized urban politics as the art of governance in which the political economy of place constrained, but did not define, the creativity of actors to both manage conflict and to achieve goals. In Stone's view, conditions of economic and social inequality among groups certainly confer systemic power to high-status groups, but political institutions are nonetheless popularly controlled, with electoral coalitions demanding benefits from their leaders for helping them to secure office.[29] This fundamental tension requires that political leaders devise mechanisms to accommodate simultaneously the electoral demands of constituents and the systemic advantages of particular groups and interests.

For Stone, the solution lies in regime politics. What makes a city governable, he writes in *Regime Politics*, is the ability of public and private sector leaders to establish an informal partnership. This "partnership and the way it operates constitutes the city's regime; it is the means through which major policy decisions are made."[30] To understand how a city is governed, according to Stone, we need to understand "the informal arrangements by which public bodies and private interests function together in order to be able to make and carry out governing decisions." These governing decisions are centrally concerned with "managing conflict and making adaptive responses to social change."[31] These sometimes tacit and sometimes overt agreements among major private interests and public actors enable city leaders to successfully define and achieve common objectives—projects like housing and commercial redevelopment, construction of transit systems, even education reform.

Subsequent to his book on Atlanta's urban regime, Stone and a number of other colleagues applied the notion of regimes and their capacity to undertake civic ventures to the notion of school reform. The difficulty of urban school reform, Stone contended, was that "education politics is not readily organized around the aim of improved school performance in educating children from lower-SES [socio-economic status] backgrounds."[32] Indeed, public "education is not simply a service over which users struggle. Education is also about jobs, contracts, career tracks, and employment opportunities.... In short, the protection of jobs and career ladders is often at the heart of how education politics is organized."[33] In order to reform this "employment regime," Stone contends that we "must establish a new set of political arrangements commensurate with the policy being advocated.... Promoting stronger academic achievement means, then, building support for schools that are driven by a performance imperative. The political challenge is to build a new set of arrangements in which academic performance is a focal concern."[34] By examining how the civic capacity of a community can transform a school system from an "employment regime" into a "performance regime," Stone and his colleagues sought to advance our understanding of the political prerequisites of school reform.

The problem, however, with Stone's formulation here is that school systems do not simply constitute regimes unto themselves, whether employment- or performance-based. Instead, they are woven into the institutional structures of cities that are themselves governed by particular regimes, and, often, the imperatives and priorities of those regimes present significant obstacles to school reform. Simply viewing school systems as discrete organizational entities ignores the fact that school systems are components of local regimes; the ability to reconfigure the incentives and work routines of schools as organizations is dependent upon ties—personal and institutional—that integrate schools into the broader regime of the community. Just as cities are embedded within an economic context that limits their autonomy, school systems, because of operational localism, are embedded within a political context that limits their own autonomy, and frequently places them in the midst of regime commitments.

Formal and Informal Connections Between Regimes and Schools

Certain institutional features of a school system may tie it more or less tightly to the local regime. If, for example, a school district lacks independent taxation authority and must request or negotiate its budget from the city's tax revenues, it obviously enjoys less autonomy. Similarly, if the officials of the school system—either school board members, or the superintendent, or both—are appointed by city officials, the system is more likely to reflect the goals and priorities of the urban regime. These two concerns—finances and personnel—structure much of the formal incorporation of a school system within an urban regime. These features are not the only elements, however, that define a school system's relationship to the local regime.

A school system may also be more or less fully incorporated into a local regime if informal arrangements and agreements create an interdependence, despite structural separation. As Stone writes, "[I]t is important to remember first that formal structures can be rearranged without altering basic relationships and second that even if formal relationships remain the same, the appearance of new players can alter how the formal structures actually function."[35] In other words, the formal relationships may determine the configuration of the playing field, but they do not necessarily determine how the game is played. If sufficient trust and civic capacity exists, a school district and a local regime could establish a set of expectations and informal arrangements that effectively negates these formal ties (or lack thereof). The characteristics of these informal agreements depends, in large part, on the overall interest regime members have in public education, an interest that will vary considerably from place to place and regime to regime.

In fact, in many locales, regime players may not take a major interest in either the administration or reform of schools within a city. While the provision of public education may be seen as an essential public service, it necessarily competes with other issues: police protection, economic development issues, transportation, housing, and local employment markets. While operational localism's fiscal structure ensures that the business community will have at least some interest in public education, that interest is more likely to be a byproduct of public education's high price tag and its direct effects on local taxation rates. In addition, the relationship between public schools and the local employment market can become an issue that regime actors worry about, depending on the nature of the interests of regime members. In general, the local provision of education is, however, most likely a secondary concern of the business community, relevant to it largely through taxation and workforce issues.[36]

But regime members are not exclusively business actors. Other private interests—whether civic groups, churches, nonprofit organizations, community organizations, or unions—all contribute to the regime's ability to anticipate, minimize, or resolve conflicts and to mobilize civic capacity. Schools, from this perspective, are cornerstones of the civic life of a community. These groups focus less on the economic returns of public schooling or the academic aspirations of schools and far more on the capacity of schools to weave the social fabric that sustains a community. To the extent that these organizations pay attention to schools and the politics of schooling, they typically focus on the civic function of schools, their socializing dimensions, and their capacity to build members of a community. Schools from their vantage point are not seen exclusively as elements of economic production, but as the sites in which communities and neighborhoods join with public officials to equip the next generation with the skills—social and otherwise—necessary for both the community and the child to thrive.

The incorporation, then, of business and community groups into the regime does not necessarily mean those groups will have an active interest or concern with education reform, particularly efforts by the federal government to change how schools operate. Regime members may take an interest in schools, but not in improving their performance. Because a regime operates across many dimensions of public life within a community and education is only one of its concerns, the regime has its own political dynamics wholly separate from the issue of public education. Thus, we need to distinguish regime politics—changes in its membership or its capacity to prevent or resolve conflict—from school reform politics, or disputes over the relationship between the schools and a local regime's political needs. Making this distinction helps us to better understand how increasing federal authority over schools may place the federal government in tension with the local regime as it seeks to reform public education.

Local Regimes and Federal Reforms

The embedding of school systems within urban regimes can make federal efforts to reform schools an indirect reconfiguration of local politics. Thus the local politics of federal education reform hinges on, first, the degree to which regime commitments and informal agreements present an obstacle to the successful reforms of schools, and, second, the degree to which federal reform objectives disrupt those informal modes of doing business. To the extent that federal reforms seriously jeopardize local regime patterns, they will face serious obstacles to implementation. In contrast, to the extent that federal reforms reinforce and entrench regime patterns and habits they will be readily absorbed and implemented. Thus the conundrum of federal education reform in the context of operational localism is the following: If the commitments of the local regime present a primary obstacle to effective learning within schools, the federal reform effort will have to undermine the existing political framework that organizes schooling within that locality. To the extent that the local school system is thoroughly enmeshed within the local regime, that process of undermining regime commitments may, ironically, destabilize the local political environment, rendering it less capable of sustaining reform in the midst of change. In such a circumstance, the federal challenge is to unsettle the local regime constructively, allowing new local actors to establish a new regime, organized in such a way as to facilitate, not hinder, federal reform objectives.

Complicating matters further, other actors besides the federal government are simultaneously seeking to reshape the political and governance environments in which schools operate. Jeff Henig has noted that much of the reform energy in public education since the mid-1980s—state governors' highly visible role in recasting state oversight of school districts, the increasing prevalence of mayoral control, the growing involvement of courts in education policy—has all aimed at breaking down the institutional insulation of schools from general purpose governance. Henig's observation is important: schools have typically been governed by single-purpose governing bodies (school boards, state boards of education, etc.), but recent reform efforts are, he contends, reincorporating school systems into the general purpose governance structures that devise and administer most policies. For Henig, this change is important; it opens schools up to the prospect of more partisan, interest-driven politicking in which logrolling and bargaining predominate. As he puts it, "In practice general-purpose governments are as often steered by partisan, ideological, and interest group politics, in a clash that metaphorically looks more like war than a New England town meeting."[37] For Henig, that change is not necessarily a bad one. Too often, he writes, single-purpose governments maintain a low political profile and are often closed systems in which professional expertise and narrowly focused interests dominate the decision-making process. As a result, other interests, perhaps more diffuse or underrepresented, are left out of the process.

In part, regime theory—with its focus on informal working partnerships, rather than formal lines of authority—renders Henig's observation somewhat beside the point: intense politicking and dealmaking occurs in both single and general purpose governments. In addition, I argue that even with the erosion of single-purpose governance structures, localism (whether single or general purpose) plays a vital and sometimes controlling role in the federal government's efforts to devise, implement, and administer its understanding of the education state.[38] But the insight of Henig's point remains: the institutional contexts of schools and school governance are changing, and it's not just the federal government that is seeking or requiring these changes—many actors are.

American Political Development and Education Policy

The changes that Henig describes within the governance structures of public education can be characterized as part of a more general process of state-building, which often requires creative dismantling of prior forms of governance. Although not generally studied by educational policy scholars, an extensive literature in American political development can help us better understand the significance of these changes in educational governance. In particular, APD's concern with the linkages between institutions and policy, the importance of sequencing in understanding institutional development, and the dynamics of state-building enable us to see broader patterns in the federal–local relationship in public education.

For each of the policy domains explored in the book—racial desegregation and integration, special education policy, English-language learners and accountability politics—I am interested in understanding how struggles over *authority* in education shape the nature of education reform and how the *sequencing* of reforms matters for policy success. The first issue, battles over who has authority within a particular policy domain, draws on the important work of Karen Orren and Stephen Skowronek. They claim in *In Search of American Political Development* that political fights over authority define the central concern of the field of political development. In their view, claims by one actor or set of actors to hold authority over a policy necessarily disrupt or dislodge an existing claim of authority. Political development, from this perspective, occurs as new contestants wrest authority from the existing players. As Orren and Skowronek put it, "political development itself involves changing the prior set of rules by which a collectivity has been governed,"[39] concluding that "in the final analysis, we are looking for changes in how people are governed."[40]

This book takes seriously the idea that the political development of public education matters for the success and viability of education reform: Battles over authority in education are closely related to the success of education reform. However, this book challenges the notion that these battles over educational authority are necessarily zero-sum. Because authority over children and their schooling emerges from multiple domains and is wielded by multiple actors, and because governance occurs through actions, routines, and behaviors that are not simple extensions of formal authority, the claims of federal actors to change the rules of public education do not diminish the authority of other actors to operate the schools in which children learn. Instead, this book argues that the political development of public education inheres in the institutional forms and political practices that emerge as local actors reconcile federal efforts to change public education with local constituencies and local regime demands. Thus, the patterned reconciliation between the policy demands of federal authorities and the political needs of local authorities is the recurring dynamic that drives the political development of public education in the United States. Because of the massive institutional fact of operational localism, local authority over education as a policy domain is not attenuated as the federal government uses administrative rule-making, federal statutes or federal constitutional interpretation to redefine local practices of education. Rather, the political development of education emerges as both sides agree (implicitly or explicitly) on consistent patterns of accommodation and partial implementation. The relatively enduring shape of that political development then shapes the conditions for the next round of reform efforts.

This brings us to the importance of sequencing in educational reforms. While Patrick McGuinn has fruitfully applied the idea of linked policy change over time— or path dependence—to federal education reform, the concept has not been applied to the interaction of federal, state and local policy change in a systematic way.[41] In this book, I examine how the choices made at an earlier stage in the federal government's efforts to restructure Alexandria's school system—particularly those choices deemed by local officials to be politically essential to the local governing structure—constrained and shaped the nature of other reforms in other domains of education policy. In other words, I am examining how the choices that Alexandria officials made in the course of first desegregating and then integrating Alexandria's schools affected the development and deployment of special education, English language-learner, and accountability policies many years later. The accounts here illustrate that both the success of federal educational reforms and the institutional shape that they take are due, in significant part, to local choices made earlier *in other reform cycles, in other policy domains.* The interrelationship of policy initiatives at the federal level and the ways that they are linked across time to politics at the local level is an important, yet neglected, aspect of studying the politics of education reform.[42]

Finally, this book's engagement with education policy from the perspective of state-building illuminates the complex nature of the American state. Stephen Skowronek's classic work *Building a New American State* takes the reconstruction of existing state forms and powers as the central dynamic of state-building in the

United States. That book, which has inspired a generation of scholarship, contends that the American state was built by the explicit actions of politicians and administrators who dismantled the pre-existing forms of state authority to fashion a more centralized and rational state structure. The expansion of national administrative capacities—and fights over who would control that capacity—hinged on an "internal disintegration of the early American state."[43] In other words, the governmental structures that existed prior to the rise of a national administrative apparatus had to be taken apart and refashioned in order for a national system of governance to emerge.

As other scholars have explored these themes of state-building in multiple policy domains, looking for the places and ways that the national government has developed and deployed national welfare and social policies, they have left education policy relatively unexplored (with the notable exception of Suzanne Mettler's masterful work on the GI bill[44]). That omission is not, I believe, merely a scholarly oversight. Instead, it reflects a particular inaptness of the prevailing models of state-building, which focus on the tendency of state-builders to centralize authority, to explain the development of public education in the twentieth century. Public education, in an institutional sense, "went local" in its earliest inception in the United States and that commitment to localism has been particularly difficult for national administrators of educational schemes to root out or overcome.[45] Using Skowronek's language, the "internal disintegration" of the prior forms of administering public education has been only partial—and for clear institutional reasons.

Anchored in a funding scheme and a process of political legitimation that relies heavily on local assent (through property taxes and school board elections), public education has remained more local than other social policies that had a similar localist bent earlier in the twentieth century. Martha Derthick's classic work on the effects of federal grants on Massachusetts's highly localized system of providing public assistance to the poor is a case in point. Derthick tells a story of the federal government seeking the cooptation and control of the Massachusetts public assistance authority in order to destroy local variation and influence in the provision of aid to poor individuals. In the end, the federal government effectively eliminated localism from the Massachusetts system: "By increasing the authority and power of the state agency and incorporating local agencies into it, the change had permanently altered the structure of [welfare] policy making and administration in Massachusetts: from now on, the state would be more responsive to federal action."[46]

In public education, federal influence has been far less pervasive, resulting in a more complex and hybrid state. As we shall see, repeated efforts by the federal government to establish priorities for locals have only partially succeeded, and only if those priorities aligned with local regime commitments. Operational localism, I contend, provides a means by which local interests are incorporated into education state, despite federal wishes.

Why Alexandria?

To some, Alexandria might seem an unusual city for a case study on the dynamics of federal educational policymaking. To be sure, Alexandria is distinctive in many ways: the boyhood home of The Doors lead singer Jim Morrison, the subject of a Hollywood movie, the quiet suburb that was the home of Vice President Gerald Ford (and for ten days in 1974, home of President Ford). Its quaint cobblestones in Old Town and its respect for its historical legacy make it a rarity among small cities. But for all its colonial charm and devotion to historic preservation, Alexandria is, in reality, a city of contrasts—a city with downtown urban poverty and affluent upper-class neighborhoods. It has a long-standing African American community and a growing population of recent Latino and African immigrants. Outside of Washington, DC, its student population is among the poorest in the metropolitan area, yet its property wealth rivals most affluent suburbs. In a region that has grown substantially over the past thirty years, its population has remained stable, growing slowly. The oldest city in the Washington region, Alexandria transcends its tourist attractions and shares common elements with cities and school districts across the nation.

A number of characteristics in particular make it an illuminating case study in which to explore long-term implementation of federal education policies. Clearly, the practical matters of undertaking a historical examination of a school district required a geographic proximity to the archives and public records of locality. Alexandria's commitment to historical preservation extends to its municipal records as well, offering a rich documentary record to draw from. To be sure, other districts within the Washington, DC area were equally close at hand (such as the school districts of Fairfax County, Virginia and Montgomery County, Maryland) but their primary self-conceptions were as suburban districts whose rapid growth in the 1970s and 1980s made them a particular kind of school district, rather than an illustrative example of tensions that are common among school districts. In a similar way, the District of Columbia is in reality *sui generis*, a unique governmental creature that was not generalizable to other cities.[47]

But Alexandria has additional characteristics that make its experiences relevant to a number of other cities in the United States. First, at roughly 13,000 pupils, its enrollment is not far from the average enrollment of school districts in the United States. This is salient because the relative balance of educational issues to other municipal concerns is an important dimension of the analysis of local regimes. To the extent that school district organizational size and complexity are part of the relationship to a local regime, then Alexandria will exhibit characteristics that are common with many school districts across the county. While large cities often dominate our discussion of educational policies in the United States the vast majority of US students are taught in public schools in suburban districts, not large city public bureaucracies. In addition, Alexandria's formal governance model is conventional: It is run through a weak mayor/city manager system with a seven-member city council chaired by the mayor and elected through at-large partisan elections. Until 1994, this city council appointed the members of the school board. After 1994, the school board members were elected directly, in non-partisan elections.[48] All told, Alexandria's moderate scale and typical institutional features enable me to trace clearly the connections between the educational system and the political regime and to track changes in school district administrative routines and procedures as federal policy initiatives take hold (or don't).

Second, Alexandria's student population is, by many measures, demographically diverse. It has a large percentage of students in poverty, a significant percentage of students whose families recently arrived in the United States, and a significant percentage of families who are affluent and whose parents have high educational attainment. Given this internal diversity, many of Alexandria's educational challenges are similar to central city school districts, but it also exhibits many characteristics of affluent suburban districts, as well as school districts in new immigrant gateway communities. Combining a professional, white-collar suburban sensibility with the challenges of being a majority-minority district with high percentages of poor and non-English-speaking students, Alexandria has elements in common with districts across the nation.

A third rationale stems paradoxically from Alexandria's proximity to Washington, DC's educational policymakers and regulators. From the early 1960s through the early years of the twenty-first century, the Washington, DC area changed dramatically, with significant expansion of the suburbs and the transformation of the District of Columbia into a global hub of migration, commercial activity, and capital concentration. Alexandria has been part of that transformation, with many of its residents working either within the federal bureaucracy or the US military, or in the plethora of contracting and consulting firms that have grown up in the DC area over the past thirty years. As a result, Alexandria as a place and a city is very much integrated into the Washington, DC culture and metropolitan governance. As both a small city and a suburb, it retains, however, a distinct identity from its adjacent neighbors, Fairfax and Arlington Counties. It is not part of the "slurbia" of strip malls and cookie cutter housing developments that characterize the exurbs of Loudoun and Prince William Counties, but is a stable, tightly knit community that has a strong commitment to its colonial and historical legacies.[49]

Because of these competing tensions, it is an ideal test case to evaluate the influence and nature of federal involvement in educational policy. If any city should be subject to the influence of federal policymakers, it should be one that is close—geographically, culturally and administratively—to the affairs of the federal government. Indeed, many of Alexandria's residents are actively involved in the ongoing operations of the federal state. They understand and take part in state-building and state maintenance on almost a daily basis, even if they do not articulate or recognize it as such. Yet, at the same time, the institutional characteristics of operational local-ism—local property taxation and local operational autonomy of schools—create a gap between the federal and the local, even when they are literally adjacent to each other. As a result, if this book identifies robust characteristics of localism driv-ing the development of the educational state in a place like Alexandria, then local-ism would, arguably, be even more influential in a locale further removed from the bureaucrats and culture of Washington. At the same time, if the priorities of the federal government within education can reorient the practices of a community like Alexandria, with its significant financial resources, a strong and clear urban identity, and well-developed political ethos and community, then the federal government's capacity to reshape local educational affairs is indeed pronounced. In short, for its size, its proximity to federal power, and its strong cultural and political identity, Alexandria is in many ways an illuminating test case.[50]

Research Design and Chapter Overviews

The book utilizes the notions of regime and political development to inform the research design. Examining one city over a roughly a fifty-year period, paying atten-tion to both the political history of the community and the introduction of new federal policy initiatives, enables me to simultaneously hold constant the state and regional contexts while examining the interaction of local regime composition and federal efforts to reform educational practices and institutions. In short, while a long-term study of one city appears to be a single case study, it has nested within it multiple opportunities to explore how federal policies interact with local regime commitments. Employing both within-case process tracing for each policy initia-tive as well as cross-case comparisons to evaluate the relative success of federal policy innovation, the book leverages the multiple regimes that have existed within Alexandria's recent past to better understand how local regime commitments shape the adoption and success of federal policy interventions in public education.[51]

Table 1.1 illustrates the emergence and persistence of different federal education initiatives during particular local regime eras within Alexandria. Using historical and archival records, interviews, and secondary accounts, this book examines these policy initiatives across time through multiple regimes in order to process-trace the conflicts between federal priorities and local regimes. By examining across policy initiatives, I also seek to draw comparisons about the relative success of federal edu-cation reforms within each regime era. Together, these within-case and cross-case examinations can give us some better analytical insights into the local factors that explain relative success or failure in federal educational policymaking.

Because I also want to explore how the federal commitment to particular policies affects the viability of particular local regimes, I also consider in this book how the implementation of particular policies strengthened or undermined the political logic

Table 1. 1 **Local Regime Eras in Alexandria, Virginia 1959–2013**

Federal education policy	Byrd Regime (1959–1966)	Post-Byrd Regime (1966–1974)	Racial Coalition Regime (1974–1995)	Metropolitan Regime (1995–2013)
Desegregation/ integration	██ Federal program priority	██ Federal program priority	▒ Program in existence, but not Federal priority	▒ Program in existence, but not Federal priority
Special education		▒ Program in existence, but not Federal priority	██ Federal program priority	██ Federal program priority
Accountability			██ Federal program priority	██ Federal program priority
Bilingual education/ELL			▒ Program in existence, but not Federal priority	▒ Program in existence, but not Federal priority

Key:

██	Federal program priority
▒	Program in existence, but not Federal priority

of these regimes. Part of the ability of federal policy to penetrate into local schools resides in its alignment (or lack thereof) with the priorities of local regime actors, which stem, in turn, from the fundamental political logics of the city and school districts. One of the virtues of this approach is that we can place federal education policies on a continuum, ranging from most disruptive to most reinforcing, according to the local logics of city and school district politics. This, in turn, can help us better understand why and how federal policies work in some places but not in others.

The organization of the chapters of the book follows the rough schematic of the horizontal process-tracing depicted in Table 1.1. Part One of the book (Chapters 2 and 3) examines the period of school desegregation and integration, roughly from 1959 to 1974. Chapter 2 documents the history of Massive Resistance in Virginia and examines closely the conduct of Alexandria school officials when confronted with court orders to desegregate and with later mandates from Health, Education and Welfare that it comply with the 1964 Civil Rights Act. The chapter anchors that examination in the political structure of the city and highlights how local authorities, particularly Superintendent John C. Albohm, struggled to find a politically viable path between what the local regime could tolerate and what federal authorities were demanding.

That struggle continues in Chapter 3, which carries Alexandria's desegregation and integration stories through the mid-1970s. Although depicted in the Hollywood film *Remember the Titans* as a difficult, but successful transition, the full integration of Alexandria was marked by violence, political upheaval, and the emergence of a new political order within Alexandria. The chapter traces both the social unrest that marked the early 1970s in Alexandria's streets and schools, as well as the radicalization of many Alexandria's youth during this time. The local political issues of school discipline and the newly emergent difficulties of educating poor students (generally black) next to affluent students (generally white) produced intense political pressure for Albohm, who was caught between increasing HEW demands to produce immediate integration and local pressure to solve the disciplinary problems in Alexandria's high schools. He responded by restructuring Alexandria's schools—creating, for the first time, a single citywide high school. While this move was adroit politically, it did not meet the requirements of federal officials. The difficult process of fully integrating Alexandria's elementary schools sparked further conflict, but after a long public debate about both the character of Alexandria's identity and its demographic future, the city finally implemented a full integration plan in 1974, twenty years after *Brown v. Board of Education*.

Part Two of the book—Chapters 4, 5, and 6—turns to the local repercussions and reception of the federal commitment to equality from the mid-1970s into the 1990s. Chapter 4 focuses on what I call the politics of exit, the flight by many white Alexandrians away from public schools and then, later, from Alexandria itself. As the more racially conservative members of the community left town, their departure helped create the foundations of a white liberal and African American coalition that would dominate Alexandria politics for the next twenty years. The chapter begins with a geospatial analysis of the relationship between desegregation and private school voucher use in the early 1960s. It then examines the attitudes of parents who responded to official school surveys as they fled Alexandria, and also traces the changing voting patterns of city residents. All told, these changes created conditions that enabled a new liberal racial coalition to gain power in Alexandria.

Chapter 5 then follows the implications of this newly emergent racial coalition by examining the reception of federal special education initiatives in the city. While Superintendent T.C. Williams had sought to use special education as a means to preserve segregated schooling, the federal expansion of special education advanced the fortunes of the racial coalition in Alexandria. This emergent regime, premised on the provision of social services as part of its racial compromise, embraced special education as a means of delivering more services to constituents. As that expansion took place, however, special education also became a vehicle by which the school system simultaneously segregated the most disruptive and challenging students (at the secondary level) and enabled white elementary-level students to maintain an accelerated academic program. Thus, the district's historical practices of overidentifying poor and African American students as special needs entrenched their segregation while at the same time retaining the support of upper middle-class (often white) parents concerned about both the discipline of students and the academic rigor of the school system.

Chapter 6 turns to federal programs for English-learners and their implementation in Alexandria. It examines the historical practices of teaching English learners in the United States and the inconsistent federal policies adopted to teach English to

non-native speakers. Alexandria saw significant numbers of new immigrants beginning in the 1980s as the Washington, DC metropolitan area became a gateway region
for immigration, but a mismatch between the needs of these students and district's
capacity or willingness to address them meant that they received little attention in
Alexandria schools. The schooling of English learners in Alexandria was the product
of both a timid federal push on English language instruction and a continuing failure to incorporate immigrant groups within Alexandria's power structure.

Part Three (Chapters 7 and 8) turns to the politics of accountability. Chapter
7 examines efforts by local activists in the early 1990s to create a directly elected
School Board, one that was more in alignment with constituent wishes. The old system, in which the City Council appointed School Board members, had produced,
in the eyes of many, a patronage-bound School Board in which members delivered votes to City Council candidates in exchange for appointment to the Board.
Efforts to create a directly elected Board accelerated in the mid-1990s as parents in
many affluent areas of town perceived Superintendent Paul Masem as unresponsive to their calls for a more demanding and rigorous school system. For his part,
Masem battled race and class tensions in the community as he sought to close the
black-white achievement gap. Chapter 8 turns to a different form of accountability
politics, one in which student test scores on state assessments, rather than electoral
representation, constituted the accountability mechanism. The chapter begins with
an overview of accountability politics and provisions in Virginia and then turns to
a detailed account of the Alexandria efforts to remove T.C. Williams High School
from the U.S. Department of Education's list of persistently lowest-achieving
schools. Focusing on the political concerns that lay just below the surface of efforts
by school officials to boost educational performance, the chapter explores how
the historical experiences of both special education and racial minorities within
Alexandria schools shaped the educational response. It also examines the profound tension between responding to the federal mandate to improve test scores
and building a school culture that reflected the multiple constituencies within T.C.
Williams's economically and racially diverse school population.

Chapter 9 concludes the book by asking what all these stories of education
reform mean—for educational policymakers, for political scientists, and for the students and residents of Alexandria. Looking both within policy domains and across
them, I contend that the construction of the education state holds significance for
each of these three groups and that the distinction between improving education
and constructing the education state should be at the forefront of all discussions of
education reform in the United States.

PART ONE

RACE AND REFORM

Perhaps T.C. Williams first realized he had gone too far when the Justice Department investigators started calling. Then again, maybe not. The Alexandria Superintendent had been in office since 1933 and was used to getting his way, so when he decided in 1958 to fire Blois Hundley, an African American cook at Lyles-Crouch Elementary School, for joining the NAACP's lawsuit to desegregate Alexandria's schools, he was probably not too concerned about the consequences.[1] As he told the School Board, "in any organization it is inconsistent and rather incongruous to have a member of the organization suing it."[2] His commitment to strict segregation was robust and, as a member of Alexandria's Old Guard, he fought as fiercely as anyone to preserve it.

The School Board certainly was not going to reverse his decision: a motion by School Board member Sarah Kerbel to rehire Mrs. Hundley died without receiving a second.[3] Nonetheless, when the U.S. Department of Justice began to inquire whether Williams had violated Ms. Hundley's civil rights by firing her for seeking to enroll her children Theodosia and Pearl, ages fourteen and twelve, in a white school, the Superintendent had to back down. Williams said his reversal had nothing to do with federal pressure, but was due to a personal reevaluation: "I felt my first action was hasty and not too well-considered," adding that by the time the Justice Department made its inquiries, "my decision had already been made."[4]

Despite her reinstatement, the reaction of the local authorities to Mrs. Hundley's efforts to undermine segregation in Alexandria highlighted the centrality of racial issues to the organization of both Alexandria schooling and politics. While the federal judicial effort to restructure schooling in Alexandria in the late 1950s was, at first, tentative, within a few years the federal assault on segregated schooling became more vigorous, boosted by both

the 1964 Civil Rights Act and the 1965 Elementary and Secondary Education
Act. Indeed, the mid-1960s saw, for the first time, an energetic federal effort
to dictate the terms of local schooling, particularly local school attendance
patterns. In Alexandria, this increasing federal authority over the racial composition of public schools undermined the city's existing power structure,
but did not topple it. The political accommodation of Alexandria's local
regime to federal pressure both allowed the federal government to strongly
influence the nature of desegregation and also limited its reach. By the early
1970s, however, the pressure—both direct and indirect—from judges and
HEW grew intense, leading to a significant reconfiguration of racial politics
in Alexandria. Unfortunately, those changes did little to mitigate or reduce
racial conflict within the city and school system. In short, the combined
pressure of court and administrative intervention forced Alexandria school
officials by the mid-1970s to incorporate African Americans not only into
previously all-white schools, but also into the local power structure.

That dual incorporation led to a dramatically changing political calculus due to rapid changes in the demographics of the city. These changes
ultimately transformed the racial order that had previously organized
Alexandria's politics, but the process took a full decade. During this transition, the absence of a new, stabilizing political order that could directly confront increasing racial conflict led to significant rancor and mistrust among
local constituents. Schools became a site in which conflicts that permeated the local political structure were identified and articulated, rather than
a site of common interests and common fates. In addition, the significant
class divisions between whites and African Americans meant that the racial
reconstruction of Alexandria's schools was seen as an academic zero-sum
struggle in which gains for poor African Americans were defined as losses
for middle-class whites.

Part One of this book follows the arc of desegregation and integration of
Alexandria's schools from the late 1950s through the mid-1970s, paying particular attention to the ways that growing federal pressures were accompanied
by local bottom-up demands for not only desegregation and integration, but
for better programs and educational offerings for African American students
in Alexandria. While the story of desegregation in Virginia and throughout
the South has been told in numerous excellent accounts,[5] Part One seeks to
link federal efforts ensuring racial equal opportunity in schooling to changes
in local political structures and local definitions of public education.

Chapter 2 follows Alexandria's movement from the Massive Resistance
era to the acceptance of tokenism in Alexandria's schools. That initial period

saw the conflicting factions of the local political regime vie for influence over the School Board and its forceful and long-serving superintendent, Thomas Chambliss Williams, known to all as T.C. Williams. Williams began serving as Alexandria's superintendent in 1933 and was, in many ways, emblematic of Virginia's mid-20th century political elite, reflecting its penchant for frugality, intolerance of corruption, dislike of political participation, and insistence on racial control.[6] His retirement in January of 1963 came as a more liberal wing of the Democratic Party in Virginia gained the upper hand in Alexandria politics. This opening allowed the School Board to replace Williams with John Albohm, a far more racially moderate superintendent, who oversaw several reorganizations of Alexandria schools that produced more or less fully integrated schools by the mid-1970s.

Chapter 3 turns to a critical juncture in this integration effort in the early 1970s. At that time, Alexandria was living through a historic transformation of the South's racial order, one that tapped into broader cultural and racial change that forced white Alexandrians to redefine their relationship with the African American community. The process in Alexandria was in many ways commendable, but it was neither smooth nor entirely peaceful. Chapter 3 pays particular attention to the issues of school discipline and the community's articulation of its own self-identity in the many public hearings that were held in the midst of these successive school reorganizations, focusing not only on local efforts to prevent federal authorities from defining the contexts of public education in Alexandria, but also the emergent class-based differences over the purposes of public education within the community.

2

Race and the End of a Regime

Introduction

The litigation history of the desegregation of Alexandria City Public Schools is per-haps among the shortest in the South. Six months after initially filing suit for the right to attend desegregated schools, nine African American students were attend-ing a formerly all-white school.[1] That short time span, however, belies the intense conflict sparked by the lawsuit and the issue of desegregation more generally. The local, state, and federal politics that led to desegregation in Alexandria were intri-cate and complex, and resistance to desegregation was fierce—particularly among School Board members and superintendent T.C. Williams. Even after the school district lost its court battle, both political and administrative school officials orga-nized intensive administrative efforts to limit desegregation despite local residents' support for racial moderation.

In part because of these conflicting forces within the city, Alexandria was, in some ways, a bystander to larger events in the story of Virginia's battle: it neither led the charge to resist desegregation nor was it the first to desegregate in Virginia. Its neighbor to the north, Arlington, admitted the first African American students to white Virginia public schools on February 2, 1959; Alexandria's initial desegrega-tion took place a week later. Nonetheless, the story of the initial steps to desegregate Alexandria's schools reveals the extent to which racial politics organized the politi-cal regime governing this small city by the Potomac, and also demonstrates a pat-tern of racial conflict that persisted long after its successful desegregation.

The entrenched nature of racial hierarchy as an organizing principle of both city and school politics meant that the federal court decision ordering Alexandria City Public Schools to comply with *Brown v. Board of Education* was a direct challenge to the political basis of the local regime. The efforts by the local regime—as an exten-sion of the statewide political apparatus headed by US Senator Harry F. Byrd, Sr.—to resist desegregation were not simply delaying tactics. They wound up establishing institutional patterns and policy routines that were difficult to undo and structured later educational conflicts within Alexandria, particularly over tracking and special education. The evasion and recalcitrance of Alexandria's school and city leaders did not simply delay justice to African American school children, but also established new institutional forms and routines that continued even after desegregation had been accomplished.

At the same time, the city's eventual compliance with *Brown* brought down the local regime, just as statewide compliance hastened the demise of the statewide Byrd organization. Desegregation recomposed Alexandria's politics by splitting its elites and realigning political loyalties of conservative Democrats. Alexandria's middle-class African American population, buoyed by the broader civil rights movement, seized that opening and began to insist on better housing, educational conditions and direct representation of its interests. By 1963, the city that the *Washington Post* referred to in 1957 as "Northern Virginia's last stronghold of conservatism,"[2] had appointed a new school superintendent who was committed to a program of compensatory education for African Americans and fostering as much desegregation as was feasible through the assignment of pupils to neighborhood schools.

This chapter recounts these developments in three sections. The first, "From Massive Resistance to Racial Tokenism, 1957–1963" examines the political logic of Massive Resistance and the techniques of resistance used to prevent desegregation, at both the state and local levels. The second section, "From Tokenism to Gradualism: Race, Poverty, Neighborhood and the Identity of Alexandria," examines the efforts of Superintendent John Albohm to address the educational effects of racialized poverty while undertaking modest desegregation within the limitations of neighborhood segregation and local expectations of "quality" schooling. The final section, "HEW and the End of Racial Gradualism," explores how the U.S. Department of Health Education and Welfare's efforts to promote desegregation under Title VI of the 1964 Civil Rights Act accelerated the racial transformation of Alexandria's schools, and brought an end to official Jim Crow schooling in Alexandria.

From Massive Resistance to Racial Tokenism, 1957–1963

Massive Resistance in Virginia was the product of a calculated campaign by Virginia's political machine—the "Organization" headed by US Senator and former Virginia Governor Harry F. Byrd, Sr.—to maintain white supremacy at all costs and deny African Americans full participation in the political, social, and economic life of the state. While Massive Resistance was deeply tied to the maintenance of a caste-based ideology of white supremacy, there was a more immediate political benefit to its organizers. The Byrd machine's long-running statewide electoral success stemmed in large part from the huge margins Organization candidates racked up in the rural southern tier of Virginia, a region known as Southside.

These margins, in turn, rested on the massive disenfranchisement of African American voters across Southside counties. The vehemence of the Organization's response to *Brown v. Board of Education* was due, in part, to the threat *Brown* posed to the machine's ability to suppress African American political participation in Southside. With better access to education, and accompanying demands for more political participation, African Americans would erode the political margins in Southside, further endangering the Organization's influence over a Virginia public already growing disenchanted with the machine's commitments to low taxes and frugal levels of governmental services. As a political machine whose governing philosophy was beginning to grow threadbare, the Organization seized on Massive Resistance both as a way to rally supporters, but also to hide its underlying political vulnerabilities.

The Organization's influence in Northern Virginia was not strong. The region grew dramatically during Washington's post World War II boom and was increasingly incorporated into a broader metropolitan economic and political structure. More recently arrived, better-educated, and more affluent, the new suburbanite residents of Arlington, Alexandria, and Fairfax County often held little regard for Byrd and his legacy. Alexandria and its Old Town denizens, however, represented the Organization's toehold in Northern Virginia. As citizens of a city older than the District of Columbia, its elite widely revered Alexandria's colonial and antebellum past; indeed, the community's attachment to the planter aristocracy of Virginia was manifest in the nearby Mount Vernon, the ancestral home of George Washington. In the late '50s and early '60s, close personal ties also connected the community's elite to the Byrd Organization. Marshall J. Beverley, Mayor of Alexandria from 1952–1955, was a cousin of Harry F. Byrd, Sr., while Alexandria State Delegate James M. Thomson was the brother-in-law of Harry Byrd, Jr. Those connections trickled down through a network of Byrd-affiliated local elites who maintained influence through their participation in the Organization, as well as their money and social prestige.

Another set of elites, more typically recent arrivals to Alexandria, was less enamored of the Organization's claims of legacy and gained their local influence through their business interests and civic associations. As leaders of medium-to-large local industrial firms, local banks, and real estate and insurance companies, these attorneys, merchants, and white-collar professionals took part in local governance through neighborhood and homeowner associations and through civic associations such as the Masons, Kiwanis, Rotary, and Jaycees. As a small city, Alexandria supported an elite coalition that was cohesive, but not single-minded. Socially and politically conservative, this elite supported school segregation, but the rise of Massive Resistance—and the Byrd Organization's fire-eating commitment to the maintenance of segregation at all costs—split Alexandria's elite down the middle, opening the door to a more liberal racial policy in order to preserve public education.

Initial Phases of Desegregation in Alexandria

Virginia's initial response in 1954 to *Brown v. Board of Education* bore only a modest resemblance to the fevered agitation of 1956–1957, the peak of Massive Resistance. The Gray Commission, appointed by Governor Thomas B. Stanley in August of 1954 to recommend a course of action in the wake of *Brown,* put forward essentially a two-pronged plan to resist and delay desegregation. As the Commission report stated: "This Commission believes that separate facilities in our public schools are in the best interest of both races, educationally and otherwise, and that compulsory integration should be resisted by all proper means in our power."[3] The first element of the plan rested on local school boards operating a program of pupil assignment to particular schools. These placements would "be based upon the welfare of the particular child as well as the welfare and best interests of all other pupils attending a particular school" and would take into account a broad range of criteria, such as the "availability of facilities, health, aptitude of the child, and the availability of transportation."[4] Through these means, the Commission asserted, localities would be equipped to respond to local desegregationist challenges in flexible ways: "[T]hese things must be in the hands of local people who know their own communities and whose children will profit or suffer by their decisions."[5]

The second element was a program of private school tuition grants for any student who sought to avoid attending a desegregated public school. This system of grants would be funded by both state and local money, with the local money being diverted, if need be, from the operating costs of the current schools. Shortly before the release of the Gray Commission Report, however, the Virginia Supreme Court struck down such private school grants, on the grounds that Section 141 of the Virginia Constitution barred public funds being used to support private schools.[6] As a result, the Gray Commission recommended that the Virginia Constitution be amended to allow private school grants. This, in turned, opened the door to a public vote on the possible steps that Virginia might take to thwart desegregation. The Byrd Organization saw its opportunity, mobilized its forces, and placed on the ballot a statewide referendum calling for a constitutional convention to amend Section 141.

In January 1956, Virginia voters approved the idea of tuition vouchers by more than a two-to-one margin.[7] Not surprisingly, the Organization and its supporters interpreted the success of that referendum as popular support for the cause of Massive Resistance, spurring them to abandon any thoughts of moderation and to move away from the Gray Commission's plan of local pupil placement. Within three weeks of the referendum, the Virginia General Assembly, having been urged on by *Richmond News Leader* editor James J. Kilpatrick, Jr., enacted a resolution of interposition, claiming to deny the Federal government any authority to desegregate Virginia's schools. Massive Resistance had arrived.

The white-hot rhetoric of interposition quickly forged a more durable barrier: a systematic state-run plan to shut down public education in Virginia if federal courts proceeded with desegregation. In late August of 1956, Governor Thomas B. Stanley called the Virginia legislature into special session to devise a legislative response to the prospect of court-ordered desegregation. The result was a package of laws designed to both thwart and delay desegregation and to shut down public education in any school district in which desegregation was imminent. First, the state assumed control of the placement of students in particular schools, under a statewide pupil placement board. Any transfers of students required the approval of the state board, thereby preventing any local school board from undertaking voluntary desegregation. In addition, the legislature approved a new plan for private school tuition grants and required the governor to seize and close any Virginia public school that confronted imminent desegregation because of a court order. The legislature also gave the governor authority to suspend state aid to any school that voluntarily desegregated. While moderates rightfully claimed that this legislative program held little chance of surviving challenges in federal court, their positions were labeled traitorous to the cause of segregation.

In Alexandria, local officials strategically used these threats of state-imposed punishment and closure in order to argue for an indefinite delay of desegregation in the wake of *Brown v. Board*, despite significant local support for racial moderation. Importantly, no local African American student sought transfer to a white Alexandrian school. In the summer of 1958, however, cracks began to appear in Virginia's wall of Massive Resistance. In August, fourteen African American students in Alexandria sought transfers to white schools. Predictably, the school district referred these applications to the statewide pupil placement board, which then denied these administrative applications for transfer. In September 1958, the fourteen Alexandria African American students filed suit in U.S. District Court in Alexandria, seeking a court order to compel their admission to white-only schools. With *Brown* on the books, and the U.S. Supreme Court upholding federal intervention in Little Rock, the legal situation of segregationists in Alexandria was weak.

Events outside Alexandria were also pushing Massive Resistance to its ultimate test. In mid-September, confronted with imminent federal court-ordered desegregation of rural Warren County High School, Governor Lindsay Almond invoked the Massive Resistance laws and closed down the school. Shortly thereafter, Almond shut schools in Charlottesville and Norfolk, leaving 13,000 students in Virginia with no public school to attend.[8] In Alexandria, meanwhile, judicial and local officials moved tentatively toward their own confrontation, while at the same time awaiting developments in Richmond that might allow them to avoid a state-ordered school closure. Two days before the Alexandria desegregation trial was to begin in late October 1958, the School Board enacted a resolution that purported to establish a race-neutral policy toward pupil assignment within the city. The resolution announced six criteria by which any application to transfer or enroll in Alexandria's public schools would be evaluated.[9] With a nod to *Brown*, the Board indicated that this six-point plan of pupil assignment would "be administered on a racially nondiscriminatory basis."[10] Partly due to the enactment of this resolution and partly because of developments on other legal fronts, Federal District Court Judge Albert V. Bryan delayed his ruling on the plaintiffs' motion for summary judgment until January 1959.

The criteria for pupil assignments adopted by the School Board were racially neutral in name only. In keeping with local regime's insistence on maintaining segregation, the Alexandria School Board relied on the administrative procedures outlined in its new six-point school assignment plan to deny African Americans seats in white schools. Each criterion was specifically related to an important and legitimate local school function, yet, collectively, they allowed the school board to deny wholesale the admission of African American students to white schools.

The first criterion addressed the geographic proximity of a school to an applicant's home. The Board would consider allowing an African American student to attend a white school only if the white school was geographically closer to the applicant's home than the nearest black school. The second criterion demanded that the district consider pupil crowding in the school to which the applicant sought to transfer; students were only allowed to transfer or attend a new school if sufficient space existed. The assignment plan's third criterion allowed the Board to consider a student's academic performance and scholarly potential—as measured by past academic achievements, performance on newly required standardized achievement tests (for older children), and "school readiness" or "mental maturity" assessments (for prospective first graders). The Board stipulated that these tests were to be administered on a "racially nondiscriminatory basis." The fourth criterion considered by the board when determining whether to grant a transfer was the health of the applicant, which could affect his or her "wholesomeness, vigor, mental capacity, association, acceptability, or learning ability and retention." The fifth—and most amorphous—standard required the Board to examine "any facts which may be available indicating emotional and social stability, or otherwise, which would in any way affect the acceptability of such transfer."[11]

In late January 1959, events unfolded rapidly. On January 19, both the Virginia Supreme Court and a three-judge panel of the Federal District Court in Norfolk, Virginia struck down the state's school closure laws and school tuition grant program, which had formed the legislative heart of Massive Resistance. While those rulings meant that Alexandria no longer faced school closure if it desegregated its schools, the School Board nonetheless held firm. Meeting in a closed executive session on January 22, the Board denied the applications of all fourteen African American students who sought to attend white schools. Compiling an extensive dossier on each student, the School Board used four of the six criteria to exclude the students.

Despite the ostensibly race-neutral characteristics of the criteria, race suffused the school board's application of them. In one case, an African American girl performed above the median score of the white school to which she was applying on the California Achievement Test, but the Board wrote:

> This girl, if admitted to the sixth grade of either the Patrick Henry or William Ramsey School, will be the only pupil of her race so enrolled. This, in Alexandria, will be a novel and unusual situation. Such a situation will constitute a disruption of established social and psychological relationships between pupils in our schools as they (the schools) have previously operated.... The situation will be an unnatural one, which, as such, cannot contribute to normal and natural progress for either this girl or for the other pupils in the grade.[12]

The School Board also denied all of the other thirteen students who had requested transfers, claiming that such moves were impossible due to geography, academic underperformance, or social disruption among white students.

Upon returning to federal District Court, some of the fourteen students had better success. Judge Bryan reevaluated the students' applications for transfer or admission using the School Board's own six criteria. Three students, he contended, lived closer to the all-black schools, so they must remain there. In two other instances, Bryan ruled, the academic performance of the students was sufficiently poor that the board was not without reason in its denial of transfer. The remaining nine students, according to Bryan, had been denied transfer or admission solely on the basis of race, and on February 4, Bryan ruled that the nine students must be admitted to three all-white schools on February 10, 1959.

On the same day as Bryan's ruling, the School Board met in executive session and voted four to one to file a notice of appeal, but it also unanimously decided that it would comply with Bryan's order if its appeal was denied (the denial came a mere three days later). Sensing the inevitable, the Board also approved a public statement that urged the "full cooperation of the citizens of Alexandria" if desegregation was required. At the same time, in an effort to ward off any mischief, the Board requested that City Council declare the schools that were targeted for desegregation "off-limits" to all persons except students, personnel, and parents.[13] On February 10, 1959, Alexandria saw the first attendance of African American students alongside white students.

Local Elite Politics and Desegregation

While white public opinion within Alexandria was generally split between racial conservatives who hoped to avoid desegregation at all costs and racial moderates willing to accept some desegregation in order to protect public education, the racial conservatives held a majority of City Council seats during this crucial initial phase. As a result, the Alexandria School Board accepted, during this time, the absolutist stance pushed by the Massive Resisters. In fact, given the alignment of local regime actors on the City Council and School Board, there was little chance the School Board would do otherwise.

Despite the close affinity between City Council and School Board over the maintenance of segregation, the position of modest accommodation was a politically popular one in Alexandria, if not a majority position. One of its most capable advocates, State Senator Armistead Lloyd Boothe, had long represented Alexandria in the state legislature and had as early as 1950 introduced legislation to repeal Virginia's Jim Crow transportation laws. His mild reformist stance, along with his willingness to tolerate a small degree of desegregation in order to keep public schools open, led to Boothe's ostracism from the Byrd Organization. To Boothe's mind, it was far better for local school officials to regulate closely the rate and kind of desegregation than to allow federal judges to order what, in Boothe's view, would be a far more sweeping and transformative desegregation.[14]

Boothe's position was far from racially liberal; he wrote in a 1957 letter to a close friend that while some remarkable individual African Americans may have the "character, intelligence and other requisites entitling them to full first-class American citizenship," the "Negro race, as a race, is very inferior to the white race."[15] And in a speech to the Alexandria Kiwanis Club in 1959 he stated that "I am a southerner, born and bred. As a result, I am a segregationist. I am not a degradationist. I have not, I do not, and shall not degrade every single American citizen who is born a Negro."[16] Nonetheless, he described the petition of fourteen African American students in Alexandria to attend all-white schools as "unwelcome news."[17] Boothe's views held significant support in Alexandria. Even constituents who may have been more racially liberal welcomed his efforts to defeat the private school tuition grants and to avoid the closure of public schools, particularly local PTA activists (who endorsed desegregation in order to prevent school closure in Alexandria)[18] and members of the Virginia Committee for Public Schools, an anti-Massive Resistance organization that fought both tuition vouchers and state efforts to close schools confronting desegregation.

Despite local support for Boothe's comparatively moderate stance, Alexandria's hardline segregationists held a dominant position in local politics, and, importantly, took steps to maintain their influence when challenged. In June 1959, the City Council voted 4-3 to remove Herman G. Moeller from the School Board. Moeller had been the sole School Board member who voted to desegregate the previously all-white schools.[19] At the time, Boothe interpreted the move as simply part of the political campaign against him as the city headed into the 1959 primary season, saying it was an effort by his opponent in the upcoming state senate race, former Alexandria Mayor Marshall J. Beverley, to "drag the public schools further into politics."[20] While the move may have been simply part of an effort to embarrass Boothe and his supporters, it also illustrates that the School Board—and contestation over its actions—mirrored many of the existing political cleavages within

Alexandria. The local elites that dominated the political landscape at this time had grown increasingly divided over whether the preservation of segregation was worth the closure of public schools. When federal courts broke the back of the state-level Massive Resistance effort, and District Court Judge Albert V. Bryan, more specifically, compelled the desegregation of Alexandria, the focus of segregationists turned to an exertion of local pressure against local Board members to continue to resist court-ordered desegregation.

The administrative face of the School Board's efforts to resist further desegregation is readily found in the rationales and justifications the School Board employed to deny admission of African Americans to all-white schools, albeit in language that was not explicitly racial. Despite the legal victory of nine African American students in Alexandria, the School Board steadfastly denied the applications of other students who wished to enroll in white schools. Four more African American students (all from the same family) were denied placement in white schools in April, 1959, and thirteen more were denied placement in white schools in October, 1959. The language of the School Board denials is, from our vantage point, both paternalistic and bigoted, but they reveal more than the bigotry of the times. The language and assumptions of the denials reveal important insights about the School Board's— and Superintendent Williams'—perspective. Their assumptions about schools, learning, and abilities are revealed in the articulations of students' capacities and potential. The denials were based upon a mix of pragmatic and normative objections; they were not (because the Court would not allow it) explicitly race-based. Thus, instead of reading about race in the denials, we read concerns about transportation and logistics, about self-esteem and accomplishments, about social effects in classrooms, about academic effects of mixing "slow" African American learners with the "advanced" white students. But no matter what reasons were offered for the School Board's denials, the results were always the same. The inability to use race explicitly as a category of denial forced the School Board to be creative about the "problems" desegregation would create for Alexandria schools. These nonracial objections to desegregation also gave credence to later popular objections about school governance that had racial ramifications, in particular claims about quality of schools, school discipline, and "natural" groupings of students.

As a first line of defense, the Board often invoked the logistical problems of desegregating schools. Transportation problems, the Board argued, would be solved more readily if the students stayed at black schools, because no transportation was provided to the white schools, while buses carried African American students directly to the black schools: "The bus going to [the black school] passes by this girl's door. There can be no inconvenience in such an arrangement. She would be inconvenienced much more by walking to the [neighborhood white school] even if she preferred it. The bus is, by far, the more convenient and protected arrangement." One boy was denied a transfer despite the fact that his home was "equidistant from Houston [the black school] and Ficklin [the white school]."

The Board reasoned, oddly, that one-way vehicle traffic would dictate the route the boy would walk to school: "It is estimated that the actual distances which have to be walked, because of the way the streets run" made the distance to the black school "somewhat shorter."[21]

When transportation was not an issue, the Board indicated a concern for the self-esteem of students who were among the top students at the all-black schools. One eight-year-old girl should not transfer, the Board contended, because while "her standing at [the black school] has been one of leadership and excellence,"; she will be "in the lower reaches of her class [at the white school], unrecognized and of no special note. This is not a good change." Another seventh-grader would find it "a frustrating and discouraging experience to pass from a position of prestige in one place to a position of low rating in another. . . . It does not appear from the record that this boy has either the ambition or the spirit to enable him to compete successfully with even the lowest of the seventh grade" at the white school. Another student would be "hopelessly outclassed" in the white school: "There is no student in the sixth grade [at the white school] who has as low an accomplishment level as this boy." At the white high school, another student "would be in a class where 99 percent of the students would exceed him in achievement and potential."[22]

In other cases—particularly when other white students had scored as low as the African American students—the School Board stressed the "burden" on the white students. "To transfer this girl to the grade [at the white school] only because there are three others in it as low in competence as she is only makes a bad situation worse. It does not profit her at all. The grade will be more heavily burdened with additional problem cases, which will intensify the slowing down effect of such cases on the grade. The more such cases there are in the grade the greater the hindrance to it." The transfer of another student "only burdens the grade at [the white school] with more problems, which tends to slow down the whole grade."[23]

Faced with such transfer denials, students and their families again filed suit, and again the Court ordered their admission to formerly all-white schools. Again the School Board appealed to the Fourth Circuit, and again the School Board lost the appeal.[24] Not until September 8, 1960 did the School Board—challenged by yet another request from an African American student—approve a transfer without first being subject to a court order.[25] Nonetheless, the process of desegregation proceeded on a student-by-student basis: still using the six point criteria adopted in November 1958, the Board assigned individual African American students to white schools only when students sought such a transfer.[26]

By the beginning of the 1962–1963 school year, the School Board had routinized this process of transferring African American students out of Jim Crow schools, but the pace of desegregation was exceedingly slow. Having lost the battle to prevent the desegregation of schooling, T.C. Williams and the School Board had settled upon a strategy of containment to limit the effects of school desegregation throughout the school system. In effect, the "moderate" position articulated by Boothe and his supporters had become de facto School Board policy. The Board's conscious efforts to contain desegregation, in conjunction with the small number of transfer requests, limited desegregation to a miniscule percentage of African American students in Alexandria. Indeed, a grand total of seventy-five African American students had been processed by the School Board in the three-and-a-half years since Judge Albert Bryan had ordered the district to desegregate, out of a total African American enrollment of roughly 2440 students in the fall of 1962.[27] The last of these individualized transfers totaled only sixteen pupils and approvals came in a June 1962 executive session in which T.C. Williams announced his retirement, effective January 1, 1963. At that meeting, Williams commented that his nearly thirty years in Alexandria as Superintendent had been "reasonably happy ones," with his mood perhaps dampened by the increasing momentum of desegregation, which he and the School Board had been forced to assist.[28]

Williams's place in the history of Alexandria schools is a complex one. A frugal and somewhat churlish administrator, he nonetheless oversaw the school district's significant expansion during the post-World War II housing boom, successfully extracting resources from the City Council. A committed segregationist, he carefully and explicitly denied educational opportunities to disfavored groups, particularly African Americans and special needs students, two groups on which he was not inclined to "waste" precious public funds. Nonetheless, Williams expressed fervent support for the ideals of public education. In his final Superintendent's Report, he urged the School Board members to focus on the larger task at hand:

> It is only through single-minded devotion to the cause of better education and the willingness to make the necessary sacrifices to realize this goal that true and enduring service is possible. Vision, sincerity, courage, unswerving devotion, insistence, endurance, and tenacity are among the qualities which are necessary for fulfillment in a cause as difficult, as intricate, and as glorious as public education is.

He concluded that "Public Education ... is the greatest of causes and deserves the best that you have."[29]

In short, T.C. Williams embodied many of the qualities and attitudes of Alexandria's white residents: a pride in the quality of its white schools, a commitment to segregation, and a dedication to the principles of public education. To many white Virginians of the time, the goals of protecting and expanding public education and of maintaining segregation were neither inconsistent nor incompatible—at least not until the federal government's efforts to desegregate public schooling placed these commitments in profound tension.

From Tokenism to Gradualism: Race, Poverty, Neighborhood and the Identity of Alexandria

The School Board's practice of allowing desegregation only through individualized approval of African American student transfers ended in 1963, after T.C. Williams's retirement, as the district began to assign both black and white students to predominantly neighborhood schools.[30] Between 1963 and 1965, Alexandria, under the direction of new superintendent John Albohm, began a slow shift to neighborhood-based school attendance zones. By 1965–1966, however, that gradual shift to wholly neighborhood schooling was outpaced by an increasingly transformative federal agenda, located this time not just in the courts, but in an energetic federal bureaucracy charged with not only distributing new federal funds for public education, but also ensuring the absence of discrimination in school districts that received those funds. By 1966, this accelerating pace of change on civil rights at the national level meant that Alexandria not only had to satisfy the court order handed down in *Jones v. School Board of City of Alexandria, Virginia* but also the terms of federal legislation (the 1964 Civil Rights Act and the 1965 Elementary and Secondary Education Act) that imposed greater demands for racial justice than the limited court orders previously lodged against Alexandria.

At the same time, many Alexandrians, white and black, pushed the School Board to adopt more integrationist policies. Indeed, the conflicts over schooling in Alexandria at this time were less a pitched battle between local school officials and federal judges and bureaucrats and more a conflict between two segments of the Alexandria population and leadership: conservatives who would tolerate desegregation only if it conformed to the existing racial and class patterns of housing in the city and a more diffuse group of white racial moderates and African Americans who advocated a more vigorous effort to remove the vestiges of Jim Crow schooling from Alexandria's schools.

As the School Board and the new Superintendent John Albohm navigated between these two groups, it confronted a series of issues that, while not directly about race, tapped into class-based racial tensions and animosities within the city. Issues such as "cultural deprivation," school discipline, athletics, and the identities of neighborhoods all challenged the capacity of local political and school officials to achieve stable outcomes that did not exacerbate existing racial tensions. In short, the political problems of the Alexandria City School Board from the mid-60s to the mid-70s stemmed largely from the race-infused class antagonisms that emerged— some intense, some minor—as the school district responded to both local calls for greater change and the federal judiciary's increasingly stringent demand that school districts achieve "unitary" status. The reluctance of Alexandria school officials to pursue strategies that would quickly achieve unitary status stemmed less from overt racial hostility than their inability to outmaneuver a local regime that was committed to the preservation of a race-based class structure in Alexandria. The white power structure's acceptance of a "better-class" African American did not translate into a wholesale acceptance of fully integrated schools, if full integration meant poor African American children attending schools with middle-class white children. The resonance of that racially inflected class conflict within Alexandria's schools continues to affect city and school politics to this day.

John Albohm and the Rise and Demise of Racial Gradualism

As John Albohm arrived in Alexandria from running the York, Pennsylvania school system, he confronted a divided white elite. A group of racial moderates wanted to turn away from the rhetoric of Massive Resistance and get on with the task of desegregation. Others still sought to extend Boothe's policy of minimizing the effects of desegregation. Simultaneously, African Americans within the community had begun to voice complaints about the quality of schooling that transcended desegregation. Organized groups had began routinely complaining to the School Board in T.C. Williams's final year as superintendent: The Alexandria Nonviolent Action Group, the Alexandria Council on Human Relations, and the Alexandria Citizens Committee for Colored Voters all lodged lengthy complaints about a range of issues, from the limited vocational opportunities at Parker-Gray High School (the African American secondary school), to complaints about the academic qualifications of teachers, to the lack of a rowing program at Parker-Gray, an athletic program of much pride and accomplishment for the white high schools in this city along the Potomac.[31]

In contrast to Williams, Albohm's response to these complaints was to deal with them head-on. Five weeks after reporting for work in Alexandria, Albohm informed the School Board that the school administration was conducting "enrollment studies" and indicated that a number of African American students would need to be moved from the two all-black elementary schools, Lyles-Crouch and Charles Houston. He indicated that "this should not be done on a massive basis," and in consultation with the state Pupil Placement Board, but it was the first step away from relying on the active petitioning of African American students to move out of these schools. In a confidential memo prepared prior to a meeting with Leonard S. Brown, Chairman of the Alexandria Nonviolent Action Group and the Alexandria Citizens Committee for Colored Voters, Albohm indicated that sixty African American students would no longer be bused out of their neighborhoods to attend Lyles-Crouch. They would instead attend their neighborhood school. In addition, he asked the principals at Lyles-Crouch and Houston to suggest to parents that their children attend the nearby, formerly all-white schools of Ficklin and Lee. Tentative and modest, these shifts were the first systemic steps taken by the Alexandria City Public School system to dismantle its dual school system.[32]

Part of the motivation may have been to avoid returning to the court-room: Leonard Brown's group, Alexandria Citizen's Committee for Colored Voters, stated in a letter to the School Board in mid-April, "what we wish to accomplish here can be achieved by either of two routes: by going to the Federal courts again, or by the action of the local Alexandria School Board. We would prefer the latter route; we are not adversed [sic] to taking the former, if the situation should call for it."[33] At the same time, Albohm seemed to be personally committed to accelerating the pace of desegregation. In a September 1963 work session with the School Board, Albohm outlined four alternatives for the Board: 1) continued segregation; 2) racially balanced schools; 3) enriched "compensatory education; 4) "accept the legal plan of integration" based on neighborhood schools.[34]

The first option he excluded as "no longer legal." The second he indicated "gets into the psychological and sociological aspects of segregation and spills over into the political, as well as the philosophical." The third would require a "super-learning" environment involving parents, teachers, and children. The fourth option, anchored in neighborhood schools, would be supplemented by "compensatory education so that Negro students are not automatically forced into an uneven learning environment." This option also would require "open opportunities" in music, school activities, recreation, PTA groups, and faculty. This fourth course of action, which the school district came eventually to adopt, accepted de facto segregation in neighborhoods but sought to undo the formal aspects of segregated schooling. To do this, implied Albohm, would not be an easy task:

> To do this will require, eventually, phasing out of Parker-Gray High School, the employment of white teachers in Negro schools, as well as the employment of some Negro teachers in white schools. The integration of science fairs, career nights, summer school, in-service training and the present teacher associations [teacher unions] … Constant improvement of the de facto schools and further improvement of housing opportunities and economic opportunities and constant upgrading of Negro teachers and curriculum, plus the involvement of Negro parents in aspects of compensatory learning.[35]

Albohm stressed in the meeting that he presented these alternatives "to keep this problem in focus" and "to review…where the present directions of Northern Virginia and the Nation at large appear to be taking us."[36] After serving as Superintendent for only six months, Albohm had laid out a desegregation vision that accepted de facto residential segregation, but sought to dismantle parallel segregated institutions and practices, such as PTAs, extracurriculars, and teaching staffs. He also linked the desegregation program to a recognition of significant achievement differences between African American and white students, achievement differences recognized by most as rooted in not only the class differences of the two groups of pupils, but the legacy of inferior segregated schools. In many ways, Albohm's efforts were remarkable, given that Virginia had only recently ended its program of Massive Resistance and that schools in Prince Edward County Virginia remained shuttered by local school authorities rather than desegregated. Importantly, Albohm sought these changes in Alexandria prior to the 1964 Civil Rights Act and prior to the enactment of the 1965 Elementary and Secondary Education Act. He spent the next fourteen years—the rest of his career in public education—trying to achieve them.

Albohm's initial acceptance of de facto segregation, which was partially a tactical concession to his political opponents and partially an accurate assessment of what the law required in 1963, eventually came into conflict, however, with the standards articulated by an increasingly impatient U.S. Supreme Court, which saw the reluctance of Southern school districts to move toward integrated schools as the continuing manifestation of Jim Crow racism. In Alexandria's case, however, the opposition to cracking de facto housing segregation stemmed in significant part from class-based apprehension over the perceived relative decline of the school system's academic reputation, compared to local private schools and neighboring affluent (and whiter) jurisdictions. These apprehensions also drew on articulations of neighborhood and school 'identity' that over time grew increasingly concerned with the values and aspirations of students.

Albohm's agenda for educational improvement in Alexandria went beyond the promotion of desegregation. Whereas T.C. Williams's frugal approach to educational administration ensured a solid attention to the basics of a secondary curriculum, Albohm sought to expand and innovate the city's educational system, particularly as the construction of a new high school was nearing completion. In a special staff meeting with high school principals and senior staff nine months after his arrival, Albohm pursued a discussion of beginning an "Honors Program in history, English, Math and foreign languages," as well as the adoption of new "majors" in art, music and possibly drama.[37] The memorandum outlining his goals for the meeting suggests that he was seeking out advice on a novel program of earning college credit in high school: "What is Advanced Placement? Can any of our high schools qualify? Should we approach this program?" He also raised questions about the role and place of special education within Alexandria schools, a theme to which he would return repeatedly in the early-to-mid-1960s.

Albohm's ambitious efforts to not only advance desegregation but to improve the rigor of high school courses, as well as the range of classes offered, was part of a consistent view Albohm held about the purposes of public education. In the December 1963 meeting with principals and senior staff, Albohm spoke of "a public school point of view." While all educators had to pay attention, Albohm argued, to intellect, scholarship, moral character, and values, "the public school educator" has additional concerns: "Public support and public policy must be [our] guidelines, respect for all people and the personality of all people ... [and] an emphasis on human improvement." In his notes, Albohm stressed the "obligations of the educated to the uneducated," noting that the "aristocracy of talent and ability in a Class System is fundamental to public education." As Albohm wrote in his notes, "The public school educator implements a pluralistic society."[38]

Albohm's efforts to realize a pluralistic society within Alexandria schools quickly ran up against serious obstacles, including both public resistance to his plans and the educational difficulties of bridging achievement gaps between African American and white students. As a result, Albohm had to temper his rhetoric, balancing ambitions against both the political and educational circumstances of Alexandria. When, for example, a citizen complained about the transfer of African American students into George Mason Elementary School, Albohm readily agreed that racial integration, in and of itself, was not a legitimate objective of the school system:

> Permit me first to state that the Board of Education here and I, as Superintendent, thoroughly agree with you that no system of manipulation of pupils for the sole purpose of racial integration is either socially desirable, or educationally desirable.[39]

When such programs exist in other communities, he added, they "appear to be brought about by political pressure rather than by an honest attempt to improve the educational program of Negro pupils."[40] He then remarked that the African American students at George Mason were enrolled there because it was now their neighborhood school.

The focus on the existing "natural" distribution of African American families among the neighborhoods of Alexandria and on the educational effects of desegregation seemed to be the primary emphases of this period of racial gradualism in Alexandria schools. Central to the school district's challenge of desegregating its schools was understanding and combating the effects of poverty within schools. Although poverty had clearly existed in Alexandria's schools, the economic mixing that accompanied racial desegregation brought the issue into starker relief and made poverty relevant to the majority middle-class white students for the first time. In the fall of 1963, Albohm requested that Cecil Belcher, the Director of Instruction, undertake a series of reports on the existing array of social services for disadvantaged children, the academic progress of the African American children who transferred to all-white schools, and the retentions of students who were two or more years behind grade level. In the course of addressing these issues, the school district's psychological services department generated, in the spring of 1964, a series of documents that highlighted the fusion of class, race, and academic progress as newly emergent concerns of the school district. These documents, and Albohm's response to them, illustrate that the three issues of academic progress, poverty, and racial desegregation became interconnected aspects of managing the shift to neighborhood schools. Without a program of addressing the educational needs of children in poverty, the academic progress of African American children moving into white schools would suffer, thereby limiting the political viability of a program Albohm knew the school district would have to undertake anyway, with or without local support.

As a result, managing desegregation became more than managing ensuing racial conflict that accompanied white and African American students attending school together. Rather it became an effort to redress the academic underperformance of growing numbers of African American children in poverty, children that the school district previously had successfully ignored, in large part through the political disenfranchisement of African Americans and the capacity of formal racial segregation in schools to remove issues from the white educational agenda. The erosion of segregation of course meant that the problems of children in poverty became the problems of administrators (and parents) in white schools. The resulting class-based conflict between whites and African Americans produced significant conflict in Alexandria over the purposes and aims of schooling. Many white parents viewed these efforts to address the educational needs of African American students as harming the interests of their own children. This perception of neglect of the educational needs of white students opened the door to significant white flight from Alexandria, even among parents who labeled themselves liberal. As the federal government began to demand more integration from Alexandria officials in 1966, these trends accelerated.

Focusing first on the experiences of the elementary students who, in the fall of 1963, transferred from de facto African American schools to previously all-white schools, the Alexandria Schools Psychological Services office detailed a number of positive outcomes for the African American children in their new schools, even though the report noted it was too early to reach a definitive assessment. Relying on descriptive data of attendance, disciplinary reports, grades, and teacher perceptions of student adjustment, the report stated "although massive adjustment problems might have been anticipated for these children, they and their teachers seemed to overcome these."[41] It further stated that two out of three students "maintained the grades they had last year or improved them" and that teachers noted more positive behavioral characteristics than negative ones. While for the vast majority of the students attendance did not worsen, the report did state, "There are serious attendance problems in this group."[42] In addition, teachers noted that over a third of the students exhibited pronounced "disinterest" in schooling, a remarkable number given that over one-half of the students were in grades one through three. The report urged further study of the adjustment of students transferring to white schools, and, in particular, urged that the school district examine the situations of those who exhibited "disinterest": "Some of these children might be improperly placed; the curriculum might not be stimulating enough; health factors may be operating. Or 'disinterest' may be masking fear and isolation."[43]

The dismay in these reports over the educational progress of African American students was perhaps only matched by the enthusiasm of the authors about the kinds of innovations the school district could offer these students. In one evaluation of an eighth-grade class at Parker-Gray High School, the author went to great lengths to detail the kinds of substantive knowledge these students were lacking: "Nine of [the students] thought the sun set in the east. Others said the southeast, north, south or 'straight.' Not one student said the sun set in the west.... The number of pounds in a ton varied, for them, from 24 to 40,000. Chile was in China, Germany, Hong Kong, Africa, Europe.... They struggled with naming recent Presidents, the color of rubies, and even the seasons of the year."[44] All of this was testimony to the conclusion that these students were "grossly underinformed and lack knowledge which belongs to the man-in-the-street."[45] Nonetheless, these students "have IQs within the range of many others who are achieving successfully" and demonstrate "exceptionally good judgment and common sense," and showed "unexpectedly good scores" on their powers of abstraction. "They *can* learn," the author emphasized.[46] Indeed, working with these students demonstrated to the author that "the IQs of these children might actually be raised by attention to areas wherein the children have been neglected or deprived."[47] A concerted program of educational strategies aimed at "culturally deprived" children, to increase both their substantive knowledge as well as their cognitive skills, would, the authors concluded, "perhaps increase these students' learning ability."[48]

The office of Psychological Services laid out one such program in a detailed assessment of the educational needs of the Old Town neighborhood, home to the vast majority of African American students in Alexandria. The report first detailed the increasing poverty of the eastern third of the city and its effects on the racial dynamics of the city: "The lack of housing for Negroes is changing the character of the Negro living in Alexandria. The proportion of old, established Negro families with middleclass [sic] income has been declining and the proportion of low income families, many without job opportunities or skills, has been increasing." In addition, "while the Negro population has not increased in proportion to the white population in the City at large, it has grown more rapidly than the white population in the Eastern population."[49] In short, Old Town was growing more black, more poor, and more troubled. Newspaper accounts during this time similarly document the extent to which housing discrimination within Alexandria led to both an increasing concentration of African American poverty within Old Town and an accelerating movement of middle-class African American households out of Old Town and Alexandria altogether.[50]

The report indicated that school district staff found these challenges daunting and that "it seemed impetuous to make any attempt to revise a traditional program" of education in the short-run. "But the staff began to share the Superintendent's convictions that (a) since the conditions in the Eastern portion are a local problem, they merited a local solution and would receive, once attacked, a united community support ... and (b) most such programs are not centered only in fiscal expenditures, but also in a redefinition of educational aims and methods."[51] This educational "redefinition" would focus on three dimensions. First, the district would tightly focus on four elementary schools within Old Town, keeping class sizes small, with the goal of "eliminating 'failure' for first graders who were entering school with various degrees of unreadiness for the traditional curriculum."[52] Relying on a framework of cultural deprivation, the staff advocated the notion that the "unreadiness [of these students] is reversible through focused, concentrated attention." Second, the "unreadiness" of these youngsters would be ameliorated by bolstering the traditional curriculum with an "abundance of materials and experiences," such as field trips and additional library materials. The aim would be to provide compensatory education through "enlarged opportunities to hear, feel, listen, speak, react, enact—in short, *experiences which middle-class children have had since toddlerhood.*" Finally, teachers in these classrooms would seek the "intensive involvement" of these students' parents in their education, attempting to overcome their "defensive hostility or wariness" about school, through "non-threatening and supportive" methods.[53]

As these reports illustrate, the challenges of desegregation confronting Alexandria during this time period quickly became a challenge of responding to educational needs of children in poverty, a task the school district had, until this point, never really undertaken. After the bluff and bluster of Massive Resistance, as federal courts got down to the nitty-gritty business of compelling the mixing of African American and white children, Alexandria was forced to respond to the educational effects of poverty in an unprecedented way. In the fall of 1964 it began the "Project in the Four Schools," a targeted effort to improve educational opportunities in the four downtown elementary schools that had the highest percentage of African American children. The aim of the program was to "meet the individual differences in learning" that arose "in some cases, out of cultural deprivation and, in other cases, out of lack of sufficient motivation, academic ability and poor housing backgrounds."[54] That response, born out of a well-intentioned desire to ameliorate decades of neglect, opened the district to political criticisms that it was weakening academic standards as it proceeded with desegregation. The effort to expose African American children to "middle-class" experiences drew greater attention to the economic differences among students in Alexandria, differences that had been largely masked in the days of formal segregation. As desegregation expanded into other schools, parents began to voice concerns about declining standards in Alexandria schools.

The emergence of racial gradualism was also marked by increased formal representation of African Americans in Alexandria politics. In the summer of 1964, the Alexandria City Council named the first African American to the Alexandria School Board. Ferdinand T. Day, a native Alexandrian and U.S. State Department employee, was among three new school board members elected by the City Council when the Board expanded from six to nine members, effective July 1, 1964. The expansion of the school board had required an amendment to the city charter and approval by the state of Virginia. Day later became chair of the School Board, the first African American to chair a school board in the entire state of Virginia.

HEW and the End of Racial Gradualism

While Day's election was undoubtedly a major concession for the old guard on Alexandria's City Council, it signaled only the beginning of major changes in the racial politics of Alexandria. Simultaneous to Day's election came Congress's enactment of the landmark Civil Rights Act of 1964. Title VI of the Act required that no entity receiving federal funds discriminate on the basis of race. Although federal expenditures on public education were small, they were still large enough to induce at least a minimal effort in much of the South to comply, and after 1965 those federal expenditures grew substantially under the Elementary and Secondary Education Act. Moreover, Commissioner of Education Francis Keppel, showing HEW's seriousness, informed state educational agencies that all federal funds for schools for the 1965–1966 school year were frozen until school districts demonstrated their compliance with Title VI. Alexandria was, according to Albohm, the first school district in Virginia to be deemed in compliance with the Act in May 1965,[55] but the ongoing challenge of meeting HEW standards proved politically more demanding than the earlier task of complying with a federal district court order to desegregate. Because HEW's standards of compliance evolved over time (largely in response to changing judicial declarations of what desegregation required) the federal agency ultimately imposed a far more transformative desegregation agenda onto Alexandria than Albohm or the school board envisioned under their gradual shift to neighborhood schools. Across the nation, Title VI, in conjunction with the 1965 Elementary and Secondary Education Act, shifted the locus of desegregation pressure away from the federal courts and into the Office of Civil Rights within the Department of Health, Education and Welfare.

In Alexandria, HEW officials used that pressure to insist on a compliance plan that challenged both Albohm's commitment to neighborhood schools and white Alexandria's notion of a neighborhood. With a new high school opening in September 1965 (on a desegregated basis), the all-black Parker-Gray High School converted to a desegregated middle school, and new elementary schools opening shortly in response to population growth, the school district in the mid-1960s had to establish three new desegregated high school attendance zones, and establish a new feeder system of elementary and middle schools. How far Alexandria would go to fully integrate its new elementary and high schools was closely watched by HEW, even as HEW's own guidelines for what constituted compliance were subject to yearly revision. Ultimately, HEW and Albohm together created a fully integrated Alexandria school system, but racial conflict and mistrust within the city persisted long after integration.

Development of HEW Guidelines

Shortly after the enactment of the 1964 Civil Rights Act, HEW faced the challenge of establishing guidelines for compliance with the Act. The HEW regulations that President Lyndon Johnson signed in early December of 1964 specified three options for school districts to demonstrate compliance with Title VI. First, a district could assert that all its programs were already fully desegregated; second, it could agree to comply with an existing final court order compelling desegregation; or, third, it could submit a voluntary desegregation plan. By allowing existing final court orders to satisfy Title VI requirements, the Johnson Administration linked judicial standards of desegregation articulated through years of litigation to the bureaucratic administration of federal aid to education. This linkage became increasingly important in the late 1960s as federal courts grew impatient with recalcitrant Southern districts and began to demand that school districts integrate completely and immediately.

The option allowing for the submission of a "voluntary" desegregation plan presented an enormous logistical challenge for HEW in the spring of 1965. With little previous experience in the enforcement of civil rights—lacking even a filing system to handle requests for information[56]—the Office of Education confronted an overwhelming organizational challenge in responding to Southern school districts seeking advice on how to comply with the law. The development of guidelines for voluntary compliance emerged only after endless negotiations, meetings, and conferences with Southern school district officials. Ultimately, it fell to a group of law professors serving as part-time consultants to the Office of Education within HEW to provide some consistency to HEW guidance by ensuring HEW advice was in alignment with numerous court decisions throughout the South.[57] After more negotiation between HEW and the Department of Justice and further revision, HEW released in late April 1965 guidelines to assist school districts that were developing voluntary desegregation plans to comply with Title VI.

While the HEW guidelines reaffirmed the ability of districts to use their compliance with a final court order as proof of compliance with Title VI,[58] they also specified in significant detail the requirements that voluntary plans had to meet. For example, HEW insisted that any freedom of choice plans apply to least four grades immediately (and all grades by 1967) and that all such choice mechanisms be widely publicized to all students. Additionally, districts were required to take initial steps toward faculty desegregation and fully desegregate all school activities and extracurricular programs. HEW also accepted geographic plans of pupil assignment that allowed students to attend their closest neighborhood school. According to Gary Orfield, these guidelines were "a charter for the reconstruction of race relations in the schools of many hundreds of communities where the Supreme Court decision had produced no change."[59]

The financial consequence for schools that were not in compliance grew substantially in early April 1965 after Congress enacted the Elementary and Secondary

Education Act. This landmark law pumped over one billion dollars annually in new federal aid through HEW, aid that was disproportionately aimed at poor southern states. Mississippi stood to lose $75 million in federal aid—a sum greater than Mississippi's total state expenditure on public education in 1963. With the stakes raised, Southern districts, particularly those that had not been subject to court orders requiring desegregation, began the hard work toward compliance.

Alexandria's Initial Efforts to Comply with HEW Guidelines

Alexandria, meanwhile, had acted quickly to protect the significant amount of "impact aid" it received from the federal government under Public Law 874. That aid, distributed to school districts with large federal facilities, totaled over $934,000 in 1963-1964, roughly 13 percent of the district's total budget.[60] In early January 1965 the district submitted an "assurance of compliance" to HEW, avowing that none of its programs discriminated on the basis of race.[61] In addition, the School Board requested (and received) from the Alexandria City Council emergency legislation taking control of its pupil placement away from the state Pupil Placement Board, a procedure allowed under Virginia law and required by the 1965 HEW guidelines concerning desegregation. Finally, in a letter to the Virginia State Board of Education that was later also sent to HEW, Albohm detailed the efforts by Alexandria to desegregate all its programs since the 1962 federal court order. He added that "some of this information may be interpreted as superfluous, however, it does indicate a tone in terms of compliance."[62] In his cover letter to HEW, Albohm further stated that "the members of our Board of Education would like to make certain that a complete picture of our school situation in regard to compliance is on file with you."[63]

Given Alexandria's uncommonly large federal revenue and its new leadership, it is not surprising that the school district took rapid steps to be, as Albohm claimed, the first district in Virginia to be deemed in compliance. But viewed from the perspective of HEW, Alexandria's actions seemed less impressive: The district had complied with a minimal court order that only addressed the admission of a specific number of individual students to particular schools. HEW's guidelines for voluntary compliance, however, required that Alexandria's voluntary plan detail specific steps to dismantle its dual system of schooling. Albohm's list of specifics may have gone beyond the court order in the *Jones* decision, but it certainly was not a systematic restructuring of Alexandria's schools. From the perspective of Alexandria's leadership, the school district's position on desegregation had significantly improved in a short time and the city was far ahead of much of Virginia and the South in general. Alexandria's position rested, however, on an acceptance of de facto segregation as a legitimate reflection of neighborhood and community preferences. Over time, those two positions would generate significant conflict between HEW and Alexandria school officials.

In the short run, the issue of neighborhood segregation played an important role as Albohm and his staff planned the opening of the new high school—now dubbed T.C. Williams High School. Indeed, the district had to decide whether new high school boundaries necessitated by the conversion of the formerly all-black Parker-Gray High School into a middle school and the opening of T.C. Williams would be drawn to maximize the desegregation within Alexandria's three high schools or would reflect the community's "neighborhoods" and thereby mirror the sharp residential segregation that confronted Alexandria in the mid-1960s.

As Albohm had expressed earlier, he saw little need to pursue integration per se as a school district objective. Adjusting school boundaries for the express purpose of "manipulating" the enrollment levels of African American students in any particular school was, in Albhom's view, as illegitimate as formally segregating schools. As he stated in a 1975 interview, the School Board in the mid-1960s was "not distributing pupils on the basis of race. We're trying to fill the schools on the basis of normal enrollment." While Albohm's position could be characterized as a commitment to racial neutrality and an adherence to the Civil Rights Act's proscription of the use of race to establish school policies, it is also true that he and members of the School Board were not interested in tackling the acute housing segregation of the city. Albohm emphasized that "the School Board's primary concern is education—not gerrymandering school districts to balance the white/Negro student ratio."[64] As a result, the School Board adopted for the fall of 1965 high school boundaries that mirrored the residential segregation of Alexandria: a virtually all-white Hammond High in the western portion of the city (0.3 percent African American enrollment), a brand-new and desegregated T.C. Williams High School in the center of Alexandria, (with 12.4 percent African American enrollment), and George Washington High in the eastern third, including Old Town, (with nearly 25 percent African American enrollment.) The plan, as described in the *Alexandria Journal*, called for "no transport of children to avoid racial imbalance."[65]

At the same time, the concentration of most African American students within four elementary schools and one high school was, to some whites, an unfair "burden" on their neighborhoods. The uneven distribution of African American students across the city's schools prompted significant concern among civic associations in white neighborhoods that were within George Washington High School boundaries, particularly those just north of Old Town. Contending that their real objection was not about racial mixing, but about the concentration of poor students within these formerly white schools, these parents and civic activists argued for new school boundaries that would not mirror existing housing segregation, but would spread the "burden" of poor African American students across a greater area in the city.

The rhetoric and politicking grew heated as Alexandria responded to the much more vigorous desegregation guidelines HEW promulgated in March of 1966. After the implementation of the geographic neighborhood school desegregation plan in fall of 1965, five of Alexandria's elementary schools remained completely segregated: Lyles-Crouch and Charles Houston remained 100 percent African American while Patrick Henry, Douglas MacArthur, and James K. Polk elementary school remained 100 percent white. The new HEW guidelines made clear that desegregation plans that employed "freedom of choice" elements (which Alexandria offered to African American students living in the Charles Houston and Lyles-Crouch attendance areas) had to produce immediate, substantive integration in order to be approved: "The single most substantial indication as to whether a free-choice plan is actually working to eliminate the dual school structure is the extent to which Negro or other minority group students have, in fact, transferred from segregated schools."[66] Given these requirements, it was clear that Alexandria would need to reconfigure its school attendance zones more substantially in order to meet HEW guidelines, particularly as very few African American students had opted to transfer out of Charles Houston Elementary School.[67]

But Alexandria's plan at this stage focused on the creation of new middle school attendance zones. A key element of the 1966 boundary reconfiguration in Alexandria was the creation of middle schools within the district.[68] Converting existing schools to middle schools and bringing new elementary buildings into the system involved significant boundary changes in the existing schools and their feeder elementary schools. The racial upshot was that the addition of a system of middle schools produced far greater desegregation in Parker-Gray and Thomas Jefferson, as well as greater desegregation of their feeder schools, particularly Lyles-Crouch. Only the racial patterns at the de facto white schools in western portion of the city would remain largely untouched by the boundary reorganization. At the same time, these new boundaries meant that George Washington High School, the neighborhood high school for the eastern third of the city, would see a significantly higher concentration of African American students than the other two city high schools.

In reaction to the plan, two predominantly white civic associations—the Del Ray Citizens Association and the Rosemont Citizens Association—organized a concerted effort to derail it. They claimed their objections did not lie in the desegregation of the schools in their neighborhood, but the increasing concentrations of children in poverty that this desegregation plan would bring to these schools. Also they worried that educational standards in these schools would suffer as a result of increasing poverty. According to newspaper reports, white parents whose children would attend a remodeled Thomas Jefferson Middle School complained that the school would be "located in a rundown neighborhood," and would draw students from six out of eight Alexandria census tracts designated as "poverty-stricken."[69] White parents who supported integration nonetheless sought reassurances from the school district that academic standards would not suffer. In a statement to Mayor Frank Mann and to the School Board, Lyles-Crouch Parents Committee urged Alexandria to turn Lyles-Crouch Elementary School into a model for the city, to make it "such a fine education facility that suburban parents would want to send their children to this downtown school."[70]

For his part, Albohm dismissed these concerns out of hand. In response to the criticisms that the new boundaries would concentrate poverty within a limited number of schools, Albohm replied that his critics wanted "to sprinkle culturally deprived children in all the City's high schools and middle schools."[71] He contended that these boundary adjustments were necessary to meet Title VI requirements and his opponents were simply former segregationists who wanted "to spread" African Americans around the city. He claimed that the only way to widely distribute African American students was to engage in citywide busing, something apparently beyond the pale for Albohm: "This community is not ready to accept busing," he told a newspaper reporter. "Why bring this down upon our city?"[72] He similarly rejected the idea of a model school for Lyles-Crouch, claiming, "We don't want just one model school. We want all of our schools to be model schools."[73]

Based on his public comments and his efforts to address the effects of racialized poverty through targeted programs in schools with high percentages of African American poverty, Albohm viewed the district's task of desegregation simply as replacing a dual system with a system of neighborhood schools, even if those neighborhood schools replicated the disparities of race and class created by the segregated system. The concentration of poverty within particular neighborhoods was an objective fact for Albohm. Some neighborhoods were better than others and neighborhood schools would, inevitably, reflect those realities. The school district's job, in Albohm's view, was to make all schools as good as they could be, but not to challenge or reorganize the existing geographic system of schooling that drew from class-and race-stratified neighborhoods. Seeking to recompose school populations was, in this view, doing more than ending a system of dual schooling—it veered toward an illegitimate challenge of class disparities within Alexandria.

Moreover, the existing power structure within Alexandria made those kinds of challenges fundamentally untenable politically for the school district. As the School Board chair at the time, Gorman C. Ridgely, stated, "The Board could not be real estate people. Our goal was education. The burden belonged to society and the community, not a School Board problem."[74] In short, Albohm's and the School Board's acceptance of the legitimacy of residential racial and economic segregation within Alexandria profoundly affected their perception of both the obligations of the district to integrate Alexandria's schools during this time and the degree of desegregation that the existing political leadership would tolerate.

At the same time, however, Albohm and the school district leadership viewed resistance to the school desegregation plan as the continuation of a Massive Resistance but in a more polite idiom. In a grant application submitted to the U.S. Commissioner of Education for an interracial staff training program on race, the school district described the nature of the opposition to the boundary changes in the spring of 1966. After noting that the resistance centered in the Rosemont and Del Ray neighborhoods, the grant application detailed the gist of their opposition: "(1) Too great a percent of low-income and educationally deprived children would occur in some schools; (2) Realigning school boundaries would result in lowering of 'school standards' (primarily directed at George Washington High School, which became the most highly integrated secondary school in Alexandria)."[75] The application added that "It must be noted that in Alexandria a high percentage of low-income and educationally disadvantaged students are Negro. Therefore, it is assumed that the substance of the allegations of the Rosemont and Del Ray Civic Associations are aimed at the interracial aspect of the Alexandria School Board's attempt to change the school attendance area."[76] Thus, any direct objection to increasing concentrations of poor students was, in effect, a race-based objection.

As Alexandria arrived at its first efforts to voluntarily comply with HEW guidelines, its school leadership sought to navigate two local pressures: the legitimacy of existing residential segregation and parental concerns about the effects of racialized poverty in the classroom. While the district accepted as legitimate—or at least not its concern—the effects of residential segregation, it also viewed arguments about "standards" in schools as a cover for racial prejudice, rather than legitimate objections to how well students were being taught. Of course, many bigots of the highest order did use arguments about standards as a proxy for their racial objections to integrated schooling. But the reluctance of the Alexandria City school district to engage in arguments about standards, along with its willingness to defuse political tensions by accepting the inevitability and desirability of economically distinct neighborhood schools, fed into middle-class impatience with racial (and economic) integration of students.

Conclusion

The results of the 1966 boundary change were numerous. First, Alexandria met the requirements of the HEW guidelines by significantly increasing the percentage of white students in formerly all-African American elementary schools. Second, opposition to the location of the Thomas Jefferson Middle School (as well as its racial and class composition) forced the school district to create only three middle schools, distributing Jefferson's population to Minnie Howard and Parker-Gray Middle Schools. Third, the school district adopted a strategy of modified tracking within classrooms—combined with enrichment and remediation for "culturally deprived" students—to respond to white complaints of lowered standards. Perhaps most importantly, however, the 1966 boundary adjustment and school reorganization represented the final end to Jim Crow schooling in Alexandria. It was by no means the end of racial segregation, nor the end of racial conflict within Alexandria schools. The 1966 boundary adjustment was, however, the framework within which both of those dynamics proceeded in Alexandria schools. The boundaries and school organization approved in 1966 stayed constant until 1971, when the combination of changing demographics of the city and more stringent federal requirements for overcoming the legacies of past discrimination demanded required further changes in the organization of Alexandria schools. Those changes emerged out of social and political contexts that were more tumultuous and confrontational, but contexts that also afforded Alexandria an opportunity to build a more responsive and democratic local political regime. The intersecting stories of full school integration, the construction of a new local regime, and representation occupy Chapter 3.

3

Racial Change, Conflict, and the Incorporation of Interests

Introduction

Despite the relative stability of Alexandria's school desegregation effort between 1966 and 1971, the city as a whole underwent significant change in the second half of the 1960s. Economic and housing changes increasingly brought African Americans into formerly all-white areas of Alexandria, particularly in the northern end of Alexandria. Del Ray, an historically working class section, saw increased black population, as did Arlandria, a newer, but still working-class neighborhood adjacent to Del Ray. And like the nation as a whole, Alexandria's citizens and leaders witnessed and participated in the social changes brought on by the civil rights movement and the rapid transformations of the 1960s more generally. These changes placed enormous stress on the local political regime in Alexandria, and the rising frustration of African Americans over their continued exclusion from the economic and political centers of the community prompted numerous calls for change and inclusion. The youth of Alexandria—like youth across the nation—were frequently at the forefront of these demands for change. Indeed, both the broader social transformations of the late 1960s and the recalcitrance of Alexandria's elite galvanized and radicalized Alexandria's youth, putting them increasingly at the forefront of street protests, rallies, and demonstrations.

The racialized generational conflict of these years held particular salience for both schools and the local regime alike. Schools became the sites of bitter contestation, in which the new demands of vocal, young, and impatient African Americans butted against an older white generation's expectations of discipline, order, and control. As Alexandria's school leaders sought to manage this unsettled disciplinary climate, white parents and political leaders increasingly saw the inability or unwillingness of Alexandria's schools to police the generational and racial boundaries that had previously regulated the community as evidence of the failure of desegregation and of declining quality of Alexandria city schools. While the turmoil of American society was worked out in Alexandria's classrooms, with many white families confronting poverty and racial conflict within "their" schools for the very first time, discipline became—in the eyes of many white Alexandrians—synonymous with quality. In addition, as elements of the local regime sought to reassert control, without incorporating or accommodating African American interests, disruptions and challenges of school authority became a form of indirect protest by some African American students. The result was an increasingly confrontational spiral: protest, followed by calls for greater discipline, leading to parental and political complaints about declining quality of Alexandria's schools, which were answered by further student protests.

Ultimately, the frustration of middle-class whites in some parts of Alexandria helped produce significant white flight from sections of the city. That demographic change, ironically, led to an erosion of the political base of white conservatives who had dominated Alexandria's political life for generations. Their rapid exit meant a shrinking pool of white conservative voters that had served as the backbone of the local regime. The middle-class white liberals who remained in Alexandria were much more ready to engage in an alliance with Alexandria's African American community, producing, by the mid-1970s, a very different kind of regime coalition, one premised on far greater inclusion of multiple interests and the provision of social services to poorer members of the community. This chapter tells that story of local regime change by focusing on the ways that local political events fused with public perceptions of school quality and HEW demands for increased desegregation to produce a reconfiguration of the local regime in Alexandria. While the Hollywood film *Remember the Titans* may have told the story of Alexandria's desegregation as a heartwarming tale of a football team that managed to see beyond race, a more accurate account of Alexandria's racial and political transformation in the late 1960s to early 1970s tells a tale of persistent violent conflict, sagging white confidence in local schools, white insecurity about the changing racial identity of the city, and, finally, a grudging acceptance of a significant role of black Alexandrians in the new regime. At key moments in those developments, the insistence of Health, Education and Welfare (and, more indirectly, the federal courts) on greater school integration presaged a fuller inclusion of African American interests in the broader local regime.

The chapter explores these issues in three sections. The first, "Racial Violence, Discipline and the Maintenance of Control" examines the state of race relations in Alexandria in the late 1960s and the extent to which desegregation was seen as synonymous (to many whites) with increasing disciplinary breakdown. The second section, "School Discipline, Racial Antagonism and the Politics of Order," turns to the efforts undertaken by the school system to address persistent racial conflict in schools, in particular the reorganization of the secondary schools in Alexandria—a change that produced, for the first time, a single unified high school. While the city apparently made progress within its secondary system, it faced enormous white resistance to a complete integration of its elementary schools, the subject of the third section, "From Secondary to Elementary: Race and the Idea of Community Schools." Changing elementary attendance boundaries required a willingness to alter "natural" neighborhoods, an inclination that not only ran counter to Superintendent Albohm's personal views, but also counter to the city's own self-identity as a white city, with a minority black population. As a result, HEW found itself forcefully pursuing in the early 1970s further integration. But with complex demographic changes underway—due to white flight, gentrification, and a declining school age population—the challenges of desegregating elementary schools prompted intense public debate over the very identity of Alexandria as a city, and as a community. That debate took place amid changing political coalitions that produced a very different Alexandria by the mid-1970s—an Alexandria that had partially incorporated African American interests into the governing consensus, even if they were clearly junior partners in the governing enterprise.

Racial Violence, Discipline, and the Maintenance of Control

"We usually don't have too much trouble with the colored."
—Alexandria Police Chief Russell A. Hawes, quoted in the Washington Post, October 1969.

On a mid-autumn evening in 1969, about ten African American boys were playing football in the street in the Arlandria section of Alexandria, at the north end of town, not far from the Arlington County line. Private Clairborn T. Callahan, a patrol office for the Alexandria City Police who regularly worked the Arlandria beat on the 4p.m. to midnight shift, stopped the boys and told them to end their game and clear the street. According to one youth present, Callahan called the boys "colored." They, in turn, insisted he should use the term "Negro" or "black." Darryl Turner, age fifteen at the time, told a Washington Post reporter, "Callahan told us we weren't black. He said Africans were black and that he never did understand why colored people got so upset when someone called them colored."[1]

A few minutes later, after most of the boys had left, Callahan became involved in a chase of a black youth, pursuing him down an alleyway, finally restraining him. At this point, a few of the original youths—still hanging out on the street corner—began asking Callahan why he was detaining the boy. As Callahan began dragging the boy back up the alleyway, the other boys followed. "The way he was dragging him, we thought he was going to hurt him or something," one of the boys later told a reporter.[2] At some point, one of the boys grabbed a piece of wood and with the youths following Callahan, the police officer turned to confront them. "When we got close to Callahan, he looked like he was scared. He took out his gun and swung around and told us to get back or he would shoot."[3] Most of the boys turned and ran, but Keith Strickland decided to walk slowly away. In response, Callahan chased down Strickland, still holding on to the other boy. While Strickland tried to slip away from him, Callahan pistol-whipped Strickland numerous times, striking him across his head. Strickland claimed he passed out about that time, but others in the neighborhood, responding to the violence, came to Strickland's aid.

A large crowd gathered around Callahan insisting that he let the boys up off the ground and call an ambulance for Strickland. Strickland's mother arrived on the scene and sought to pull her son away from the officer, at which point Callahan shoved her to the ground, sparking other bystanders to intervene. Eventually, five people were arrested as a result of the melee and Callahan had to navigate his way out of a crowd of nearly thirty bystanders. In his initial arrest report, Callahan stated that he came under an assault of hurled bricks and bottles and that the fourteen-year-old Strickland had struck him with a board.[4] Strickland claimed he had taken the board away from another teenager because "we didn't want any trouble."[5] Indeed, many of the black residents of the neighborhood insisted that it was Officer Callahan who had gone looking for trouble, escalating the conflict unnecessarily.

The response of Alexandria's black community to the violence ranged from organized mass protest to outbursts of vandalism and firebombings. A conflict that began with teenagers insisting that a police officer respect the word they chose to assert their racial identity grew into a citywide effort to demand respect for the entire black community. Led by a number of African American church congregations and the local chapter of the Urban League, citizens organized a march of roughly one-hundred people to the police station, where they demanded the resignation of Police Chief Russell Hawes, a thirty-nine-year veteran of the Alexandria police force, and Private Callahan.[6] Two days later, a group of 150 African Americans voiced outrage at the beatings at a City Council meeting, again demanding Callahan's dismissal. According to the Washington Post, "The standing room only crowd in the Council chamber was the largest black audience ever to attend a council session, observers said."[7] Nightly street disturbances also erupted, with firebombings regularly taking place in Old Town and downtown areas of Alexandria, sometimes targeting politically prominent establishments; Vice Mayor Eugene Zimmerman's electrical contracting business was "hit by a Molotov cocktail," according to the Washington Post.[8] In sum, over eighteen firebombs were thrown in the month after the beating, according to press reports.[9]

This outrage over a police beating emerged from a political context of rapid political and racial change in Alexandria. These changes in the late 1960s and early 1970s were most evident in the north Alexandria neighborhoods of Del Ray and Arlandria, where the Callahan-Strickland incident took place. Long working-class communities, many of their residents earned their living in the railyards at the northeastern edge of the city. Virtually all white in the 1950s and early 1960s, the neighborhoods underwent a rapid racial change as black Alexandrians moved from their historic neighborhoods near Old Town into Del Ray and Arlandria. In Arlandria, whites began to move out after a series of floods from nearby Four Mile Run inundated the area and as black in-migration accelerated.[10]

Because these conservative white working-class neighborhoods provided significant support to the "Old Guard" establishment in Alexandria, the sudden exit of white conservatives from Arlandria and Del Ray accelerated the destabilization of the long-governing local Democratic establishment with its firm ties to the statewide Byrd regime. In addition, many of the white residents who remained behind in Del Ray and Arlandria grew increasingly frustrated with local Democratic leaders, whom they saw as unnecessarily accommodating to black residents—particularly on the school desegregation issue. And if the Old Guard was increasingly ineffectual, the "New Guard" wasn't any better: Democratic city leaders who argued for greater inclusion of black interests were generally seen as representing a new kind of Alexandria Democrat—professional, white-collar workers, many college-educated, moving into Alexandria as the older city was incorporated into the suburbanization of the Greater Washington, DC area.[11]

Thus, from the perspective of those white residents of Del Ray and Arlandria who were opposed to a greater inclusion of black interests in Alexandria, the political options were less than optimal: an increasingly isolated Old Guard, weakened by the civil rights movement and a faltering statewide Byrd regime; and a liberalizing, predominantly upper middle-class professional Democratic party, one that increasingly resembled the northern wing of the national Democratic Party. Neither option appealed. The splitting of the local Democratic Party allowed Republicans to make significant headway in a community in which a Republican had not won a seat on the City Council since Reconstruction. Republican exclusion from the Council ended in 1967, when Wiley F. Mitchell, a young attorney for the Richmond, Frederick, and Potomac Railroad, won a seat on the Council. A year later, Mitchell was joined by another Republican, Harry S. Flemming, who won a special election to replace deceased Old Guard member James M. Duncan.[12] Although racially moderate, these GOP newcomers invariably supported local financial and commercial elites.

The resulting cleavages on the City Council compounded internal Democratic Party differences, as the liberal wing battled the Old Guard for control of the City Council, sometimes aided by racially moderate Republicans, some of whom received backing from black leaders suspicious of the Democratic establishment. At the same time, the rise of racially confrontational Southern Republicans (such as U.S. Representative Joel Broyhill, who fought desegregation in Congress) gave solace to the Old Guard who substituted a racial line for a party line. Pursuing Nixon's Southern strategy and at the forefront of the historic realignment of the American South in the 1970s and 1980s, these racially conservative Republicans offered a fourth option to Alexandrians who sought to slow the pace of black inclusion.

As this fragmentation of elites played out in the late 1960s, the Callahan-Strickland episode and the growing reluctance of African Americans to remain quiescent sparked a mobilization of the African American community. In its initial reporting of the incident and subsequent black mobilization against police brutality, the *Washington Post* labeled the African American demands that Callahan be arrested and charged with assault "almost a revolution in police-community relations in Alexandria."[13] The mobilization of Alexandria's African Americans against police violence led them to challenge directly the exercise of power by white elites in a city where direct racial confrontation was rare, if not nonexistent. As that willingness to challenge existing authority extended into Alexandria's schools, it soon placed the community's youth on a collision course with the priorities of the local regime.

The Murder of Robin Gibson and Youth Radicalization

On the evening of May 29th, 1970, only eight months after the Callahan-Strickland incident, a George Washington High School junior named Robin Gibson walked into a 7-Eleven store at the corner of Commonwealth Avenue and West Glebe Road in the Arlandria section of Alexandria, a little over two blocks from where the Callahan-Strickland confrontation took place. According to John L. Hanna, the twenty-four-year-old white manager of the store, he and Gibson had had a couple of conflicts since Hanna began working at the store at the beginning of May. That night, however, the conflict escalated out of control. According to eyewitnesses, the men exchanged words—apparently over allegations that Gibson was shoplifting razor blades—and then Hanna shot the nineteen-year-old black man in the chest and neck, killing him.[14] As Gibson lay dying, Hanna placed a "hawk-billed" knife in the pool of blood next to Gibson's body. According to newspaper accounts, he told a police officer who arrived on the scene that he had placed the knife next to Gibson.[15]

Gibson's murder sparked outrage among African Americans in Alexandria. For six consecutive nights following the shooting, black Alexandrians resorted to fire-bombings, overturning of cars, rock-throwing, and vandalism to protest the killing. It was the worst racial violence Alexandria had seen in a challenging decade of racial transformation. While the Callahan incident had prompted black outcry, particularly against police brutality, the murder of Robin Gibson—and the subsequent legal proceedings—produced a severe crisis of legitimacy for the local regime, and led to a rejection of Alexandria's elite among African Americans, particularly the young. In short, the prosecution and outcome of the Gibson case convinced many young Alexandrians that the local regime was incapable of yielding justice for black Americans.

The incumbent city leaders were taken aback by the vehemence of the reaction of black citizens to Gibson's killing. Coming less than two weeks before a City Council election, the disturbances unsettled the candidates, particularly those in the liberal wing. Mayor Charles Beatley, regarded as a moderate Democrat, told a group of white voters at a campaign event that when he arrived that night at the scene of the shooting, he found a "crowd of mad, irrational people." While he acknowledged that their sentiments were not unreasonable, he said Alexandria had "white frustrations" as well.[16] In an interview with a reporter, Beatley amplified his comments at the voter's forum, stating that "the white community will accept some things that the black community won't accept," adding that "most people in the black community are very rational.... They will understand that these kinds of things happen and life must go on."[17]

Other City Council members felt black frustrations were completely unfounded, that the city had in fact done much to improve the lot of black Alexandrians in recent years. Addressing a group of African Americans at a City Council meeting during the disturbances, Vice Mayor Eugene Zimmerman said, "Look at what we've done for you. Look at all the public housing you have here.... You're a lot better off in Alexandria than in Arlington and Fairfax," two adjoining jurisdictions.[18] Not surprisingly, black leaders found such comments patronizing: According to the *Washington Post*, one black Alexandria lawyer stated, "They've got to stop saying that because we're black they're doing us a favor to give us a break."[19]

The outpouring of violence, frustration, and grief proved to be a potent force in Alexandria politics. Newspaper accounts estimated that over 1,500 individuals attended Gibson's funeral,[20] which took place only days before a City Council election. That mobilization spilled over into Election Day, when black turnout out doubled from the 1967 City Council race, from 1000 voters to 2000.[21] All told, citywide turnout jumped nearly forty-five percent, and three incumbent Democrats were turned out of office. In their place, voters elected Ira Robinson as the first African American to Alexandria's City Council and added another Republican and a liberal Democrat who had served as research director on the Kerner Commission Report on racial riots in the United States. A conservative Democrat replaced Zimmerman, who unsuccessfully challenged Mayor Beatley in the Democratic primary. While the voter's repudiation of the Old Guard's position was clear, it was less clear how the new liberal Democratic wing would find common ground with the three Republican members, particularly since, as the *Washington Post* put it, Robinson held "the controlling vote on any issues that divide the seven-man Council along party lines." The results electrified the Republican Party in Alexandria, which felt that its long exile from an effective role in city politics had at last come to an end.

Despite these political changes, long-standing racial practices and norms proved hard to alter. As the city's mood cooled and the trial of John Hanna proceeded, cynicism among African Americans was widespread. As one city council member put it, "There is a feeling that a white man can kill a Negro and not likely be brought to justice." While the councilman added, "I don't think that is true—not today, not in Alexandria," events in the courtroom seemed to confirm the worst suspicions of many black Alexandrians. Indeed, the legal proceedings illustrated to black Alexandrians that the local system of justice was not even-handed.

During the trial, Hanna claimed he shot Gibson in self-defense. The jury of twelve white men deliberated for eleven hours before it returned to the courtroom, informing the judge that it had failed to reach a verdict in this case, because one juror refused to convict, on any grounds.[22] After the hung jury was announced, Wendell Evans, a local youth activist, told a reporter for the *Washington Post* that there was no way that a "white judge and a white jury in a courtroom decorated with a Confederate flag will give the same kind of justice to a white defendant that they would to black one in the same case."[23] Six weeks later, John H. Kennahan, the Commonwealth Attorney responsible for prosecuting the case, announced a plea bargain for voluntary manslaughter that carried a maximum sentence of five years in prison. The next day, Judge Franklin Backus sentenced Hanna to five years in prison, but suspended three years of the term, making Hanna eligible for parole in six months.[24]

In response to the light sentence, the youth of Alexandria rallied in protest. Four-hundred- and-fifty of Gibson's classmates attended a memorial service at Roberts Memorial Methodist Church on what would have been Gibson's twentieth birthday, two days after the sentencing of Hanna. That memorial service produced fiery rhetoric and a denunciation of white Alexandria and its legal system. Rev. Samuel NeSmith, pastor of Roberts Memorial, told the congregation that Hanna's sentence was "a blow to the dignity and pride of a free society, especially black Alexandrians." He added, "This is how Alexandria became an all-American city—by keeping niggers in their place." The student leaders in attendance were no less confrontational. Robert Callahan, president of the George Washington High School Sophomore class: "The so-called Christian white people who push the blacks aside in this city are going straight to hell." In response the audience stood and cheered, according to the *Washington Post*.[25] After the memorial service, about 250 youths marched peacefully to City Hall, where they met publicly with Commonwealth Attorney John E. Kennahan, who prosecuted the case and agreed to the plea deal. Kennahan defended his office, telling the group, according to the Post, "You know perfectly well that this was the most vigorous prosecution of a white defendant accused of killing a black man ever to take place in this courthouse."[26]

School Discipline, Racial Antagonism, and the Politics of Order

While John Hanna's trial was proceeding, Alexandria schools were in turmoil, reflecting many of the racial conflicts present in the city. The early stages of desegregation had proceeded more or less peaceably in Alexandria, but now the mood was darker and emotions were raw. As racial tensions in the city spilled into Alexandria's classrooms and gymnasiums, the schools became a symbolic battleground in which the various elements of Alexandria's now fragmented local regime sought to assert control. At the same time, schools became an important policy tool by which local leaders sought to mitigate the worst aspects of Alexandria's racial divisions. Competing definitions of racial justice played out on a daily basis, with school administrators, city officials, parents, and teachers all grappling with the contradictory challenges of acknowledging present and past racial harms, maintaining existing norms of student behavior, and seeking to change student attitudes and prejudices.

At the same time, many African American parents and students perceived any continuation of past school policies as simply an effort to maintain racial hierarchies, but in a more neutral language. These multiple claims and agendas found expression in school-level battles over two issues: discipline and school quality. Because both issues arose most prominently within the context of racial conflict in schools, they came to embody the substance of the political and educational meanings of school desegregation. As school district officials engaged the questions of discipline and quality they not only placed the school system at odds with the priorities of the old regime, but they indirectly hastened its demise. The resulting clash produced what I call a "politics of order," a term I use to explain the policy decisions adopted by school officials in Alexandria that sought simultaneously to placate whites worried about the reach of substantive changes in the school system and to accommodate black demands for a robust and meaningful equality. The signature policy achievement of the politics of order was a complex redesign of secondary schooling in Alexandria. The political compromise behind this redesign was to unite all Alexandrian students under one fully integrated high school, but simultaneously avoid the difficult decisions of integrating all-white elementary schools. Not until HEW forced the Alexandria school system to fully integrate at all levels did the politics of order shift into the politics of exit, the subject of the next chapter. The politics of order emerged out of a context of intense racialized conflict in Alexandria, and in order to understand its dynamics we need to explore the rationales behind white repudiation of school officials' efforts to integrate and black confrontation with those same officials over the slow pace of piecemeal reforms.

White Repudiation, Black Confrontation

On a Sunday night, in early November 1970, a group of roughly twenty "white youths and men" gathered on the grounds of George Washington High School in Alexandria. According to police reports, they ranged in age from fifteen to thirty-five years old. They brought with them an eight-foot high cross, constructed of two-by-fours and wrapped in cloth. Newspaper reports do not indicate whether the cross was soaked in gasoline before someone in the crowd ignited it, but a short article in the *Washington Post* noted that Alexandria police officials chose not, on this night, to arrest anyone for the disturbance. The *Post* did report that "individuals identified themselves as members of the American Nazi Party."[27] The *Alexandria Gazette* reported that shortly after the group left the high school they were sighted erecting another cross to burn, this time behind Maury Elementary School a few blocks away.[28]

These were not the first crosses to be burned on the grounds of an Alexandria school in the fall of 1970. A little over a week earlier, on Friday, October 23rd, also at the grounds of Maury Elementary School, a group of "youths scattered from the school" as officers arrived to investigate reports of a burning cross.[29] That night, at the Alexandria Holiday Inn, the National Association for the Advancement of Colored People (NAACP) was holding the opening events of its Virginia state convention, being held for the first time in Alexandria.

Both the NAACP convention and the cross-burnings occurred in the midst of a vocal public campaign by white supremacists to discredit Alexandria's school leadership. Thirty members of the National Socialist White People's Party (formerly the American Nazi party) picketed in front of Albohm's house in early November 1970, claiming that school district policies tolerated "black terrorism" in Alexandria's schools. Albohm also reported receiving several "irritating and threatening" phone calls at his home.[30] Those recorded phone messages called Albohm and George Washington High School Principal Richard Hills "traitors to the white race."[31] At a mid-November School Board meeting, Claude L. Haynes, Jr., head of the American Independent Party in Alexandria and supporter of George Wallace's 1968 presidential campaign, circulated a statement calling for Albohm's dismissal or resignation. Existing school policy, claimed Haynes had produced "lower achievement levels and … a breakdown of discipline, morale, and race relations." He added that recent events showed that "The collapse of discipline was allowed to progress so far that it can no longer be hidden."[32]

While white supremacists were extreme in their language, other city officials also took Albohm and the School Board to task, particularly over the issue of discipline. Commonwealth Attorney John Kennahan, who served as the School Board's own lawyer, publicly criticized Albohm and the School Board during the November 4 board meeting for not pursuing legal action against students accused of assault or vandalism. He indicated that school officials had dropped charges against students against his advice. According to press reports, Kennahan stated that "The police power of the state cannot be diminished or compromised by school officials for any student for any reason."[33] After the meeting, he told reporters that he went beyond his charge of giving legal advice to the Board in order to encourage teachers to "stiffen up on discipline."[34]

Members of the board took exception to Kennahan's public scolding and to its "law and order" tone. School Board Chair Ferdinand T. Day decried the Republican Commonwealth Attorney's use of schooling as a political platform to incite voters.[35] Kennahan's views, however, were not unrepresentative of many Alexandrians. The first Republican ever elected Commonwealth Attorney in Alexandria, Kennahan enjoyed broad range of support within the community, including both Claude Haynes and the Black Community Action Council.[36] His views on discipline found resonance among several groups particularly among some Del Ray residents, whose neighborhood was part of the George Washington High School attendance zone, and who were angry at the accelerating speed of integration in the neighborhood. In a 1969 Washington Post article on disciplinary problems at George Washington High School, PTA President Jack Clark told a Washington Post reporter, "The trouble started with the speed of integration forced on both white and black." His wife Susan Clark added, "What the whole thing boils down to ... is that they do not have enough discipline.... Everything will fall into place if we could get discipline back into the schools."[37]

Although many parents saw disciplinary issues as separate from the moral and legal imperative to desegregate, the issue of discipline frequently devolved into arguments about how best to control black children. The disturbances in Alexandria's schools were real, but the fundamental issue revolved around respect and identity. In one incident, a shoving match broke out between black and white students in the midst of a debate over the impeachment of the white senior class president of George Washington High School, who had called the school's African American homecoming queen "a nigger." An initial vote against impeachment was met with cheers from white students, and at a second meeting demanded by black students, sharp words escalated into a brief scuffle between black and white students.[38] After the principal removed the class president from office, students elected a popular African American football player to take his place.

At T.C. Williams High School, Albohm met with students to exchange views with students on disciplinary issues. After the talk, many students jeered and booed Albohm, who had urged students simply to "settle down" and return to their classes. A group of forty African American students persisted in questioning T.C. Williams's principal Arnold Oates and Albohm, with one student saying, "I'm tired of being told to go to my room.... I've been in this school for three years and I'm tired of being put in rooms, shuffled from class to class. I want to talk now."[39]

Despite black student concerns about respect, conflict suffused the school system. The conservative Alexandria Gazette focused on the number of violent incidents, stressing the rising rate of bathroom burglaries and assaults among students.[40] For their part, black students had taken to "liberating" particular bathrooms at George Washington High, allowing only African American students to use them.[41] Sometimes more violent episodes took place: A black student, demanding money, cut a white student with a knife while riding on a school bus serving Parker-Gray Junior High. In response the victim's father publicly demanded Albohm's resignation at a School Board meeting—the same meeting at which Kennahan urged the School Board to take a hard line on prosecuting disciplinary cases.[42] In one day, three bomb threats (all false) were made against Alexandria schools.[43] Numerous other minor incidents may have been the result of the usual conflicts among teeenagers, but because they involved a black and a white student, they took on new importance in the context of racial tension. In both the schools and the city at large, these minor conflicts were viewed through the lens of a racial power struggle among various actors within the city, including students and adults.

From the perspective of black parents and students, the linkage that white supremacists made between desegregation, discipline problems, and declining academic standards made the actions of school officials highly suspect. Perceptions that black students were subject to harsher punishments than similar violations by white students sparked further discontent. On December 10, 1970, about a month after Kennahan urged greater disciplinary enforcement—and less than two weeks after a hung jury failed to convict John Hanna—school officials suspended a George Washington High School student for standing on a table in the school cafeteria. In protest, a group of about fifteen black students poured roofing tar on the floor of a boy's bathroom and then set it on fire, "not causing a large fire but igniting one which gave off a very sooty appearance and noxious fumes."[44]

Often the staff seemed unprepared to deal with the changes Alexandria schools were undergoing. At GWHS, in 1969, over half of the teaching staff was more than fifty years old; only eight of the school's ninety-one teachers were African American. In general, one teacher told a reporter, "I'm not sure that many of the teachers have been prepared adequately for integration."[45] In addition, none of the principals at any of the city's high schools or middle schools were African American. From the perspective of black students, the racial and generational gulfs between teachers and students made schooling conflicts a personal insult: "There are too many old people in the school," one black ninth-grader told a reporter. "If you walk into the library they ask you what you want there. 'No, no, get out here.' Then they say, 'come here you poor boy.' My name ain't 'boy'. My name's not 'boy.'"[46]

Teachers, however, felt increasingly vulnerable to student unrest and bargained successfully for greater powers to exclude disruptive students from their classes. In January 1971, Albohm announced that the new teacher's contract granted teachers the unilateral right to expel a student from his or her classroom, permanently. According to the *Washington Post*, these teacher-held powers to bar a student from the classroom were unprecedented in the Washington area.[47] From the perspective of the black community, however, these powers would simply allow teachers to bounce students from their classrooms, without actually addressing their educational needs. City Councilman Ira Robinson, the first African American elected to Alexandria's City Council, assailed the new powers, claiming that Albohm was simply devising a repressive policy of control, rather than devising strategies to better teach students. Robinson called for the School Board to fire Albohm because of his failure to realize that when elementary schools "advance children who cannot read or who read poorly to middle school, then [on] to high school, the likelihood that those children will become disruptive is greatly increased." Alexandria's discipline problems, Robinson argued, stemmed from its failure to address basic illiteracy among many poor African American students.[48]

For its part, the leadership of Alexandria Public Schools sought to assure white parents that disciplinary problems were not as widespread as press reports indicated and that this was not a problem of schools alone. Indeed, Albohm and other district officials often stated that schools merely reflected, rather than generated, social conditions. Both Assistant Superintendent Raymond Sanger and Albohm contended that Alexandria's schools were affected by the same pressures and conflicts that were disrupting college campuses and American society in general. This was a generalized crisis of authority, not a breakdown of school discipline, they claimed.[49] Sanger and Albohm insisted that only a small percentage of students caused the bulk of the disciplinary conflicts. Albohm stated that if, out of 1700 students in a high school, "we remove seventeen students from time to time who are above compulsory school age, who have demonstrated their unwillingness to learn in our system and demonstrated the necessity of removal, this would be the end of the problem."[50]

HEW Asks for More: Federal Pressure Meets Local Politics

Despite Albohm and Sanger's efforts to claim that the racial conflicts affecting Alexandria's schools were driven by outside influences, pressures grew on school administrators to make a significant change in the organization of Alexandria's schools. The growing disciplinary crisis combined with increasing racial imbalance at the secondary level and increasing HEW scrutiny of Alexandria's racial attendance patterns meant that Albohm needed to restructure significantly Alexandria's schools. The proposed reform, dubbed the 6-2-2-2 Plan, was a watershed moment in Alexandria's schooling history, but it emerged more out of local concerns than federal pressures. The new plan involved keeping the existing elementary school structure (grades Kindergarten through Six) largely intact, but altering the composition of the middle and high schools. The secondary scheme would begin with neighborhood-based two-year junior high schools (grades Seven and Eight), continue with two existing high schools (Hammond High and George Washington High) converted to Ninth and Tenth grade only and culminate with all Alexandria students attending one common high school in grades Eleven and Twelve, at T.C. Williams High School. By merging all high school juniors and seniors into a single school—and by ensuring that all middle schools and ninth to tenth grade high schools had equal ratios of black and white students—Albohm designed a fully integrated secondary school system that he hoped would both alleviate white flight and defuse black concerns about being relegated to declining schools.

Three pressures led Albohm to develop the 6-2-2-2 Plan. First, the growing numbers of African Americans in both the George Washington High School attendance areas and its feeder elementary and junior high school clearly indicated that George Washington would very soon be majority black, leading to an ever-accelerating exodus of whites from the high school. This resegregation particularly affected formerly all-white elementary schools near downtown that were rapidly becoming majority African American. Second, the U.S. Department of Health, Education and Welfare Office of Civil Rights was stepping up its review of conditions in Alexandria. Focusing primarily on faculty assignment, HEW officials were also increasingly concerned about the apparent failure of Alexandria City Public Schools to address the reemergence of nearly all-black schools, particularly among elementary schools in Alexandria. Third, the continuing agitation of a number of African American students, increasingly radicalized by both events in Alexandria and across the county, made it difficult for Albohm to pretend that "disciplinary" problems were the product of a few overage miscreants looking to evade rules they found confining. Instead, the students repeatedly disrupted the traditional norms of student behavior in a purposeful effort to prompt significant changes in staffing, curriculum, and facilities. Their persistent challenges showed that merely cracking down would not eliminate the frustrations and anger of young black students, particularly at GWHS. Said one black student activist about the demands of GWHS black students, "With us, it's a different thing. . . . The white kids had everything from the beginning. Now the blacks are trying to get it. We have to make these demands for our self-respect."[51]

The pressure from the HEW's Office of Civil Rights began to emerge in December of 1970 with a site visit from HEW officials who met with Albohm and other district officials to discuss the racial patterns in Alexandria's school and the state of faculty segregation among elementary and secondary schools. In 1966, Alexandria had approved a series of elementary boundary changes and created, for the first time, three middle schools. These changes had produced enough racial mixing in Alexandria schools to satisfy the newly toughened HEW Guidelines.[52] The succeeding five years, however, had seen dramatic changes in the racial composition of many of the elementary schools, as well as growing concentrations of African American students at Parker-Gray Middle School and George Washington High School. Table 3.1 shows the changes in the black-white racial composition of Alexandria's elementary and secondary schools between 1966 and 1971.[53] The de facto resegregation of African American students in the East Side elementary schools was particularly glaring to HEW officials.

Moreover, as Alexandria concluded the construction of two new schools, John Tyler on the West Side and a replacement school for Charles Houston on the East Side, HEW officials began to look very closely at the attendance patterns of the new schools and their surrounding neighborhoods. What they saw was a strong pattern of resegregation that placed Alexandria in jeopardy of running afoul of recent court rulings. Those rulings—in particular the U.S. Supreme Court decision in *Green v. County School Board of New Kent County* in 1968—required immediate compliance from school districts that had formerly operated Jim Crow schools. In *Green*, the Supreme Court declared that the *Brown* decisions in 1954 and 1955 had imposed on school districts "the affirmative duty to take whatever steps might be necessary to convert to a unitary system in which racial discrimination would be eliminated root and branch."[54] A "freedom of choice" plan that simply allowed black students to attend formerly all-white schools (the kind of plan Alexandria had operated prior to 1966) was not sufficient to meet compliance with the *Brown* decision. Keeping the existing boundaries of neighborhood schools would only

Table 3.1 **Change in Black Enrollment in Alexandria's Elementary Schools, 1966–1971**

	Percent Black 1966	Percent Black 1971	Percent Chg. in Black Enrollment 1966–1971
East Side Schools			
Theodore Ficklin	42.8	80.3	37.5
Jefferson-Houston	100.0	94.6	−5.4
Cora Kelly	19.6	80.0	60.4
Maury	1.2	8.4	7.2
Mt. Vernon	5.3	27.2	21.9
Robert E. Lee	28.2	83.2	55.1
Lyles-Crouch	100.0	74.3	−25.7
Central Schools			
Charles Barrett	1.1	1.9	0.8
Stonewall Jackson	1.2	31.9	30.7
Douglas MacArthur	0.0	7.4	7.4
George Mason	2.9	2.6	−0.3
West Side Schools			
Patrick Henry	0.0	6.8	6.8
James Polk	0.0	0.0	0.0
William Ramsey	1.1	1.7	0.6
James Tyler	0.0	1.6	1.6
Special Education Facilities			
Trainable Center	25.0	43.1	18.1
Prince St.	58.7	Closed	

exacerbate the resegregation of Alexandria schools. Its past failure to fully deseg-regate and achieve a "unitary status" meant that the Alexandria City School Board was now, arguably, under the same mandate as New Kent County: "The Board must be required to formulate a new plan and ... fashion steps which promise realistically to convert promptly to a system without a 'white' school and a 'Negro' school, but just schools."[55]

In early December 1970, Alexandria's upcoming ribbon-cutting at two new elementary schools—one all white and one virtually all black—prompted a visit from HEW officials, a site visit that was unprecedented in Alexandria's history of desegregation. Following that visit, HEW officials outlined in a letter to Albohm the steps that the Alexandria City School Board would have to take in order to be in compliance with Title VI of the Civil Rights Act. Eloise Severinson, the Region III Civil Rights Director at HEW, indicated that there were two areas that concerned HEW: the enrollment of only fifty whites out of a total enrollment of 860 at the new Jefferson-Houston Elementary school (replacing the formerly all-black Charles Houston School) and persistent absence of black teachers at several schools in the city. HEW recommended that the school district "reconsider" Jefferson-Houston's attendance zone "for the purpose of increasing white enrollment so that as stable a situation as is possible will result" and requested revised teaching assignments at several schools in the city. Indeed, HEW warned that Alexandria officials that "substantial changes" in the teaching assignments at these schools would be needed before the district would be found in compliance with Title VI of the Civil Rights Act and federal court decisions.[56]

The growing pressure from HEW came at precisely the same time that African American student demands at George Washington High School and Hammond High were becoming increasingly vocal and pressures grew on Albohm to "solve" the disciplinary problems in the high schools. In late March of 1971, black student leaders at George Washington High School held a series of unauthorized, all-day "rap sessions" in which they developed a list of demands to present to district and school officials. Demanding a black principal at the school, a more relaxed disciplinary regime, more black teachers, and more classes in black culture (along with the perennial demand for better school lunches), the students skipped classes to attend the sessions.[57] In response, Principal Hills suspended eleven of the students who attended the meetings. Hills insisted the suspensions were not in retaliation to the student demands, but "a sincere effort to continue even-handed enforcement of school rules and standards."[58] Two days later, Hills' efforts to produce an orderly educational process backfired when a black student struck Principal Hills after he told a group of black students holding another unauthorized meeting to return to classes or be suspended.[59] Later that night, roughly one-hundred people turned out at a Rosemont Citizens Association meeting to discuss issues of discipline at neighboring George Washington High School. According to the *Washington Post*, no blacks attended the meeting, but many of the speakers called for a "crackdown" on disciplinary problems at George Washington.[60]

In his own meeting with student leaders, Albohm conceded the legitimacy of some of their demands, but drew the line on discipline: "Demands for relaxed discipline may reflect the values of some of these black students, but we don't think it reflects the values of most blacks, including parents," Albohm told a reporter. The disciplinary problems at GW stemmed, according to Albohm, to frustrations of both blacks and whites over the changes that had occurred within Alexandria's schools: "Blacks remember when their children dominated the athletics, social events, and prizes at Parker Gray (the former all black high school) and whites believe their high school (George Washington) has declined from standards of excellence and achievement." [61]

The solution, to Albohm, was a new kind of school—a school that officials were already planning. "What we will have to build is a new school in a town that has become urban rather than suburban."[62] The forces that induced Albohm to design a "new school" that reflected the racial realities of Alexandria and the expectations of a post-civil rights era nation stemmed from an intense confluence of localist demands and federal constraints. This new school—the subject of the Hollywood film *Remember the Titans*—exemplified, in many ways, the "politics of order" that Albohm sought to achieve. Its origins lay in three sets of competing demands. First, Albohm needed to defuse the continual pressures from activist black students, particularly at George Washington High School, many of whom were highly suspicious of city leaders and sought more than mere toleration from school authorities. While Albohm could not offer them the full incorporation into educational governance that they sought, he could present them with an opportunity to create a new school culture and climate at T.C. Williams. Secondly, pressures from white parents, increasingly dismayed over the continuing tumult within the city schools, made it necessary to speak simultaneously of order and academic excellence in the design of this new school. Throughout the community debate over the 6-2-2-2 plan, Albohm repeatedly stressed the academic benefits of dividing the high school years into two stages, even though many parents did not find the logic compelling. Finally, the continuing oversight of HEW's Title VI enforcement placed an ever-present pressure on the school district to integrate fully its faculty, address resegregation and eliminate the racial identification of elementary schools. As a result, the district faced a clear federal mandate to recompose school teaching staffs and reconfigure school attendance zones. The 6-2-2-2 plan enabled Albohm to shuffle teachers and boundaries without appearing to be merely complying with HEW orders. The changes, however, did not fundamentally address HEW's most clearly developed objection to racial inequities in Alexandria's schools: the growing resegregation of elementary schools.

These three sets of demands were in many ways competing, and given Albohm's limited political space, the localist demands ultimately trumped the federal imperatives. Ironically, the localist politics of order meant that Albohm had to pay attention first and foremost to the city's high schools, even though HEW did not consider the city's high schools to be the central problem. HEW was most concerned about faculty assignments and continuing racial divides among elementary schools. Albohm realized that a wholesale elementary integration—in the midst of significant racial turmoil in its high schools—would accelerate white flight. As a result, he sought a solution to the district's upheaval through a secondary school system reorganization, even though HEW was most concerned about continuing segregation (and resegregation) of elementary schooling.

Albohm's sense of urgency was reflected in the School Board as well. Norman Schrott, Alexandria City School Board Chair from 1970 to 1971, stated in a 1975 interview that "the school system could not remain the way it was. Poor morale and discipline within some of the schools was tearing the system apart. We needed to find some way to improve morale, discipline, and academics. There was such a sense of urgency and need."[63]

From HEW's point of view, however, the central element of the 6-2-2-2 plan, the proposed unified high school, was really beside the point. From the federal perspective, the plan was essentially a solution to a nonexistent problem since a common high school in Alexandria did not address continuing segregation at the elementary level. In its communications, HEW had made clear that its concerns about Alexandria stemmed from segregation in elementary, not secondary, schools. From Albohm's perspective, however, the most pressing problem he faced stemmed from student unrest and discipline issues emerging out secondary schools, both of which contributed to the ongoing political turmoil in Alexandria. Albohm adroitly harnessed HEW pressure to propose a solution to a locally defined problem, not a federally defined problem. The result was a structural transformation in Alexandria schools that helped redefine the city's identity, but left unaddressed, for the time being, growing resegregation in elementary schools. The creation of a single, city-wide high school at T.C. Williams fused the fates of black and white high school-ers and represents to this day, within Alexandria, the city's progress toward racial accommodation and unity. It just wasn't what HEW had in mind.

T.C. Williams High School and the Hope of Unity

The goal of the 6-2-2-2 plan was evident from Albohm's confidential memorandum to the Board of Education written prior to the public disclosure of the plan. Although he framed the issue as one of compliance, the first section of the memorandum was entitled "Considerations Other Than Compliance." There he writes,

> The schools are being held accountable for social and political changes not of the schools' making. Budget stresses; racial conflicts; resegregation; militancy on the part of white and black students; parent concerns with the drug scene; court orders involving extension of adult civil rights to pupils in schools; teacher strikes; irrelevant curriculum offerings—all interfere with the basic purpose of public education, which purpose is to provide an education in citizenship, and an education in skills and in learning toward the end of good citizenship and the ability to make a living and contribute to American society.[64]

He continued, stating that "Alexandria, similar to many communities above 100,000 [in] population ... is also subject to the major problems of resegregation;

some aspects of irrelevant curriculum practices; budget pressure; and overall community tensions—all of which reflect themselves in the programs and practices of the school system." Thus, while compliance with HEW Title VI regulations provided a context for recomposing Alexandria's school system, local considerations shaped to a considerable degree the magnitude and content of those changes.

This confidential memorandum formed a draft of the four public proposals for structural reforms that Albohm presented to the Board on May 5, 1971. While Albohm and his staff did not formally endorse any one of the four proposals advanced at the meeting, it was clear that the 6-2-2-2 plan was Albohm's preferred choice. The presentation of the plan's advantages ranged from increased efficiencies in course offerings to a reduction of "intra-city rivalries and tensions" and a new focus of "city loyalties on one major central high school," along with the development of the "leadership potential" of ninth and tenth graders.[65] The Director of Secondary Education, John R. Stubbings, indicated that the concentration of eleventh and twelfth graders in one school (along with the concentration of ninth and tenth graders at Hammond and George Washington) afforded "opportunities for significant instructional improvements" because the district could allocate teachers and course offerings "in a more efficient manner once we have more students together with similar needs and interests."[66]

In addition to focusing on the instructional and educational advantages of the 6-2-2-2 plan, Albohm and his staff stressed the competitive advantages T.C. Williams sports teams would have. Director of Athletics William Blair told the Board, "If this plan is approved, juniors and seniors throughout this city will be blended into one great high school whose entire sports program will be second to none in Northern Virginia and comparable to the best in this state."[67] Alluding to a number of violent conflicts that had plagued sports events at the city's high schools over the past year, Blair also expressed confidence that the new common high school would reduce intra-city rivalries and foster greater cohesion within the community.

In many ways, the common high school proposal was an effort to not only meet HEW demands that faculties and schools be better integrated, but to anchor the educational experiences of all Alexandrians within a common space. Albohm insisted that all four proposals—which ranged from the 6-2-2-2 plan to modest boundary changes to more aggressive recomposition of the current high school populations to ensure a 30 percent African American enrollment at all three high schools—would satisfy HEW. But it was clear to Albohm at least that only a unified high school would simultaneously allow the district to fully integrate the teaching staffs, promote a broad integration of pupils within the secondary school system, and ensure that none of the three high schools evolved—because of demographic shifts—into a "black" high school, a designation that George Washington High School was only a few years away from given the prevailing demographic trends.

The opponents of the plan—particularly members of the Old Guard—felt that Albohm was going too far too fast. The 6-2-2-2 plan, they contended, was unnecessary, given that other proposals would also keep Alexandria City Schools in compliance with HEW. A more modest change of boundaries would prevent the wholesale transformation of the secondary school system. During the public comments at the May 19 School Board meeting, former Alexandria mayor Marshall Beverley (a cousin of Harry F. Byrd, Sr.) was the first person on the list to speak. He immediately questioned the necessity of the entire enterprise. He queried whether the Board had sought the legal of advice of Commonwealth Attorney John Kennahan as to whether the Board was under any obligation from HEW or the courts to develop any plan. Later in the meeting, Kennahan responded to Beverley's questions, point by point, stating at one point, according to a transcript of the meeting: "I don't doubt that 6-2-2-2 would be in compliance. I don't doubt that the other plans would be in compliance, but there is nothing that has come before me, either in correspondence or in our conversation [with HEW officials], which specifically says that the school system is not in compliance at this time." He added, "I can't say as a legal matter that anything has at this time been directed by HEW."[68]

Kennahan's open disagreement with Albohm over the need for the 6-2-2-2 plan (or any other plan) stemmed, in part, from a difference in perspective; from a strictly legal standpoint, Alexandria was under no direct legal or administrative order to either alter its boundaries or adopt a new organization of its secondary schooling. However, given the both the direction of Alexandria's demographics and HEW's adoption of *Green v. County School Board of New Kent County's* insistence on immediate, full integration within former Jim Crow districts, it would only be a matter of time before some kind of federal official—either judicial or administrative—would be requiring (or imposing) significant changes. Kennahan's position echoed an earlier Old Guard line of resisting all integration until the last possible moment.[69]

On the other side, the possibility of renewed desegregation litigation was raised by community African American leaders in their comments to the School Board during the May 19 debate. According to the detailed minutes of the public debate, Melvin Miller, an African American Alexandria attorney, pointed out that recent decisions of the Fourth Circuit had ruled that "all deliberate speed" was no longer an acceptable pace of integration. Instead, desegregation plans were being imposed within thirty or sixty days. According to the minutes, Miller reminded the Board that "it only takes one plaintiff in court the day after school opens and I would suggest to you that you will have to revamp your entire system within thirty to sixty days."[70] In his written comments submitted to the Board, Reverend Samuel E. NeSmith, minister at Roberts Memorial Methodist Church in Alexandria, endorsed Miller's position, but made clear that integration, in and of itself, was not the highest priority of the African American community: quality education was. He argued that "If no changes are made to ensure quality education for all students, none of the proposed plans will work." He went on to detail the range of needs that would have to be met within the district to deliver that quality education: a robust program of reading and language skills; teacher sensitivity training; and increased numbers of African

American principals, counselors, and coaches. Reorganization of the secondary system alone—without an attention to the quality of education delivered—will not solve the problems facing Alexandria's high schools, NeSmith claimed.[71]

As the School Board members turned to debating the reorganization, it became apparent that their own motivations for reform stemmed less from responding to HEW's pressures to better integrate faculties and elementary schools than meeting a local understanding of what quality education looked like. The spate of disturbances in high schools and concerns about declining quality were, according to the words of School Board members, more important than meeting a federal standard of integration. While pragmatic concerns such as costs of busing and a quick timetable to implement the new scheme by September did come up, the issues of racial equality in educational opportunity, as well as community resegregation, were equally prominent. In his extended comments recorded verbatim in the minutes, School Board member Carlyle Ring began by noting that "our obligation is to provide quality education. Incidentally, the State Constitution states that that is our obligation. But quite independently, I think it is self-evident that this is our obligation."[72]

Turning from the local nature of the school board's obligations to its legal obligations, Ring stated "the legal complications that lie in the background are certainly factors that we need to take into account but I do not see how they should or could be a prime consideration by this Board.... Obviously, we must be mindful of what the Federal Law [sic] may require. To my mind our responsibility transcends what our legal requirements may be to meet the minimum standards." He added a few lines later, "we cannot feel that our obligation to quality education is met because of what the HEW may or may not be insisting that we do.... The Board's consideration has been prompted by consideration primarily of what we need to do in order to equalize educational opportunities in the city."[73] He concluded his comments by stating that in formulating the plans "[W]e are not concerned about the legal requirements as such, but we were concerned about quality education.... Our consideration of the 6-2-2-2 Plan or any plans, in my judgment, is not based upon any compulsion at this time by HEW."

Following upon Ring's comments, School Board Member William B. Hurd, while professing to still be undecided about which way he would vote, indicated that HEW's position held little relevance to him, even though he supported desegregation:

> I do want to make it clear that I am not interested in compliance with some HEW standards. We as members of this Board have an obligation under our own oath to attain both desegregation and quality education in Alexandria. Nor ... do I think we have to wait to be pushed by a bureau in Washington or a Federal Regional Office (sic) anywhere, that we act only as someone else requires us to act. We can attain desegregation in the

secondary system without 6-2-2-2. The question is which plan provides the best educational program, and that is what I have to decide for myself here tonight.[74]

In the end, Hurd joined with a unanimous Board in approving the 6-2-2-2 plan. While there was a realization that growing resegregation would most likely prompt either a more aggressive HEW involvement or direct judicial intervention, the sentiment expressed by Board members was that this proposal was an Alexandria response to an Alexandria issue, enacted with the aim to improve educational offerings, reduce resegregation within the secondary program, and, in so doing, promote greater educational opportunity in the city.

In short, the adoption of the 6-2-2-2 plan emerged, in part, from increasing numbers of African American students within one part of the secondary system, along with the reaction of white families in the George Washington attendance zone to the notion that they might soon be in a minority. That dynamic, combined with an awareness that either HEW or federal courts could assume control of the issue in the near future, induced a new model of secondary education within Alexandria. T.C. Williams High School, named after an ardent segregationist, soon stood as a symbol of a racially unified community, whether or not it existed in reality. While that symbolism did not eliminate racial conflict in Alexandria's schools, it helped defuse some of the racial tension that had plagued Alexandria's high schools the previous year. At the same time, the school system's reluctance to redress segregation in elementary education continued to sow distrust within the African American community and prompted a more tense confrontation with HEW in the years ahead.

From Secondary to Elementary: Race and the Idea of Community Schools

As the school district and the city turned to implementing the 6-2-2-2 plan, HEW pressure on the elementary school front threatened to add to Albohm's woes: In a letter dated June 24, 1971 (only a month after the School Board adopted its new secondary school plan), Regional Civil Rights Director Eloise Severinson informed the school district that "at the elementary level there remain areas in which your projections do not appear to meet the requirements of current law"—despite the fact that the secondary school reorganization plan and accompanying faculty reassignments appeared "to be in accord with current law." In particular, Severinson focused on the racial disparities in staffing and enrollments in Alexandria's elementary schools. The opening of the new Jefferson-Houston school was, according to HEW, "in reality a continuation of the former virtually all-Negro Houston School. This situation appears to result in the continued racial identifiability of a formerly Negro school."

In addition, Severinson wrote, the African American enrollments at four other elementary schools were "highly disproportionate," with black enrollments topping 70 percent. The letter detailed the ruling of the recent *Swann v. Charlotte-Mecklenburg Board of Education* decision and concluded by invoking the prospect of citywide elementary busing: "It appears clear that measures such as those utilized in the *Swann* case would be applicable in your school division."[75] Severinson requested that Albohm submit by July 10 a plan to "accomplish full compliance."

Initially, the Board dodged Severinson's request, seeking a delay because three new members had recently joined the Board. In the letter, Albohm also requested to meet with HEW officials to "discuss the matter in detail."[76] On July 20, 1971, Albohm and Deputy Superintendent Raymond Sanger met in Albohm's office with Ernest King and James Wego, both HEW officials at the Region III Office of Civil Rights in Philadelphia. Detailed minutes of that meeting indicate that Albohm and Sanger were not only frustrated with the apparent inability of HEW officials to appreciate the local contexts of desegregation in Alexandria, but also their unwillingness to see the importance of the secondary school reorganization. The minutes provide a revealing glimpse into the process by which Alexandria's officials reconciled federal demands to local governing needs.

Albohm began the meeting by noting that he was uncertain what the Board's sentiment about further elementary integration would be and that there was further uncertainty over what compliance actually meant. He noted also that a lawsuit against the 6-2-2-2 plan was complicating matters[77]: "A new question has arisen in our community and that is on our [law]suit that is pending. People have made various charges, such as that we are already in compliance and it was unnecessary for us to do anything now." Wego replied that the "law [on compliance] has certainly evolved," but that since the *Swann* case in March "the burden of proof is on the school division" to show it is in compliance. He also stated that since that decision, HEW had been in contact with thirty-five school districts in Region III alone about their compliance.[78]

Then, in a revealing question, Albohm shows that he was only now coming to grips with the difference between ending segregation and achieving integration. He asked, "Is compliance a permanent status?" and Wego replied, "No, it is not. It has always been subject to review. The law has been further clarified in meaning," reflecting the evolving state of both judicial rulings and HEW regulations on what constituted compliance.[79]

At this point in the conversation, the HEW officials turned to the question of whether a school is a racially identifiable school. The issue quickly focused on the Jefferson-Houston school, which was interpreted by HEW officials as a replacement for the formerly segregated Charles Houston Elementary. Mr. Wego stated: "the letter you sent us [indicated] that Jefferson-Houston school is a replacement of Charles Houston. If that fact is interpreted that it had been a black school, it is now a [de jure] segregated school."[80] Albohm then asked, "If that fact [about Jefferson-Houston's de jure status] is open to reasonable discussion on each side, how do we clarify that?" Wego responded, "The burden of proof would be on the school district [to prove it is not the product of de jure segregation]."

Albohm and Sanger then turned to demographic changes in the city, mentioning Cora Kelly Elementary, a school located in the Del Ray neighborhood, and Robert E. Lee Elementary, at the southern end of Old Town. Both schools had seen a rapid influx of black students and an exodus of white families. King from HEW indicated that this new segregation "would be an area of close scrutiny" by his office. Sanger objected that the changes stemmed from "upgraded housing for black people" as they moved out of Old Town, producing "a complete turnover in row housing."

At this point, King indicated that HEW did not consider Alexandria to be a passive observer of demographic patterns as it planned for future school sites: "It was your [original] intention to locate a junior high school at [Jefferson-Houston] which would have been much easier [to integrate], but by action of the city it was made an elementary school. There is 89 percent black enrollment [at Jefferson-Houston]. This creates a pretty strong presumption that Jefferson-Houston is tailored to a black neighborhood. The problem is location of schools—site selection is a School Board burden and has been so in the past."[81]

Albohm then shifted tack, turning to the secondary school reorganization in order to show the good faith of Alexandria City Public Schools, noting that "under our reorganization of 6-2-2-2 Plan ... grades 7–12 will be attending fully integrated schools. Would this be considered sufficient to indicate intent as far as School Board policy is concerned?" The School Board, he added, voted unanimously "to integrate the high schools and bring [them] within the racial ratio of the city, which is in keeping with the *Swann* decision. Is this not sufficient to indicate intent as a well as official policy of desegregation on the part of the Alexandria School Board?"[82] Despite this plea, HEW officials returned to the problem of elementary education and the need for integration throughout all schools in the system. Wego simply replied, "It is not sufficient to indicate [integrated] K-12 grade schools."[83]

After the discussion turned to logistics concerning busing, Deputy Superintendent Sanger reached the limits of his patience. His frustration over HEW refusal to give Alexandria credit for its secondary school reorganization is palpable in the minutes. Sanger: "I am concerned that we are making this major change in a secondary level. We have done more than anyone. The three middle schools are 30 percent black and 70 percent white. The secondary schools too—82 percent white and 18 percent black. Who will do the job at the elementary level? Don't we have time to work this out?" Despite this plea, Wego simply stated, "There is not much time."[84]

Sanger did not give up, however, and tried to portray the need to delay elementary integration as essential to the viability of the city: "I feel it [the secondary school reorganization] is going to save a section of the city [around George Washington High School] because we have had a major move-out of solid citizens.

We are hoping this will arrest the situation and stabilize the community. If we were to integrate more our predominantly Negro elementary schools, it would confuse the issue. The Board has had their hands full because of the suit and we have not gotten into the elementary problem. I would like to delay the elementary problem for a while. We would like to do it right."[85]

As the discussion turned to feasible techniques of elementary integration, given the existing demographics of the city, Albohm identified some of the obstacles the district faced: The "feasibility of going further" with integration, Albohm stated, "gets into neighborhood psychology. The same 9th, 10th, 11th and 12th grade pupils attending [George Washington, Hammond and T.C. Williams] instead of the nearest high school and middle school are now being moved greater distances. This is causing parent concern as evidenced by the [Sando] suit. Real estate values are another factor to consider."[86] Albohm's long-standing commitment to the idea of neighborhood schools and his own reluctance to disturb "natural" neighborhood patterns of class and race at the elementary level aligned clearly with the preservation of vestiges of Alexandria's old segregated school system. HEW's effort to push Alexandria's elementary system into a unitary status clashed with Albohm's perceptions of the limits of schools to overcome the racial and class realities of neighborhoods. And at last, he, too, reached the limits of his patience and laid out the positions of his local opponents:

"We do not indicate unwillingness to cooperate with you. We are getting phone calls from very prominent people [in Alexandria], who do not have children in school, who are officials in the Federal Government and who are nationally known.... All I am getting from outsiders, from the School Board, City Council members, prominent people, is caution. [They tell me] 'You would be better off to take a stand, not to be so compliant.' 'Buy time.' 'Set up a program that would be a step program rather than you going all out now.'"[87] Albohm went on to imply that the secondary school reorganization has been politically costly to him and the School Board and that he faced severe political obstacles: "We have lost white support. We have lost black support. Parents think we have not kept promises.... I am trying to indicate the box we are in. There is a caution on our part and maybe a caution on the part of the School Board and the community because of the [existing] power structure and [the possible] Federal injunction" in the Sando suit.[88]

The "power structure" of Alexandria and its pressure to slow down elementary integration placed real constraints on both Albohm and HEW as the city's school system sought to reconcile the demands of the local political forces with the mounting Supreme Court and HEW pressure to undo all vestiges of segregated schooling. The sweeping changes of Albohm's secondary school reorganization required that he expend significant political capital to ensure its passage. He made that expenditure because the "politics of order" compelled him to confront decisively the issues of discipline and student agitation in local high schools. But the consequence was that when HEW came asking for more, Albohm felt he had limited political standing to deliver what HEW officials were seeking.

The costs of Albohm's decision to first pursue secondary school reform, rather than elementary reform, were not lost on HEW. Near the end of the meeting, Wego commented, "The irony is that a *Swann* letter would have come if you had not reorganized. The Jefferson-Houston [Elementary School] situation is there and is still there. We need a communication soon. The burden is placed on you."[89] What Wego was trying to make clear was that the *Swann* decision—and HEW's alignment of its compliance enforcement with the standards articulated in *Swann*—required immediate elementary school integration, independent of both the secondary school reorganization and the political costs that accompanied that reorganization. In short, HEW, from the start, had been focused on the need for elementary integration, but the local political pressures demanded secondary school reorganization. This structural reform was not only politically costly, but the high financial costs associated with the creation of a common, unified high school also made elementary school integration harder to achieve in the short run.

According to HEW officials, however, there would be no "long run." The minutes of the July 20th meeting end with the following exchange:

MR KING: Whatever you decide to do, you need to decide between now and the first of September.

MR WEGO: We will have to have an answer by the last of July.

DR ALBOHM: What alternatives do we have? Do we describe any plans that the School Board would have?[90]

The last line of the minutes read: "The meeting adjourned at 4:00PM. It was entirely cordial."[91] At the end, Albohm was left with posing questions, seemingly to himself, about ways the school district could simultaneously satisfy HEW and the local power structure. The growing tensions made it far less likely that he would be able to placate both.

A week after Albohm met with Wego and King from HEW, he mailed a letter off to Eloise Severinson, the Regional Civil Rights director in Philadelphia, who had sent out the "*Swann* letter" in late June, indicating the need for further compliance. Albohm's brief response relied upon the Sando litigation as a justification for delay. Because a central element of the lawsuit was the constitutionality of the secondary school reorganization, Albohm contended, he would be unable to respond to HEW's request for a plan until after the court decision.[92] Shortly after receiving the letter, HEW officials agreed to delay their compliance requirements until after the Sando litigation ended.[93] And although that litigation effectively ended at the end of August, when Federal District Court Judge Oren Lewis ruled in favor of the 6-2-2-2 plan, HEW continued its "watch-and-see" response to events in Alexandria.

Part of HEW's hesitation may have stemmed from the disturbances that plagued Alexandria's schools in September 1971 under the new secondary organization. While T.C. Williams was calm, Hammond High and later George Washington High saw numerous fights and conflicts among students. At Hammond High, whites threw rocks at buses carrying African American students from East End schools, and throughout the first week of school sporadic fights broke out among students. At Hammond, four students—three whites and one black student—were arrested on the second day of school, with charges ranging from disorderly conduct to carrying concealed weapons. That evening, at a regularly scheduled School Board meeting, tempers grew heated among parents. One white parent declared that he was withdrawing his daughter from Hammond, saying "until you people remove this black animalistic element my daughter will not go back there."[94] A black parent commented that she was "shocked to be in an audience of people who refer to my children and race as animals," noting that many black students also suffered abuse at Hammond at the hands of whites.[95]

As September wore on, the mood at Hammond and George Washington grew calmer. In part, the secondary school reorganization became easier to accept with the success of T.C. Williams's Titans football team, which went undefeated and won the Virginia state championship in its inaugural season as an 11th and 12th grade high school. Prior to the Titans' championship season, athletic events had proved to be contentious and fractious affairs within Alexandria. In 1969, during tensions over the Private Callahan-Keith Strickland incident, firebombings broke out after a Hammond-George Washington football game that saw groups of fans throw rocks at each other at the conclusion of the game.[96] The recurring violence and disturbances associated with football games that season forced the school district in the fall of 1969 to move all Friday night games to afternoons to minimize violence. Other sports were not immune. In February 1971, George Washington fans harassed and struck visiting spectators and cheerleaders at the conclusion of a game between Arlington's Washington-Lee boys' basketball team and George Washington High School. (The visiting team's locker room was also burglarized while the teams played.) As a result of the fracas, George Washington was officially warned by the Virginia High School League, potentially preventing it from participating in or hosting league events.[97]

Athletics were both a source of pride and tension in various sections of the city and the new secondary school organization sought to harness those attachments and promote a common identity for Alexandria's youth. Importantly, the interracial coaching staff of the Titans football team, although not without its own tensions, fostered an atmosphere of racial respect on the team, most notably through a week-long training camp at Gettysburg College prior to the season. That atmosphere extended to the T.C. Williams campus in September: At the start of the school year, members of the football team patrolled the hallways, wearing team jerseys, to minimize conflict at the school. As John Stubbins, director of secondary education, told a *Washington Post* reporter, "[I]t's pretty obvious that there's been a tremendous spillover into the entire system because of that team.... The parents are thrilled to death to see these kids getting along and it's really helped. A lot of minds have been changed at the dinner table, believe me."[98]

Fewer minds could be changed, however, when it came to addressing resegregation in Alexandria's elementary schools. After the court decision came down in August 1971 approving the secondary school reorganization, HEW let the matter rest for a few months and then resumed communications with Albohm about his plans. The controversy this pressure prompted—along with the political backlash and lobbying against HEW—highlights the continuing ability of the local regime to resist incursions into neighborhood-based schooling in Alexandria. It also illustrates Albohm's sensitivity to local considerations prior to overseeing the HEW-required integration of elementary schools.

The renewed attention to elementary schools in Alexandria began in late January 1972 when HEW Civil Rights Director J. Stanley Pottinger picked up the phone to ask Albohm what the status of Alexandria's desegregation plans were. During that phone call, Pottinger heard Albohm to say that he was preparing new attendance plans that would leave Alexandria with no elementary school with a black enrollment higher than 50 percent.[99] This figure would have represented a major integration of all Alexandria's elementary schools since five of the fourteen elementary schools at the time had black enrollments ranging between 70 and 95 percent. Pottinger then memorialized that conversation in a letter to Albohm dated February 3rd, stating his understanding that under all of the plans being developed "no schools would have a majority of Negro or other minority children."[100] Given the existing residential segregation within Alexandria, the elimination of all majority-minority schools was only possible under some kind of busing scheme. The implication of Pottinger's letter, then, was that all of the plans Albohm was developing required busing outside of existing neighborhood school boundaries.

Albohm did not publicly announce the letter's arrival for over two weeks. Then, shortly before midnight, as the regularly scheduled February 23 School Board meeting wound down, Albohm publicly announced that he had received correspondence from HEW concerning elementary school integration and that a reply was needed.

Katrina Ross, an African American Board member who was appointed in July 1971, then moved that Albohm prepare plans and analyses for the Board's consideration that would meet the concerns outlined in Pottinger's letter. At this point, for the first time in Albohm's tenure, the School Board divided over the proper response to HEW's mandates. Board member Carlyle Ring offered a substitute motion, declaring that while the school district was committed to the "objectives of equal educational opportunity and a quality education for all Alexandria students" it was the Board's intent "to maintain our policy of neighborhood elementary schools" and that the Board had "no plans to cross-bus youngsters between elementary schools."[101] The board then engaged in a "45-minute, emotionally charged debate"[102] on the two motions. Eventually, in a 4-3 vote, Ring's substitute motion lost and Albohm was charged with developing options for the Board's consideration at its next regular meeting.

Fortunately for Albohm, HEW again backpedaled, obviating any immediate need for him to submit plans for elementary integration. Less than a week after the divided School Board vote, Albohm received another letter from Pottinger dated February 28th, this one stating that "there may be some misunderstanding as to the purpose of my February 3 letter to you." Pottinger then went on to state that he now understood that any integration plans being developed by Alexandria were "premature" and that no determination had been made, as of yet, whether such plans were even required.[103]

While Pottinger may have misunderstood Albohm in their late January phone conversation, it is equally plausible that Albohm sought out federal pressure in order to force the School Board into action. In an interview with the *Washington Post* about HEW's reversal, Albohm said that he told Pottinger in their January conversation that without federal pressure, he would not pursue further elementary integration. According to the reporter, Albohm "told Pottinger in a late January telephone conversation: 'I'll need you to write me to initiate me to present alternatives (to the city's neighborhood schools)...I'm not going to initiate it on my own.'"[104] Whether Pottinger indeed misunderstood Albohm or Albohm sought a clear directive from HEW in order to overcome local pressure, the fact that local establishment figures could quickly undermine Pottinger's position meant that Albohm faced severe local opposition and was not going to immediately undertake elementary integration on his own.

Local Responsibilities and Local Priorities

All of this happened so quickly that the Alexandrians who flocked to the March 1, 1972 School Board meeting to argue against elementary integration found themselves listening to Albohm announce HEW's reversal. That did not stop them, however, from denouncing elementary integration during the public comments. At the opening of public comments, Donald Baldwin, leader of the Alexandria Committee for Quality Education, quickly rose and blasted Albohm for scheming with Pottinger to increase HEW pressure on Alexandria. He claimed that "busing of elementary school pupils" was not the intent of [HEW], "but that it was merely a vehicle which the [school] administration was using to bring this matter before the [School] Board." Baldwin went on to contend that busing was simply not on HEW's agenda; it was solely on Albohm's agenda:

> I think they [the School Board members] should know that [elementary busing] is not the request of the Office of Civil Rights Department of HEW. It is not the position of the Secretary of HEW to require that we further organize our schools

.... [T]he director of the Office of Education [has stated] that we should concentrate on quality education, and not spend too much time on considering sociological experimentation and spending taxpayers money on unnecessary busing, unnecessary costs [that are] doing nothing but lowering the quality of education in our schools.[105]

Such sentiments were similar to those expressed elsewhere by Baldwin, whose group joined forces with other roughly 150 other local organizations to form the National Council Against Forced Busing in early 1972. In a letter to the *Washington Post* in June, 1972, he contended that "the reorganization of Alexandria's secondary schools last year to achieve racial balance is not working. The quality of education in our public schools has gone down, and no one is happy with it—blacks or whites. Busing is not the answer."[106]

No matter who was responsible for proposing busing for elementary students, the opponents of the plan were adamant that it was poor educational practice. The opponents of busing stressed that disruption of local neighborhoods and the disruption of classrooms were too high a price to pay for any benefit that greater racial mixing in school might achieve. Jim Thomas, President of the George Mason Elementary PTA, stated that 95 percent of its membership was opposed to busing and that "In our opinion, Gentlemen, the school is a part of the community or neighborhood much like a church ... and is the center of neighborhood activities. When children are taken away from the neighborhood, it breaks down the community spirit and cohesiveness."[107] Archie Saban filed a statement with the School Board that declared that any proposal to "compel racial balance" can only "be achieved by force and by the disruption of the educational process and increasing racial divisiveness." Moreover, greater integration will "extend to the primary schools the breakdown in discipline and morale now prevalent" in the secondary system. Finally, he claimed that promoting racial balance offers "no hope of improving the quality of education" in Alexandria. In fact, he claimed, these measures—in Alexandria and elsewhere—have been accompanied by lower quality education."[108]

Others in Alexandria, however, defined quality education as the provision of greater equality in educational offerings, and saw busing as one way to achieve that quality. Despite the loud chorus against busing, other voices—particularly white liberal voices—expressed the view that greater inclusion and greater educational opportunity were local responsibilities independent of any pressure by HEW or federal courts. John Rothburg, President of the Alexandria Council on Human Relations, told the School Board at the March 1 meeting,

[A]lthough the Federal Government—Executive Branch, Legislative Branch [and] Judicial Branch (sic)—can make our job in Alexandria an easier one in some ways or more difficult in some ways, we are Alexandrians and we are talking about a not-so-hypothetical problem ... we are talking about education in Alexandria. The problem we have is the problem of providing a better education for every kid in this city, and that is a problem that we—the citizens of this community, the School Administration, the School Board—we are the ones who have to solve that problem. This [HEW action] can help us or hurt us. But basically it is our problem, and it won't go away.[109]

Rothburg's construction of the political and educational problem facing the Alexandria City Public Schools hinged on the very idea of operational localism. The need for local school authorities to provide equal educational opportunities was a given for Rothburg; indeed, they were the only ones who could provide it. Federal authorities may make that task easier or harder, but it was responsibility of those citizens who funded schools and elected school board members. In many ways, Rothburg's position showed how the civil rights movement and the integration of schools throughout the South had changed the discourse surrounding education, creating a norm that a two-tiered, formally unequal structure of education was no longer desirable or even politically tenable. On the other hand, the enduring notion that locals, not federals, bore the responsibility for ensuring the provision of the actual educational experience—equal or unequal—reveals the continuity in American educational governance, the expectations of local self-determination that grow out a locally funded, locally elected (or selected) school board.

In short, the reaction to the notion of elementary busing—while not formally on the agenda—showed that Alexandria was increasingly of two minds about racial integration at the elementary level. On one side was a vocal, predictable, and strident opposition, but on the other side we see the emergence of a localist, racially moderate position (albeit a minority position) that at least was not unilaterally opposed to the idea of busing. While the crowd at the School Board meeting sometimes jeered a supporter of busing, John Alexander, President of the Alexandria PTA Council, expressed the conviction that a sizeable percentage of the community actually supported the practice:

There is, I believe, strong community support for school integration at the elementary level in Alexandria. It may not be a majority but it is a sizeable group. The opposition, it seems to me, is more vociferous than real. Alarmist phone calls should not be accepted as truly indicative of our community's overall sentiment.[110]

In the end, however, the School Board authorized Albohm to "keep under study ways and means of fulfilling the School Board's commitment to equal educational opportunities for all Alexandria pupils."[111] Later in the month, the Board created an "Ad Hoc Committee re the Study of Elementary Education in Alexandria" to review proposals developed by Albohm's staff and to gather the views of parents and the community. Local forces opposed to elementary education had, once again, shown an ability to repeatedly delay the federal judicial mandate.

Political Regime Seeks to Reassert Control

That clout was exercised yet again a few months later when conservatives on the City Council replaced liberal members of the School Board with strong opponents of busing. In June 1972, Ferdinand Day, the chair of the School Board and its first African American member announced his intention to retire from the board, after eight years of service.[112] With Day's departure, the City Council selected Hanford Edsall, a white resident of the West End who was supported by busing opponents.[113] Edsall's selection stoked the ire of black Alexandrians who sought to preserve the existing black representation on the Board and who grew increasingly frustrated with the pace of reforms at both the School Board and Council level.

Their ire grew to a near fury when in October of 1972, the City Council, faced with replacing School Board member Jack W. Carlson, who had resigned mid-term, selected Thomas F. Johnson, a former President of the Alexandria Hospital Board and a prominent opponent of busing.[114] The appointment of Johnson was particularly upsetting to the Black community because it had rallied behind Rev. Samuel NeSmith and lobbied heavily for his appointment, in order to restore African American representation on the Board.[115]

In the wake of Johnson's appointment, relations between the black community and the white leadership of Alexandria grew more difficult. Katrina Ross, the sole remaining African American member of the school board and its Vice Chair, announced her resignation from the Board in protest over Johnson's appointment. In a public statement at a School Board meeting in which she announced her resignation, she blasted the City Council, saying its actions had embarrassed the entire city and were reminiscent of "the old way of thinking" that harkened back to "action taken by Alexandria and school officials years ago in the late fifties."[116] She added that the Council's refusal to add another African American member to replace Day and its insistence on appointing anti-busing candidates would only "further isolate the black community from the decision-making process of the City."[117] She concluded her comments by asking that black Alexandrians boycott the School Board selection process: "I personally ask every black in this City not to apply for the position I leave vacant, under any circumstances. As long as we are expected to have representation with only one black and deliberately appointed conservative white Board, we gain nothing. Blacks are not tokens and no black in this City is going to be used as one."[118]

HEW Forced to Enforce

Alexandria's perennial opponents to busing, however, soon found a formidable foe in Judge John H. Pratt, a U.S. Federal District Court for the District of Columbia.

Since 1970, Pratt had been overseeing an NAACP lawsuit against Health, Education and Welfare for failing to enforce Title VI of the 1964 Civil Rights Act. After a ruling in November 1972 that found HEW had not enforced federal law,[119] Pratt issued a declaratory judgment and injunction on February 16, 1973 against HEW, ordering it to commence enforcement proceedings against Alexandria City Public Schools (and some forty other school districts) within sixty days.[120] Those enforcement proceedings, which Stanley Pottinger had slowed in January 1972 after the issuance of the *Swann* letter in 1971, would result in the termination of federal funds to Alexandria if its elementary schools continued to contain "vestiges" of state-required segregation. Those vestiges were most pronounced in the new Jefferson-Houston Elementary School and four other elementary schools that had over 70 percent nonwhite enrollment. With the long-delayed HEW enforcement now a pressing concern, the Alexandria City School Board's attention returned to the dilemma of elementary integration that met federal judicial requirements.

A few days after the Pratt ruling, the Alexandria Chapter of the NAACP ratcheted up the pressure by providing to the School Board its own plan for elementary integration, which involved extensive pairing of crosstown elementary schools and two-way busing of children. Mr. Urquehart Dixon, chairman of the Education Committee of the local chapter, indicated that without significant movement by the School Board, the NAACP would be filing a lawsuit later in the spring to compel compliance with Title VI and the *Swann* decision.[121] The next day, the Board authorized Albohm to retain the law firm of Armistead Boothe to provide legal counsel about the reorganization of elementary schools.[122]

The lawyers at Boothe's firm soon came to the conclusion that Alexandria had little choice but to adopt some kind of integration plan. In a three-hour closed-door session with the School Board, attorneys Waller Dudley and Tom Brown offered a frank assessment of the District's legal options. In light of the Pratt ruling, the Supreme Court's *Swann* decision, recent decisions coming out of the Fourth Circuit, and the persistence of racial segregation in Jefferson-Houston and Lyles-Crouch Elementary schools, the School Board faced a very difficult legal climate if it chose to do nothing. At a minimum, it would confront imminent Title VI enforcement proceedings seeking the termination of federal funds, as well as a probable lawsuit by the local chapter of the NAACP. Equally importantly, Dudley told the Board, the school district would most likely lose both of those legal battles: "I do not believe Alexandria could really convince the court that it has a unitary school system.... [N]o attempt really has been made apparently to desegregate the elementary schools and I think it would be hard to convince the court that what you did in the 1966 and 1967 session made you a truly unitary system...."[123] In later press reports, an unnamed source indicated that at this meeting "the lawyers were pretty convincing that something had to happen" if Alexandria wanted to control its own desegregation plan.

Despite the clarity of the legal position, both Dudley and the School Board members expressed concern over the local electoral politics of responding to

HEW's enforcement letter. As he weighed the pros and cons of waiting for an HEW enforcement letter before adopting a plan, Dudley stated:

> Again, I would point out the fact that we are having an election in town on May the 1st and that ... any action the Board takes publicly at this time is certain to become something to which every candidate will feel obliged to respond. I think it would be unfortunate for the matter to become a political one ... which would certainly happen if the Board at this time were to act in the absence of a specific requirement of some sort.[124]

Although Dudley indicated that he shouldn't be giving out political advice and should probably stick to providing legal counsel, his concern with the politics of elementary integration and its intersection with local electoral politics highlighted the need to align federally mandated integration with the imperatives and concerns of local politicians. At this late stage in the struggle to integrate Virginia's schools, few individuals from the Old Guard believed that outright resistance could preserve all-white schools. Nonetheless, the political need felt by School Board members and their lawyers to create a perception that elementary integration was not their choice, but was being forced upon them, shows the continuing capacity of the existing regime to implicitly order the agenda of education reform. Albohm hinted at the pressures that awaited them when he told the Board, "I understand the timing of all this. I understand what Mr. Dudley I think said all night.... I think from the public point of view we would all be a lot better off around here if we got a letter pushing us one step further."[125]

The Endgame

Albohm got his wish for an HEW enforcement letter only a few days after the Board requested his proposals for integration plans.[126] Armed with notice from HEW that the federal government would initiate begin procedures that could result in the termination of federal funds on April 17, Albohm presented to the Board seven integration plans on April 4. As introduced, none of these plans enjoyed the support of a majority of School Board members. Albohm's strategy in putting forward such a wide range of options was, most likely, an effort to force the Board to compromise and develop a plan that enjoyed significant support within the community. The conservatives' first reaction, however, was to make a motion directing Albohm to survey all Alexandria parents in the public school system on all seven plans. While some saw the tactic simply as a means to delay the inevitable, School Board member Thomas Johnson defended the motion as means of hearing from the people: "I think this Board is responsible to the community and to the City Council. We have got to leave no stone unturned to ... give this community every opportunity [to express their views] even if we have to go to them and ask them specifically what their opinion is and sort of force it out of them."[127] The motion was defeated 5 to 4, but it indicated that strong divisions within the Board could make compromise difficult.

Part of the conservatives' support for polling the public at large may have stemmed from the fact that politically active Alexandrians—those motivated to attend School Board hearings and City Council candidate forums—were no longer stridently opposed to busing. Many of those appearing at School Board meetings echoed the sentiments of Dick Warden, who had four children enrolled in Alexandria public schools. After indicating that he did not endorse any one particular integration plan because he had questions about all of them, he urged the board to "combine the best elements of the various plans to achieve a *fully integrated elementary school system* and to make equality of educational opportunity a reality for all children in Alexandria." He added that "Alexandria has never set records for speed in dealing with race relations, but neither has it been a community which has said, 'Never.'"

Warden went on to say,

> The hour is late; it has been nineteen years since the Supreme Court said segregated education is inherently unequal. And we still have the vestiges of segregation in our community. We should now make up for lost time; we *are* legally required to remove the vestiges of the segregated system, but we should forget about minimum requirements and do what is right for our children. What is right, in our judgment, is to integrate our schools as thoroughly as possible and to do what ever is necessary to assure that all children in our system—black and white alike from all economic levels—will have an equal chance for a quality education and to fulfill their maximum potential.[128]

At the same time, the opponents of busing contended, as attorney Waller Dudley correctly predicted they would, that Alexandria was under no compulsion to integrate its elementary schools because it was not under a current court order to do so. Gerald Little, of the Alexandria Committee for Quality Education, argued that the School Board "cannot know what the law requires of Alexandria without taking the case to the court of last resort, since in the end the law will be what that court says it is."[129]

The resistant stance advocated by the Alexandria Committee for Quality Education, was, however, an increasingly isolated one. Indeed, Dudley's fear that elementary integration would become a consuming issue in the May 1, 1973 City Council election proved ill-founded. Reflecting a sense of inevitability that some form of busing was needed to achieve integration, there was little debate among the candidates on the issue. Nora Lambourne, a Democratic City Council candidate, told a reporter, "People just seem less and less combative about busing." She added that "Nobody thinks its great, but there's more and more acceptance that we'll have to have some."[130]

During the last two weeks of April, School Board members modified and refined several of Albohm's proposals. The conservatives, particularly Erwin Bondareff and Carlyle Ring, advocated for two separate plans, both of which sought to minimize busing and primarily targeted the racial composition of the two "downtown" schools of Jefferson-Houston and Lyles-Crouch. After the announcement of the Board proposals at the May 2 meeting, the NAACP indicated that none of them met its satisfaction and that its patience was wearing thin. NAACP member and long-time black political figure Melvin Miller told a reporter for the *Washington Post*, "We'll be talking to our lawyer before May 9," the date the Board had set for its final vote. In all the current Board proposals, Miller said, "the weight of busing is going to fall on the poor blacks of this city. This is not only unacceptable to the black community but something I do not think this board wants to go on record as supporting."[131]

After further debate on May 9, the Board decided to delay its final action until May 14. At the beginning of the May 14 meeting, Albohm finally revealed his cards, putting forward a carefully drawn detailed plan that contained elements of several of the plans previously debated. Albohm's plan was a broad, sweeping proposal that incorporated much of the NAACP plan emphasis on pairing elementary schools, along with a number of boundary changes that had previously not been extensively discussed in public. With the addition of the Superintendent's proposal the choices quickly boiled down to two proposals: Ring's modified plan and Albohm's. Both plans achieved roughly similar levels of racial mixing, but Ring's plan relied more heavily on busing black students out of their current neighborhoods, while Albohm's plan relied more heavily on busing both blacks and whites to crosstown paired schools.

In the end, it was this greater sense of shared burden that swayed Colonel Henry Brooks, long regarded as a swing vote on the Board, to opt for Albohm's plan, giving it a narrow 5-4 victory. As Brooks told a *Washington Post* report, "The difference was that more of the kids that Ring bused were black. I told them it was a moral issue and I found it hard to overcome. The two plans were very, very close—the thing was to look at who bore the burden of it all."[132] With the approval of Albohm's plan, HEW halted its termination of federal funding proceedings. More significantly, however, the local political forces that had sought first to resist and then to contain black and white integration within Alexandria were defeated. Segregation, formerly a unifying principle of Alexandria's political and educational leaders, was, fourteen years after the first black student entered an all-white school, no longer the basis by which Alexandrians organized their schools. This is not to say that racial conflict or racial politics was now absent from the Alexandria scene; far from it. But the regime that was premised, first, on the segregation of blacks from whites and, second, on the unequal provision of public benefits and goods to blacks and whites was now undone.

The consequences of that undoing were soon felt on the School Board. Roughly a month after the elementary integration plan, Dr. Erwin Bondareff, who voted against the plan, announced that he was withdrawing his three youngest children from Alexandria's public schools. "What we've done is lower the education level significantly," he told a reporter. "It's not a vindictive thing, but if I did anything else, I wouldn't be true to my own statements."[133] While Bondareff expressed confidence that his decision to withdraw his children would not hurt his chances for reelection to the School Board, others felt differently, including the City Council, the body that selected Alexandria's School Board. In an eight-way race for three seats, Bondareff came in fourth. The vote was, according to City Council member Ira Robinson, "a strong vote of confidence"[134] in favor of the integration plan. In addition to returning Colonel Henry Brooks to the School Board, the Council also selected Shirley Tyler, the NAACP member and community activist who had long been vocal on issues of race in Alexandria's schools. Mayor Charles E. Beatley expressed satisfaction over Tyler's selection, saying "she's the black middle class in Alexandria."[135] By assuring the representation of the affluent West End with the selection of Claudia Waller, a majority of the Board regarded Bondareff's refusal to accept integration as sufficient reason to not reelect him. One political observer told the *Post*, "There just was no way to interpret what he did as having faith in the system."[136] Or, as Ira Robinson, Alexandria's first Black councilmember, put it, "The hard questions have now been answered."[137]

Conclusion

The saga of reconstructing Alexandria's school system from a Jim Crow system with two all-black elementary schools and an all-black high school to an integrated school system with a single high school in many ways looks similar to the accounts of integration across the nation. Alexandria's experience was typically southern, marked by Massive Resistance and a long-running and fierce political and administrative resistance to mixed race schools. The chronology also followed a pattern seen elsewhere in the South: no desegregation until roughly 1959, a few years of modest tokenism, more substantial desegregation after 1966, a keen opposition to a program of busing, substantial integration once busing commences in the early 1970s.

Within those general patterns, however, a number of factors shaped the local response to the *Brown* mandate: the local characteristics of school disciplinary issues, the political agility of Superintendent John Albohm and the one-high-school solution, the persistence of reactionary racism in the form of a neo-Nazi presence in Northern Virginia—all of these shaped the local reaction to the federal requirement of racial integration. In turn, those local characteristics also conditioned the reception of new federal requirements in education beyond racial integration. The federal imposition of an expectation of equality soon expanded to special education and the instruction of students who speak languages other than English. Part Two of this book tracks the local reactions to the new federal commitment to equal educational opportunity, first focusing on white flight and the recomposition of the Alexandria electorate. This transformation of Alexandria's political base, in turn, induced a significant regime change in local politics. This new regime was much more focused on the provision of services, which resonated with the federal commitments to students with special needs. At the same time, the federal effort to provide greater educational equity to non-English-speaking students was stymied by both a tepid federal commitment and the exclusion of new immigrants from the local political structure in Alexandria, an exclusion that is contested still.

The conflicts engendered within the integration struggles in Alexandria set off a cascade of political changes that later intersected with other educational reforms pursued by the federal government. The next three chapters lay out that story of political restructuring and policy reception in an effort to show the complex interplay of federal policy innovation and local regime reception.

PART TWO

THE LOCAL POLITICS OF THE FEDERAL COMMITMENT TO EQUALITY

By 1973, the year that Alexandria fully integrated all of its elementary and secondary schools, the resonances of the federal judiciary's twenty-year campaign to end formal segregation of public school children were echoing through communities in the North and the South. With busing approved as a remedy in 1971, the integration of US schools was proceeding apace, but it was not only racial attendance patterns that were changing in US schools. The idea that the federal government could expand the educational opportunities of students who had been previously excluded from schools or whose educational needs had been fundamentally ignored by local districts because of cost or inconvenience sunk in deep roots in the early 1970s.

At roughly the same time that racial integration reached its most transformative phase, the ideal of greater educational opportunities for other students gained purchase in the federal policy arena. With a series of court decisions in the early 1970s, federal courts expanded tentative commitments to offer more opportunities to English-learners and students with special needs. While Congress appropriated roughly $12.5 million in fiscal year 1967 for states to launch new programs for the education of handicapped children, nothing required states to participate in or to provide such programs. Similarly, in 1968 Congress enacted the Bilingual Education Act to help create better educational opportunities for students who did not speak English. These two programs—as important as they were—simply offered money to states if they wished to participate; no obligation was incurred. But in a flurry of court decisions in the early 1970s, the principle that federal courts could and would protect the constitutional rights of students flourished and federal district courts handed down important decisions that obligated local school districts to attend to the educational needs of these students.

Part Two of this book turns to this expansion of the federal agenda of educational equality and its implications for local school districts. The consequences of this expansion, anchored in the civil rights paradigm, were extensive, but they also operated against the backdrop of the continuing political change that school integration was prompting. Indeed, it was not readily apparent in the early 1970s what the political ramifications of these new attendance patterns would be. While Boston's bitter battles still lay ahead in 1974, Atlanta's largely calm desegregation in the early 1960s belied an accelerating white flight which, Kevin Kruse argues, transformed the political agenda of Southern suburbs, and changed the face of the conservative movement more broadly. In Alexandria, a similar dynamic was at work, although in Alexandria's case the effect was to transform a politically conservative bedroom community into the standard-bearer for liberal politics in Northern Virginia. This change, which emerged out of the context of school-based white flight from Alexandria, held consequences for the expansion of the federal equality agenda in school reform.

In short, the collapse of the Byrd regime and the political fallout from integration in Alexandria produced a governing regime that was premised on racial coalitional politics within Alexandria. At the same time, the dynamics of white flight made school officials deeply anxious about retaining white parents who were most concerned about perceptions of declining school quality. This rise of a more liberal racial coalitional regime, combined with an administrative attentiveness to concerns about declining school quality, fueled local support for an expanded set of programs for special needs students. The expansion of offerings for special needs, while at first resisted, was later used as a means to anchor the support of politically liberal constituents, as well as those who worried publicly about declining quality of Alexandria schools. Often the two groups were one and the same.

In contrast, the federal government's efforts to ensure that English-learners were afforded high quality educational opportunities were, for the most part, neglected in the 1980s and 1990s, partly because of tepid federal enthusiasm for the project, but also because of the incomplete incorporation of new immigrants—many of whom were undocumented—into Alexandria's power structure. Despite the transformative nature of immigration in the Washington, DC area and Alexandria, in particular in the 1980s and 1990s, the political invisibility of these new immigrants meant that there were few opportunities to make claims on local authorities. In addition, many of these immigrant groups lacked the social and political capital to accelerate their inclusion into the local regime. This invisibility defined much of the educational experience of English-learners until the federal government insisted that Alexandria document the educational outcomes of English-learners under the new federal accountability requirements of No Child Left Behind. This imposition of accountability requirements meant, however, that Alexandria City Schools was forced to undertake a narrow test score intervention to satisfy the demands of federal accountability. As a result, the fundamental needs of these students were left significantly unaddressed by either federal mandates or local responses.

Part Two of this book moves through these three themes in three chapters. Chapter 4 addresses the nature of white flight in Alexandria, first through the voucher system under Massive Resistance and later in the early 1970s as concerns about school quality reached a peak. These demographic changes produced a rapid and dramatic swing in the political orientation of Alexandria's residents and created a fundamentally more liberal electorate. This, in turn, opened the door to the greater provision of social services. Chapter 5 addresses the creation and growth of one those social service provisions: the education of special needs students. Beginning with the efforts of Superintendent T.C. Williams to confine African American students to classes for the "under-achiever", the chapter traces the racially tinged adoption of special education programs in the 1970s, including the creation of services for "Gifted and Talented" students that won quick approval. This program, however, exacerbated the white-black educational gap within the district, a gap entrenched in the 1980s through a pervasive system of academic tracking of students. Chapter 6 then turns to the federal government's efforts to ensure that English-learners received better instruction—first through the *Lau* decision in 1975 and later through the expansion of the Bilingual Education Act. These federal efforts were trimmed back, however, in the 1980s, just as Alexandria's English-learner population expanded significantly. With minimal federal pressure and even less local incentive, the ability of the education state to provide services to English-learners proved largely inadequate through the 1990s. The chapter then turns to the advent of accountability mechanisms as a means to ensure that districts meet the educational needs of English-learners.

In sum, these three chapters trace the radiating local effects of the federal commitment to equality in education—first on local demographics and then on specific school offerings to students with special needs and

English-learners. The story is one in which local political priorities structured the reception and reaction of schools and communities to federal educational policies. The federal schoolhouse, begun with a foundation of racial equality, has expanded, but the nature and shape of that expansion is limited and defined by local imperatives.

4

The Politics of Exit

Introduction

In the fall of 1961, four young children prepared for the new school year in Alexandria. Two of the children, a boy entering fourth grade and a girl starting fifth, lived one block apart on Crown View Drive, a quiet residential street in the central part of Alexandria. The other two lived about a mile away, near Quaker Lane, one entering fourth grade at a new school, while the other was starting third grade. While the four children were about the same age, living near each other, their experiences that Fall were radically different. Jack Ford, the boy who lived on Crown View Drive, was the son of then Congressman and future US President Gerald Ford, but he nonetheless experienced a stereotypical suburban elementary classroom, going to an all-white, highly regarded public elementary school with other students from affluent, well-connected families. The family of the girl down the street from the Fords, however, made a different choice for their daughter: She attended a private school at public expense, her family deciding to utilize a state voucher program enacted under Massive Resistance to subsidize the cost of her attendance at a private school in Fairfax County. After two semesters, there is no further record of the family's use of the program. It is quite possible the family moved out of Alexandria, into rapidly growing Fairfax County.

The other two children—a boy and a girl—both attended integrated schools, but under very different circumstances. The girl's family used the private school voucher to defray the costs of enrolling her in Burgundy Farm Country Day School. Although a private school, Burgundy Farm was the first school in the entire state of Virginia to desegregate; according to school documents it desegregated in 1950. Eric Sevareid, CBS radio and television reporter and chronicler of the civil rights movement, helped found Burgundy Farm in 1946 and sent two of his children there. In a radio commentary on the February 10, 1959 desegregation of Alexandria City schools, Sevareid stated, "We integrated that little school, not as a challenge to anybody, not as a precedent, but because it seemed a good thing to do on behalf of our own children, who must learn to live, after all, in a country that doesn't belong to any particular group."[1]

The fourth child, a boy entering fourth grade, lived only a few blocks away from the girl attending Burgundy Farm—but a world apart. He lived in a highly impoverished African American section of Alexandria called Mudtown, and was one of the first African American students to attend Minnie Howard Elementary School, his neighborhood school. Although Minnie Howard was close by, his own immediate neighborhood was vastly different from the rapidly developing suburban landscape surrounding Minnie Howard Elementary. An African American pocket of rural poverty, Mudtown was not connected to the municipal water supply, had no sewer system and was accessible only via unpaved roads. The previous year he had been bused every morning nearly four miles to Lyles-Crouch Elementary, one of the two African-American-only elementary schools in the city. In the fall of 1961, however, he was the only African American boy in his fourth grade class at Minnie Howard.

The experiences of these four children—who all lived within one mile of each other—highlight four very different dimensions of the parental responses to Alexandria's early stages of desegregation. Both the federal imposition of desegregation and Virginia's program of Massive Resistance destabilized the ability of local government to control where students attended school at public expense—whether it was African American students exercising a grudgingly extended and difficult to use "freedom of choice" or affluent white parents using public funds to defray the costs of private school enrollment. Court-ordered desegregation—and its accompanying educational changes—led many Alexandrian parents to consider exiting from Alexandria's public schools. Those exercising the exit option, only a trickle under the voucher scheme in the early 1960s, accelerated in the early and mid-1970s as the pace of integration grew and the city underwent significant demographic change. In the early 1970s, however, the nature of the withdrawal was different: Rather than simply remaining in the city of Alexandria and enrolling their children in private schools, the new exiters were moving out of the city entirely, further unsettling the prevailing demographic and political patterns of Alexandria. Together, both the early flight to private schooling among Alexandria's wealthier residents as well as the broader exodus in the early to mid-1970s significantly changed the city's relationship to public education. It also changed the political calculus of Alexandria's political leaders, particularly those who emerged in the wake of white flight from Alexandria.

The exit to private schools, while only affordable to upper middle-class households, created patterns of school attendance in which class—not race—was the predominant marker of students, and preserved the notion that good schools were composed of a certain class of students. Similarly, the flight to rapidly growing suburbs of Fairfax and Prince William Counties was more than a flight from racial integration; often it was flight from the poverty of these African American students. In both forms, however, the exits of white Alexandrians from public schooling eroded the local elite's ability to sustain support for public education. Both the provision of anti-desegregation vouchers by the state of Virginia and the white flight of families with children represented an indirect assault on operational localism, the first because it attacked the normative ideal of "common schooling" paid for by the public and the second because it represented a rejection of the emergent political status of Alexandria's African American residents.

Both developments also had deep political significance. While the late 1960s and early 1970s were a period of rapid social change in both Alexandria and US society at large, and white flight was only one part of those changes, the departure of middle-class families to both neighboring jurisdictions and to private schools affected the political underpinnings of Alexandria in important and unanticipated ways. The growth of the private school sector partially disconnected affluent and influential city residents from public schooling, creating patterns and traditions of private school attendance that persist to this day. The result was a wider gulf in Alexandria between local elites and school politics. Similarly, the later and broader white flight from the city reshaped the political foundations of local schooling, fostering a more liberal political environment within Alexandria. The two phenomena—Massive Resistance-inspired tuition voucher use and white flight a decade later—are illustrative of the same political change that Kevin Kruse relates in his book on white flight in Atlanta, in which he employed a "community-level approach to demonstrate the interconnected nature of different stages of white resistance."[2] As in Atlanta, Alexandria's conflict over to desegregation induced a white flight that had regional political consequences. For the purposes of school politics, however, the operational localism that organizes resources and students transformed white flight into a mechanism of liberalization of Alexandria's politics.

In Alexandria, withdrawal from desegregated schooling—whether to private schools or to predominantly white outer suburbs—recast and restructured the relationship between city governance and school governance. In particular, in the 1970s, as the city remained predominantly white but increasingly populated by older residents and single residents, its schools became predominantly minority. With the departure of households opposed to integration, the population of Alexandria grew increasingly liberal during the mid-1970s and 1980s and the nature of the governing coalition that dominated Alexandria politics during this time reflected that increasingly liberal bent. The new political regime that emerged in the mid-1970s was far more racially moderate and increasingly focused on the provision of social services and a liberal social agenda. White flight enabled a more progressive coalition to challenge the remnants of the Byrd regime that dominated Alexandria until the late 1960s and, ultimately, to gain office.

As the number of African American students equaled white students in the mid-1970s, this new coalition put into place its own regime, one firmly Democratic and the standard bearer for liberal politics in Northern Virginia. Both the physical relocation of politically conservative families from Alexandria and use of private schools by affluent families within Alexandria opened a political space for a new regime that was more anchored in the politics of service provision than the Byrd regime. This more liberal political environment helped establish a racial coalitional regime in the city that not only incorporated African Americans into the local governing regime but also provided more city services—both within schools and outside—to middle-class and poor residents alike.

In the midst of the exits, however, local officials took numerous steps to minimize the effects of both forms of exit from schooling. The politics of exit—what I define as both the political measures taken by local officials to minimize exits and the ensuing political consequences of those exits—significantly shaped the nature of educational debates within Alexandria during this time period. Moreover, the federal educational policies of both racial integration and special education were filtered through the local politics of exit. At first, the politics of exit constrained the ability of Alexandria officials to comply with HEW integration mandates, but later, as local politics liberalized because of the consequences of exit, local demands for more public services resulted in a far smoother adoption of federal and state special education policies, as we shall see in Chapter 5. In both local responses, however, the shape of the educational state was largely outside the control of federal authorities. The localist politics of exit both thwarted and advanced the federal policy objectives, but for reasons wholly independent of federal actions or aims.

This chapter explores the characteristics of both forms of exit (voucher use and residential relocation), examining their effects on the nature of the political regime in Alexandria. The first section, "Desegregation and Tuition Voucher Use, 1959–1964" uses geographic information systems (GIS) mapping techniques to argue that desegregation catalyzed class anxieties in Alexandria's affluent neighborhoods. The second section, "The Rationales of Exit," turns to reasons offered by parents who left Alexandria schools in order to understand the dynamics of their dissatisfaction with Alexandria schools in the early 1970s. Together the voucher usage and explicit exit rationales of parents reveal that class played a significant role in the flight from an integrated Alexandria school system. While rates of participation in the voucher system were higher in more affluent neighborhoods, they were significantly higher in affluent neighborhoods undergoing desegregation. Similarly, parents withdrawing their children from Alexandria schools frequently expressed the opinion that their concerns were driven by what they saw as the behavioral consequences of poor black children being educated alongside white, middle-class, or upper middle-class children. In the third section, "Demographic Change and the Restructuring of the Alexandria Political Regime," I examine the nature of political and voting changes in Alexandria in the wake of white flight, showing that the liberalization of Alexandria was largely complete by 1980, a few years after the full integration of Alexandria's schools. Overall, the exits from public schooling in Alexandria constituted an important local reaction to federal educational policy initiatives, and presented a major challenge to the incorporation of federal educational reforms into the local school operations. At the same time, the persistent federal effort established a political context that made the next federal educational initiative—special education—an easier policy innovation.

Desegregation and Tuition Voucher Use, 1959–1964

As one part of its campaign of Massive Resistance, the Virginia state legislature created a private school tuition grant program in August 1957. This program provided flat grants of $250 per year ($275 for high school students) to enable students to attend private schools, but only if the state closed their schools because it was under a federal court order to desegregate.[3] When the Virginia Supreme Court struck down that tuition grant as unconstitutional, the state legislature adopted a revised tuition grant program that was open to all students in the state, regardless of whether the district was undergoing desegregation.[4] At its core, the voucher program was an effort, in the words of Governor J. Lindsay Almond, Jr., "to prevent any student from being compelled to attend a racially mixed school."[5]

In Alexandria, the voucher program began in the fall of 1959 with sixty-two students, seven months after the initial desegregation of city schools. The program grew steadily over the course of its five-year run, and by the spring of 1964—at the peak of the program in Alexandria—the voucher scheme paid (at least partially) for the tuition of roughly 200 students at private and out-of-jurisdiction public schools (See Figure 4.1). In the fall of 1963, the first year that Alexandria City Schools assigned some African American students directly to all-white neighborhood schools,[6] new entrants to the program surged to over one-hundred students.

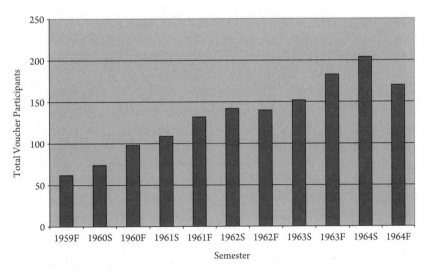

Figure 4.1 Total voucher participants by semester, fall 1959–fall 1964

Collectively, 557 students received a voucher at some point during this five-year period. Even at its peak in the spring of 1964, however, the voucher program enrolled only a little over one percent of Alexandria's public school population. This relatively small number of voucher recipients, could be explained by a number of factors. First, there may have been insufficient space in the private school system to allow greater numbers of students. Second, the voucher's subsidy may not have been high enough to make private school tuition affordable to a large number of Alexandrians. In 1964, the *Washington Post* reported that tuition at the Congressional School, just outside Alexandria, was $700 a year for the elementary school, meaning that at the end of the program, the voucher covered over one-third the cost.[7] Third, the relatively low levels of participation may have meant that Alexandria parents valued a public school education over a private one, for a variety of reasons. Whatever the rationale, it is clear that overwhelming percentages of students did not take part in the voucher program. At the same time, the absolute numbers of students grew inexorably over the five-year period of the program's operation.

The families in the program selected a wide range of schools, with 557 students using the vouchers at approximately eighty different schools. (See Figure 4.2.) While one school, Congressional School, enrolled twenty percent of the voucher recipients, the remaining students were distributed widely across a number of schools, including a substantial number of students at out-of-area boarding schools. These schools included both traditional southern boys military academies, as well as elite New England prep schools such as Philips Exeter and Philips Academy. As a result of these enrollments, many Alexandrians criticized the program for simply subsidizing the private school choices of elites. While it is impossible to determine whether

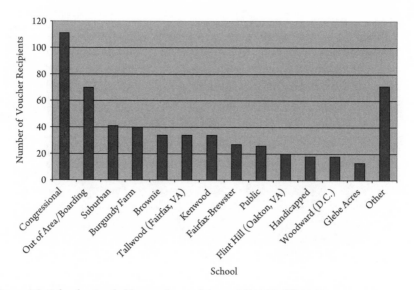

Figure 4.2 Schools attended by voucher recipients, fall 1959–fall 1964

students were already enrolled in these schools prior to receiving the voucher, it is clear that boarding schools were a common school choice among voucher recipients. In addition, it is important to note that local area public schools (including schools in Washington, DC and Fairfax County) were among the top enrolling schools. Significantly, DC public schools were substantially desegregated by this time, although residential segregation in the capital city still limited the extent of racial mixing in DC schools.

The desegregated local public and private school choices of many of the voucher families—as well as the non-southern private school choices—raise an important question: To what extent did families in Alexandria use the vouchers to send their children to desegregated schools? The local school that enrolled the third-largest number of voucher students, Burgundy Farms, was, according to its website, racially integrated in 1950.[8] In 1964, Burgundy Farms enrolled eighty-three students who received vouchers from Alexandria, Arlington County, and Fairfax County, out of roughly 1000 tuition grants distributed in those jurisdictions.[9] While many families who used the vouchers undoubtedly sought to enroll their children in segregated schools, it is clear that the motives of voucher recipients were not homogeneous. A significant portion of voucher recipients used the program to subsidize enrollment in public and private desegregated schools. Superintendent Albohm noted in a Fall 1964 report recommending the suspension of the program that eight of the forty-five participating schools in the 1963–1964 academic year were known to be desegregated.[10] Given this figure, combined with the numbers of vouchers granted to students enrolled in schools known to be desegregated, it seems fair to estimate that at least fifteen percent of voucher recipients attended desegregated schools, a circumstance most likely not what the designers of Massive Resistance had in mind.[11]

This gap between the original aims of the voucher advocates and the use of the voucher by Alexandria families raises, then, an important question about the nature of exit from Alexandria's schools during this time period: Were the families that obtained these vouchers even confronting an immediate desegregation of their neighborhood school? Given the fact that a significant number of families used the voucher to send their children to desegregated schools, how did Alexandria own public school's desegregation affect the use of vouchers?[12]

Where did Desegregation and Voucher Students Live?

Let's first look at the geographical relationship between voucher recipients and African American students who sought to desegregate Alexandria's schools. Figure 4.3 shows us a map of Alexandria with the locations of both elementary voucher recipients (denoted with small circles) and the African American elementary students who petitioned for enrollment at historically all-white schools between 1959 and 1964 (denoted by stars).

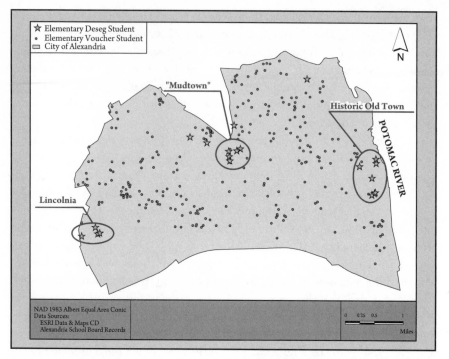

Figure 4.3 Alexandria, Virginia: Desegregated elementary student and elementary voucher recipient locations

Figure 4.3 shows clearly that the African American students who initially desegregated Alexandria's schools were clustered in three areas—in historic Old Town in the eastern half of the city, next to the Potomac River; in an area then referred to as "Mudtown," a poor, formerly rural pocket of African American homes in the central portion of the city; and in Lincolnia, an African American neighborhood on the far western edge of Alexandria. In contrast, voucher recipients were scattered throughout the city, without any readily apparent clustering in particular neighborhoods.

Of course, the direct spatial proximity among voucher recipients and desegregating students is mediated, for purposes of school desegregation, by the geography of school attendance zones. The pooling of students into school attendance zones—rather than mere geographical proximity to each other –was more likely to be salient to voucher recipients who were responding to desegregation. If desegregation were driving their use of vouchers, then we would expect that there would be higher numbers of voucher recipients at those schools undergoing desegregation at the time.

African American students who sought to desegregate Alexandria's public schools were, during this early period of desegregation, clustered in only a few schools. Because of residential segregation, the African American students who petitioned to desegregate lived within the attendance zones of four formerly all-white elementary schools.[13] The desegregated and still all-white elementary school attendance zones are outlined in Figure 4.4

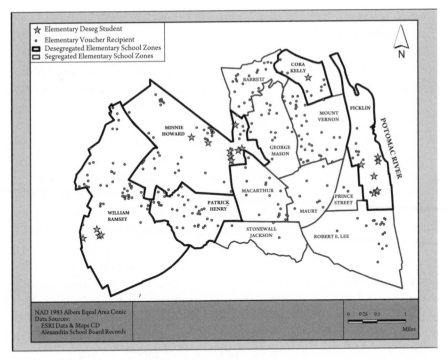

Figure 4.4 Desegregated elementary school attendance zones

The map shows distinct clustering of dots in the western half of the city, with Patrick Henry and William Ramsey seeing both desegregated students and a modestly denser clustering of voucher students. At the same time, we also see voucher students well-represented in Mount Vernon, Barrett, and MacArthur schools, which enrolled no African American students during this time period. Similarly, we also see relatively few voucher students coming out of the Ficklin school attendance zone, despite the fact that Ficklin had one of the highest rates of desegregation in the city. Figure 4.4 suggests that that while there was a geographic relationship between voucher use and the immediate prospect of desegregation within particular school zones, the willingness of families to use vouchers was not *solely* driven by exposure to African American students at one's local school. Many of the voucher recipients lived within school attendance zones that enrolled zero African Americans pupils. At the same time, schools that saw relatively high numbers of desegregating African American students also saw comparatively few voucher students.

Explaining the Relationships Between Voucher Use and Desegregation

This simple visual inspection of these two maps is obviously not conclusive. We see some school zones where there appears to be a relationship between desegregation and voucher use, but other school zones where the relationship is not apparent. Regression analysis, however, allows us to better explore the interrelationships between residential patterns, voucher use, and desegregation in Alexandria. By combining the data we have about where voucher and desegregation students lived with U.S. Census data on the underlying demographic characteristics of their neighborhoods, we can more precisely understand how the racial and class characteristics of neighborhoods were linked to the desegregation of schools and voucher use.

Table 4.1 below shows the results of an Ordinary Least Squares (OLS) regression to test three possible explanations of voucher use within Alexandria Census blocks from 1959 to 1964. All of the models control for the population within each Census block, simply because more residents within a block will generally result in greater voucher use. The first model seeks to explain the rate of voucher use within Census blocks by only examining two additional factors: the percentage of nonwhite residents within a Census block and whether or not that Census block lies within a desegregated elementary school attendance zone. The second model adds one more variable, the average cost of housing within the Census block. This housing cost index captures the average income of the residents of that block, a characteristic not directly reported in the 1960 Census of Housing. Finally, the third model adds one more variable, an interaction term that looks at the effect of the housing cost variable only in cases where desegregation was occurring. In other words, the interaction term tests the idea that upper-class neighborhoods undergoing desegregation used vouchers at higher rates than similar neighborhoods not being desegregated.

The results are striking. All else being equal, the analysis indicates: 1) voucher use was moderately higher in neighborhoods undergoing desegregation; 2) voucher use was moderately higher in neighborhoods with higher housing costs; and 3) voucher use was substantially higher if both conditions were true—that is, voucher use was substantially higher in high cost neighborhoods undergoing desegregation. What is noteworthy about the differences among the models is that racial composition of the Census block becomes less significant, on its own, as the models factor class measures into the analysis.

Let's start with the simplest model and proceed to the most complex. Model 1 shows us that neighborhoods with higher percentages of nonwhite residents had lower rates of voucher use. This tells us, conversely, that neighborhoods with higher percentages of white residents had higher rates of voucher usage. In addition, the model shows that neighborhoods undergoing desegregation had higher rates of voucher use, with both variables significant at the 0.01 level. This model—which is basically a racial exposure model—suggests that the use of vouchers was linked in a significant way to the experience of desegregation and to the whiteness of the neighborhood. In other words, the use of vouchers within a neighborhood dropped as the percentage of nonwhite residents increased[14] and increased if that neighborhood was within a school zone that was being desegregated.

But race was not the only salient factor within Alexandria's desegregation struggle. As the accounts of desegregation in Chapters 2 and 3 showed us, class

Table 4.1 **Standardized Coefficients and Significance Tests for a Series of OLS Regressions on Number of Elementary School Vouchers per Census Block, Alexandria, VA 1959–1964**

	Model 1 Race Only		Model 2 Race and Housing Cost		Model 3 Race, Housing Cost, and Interaction	
	Parameter Estimate	T-score	Parameter Estimate	T-score	Parameter Estimate	T-score
Total population	0.39124**	4.62	0.37635**	4.64	0.35718**	4.74
Percent non-white	−0.09851**	−5.65	−0.03411	−1.53	−0.02771	−1.16
Desegregation dummy						
=1 if block is in desegregated school zone; = 0 otherwise	0.13603**	2.59	0.14399**	2.77	−0.34872**[b]	−1.87
Housing cost index[a]	–	–	0.15785**	3.86	0.07991**	3.52
Interaction of housing cost index and desegregation dummy	–	–	–	–	0.52394*	2.52
Intercept (unstandardized)	−0.08006	−0.85	−0.90642**	−3.64	−0.49279**	−3.67
R-squared	0.2226		0.2270		0.2497	
Lowest Ramsey's reset p	<0.0001		<0.0001		<0.0001	

Standard errors robust to heteroscedasticity.
N = 618 Census blocks (sample excludes blocks with zero population or zero housing cost index.)
[a]Housing cost index = Weighted average cost of rented and owned properties.
[b]Desegregation dummy is jointly significant with interaction variable.
*p < 0.05.
**p < 0.01.

considerations seemed to play an important role in the nature of white opposition. Both Models Two and Three incorporate class into the analysis by using the housing costs of each Census block as proxy for class. With this class variable included, Model Two shows us that the percentage of nonwhite residents in a neighborhood *does not* show a statistically significant relationship to voucher use. Importantly, however, census blocks with higher housing costs do exhibit higher rates of voucher use under Model Two. This finding suggests that class (as indicated by housing costs) was a better predictor of voucher use than race *per se*. In other words, voucher use was not higher in white neighborhoods than in nonwhite neighborhoods, but voucher use was higher in more expensive neighborhoods, controlling for neighborhood racial composition. Importantly, in Model Two, the experience of desegregation itself was linked to higher rates of voucher use, just as it was in Model One.

Finally, Model Three takes this analysis further by exploring the interaction of higher housing costs and the experience of desegregation. As in Model Two, the percentage of nonwhites in a neighborhood is not associated with higher rates of voucher use. Also, as in Model Two, Model Three shows a statistically significant relationship between housing cost and voucher use, although the effect size of the relationship is considerably smaller. But what it is striking about Model Three is how the combination of higher housing costs and the experience of desegregation yields much higher rates of voucher usage. Families living in more affluent census blocks *and* undergoing desegregation applied for vouchers at much higher rates than families living in census blocks with lower housing costs and also undergoing desegregation. In fact, when we hold constant the population and racial composition of a census block, a one-unit increase in the housing cost index in desegregating neighborhoods produced voucher rates 6.5 *times higher* than a one-unit increase in housing costs among all census blocks. The bottom line: families living in high-cost housing blocks undergoing desegregation obtained vouchers at much higher rates than families living in similarly priced housing, but *not* undergoing desegregation.

This analysis suggests, then, that the use of vouchers in a neighborhood was not simply the result of white families undergoing desegregation, or, for that matter, the reliance of affluent families on state funds to subsidize their private school enrollments. Instead, the results of Model Three show that in more affluent neighborhoods, voucher rates surged when desegregation took place, but that in equally affluent neighborhoods voucher use was not nearly as extensive if that neighborhood was not undergoing desegregation.

This finding suggests an important inference: the commitment to Alexandria's public schools among families living in more affluent neighborhoods was—to some extent—conditional upon their children not undergoing desegregation. Desegregation in their local school, it seemed, tested affluent Alexandrians' commitment to public school in a way that desegregation across town did not. It is important to remember two limiting factors here: the overall low rate of voucher use across Alexandria and the fact that the vouchers did not, typically, cover the complete cost of private schooling. The first reminds us that the vast majority of Alexandrians did not use vouchers to attend another school. Either they remained committed to public education or did not feel that state funds should subsidize their children's private schooling. The second factor reminds us that the cost of private schooling probably prevented some middle- or lower-income Alexandrians from utilizing the voucher. It is entirely conceivable that middle- and lower-income whites in Alexandria were as equally conditionally supportive of public education as their more affluent neighbors, but lacked the financial means to utilize the private school exit option, even with the voucher's assistance. Nonetheless, this analysis shows that certainly among affluent neighborhoods the experience of desegregation was a significant factor in the likelihood of exercising the voucher. The bottom line is that in neighborhoods where household resources likely existed to send children to private schools, desegregation accounted in a significant way for the rates of voucher use.

The dual cleavages of race and class in these early stages of desegregation profoundly shaped white concerns over the educational effects of racial mixing within Alexandria schools. The school voucher data presented here suggests that residents in predominantly white neighborhoods at the upper end of the economic distribution were either more concerned about desegregation than residents in racially mixed or lower income neighborhoods, or they had more resources to take advantage of the state-provided subsidy for private education. Either way, within higher-priced neighborhoods, desegregation of local schools seemed to trigger resort to vouchers much more readily than in lower-priced neighborhoods.

This class-based concern about desegregation found expression even among those not choosing to enroll their children in private school. Some white supporters of desegregation expressed concerns about the effects of effects of African American poverty on white students within the school system. One Alexandrian wrote in a letter to Gorman Ridgely, Chair of the Alexandria City Board of Education, in the summer of 1963, "we are quite prepared to see an equitable distribution of colored pupils in our Alexandria school system," adding that, "We think our best interests as citizens are served by moving to a truly integrated school system as soon as possible." At the same time, that support was tempered by a concern that such integration not yield unwanted families: "We will always have a considerable colored population, and we believe that offering superior school opportunities is the best way to attract able, talented, high-income young colored people who will contribute to our tax base and broaden our cultural base."[15]

Often, the white liberal position on desegregation focused on the need to attract the "right" kind of African American students and their families in order to sustain high academic standards within the school system. The concerns about the curricular and classroom effects of African American poverty on white students persisted throughout the 1960s and 1970s, and, in the eyes of some, the school system's inability or unwillingness to maintain high academic standards in the face of integration became a rationale to exit Alexandria City Public Schools. As a result, school officials persistently sought to dispel the perception that desegregation would only yield a school system with lowered standards. That story is linked, in important ways, to efforts to prevent the demographic shifts from becoming politically destabilizing to the local regime, but in the end, integration meant the incorporation of

African American interests in local governance. In the eyes of white conservatives, as a result, that political incorporation became sufficient reason to exit Alexandria, independent of integration's effects on schools and learning.

The Rationales of Exit

Virginia's public support for private segregated schooling ended in early 1965 when federal courts struck down the use of vouchers at segregated private institutions. As school desegregation accelerated in the early 1970s, moving out of the city, rather than enrollment in private schools, became an increasingly common reaction to Alexandria's integration, at least among white households in Alexandria. The full extent of this change, while forecast by outside consultants, unsettled school officials who were forced to alter their view of Alexandria as a predominantly white suburban school system. As they grappled with this change, school officials undertook a survey of families who exited, in an effort to understand why they were leaving. Their answers comprise the bulk of the second section of this chapter. While many of the respondents offered typical reasons for the shift—relocation because of work, moving to a bigger house to accommodate a growing family, a preference for a religious education, perhaps a death in the family—others gave reasons more directly related to the experiences of desegregation: an objection to busing, a concern for the changing school environment because of the increased number of poor students in formerly all-white schools, worries about declining standards, and racial conflicts among students. In their initial reporting of this survey, school officials emphasized the mundane and typical reasons for leaving and massaged the data to project an image of public satisfaction with Alexandria schools. In this section of the chapter, these survey answers have been accurately retabulated to peel back the shiny public relations veneer school officials applied to the numbers. This reassessment of the survey gives us a window into some of the reasons the percentage of nonwhite students in Alexandria schools jumped from 31 percent in 1971 to 52 percent in 1976.[16]

This transformation was not unpredicted. Indeed, outside consultants hired by the school system found that changing residential patterns in the city—apart from white flight—would alter the school system composition within a few years. In the midst of the School Board's efforts to delay elementary school integration, Superintendent Albohm successfully urged the Board in May 1972 to hire an outside consultant to provide a dispassionate analysis not only of the school district's efforts to provide equal educational opportunities, but of the entire elementary program and its relationship to the City of Alexandria.

This in-depth study, conducted by Engelhardt and Engelhardt Consultants, ranged from an examination of existing school facilities to current curriculum and instructional practices to zoning, housing, demographic trends, and infrastructural developments within the City. The authors of the study specifically sought out parental, teacher, and administrative views, meeting with over 200 citizens in a variety of settings, and seeking to ascertain desires of residents and the capacity of the City of Alexandria and Alexandria City Public Schools to meet those desires. Their findings would not, however, please many of those parents who sought to further delay integration.

The Engelhardt Report arrived in January 1973 at nearly 200 pages long, with conclusions that stunned many residents of Alexandria. While the School Board asked Engelhardt and Engelhardt to examine eight facets of the elementary program, its findings on pupil population trends and its recommendations regarding equal educational opportunity within Alexandria schools sparked the greatest controversy. The report predicted not only declining elementary enrollments in Alexandria schools through the 1970s, but an accelerating nonwhite percentage, with minority students becoming a majority of all elementary students by the 1976–1977 school year.[17] (At the time of the report, nonwhite elementary enrollment stood at roughly 37 percent, while the total nonwhite enrollment in Alexandria schools was 33 percent.[18] In the 1970 U.S. Census, the black population of Alexandria was 15 percent.) The rapid growth of nonwhite enrollment was driven, according to the Engelhardt Report, by the increasing numbers of single residents and older couples who were largely white, along with growing numbers of nonwhite families residing in newly constructed high-rise and garden apartments. Thus, while the population of Alexandria was predicted to grow, it would become an increasingly nonwhite city and the schools would become predominantly nonwhite within a few short years. Given this racial transformation of Alexandria's schools, the authors of the Engelhardt Report recommended a robust program of integration to ensure equal educational opportunity for elementary students: every elementary school should have at least 25 percent nonwhite enrollment. With seven of Alexandria's sixteen elementary schools enrolling less than 15 percent nonwhite students, this would require a significant shift of the existing elementary population.[19]

The Engelhardt Report ignited a firestorm of controversy. Engelhardt's projections made Page One of the *Washington Post* and school and city officials quickly disputed the projections, but could not offer alternative figures to counter Engelhardt's report. According to the *Post*, Alexandria officials had "never before undertaken an analysis of population changes in Alexandria or attempted to forecast trends in the racial makeup of either the total population or school population." Similarly, anti-busing foes complained that the report made busing a foregone conclusion, even though Engelhardt did not specify the means by which Alexandria City Schools should achieve the goal of at least 25 percent minority students in every elementary school. Donald Baldwin of the Alexandria Committee on Quality Education wrote in a letter to School Board Chair William Hurd that Engelhardt's 25 percent figure would trigger an exodus of middle-class families from Alexandria, and "that Alexandria would soon become another Washington, DC,"—adding that "no one wants that."[20]

Tallying Discontent

Despite the controversy over the Engelhardt report, it soon proved prophetic. During the summer of 1974, a year after Alexandria implemented a comprehensive elementary busing plan, nearly a thousand families either moved out of the Alexandria City Public School system or enrolled their children in private schools. The sudden departure of such a large number of families prompted the school district to survey those who had left. While the survey instrument was not, in many ways, ideal, it provides us with a picture of Alexandria City schools, from the perspective of those who were increasingly disaffected with it. In its press releases, ACPS portrayed these departures as not out of the ordinary and only marginally related to the processes of integration. A re-analysis of the surviving original survey forms, however, shows that the district underreported the extent to which parents viewed integration as part of an overall decline in the quality of Alexandria City schools, particularly among parents who enrolled their children in private schools.

As school resumed in the fall of 1974, school officials noticed that 937 families (totaling 1,039 students) had removed their children from Alexandria City Public Schools. In response the school system mailed out a survey to help determine why those families had left, receiving returns from 474 families. While the survey did not collect any demographic information on respondents, it did query them about where they had moved and their reasons for withdrawing their children from Alexandria schools. In the press release detailing the results of the survey, the school district broke the responses into three groups: those that moved away from the metropolitan area, those that moved within the metropolitan area, and those that did not move but had enrolled their child (or children) in private schools. The district reported that 40 percent of respondents had moved away from the metropolitan area entirely, 36 percent had moved within the metropolitan area, and 24 percent had enrolled their children in private schools.

The reasons that these groups offered for their departure differed substantially: 60 percent of all those who moved out of the metropolitan area cited a change of employment as the reason, whereas only 6 percent of those who moved within the metro area cited a change of employment as a reason for their move, and none of the private school enrollee families did so.

Table 4.2 summarizes the reasons for each group that that the school district reported in its press release. Based on the survey results reported in this table, personal and work-related reasons accounted for 82 percent of the family decisions to move outside the metropolitan area. Similarly, for those who moved within the metropolitan region, 73 percent did so because of housing or economic or personal reasons. What the school district sought to convey with reporting these findings this way was the clear implication that desegregation and busing—or the quality of schooling in Alexandria—was not the primary motivation for exit. In contrast, however, those who remained within Alexandria and enrolled their children in private

Table 4.2 **Results as Reported by ACPS of 1974 Survey of Alexandria Parents;** *N*
            in parentheses

Reason for Child's Departure from ACPS	Parents Who Moved Away from Metro Area	Parents Who Moved Within Metro Area	Parents Who Enrolled Children in Private School	Total Reponses
Change in employment	60% (114)	6% (10)	0%	26.16 % (124)
Housing or economic reasons	11% (22)	50% (85)	0%	22.57% (107)
Desegregation and busing in the Alexandria school system	3% (6)	13% (22)	40% (46)	15.61% (74)
Quality of education in the Alexandria school system	2% (3)	6% (10)	16% (18)	6.54% (31)
Other education reasons	2% (3)	2% (4)	18% (21)	5.91% (28)
Other personal reasons not related to the Alexandria school system	22% (42)	23% (40)	25% (28)	23.21% (110)
Totals	40.08% (190)	36.08% (171)	23.84% (113)	100% (474)

schools were significantly concerned with desegregation, busing, and the quality of schooling. Of those families who had enrolled their children in private schools, the Alexandria City Public Schools reported that 40 percent of them cited busing or desegregation or quality of schooling as the reason for their departure. Another 16 percent cited concerns about the quality of schooling in Alexandria. According to the school district's tallying, private school enrollees were much more concerned about desegregation and busing than those who moved.

These figures, however, do not accurately convey the depth of parental concern about the quality of schooling. Although not all the survey returns still exist within the Alexandria school system archives, 209 original returns were located. Of these, the majority were returns from private school enrollees. In fact, 105 of the original 113 returns categorized as private school enrollees were recovered, nearly 93 percent of this category of respondents. A re-analysis of those original 105 returns indicate that the school district did not faithfully tally *all* the reasons parents withdrew their children from school. Many families indicated multiple reasons for withdrawing their child (or children), but those multiple rationales were not reported by the school district. Instead, school officials only tallied one reason for each family, skewing the findings of the survey.

If we reexamine the concerns of parents who enrolled their children in private schools (the group for which we have almost 93 percent of the original returns), we find that quality of education was a much larger concern than the school district indicated in its report of the survey. This re-tallying of *all* the reasons that parents listed as reasons for enrolling their children in private school provides us a much

Table 4.3 **Re-Tabulated Results of Existing Returns from 1974 Survey of Alexandria Parents; *N* in parentheses. Multiple responses recorded**

Reason Listed for Child's Departure from ACPS	Parents Who Moved Away from Metro Area	Parents Who Moved Within Metro Area	Parents Who Enrolled Children in Private School
Change in employment	23.8% (5)	4.8% (4)	Not an option on survey
Housing or economic reasons	9.5% (2)	38.6% (32)	Not an option on survey
Desegregation and busing in the Alexandria school system	23.8% (5)	31.3% (26)	45.7% (48)
Quality of education in the Alexandria school system	23.8% (5)	20.5% (17)	52.4% (55)
Other education reasons	0	4.8% (4)	30.5% (32)
Other personal reasons not related to the Alexandria school system	38.1% (8)	44.6 (37)	22.9% (24)
Total returns found	21	83	105
Total number of answers given	25	120	159
Percentage of survey returns found	11.1%	48.5%	92.9%

different picture than the one portrayed by the school district. Over 52 percent of the parents who enrolled their children in private school did so at least in part because of concerns about quality of schooling. ACPS reported this figure as only 16 percent.[21]

In addition, the percentage of parents who explicitly linked desegregation and busing to their concerns about the quality of education in Alexandria's public schools was quite high: Fully 69 percent of those who indicated that desegregation or busing was a reason for leaving also indicated that quality of schooling was a concern. Overall, 31 percent of all respondents indicated that busing and/or segregation combined with quality of schooling were the reasons they exited the public school system. In short, a large percentage of parents who placed their children in private schools perceived a linkage between busing and desegregation and concerns about the quality of education in Alexandria—and it was precisely this perceived linkage that school officials downplayed in their reporting of the results of the survey.

If we turn to the rationales of the parents who enrolled their children in other public schools within the metropolitan area, we cannot be as confident that the school district underreported the concerns about quality of education for the simple reason that a smaller percentage of those survey returns still exist within the archives.[22] Still, even with fewer than half of the surveys of parents who moved still available for re-analysis, it is clear that school officials misreported the survey findings. Again, the primary discrepancy lies in the underreporting of those parents who cited both quality of education in Alexandria's schools and opposition to busing as a rationale for moving within the metropolitan area: in the school district's results (found in Table 4.2) only 13 percent of respondents indicated busing was a reason for their exit, but the re-tallied surveys show that over 31 percent indicated that busing was among their reasons for leaving. Similarly, ACPS reported that only 6 percent of exiters stated that school quality was the rationale, but the re-tallying indicates the figure was close to 20 percent.[23] Thus, it appears that the school district systematically underreported the complaints about school quality and busing made by parents moving their children from ACPS to both private schools and to public schools outside of Alexandria.

A number of parents wrote extensive comments on their survey, explaining in greater detail why they decided to exit Alexandria's city schools. Despite the fact that the one-page survey had no space on the form for comments, these parents felt compelled to explain their actions in greater detail; as a result, these comments are probably best viewed as a measure of the intensity of feelings among some parents.

Among the survey forms located in the Alexandria school archives, roughly 18 percent of parents took the time to write comments. By coding these unsolicited comments into common themes we gain a window on the most pertinent explanations families offered for leaving Alexandria's schools. The results are striking: nearly half of all families who wrote comments cited low standards and discipline within the schools. Nearly a quarter of the families indicated that they had concerns about their children's safety at school. About 15 percent directly expressed busing as a central concern and another 6 percent highlighted racial issues as a reason for their departure. Roughly 16 percent cited pedagogical reasons for their child's departure. Table 4.4 lists the most common complaints detailed in the comments, with the quality of education offered in Alexandria's schools and the safety of children while at school topping the list.

Table 4.4 **Categorization of Written Explanations for Exiting Alexandria Schools, 1974**

	(N)	*Percentage of All Rationales*	*Percentage of Surveys*
Low standards and/or discipline in schools	46	29.3	46.9
Concerns about physical security	23	14.6	23.5
Learning style of child	16	10.2	16.3
Opposed to busing	15	9.6	15.3
Despite exit, expressed support for public schools	13	8.3	13.3
Religion	12	7.6	12.2
Racial Issues	6	3.8	6.1
Issue specific to a particular school	5	3.2	5.1
Family circumstances	5	3.2	5.1
Schools unresponsive/Nothing to offer	3	1.9	3.1
Child's desire	3	1.9	3.1
Concerns about child's development	3	1.9	3.1
Inadequate supplies/facilities	2	1.3	2.0
Miscellaneous	2	1.3	2.0
Socioeconomic objections	1	0.6	1.0
Geographic proximity	1	0.6	1.0
Sports	1	0.6	1.0
Total number of rationales given	157		
Total number of surveys with written comments	98		

But beyond the frequency of various complaints, the tone and language of parental concerns is strong and evocative. A few quotes illustrate the range of concerns parents expressed:

- "During the school term 73–74 at George Mason, my son was picked on *all* the time. After numerous complaints nothing much was done. He went to summer school for half the session—after being picked on there severely and almost a broken limb, I removed him from your school system. Perhaps if interested, *you* might be aware of the problems."
- "Black student fights! Hard enough for a child to learn, but to go to school in constant fear is *too* much."
- "I do not feel that my child (nor his mother and father) had *anything* to gain, socially or educationally, by riding a bus to Lyles-Crouch. With each passing day, I am more satisfied with our decision to remove him from the public school system."
- "Quality of education in the Alexandria School System. Many students graduate unprepared for college or other types of further education."
- "The lack of discipline exhibited by the school in coping with student misbehavior as a result of busing made me worried for my children's safety and well-being."
- "Quality of education in the Alexandria School system has brought down to a totally unacceptable level. Lack of learning environment and total breakdown of discipline."
- "Quality of education in the Alexandria school system. Lack of discipline reduced quality of education. Standards were lowered in all areas."
- "Quality of education in the Alexandria school system—a degradation resulting from the busing."
- "Primarily the busing."
- "Location of school in bad part of Alexandria."
- "The Alexandria School System has deteriorated to a totally unsatisfactory level, both in class and in the school itself."
- "My children received an excellent education while in Alexandria schools for four years. Desegregation of elementary schools was very difficult for one of my children who was in a poor classroom situation. However, she did continue to progress in reading and mathematics and to enjoy going to school. I think it is too bad we were forced to bus our children across the city, but in the long run I don't feel it should adversely affect the quality of education for our children."
- "Last year, various factors contributed to a classroom atmosphere which was not conducive to learning. These include classroom discipline problems, harassment by other students, and the inability of teachers to cope with a wide range of student academic abilities—particularly in reading and arithmetic. Academic shortcomings were typified by a misguided attempt to teach fractions to my son (and other average or above-average sixth graders) on a do-it-yourself (i.e., teach yourself) basis.

- "Busing only. My daughter could have walked to her ninth grade school. No foreign languages were offered in the Middle School. My daughter was exposed to abuse from other students as well as having valuable personal items stolen which the school did nothing about."

In many of these descriptions, the difficulties of integration produced a cascade of interrelated complaints. According to some parents, busing induced conflicts among students that the school system was not prepared to handle adequately. As result, many parents felt that their children were under constant threat of violence or intimidation. Moreover, many parents also considered disciplinary problems, particularly inconsistent discipline, to be a source of tension among students that was compounded when teachers had to confront different levels of academic preparation and achievement. In short, busing—and the school district's inadequate preparation for the consequences of busing—sparked parental concerns about school safety, discipline, and academic standards.

While it should be stressed that these written comments came from a group of parents who were likely the most disaffected, underlying many of their concerns was a broader sentiment that changes in Alexandria's school system were not just linked to racial integration but to an inability of the school district to address the newly salient differences among students. From this perspective, race was really a proxy for class disparities among students, particularly the way that class inequalities among black and white students led to divergences in educational achievement and the expectations of the school system for the academic achievement of its students. One comment in particular encapsulates this progression from acceptance of racial integration to opposition to the consequences of class integration of students:

> Not desegregation as such—our neighborhood school, because of pairing, went from drawing mostly in single-family residential to public housing and low-income families—color doesn't matter—it's the change of atmosphere and discipline problems that arose. Quality has suffered in schools my children go to because of #1 (above) [i.e., desegregation]. Gifted child programs at Jackson (which both my children were accepted in) can't touch the one at Barrett [on the West Side of Alexandria] and others. Our other child will probably be taken out of public schools next year and youngest will probably never attend because more and more high achievers are being taken out and quality will suffer more.

The racial integration of Alexandria's elementary schools broke down what had been a relatively high degree of economic segregation between East Side and the West Side students. That economic integration, in turn, created conflict beyond the direct racial conflict seen at the high school level two years earlier. As a result, opposition to elementary integration among whites included both old-style commitment to formal segregation, as well as those parents who felt that that Alexandria's inability to manage the diverse educational experiences and expectations of students and families had harmed the quality of education in Alexandria. Thus, while "quality of education" could be and was seen as a code word for outright racial antipathy, it also encompassed a range of complaints that stemmed from the increasing economic diversity in Alexandria's elementary schools and the ensuing gulfs in academic achievement and expectations for students.

Demographic Change and the Restructuring of the Alexandria Political Regime

Taken together, the District's survey results and the written comments of parents reveal a broad vein of dissatisfaction with Alexandria's public schools that school officials took great pains to obscure or minimize. What officials could not minimize, however, was the bottom line effect on school enrollments, particularly in the western half of the city, where flight to private schools was increasingly common: three elementary schools lost 40 families to private elementary schools, in just the summer of 1974 alone. Across the city as a whole, 256 elementary students left for other suburban public schools that same summer.[24] Over time, the exiting students—combined with a shrinking school-age population (due to the end of the baby boom)—led to rapidly dwindling enrollment figures in the 1970s and 1980s. Figure 4.5 shows the extent of this drop, both in absolute numbers, as well as a percentage of the city's total population. From 1970 to 1990, Alexandria's enrollment declined from just under 20,000 students to less than 10,000, and as a percentage of the city's overall population, the drop was even more staggering: from 17.4 percent to 8.3 percent.

Of course, these shrinking school enrollments were not isolated from broader social and demographic shifts within Alexandria. These declines in school enrollment, in part, reflected changes in Alexandria's population overall, which shrank from 110,938 in 1970 to 103,217 in 1980, a decline of 7 percent.[25] Two aspects of Alexandria's population decline over the 1970s stand out. First, the 1970s were, in general, a period of significant growth in both Virginia as a whole and in the Washington, DC metro area. Virginia saw a 15.0 percent population growth during the decade, while the DC metro area as a whole grew 7 percent. More strikingly, the Virginia portion of the Washington DC census region, grew 20 percent in those ten years, according to census reports. For Alexandria's population to have fallen 7 percent, while its adjacent neighbors grew by 20 percent in the same period, indicates that Alexandria faced different demographic pressures than other parts of Northern Virginia.[26] The second point worth noting during this period of population decline was the *growth* in the number of households: from 42,477 households in 1970 to 49,004 households in 1980, a growth of 15.4 percent.[27] The growth in households,

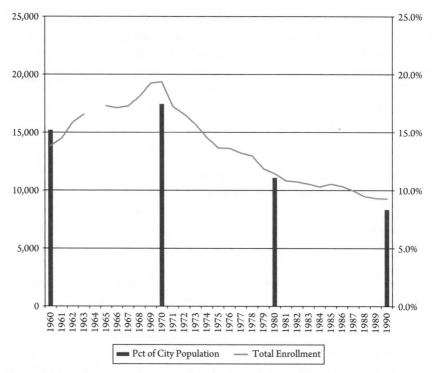

Figure 4.5 Alexandria city public school enrollment, total and as percentage of city population, 1960–1990. Sources: Virginia State Board of Education, Annual Report and City of Alexandria, Virginia, Office of the City Manager. Annual Report. Data missing for 1963.

coming during a period of population decline, came about as more single residents and elderly couples without children moved into the area. Indeed, the percent of the population that was under the age of eighteen fell from 27.6 percent in 1970 to 18.3 percent in 1980.[28] Thus, as the baby boom busted, or as parents with children moved out, singles and older couples moved in, increasing the overall number of households, but not increasing the population.

These changes led to an unusual political economy for Alexandria schools. With increasing numbers of households, and rising housing prices, property tax receipts remained robust, despite the declining population. As a result, the typical effects of white flight from major cities were not felt acutely in Alexandria, despite the fact that Alexandria's schools underwent the kind of racial transformation that Washington, DC saw at roughly the same time. Thus, while the racial composition of Alexandria, as a whole, changed only modestly in the 1970s, the racial composition of the city schools changed dramatically and rapidly. Blacks comprised 15.1 percent of the city's population in 1970, and 22.3 percent of the population in 1980. In the schools, however, black enrollment jumped from 20.2 percent in 1970 to 46.2 percent in 1980, according to U.S. Census reports.[29] In addition, increasing racial complexity emerged in Alexandria during this period as well: The nonwhite enrollment in Alexandria schools increased to 58.9 percent of all students by 1980, according to city figures.[30] In most other cities, this kind of rapid racial transformation would have led to other kinds of budgetary and fiscal stress. Due, however, to the growth in the number of households, Alexandria as whole remained fiscally viable (although certainly strapped by the recessions of 1973–1974 and the early 1980s) even as population shrank.

Despite the lack of long-term fiscal stress, these demographic shifts did, however, play a significant role in both restructuring Alexandria's political regime and in the commitment of Alexandria's political leadership to provide greater levels of public services to its constituents. Although racial conflict continued within Alexandria's schools during the late 1970s and into the 1980s, the influence of African Americans within city governance continued to grow. At the same time, this period saw the first influx of a significant Latino and immigrant population into Alexandria, a development that would further change the demographics and politics of the city in the 1990s and on into the 21st century.

The most prominent change in the composition of the local regime began in 1970 with the collapse of the conservative Democratic hegemony on the City Council and the rise of a progressive Democratic faction, as well as the emergence of a competitive Republican party within Alexandria. The one-party Democratic regime that organized Southern politics through most of the 20th century crumbled at both the state and local level by the end of the 1960s. In 1964, Democrats held all seven votes on the Alexandria City Council (The council consists of six members, plus an elected mayor). The election of 1967 saw the first Republican elected to Alexandria's City Council since Reconstruction and in 1970 three Republicans were elected, along with an African American who ran as an independent. For the first time in the 20th century, elected Democrats held a minority of City Council votes in Alexandria. As the Democratic Party within the city sought to recover, it shifted away from its conservative southern past and became part of the liberal wing of the national Democratic Party. In 1973, Democrats elected Beverly Beidler and Nora Lamborne, the first two women elected to the City Council in Alexandria's history. The 1973 election also saw the reelection of Melvin Bergheim, a liberal member who had served as staff director for the Kerner Commission, and when Republican Wiley Mitchell resigned from office in mid-term, Bergheim succeeded him as Vice Mayor.

The growing popularity of the Republican Party throughout the rest of Virginia was not entirely paralleled in Alexandria, but local Republicans enjoyed a vigorous presence on the City Council, gaining numerous supporters on the West Side of Alexandria, and benefiting from the statewide success of Republican gubernatorial and Presidential candidates in the early 1970s. Although they did not match their 1970 success in 1973, by the late 1970s and through the mid-1980s they held a competitive position against Democratic City Council candidates, placing three Republicans on the City Council in 1979 and again in 1985.

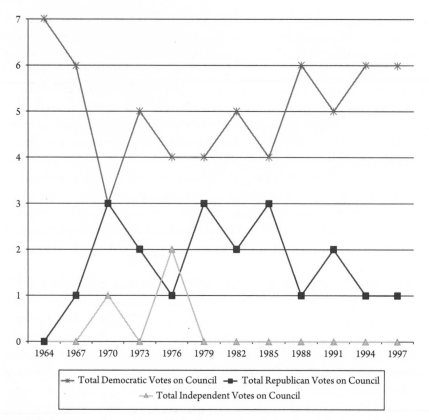

Figure 4.6 Partisan composition, Alexandria City Council, 1964–1997. Source: Alexandria Registrar of Voters.

These Alexandria Republicans, however, were not of the same ideological stripe as those that held sway at the state level. Generally moderate and pro-civil rights Republicans who shied away from conservative social issues, these Alexandria Republicans differed on a number of issues from Virginia Republican leaders. Indeed, David Speck, a Republican City Council member who won office in 1991, opted not to seek reelection in 1994 and then changed his party affiliation in 1995, citing what he felt were extreme views of state Republican party leaders.[31] Speck later won a special election in 1996 as a Democrat to fill a vacancy on the Council and was reelected as a Democrat in 1997.

Part of the challenge facing Republicans in Alexandria in the 1970s and early 1980s was the increasingly liberal views of Alexandrians, especially when compared to the state as a whole. When we compare the percentage of votes won by Democratic presidential candidates in Alexandria with the vote share they won at the state level, we see that Alexandrians and Virginians largely moved in sync until the early 1980s, although Alexandria had a higher level of baseline support.

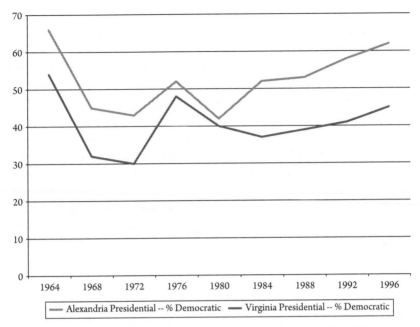

Figure 4.7 Democratic presidential vote, Alexandria and Virginia, 1964–1996.
Source: Alexandria Registrar of Voters.

As the one-party system of the South crumbled in the late 1960s, the Democratic Party presidential vote hit its lowest point in both Alexandria and Virginia in 1972, and then climbed and fell in 1976 and 1980, respectively, with the candidacies of Jimmy Carter and Ronald Reagan. After 1980, however, Alexandrians and Virginia as a whole moved in very different directions, with the Alexandria Democratic Presidential vote share spiking while it continued to drop across the state. Alexandria's Democratic presidential vote share climbed above 60 percent in 1996, while in the state at large it remained in the mid-40s. This wholesale local shift to strong liberal Democratic majorities hurt local Republicans after the mid-1980s, when a number of retirements removed the incumbency advantage from Republican City Council candidates. Indeed, between 1988 and 1997, Republicans held more than one seat on the seven-person Council only for two years (from 1991 to 1993), when they had two seats.

By the mid-1980s, the progressive Democratic hold on Alexandria was largely complete. Alexandria no longer moved in synch with a more conservative Republican Virginia and its city government pursued policies that were far more liberal than had been historically popular. While the pro-development agenda continued to dominate the suburb's commercial sector, the attention to the provision of services and poverty issues gained much headway, even in the midst of the economic downturn in the early 1990s. The appointment of Vola Lawson as a city manager in 1985 in many ways epitomized the shift. The first woman to serve as Alexandria's

city manager, Lawson got her start in city politics working as a community organizer in Arlandria, and later managed Ira Robinson's successful 1971 bid to become
the first African American on the Alexandria City Council since Reconstruction. In
the 1970s, she served as Assistant Director of Alexandria's Economic Opportunities
Commission and later Assistant City Manager for Housing. During her 15-year
stint as city manager, she cleaned up a corrupt police force and was widely esteemed
for preserving city services in the face of recessionary budget pressures. She was,
in fact, both the product and an agent of Alexandria's progressive politics. As she
said in a 2009 oral history, "When we moved here in 1965, Alexandria was a sleepy
Southern town, very much a stronghold of the Byrd machine. And it was wonderful
to live here during the next several decades because during this period of time, the
city really changed into one of the most progressive places in the state of Virginia."[32]

Conclusion

This chapter argues that the desegregation and integration experiences of Alexandria
drove a politics of exit that, in turn, transformed the politics of the city. While the
arguments over school quality and discipline in Alexandria's schools in the early
1970s often only thinly masked outright racial hostility, they also prompted a number of white middle-class families to either enroll their children in private schools in
the area or to move beyond Alexandria's city limits. The dynamics of this exit culminated in a major demographic change within Alexandria, a change that had enormous
local political consequences. An effort in the late 1960s to annex major portions of
neighboring Fairfax County could have forestalled that exit, but Alexandria lost the
annexation bid.[33] Had it been successful, the annexation would have produced, geographically, the largest city in the greater Washington, DC area and possibly enabled
white Alexandrians to relocate within a larger city, albeit one more racially and economically divided. But Alexandria's boundaries remained more or less constant from
the mid-1950s on, and, as a result, the 1970s white flight profoundly altered the
local political calculus. As Virginia turned solidly Republican in the 1970 and 1980s,
Alexandria became less and less representative of the Old Dominion as a whole, and
instead became an outpost on Virginia soil of a liberal metropolitan Democratic sensibility, a sensibility that helped forged a new Alexandria regime.

This political dynamic yielded a local regime that was far more liberal and that
partially incorporated African American interests into both school and city politics.
As the departure of significant numbers of white middle-class families with children
combined with the influx of singles and older couples without children, the number of conservative voters within Alexandria—whether conservative Democrats
or Republicans—dropped. This, in turn, gave greater influence to liberal voters
more likely to support expanding local public services and helped produce a moderate business elite more concerned with navigating a pro-growth agenda within

Alexandria's historically sensitive preservationist movement than with keeping tax rates low.

As we will see in the next two chapters, these demographic and political shifts—which emerged largely in response to federal integration requirements—held consequences for other federal educational policies, in particular special education and programs for English language learners. Alexandria's program of special education, anchored initially in a program of "desegregation containment," had deep racially divisive roots, but it also appealed to an increasingly liberal constituency, which both sought more services for their children and also supported federal programs that, on paper, promoted greater equality of opportunity. As we shall see in Chapter 5, the initial clashes over special education policies in Alexandria stemmed from the difficulty school officials had overcoming the racially exclusionary elements of special education while at the same time providing additional services to students who genuinely needed them. Moreover, programs for gifted and talented students, typically administered as part of special education services, served to further segregate students within schools and became a form of de facto racialized tracking of students, which only further expanded a black-white test score gap.

At the same time, the arrival of large numbers of Central Americans in the 1980s and later Mexican and East African immigrants to Alexandria further complicated the demographic changes in the community and the school system's ability to respond to the needs of its increasingly diverse students. While African Americans in Alexandria achieved an increasingly influential political presence in Alexandria over the 1980s, new immigrants did not. Isolated by poverty, language, and, frequently, their undocumented status, many of these community members could not (or chose not) to mobilize to seek better services from an increasingly liberal regime. Simultaneously a tepid federal program of services for English-language learners, combined with a contradictory federal immigration regime that created strong incentives for immigrant families to not place demands on local governments, meant that there was little top- down or bottom-up pressure to incorporate the needs of immigrant students and constituents into local services, despite the political inclination to do so. As we see in Chapter 6, this weak and contradictory engagement of the federal government in the educational offerings for immigrant students meant that there were few challenges to the local regime's priorities, effectively pushing the concerns of non-English speakers aside. Not until federal accountability politics increased the pressure on local school officials to respond to the educational challenges facing immigrant students did Alexandria schools undertake serious efforts to provide services.

In sum, the experiences of desegregation and integration in Alexandria set into motion a number of demographic and regime changes that had long-lasting effects. For the purposes of federal educational policymaking, these changes set the contexts for the next rounds of educational state-building, even as complaints about the inadequacies of racial equality in Alexandria continued into the 1980s and 1990s.

5

Special Education and the
Politics of Services

Introduction

The arrival of the letter should have been a cause for celebration, but perhaps Alexandria City Public Schools Superintendent John C. Albohm was simply weary from the fight. When he opened the letter dated June 13, 1973 from Peter Holmes, Director of the Office for Civil Rights at Health, Education and Welfare, informing him that Alexandria was in compliance with Title VI of the 1964 Civil Rights Act, Albohm wrote a brief cover memo to circulate the HEW letter to the School Board. He informed Board members, "For the record I will have to report this at the School Board meeting next Wednesday under the Superintendent's Report."

His somewhat dour and dutiful tone seems a bit odd. Only a month earlier, Albohm had shepherded through the Alexandria City School Board a long-delayed school reorganization plan that fully integrated its elementary schools, the final stage in a long process of compliance with *Brown v. Board of Education*. After HEW reviewed these changes, Holmes wrote to Albohm that the school district was in compliance and "your file is being returned to our Philadelphia Regional Office." But given the tone in the cover memo, Albohm was not entirely pleased. Perhaps he was annoyed at the prospect of ongoing supervision, as Holmes did indicate that "Staff from that office will be visiting your district shortly after the beginning of the 1973–74 school year to review the implementation of your plan."

Or perhaps one sentence in the letter struck Albohm as worrisome. Wrote Holmes, "In addition, because of the disproportionate enrollment of minority students in special education classes, the Regional Office will wish to review your district's referral and assignment procedures for such classes."[1] Given Alexandria's difficulties in fully integrating its schools, and recent agitation from members of the community over the need for more special education offerings, perhaps the last thing Albohm wanted were the Feds nosing around a special education program with a historical legacy of racial bias. As this chapter will illustrate, the origins of

Alexandria's special education program lay in a policy of "containment" in which Superintendent T.C. Williams and the School Board utilized separate special education programs to minimize desegregation in Alexandria schools. The unanticipated consequence of this effort, however, was the identification of a large group of white students who needed special services as well. Given this unexpected demonstration of need, and growing community demand for special education services, the program grew, boosted in part by state laws banning school districts from excluding special needs students.

The growing federal role within the field of special education—most notably in court decisions in the early 1970s and then the 1975 Education for All Handicapped Children Act (PL 94–142, 1975)—put Alexandria, however, in a position of expanding expensive programs in the midst of tight budgetary times. But in the post-civil rights era in Alexandria, as African Americans gained a toehold in the political structure in the community, the expansion of special education served a double-edged function that overrode any budgetary objections of School Board members or City Council members.

The expansion of special education services in the mid-1970s and through the 1980s—and the accompanying expansion of the federal role in local education—was largely unquestioned because it conformed to the priorities of the emerging racial coalition in Alexandria. In short, special education was one-half of a local bargain struck in order to simultaneously build a racial coalition to govern Alexandria schools and to retain white middle-class parents. Combined with a "talented and gifted" program (initially treated as part of special education) and a de facto policy of academic tracking, special education both appealed to liberals' desires to expand social services in the community and conservatives' efforts to keep high-performing students segregated from low-performing students.

This is a story told in four parts. "The Racial Foundations of Special Education in Alexandria" examines the origins of special education programs in Alexandria, focusing on Superintendent T.C. Williams's use of systemwide testing during the early days of desegregation to document the academic limitations of African American students in order to justify their continued segregation from whites on "academic" grounds. That plan, however, backfired as the testing regimen uncovered widespread academic deficiencies among white students, thereby prompting a new effort to boost "school readiness" for all children. "The Federal Commitment to Students with Special Needs" then turns to the federal government's involvement in special education law, focusing on the interaction of Virginia state law and federal law, as well as highlighting major issues that confront all programs to provide assistance to students whose needs are distinctive.

"Special Education and the Emergence of the Grand Compromise" explores the response of Alexandria schools in the early 1970s to new Virginia regulations and federal case law on the provision of special education to all children. These new regulations forced Alexandria to confront its complete disregard of students with learning disabilities, as well as emotionally disturbed students. This section explores how the few existing programs for emotionally disturbed students were used largely to discipline students, and given the racial disparities in school discipline, generated racial disparities in special education. At the same time, the district created a "talented and gifted" special education program, which, along with "ability grouping" and academic tracking, helped perpetuate a two-tiered system of education within Alexandria schools, despite thorough racial integration at the school level.

"Growing Budgets, Declining Enrollments, Happy Constituents" concludes the chapter by examining briefly the budgetary growth of public education as a whole in the city, despite shrinking revenues from federal and state governments and despite dwindling enrollments. This growth—along with increasing numbers of students with special needs—was linked to the growth of a city government increasingly committed to offering more services to its constituents. From this vantage point, special education "stuck" in Alexandria, in part because it helped the consolidation of a local regime in which City Hall sought another way to expand its portfolio of services to residents, even as its discriminatory origins were not entirely overcome.

The Racial Foundations of Special Education in Alexandria

In their efforts to block the desegregation of Alexandria schools in the late 1950s, Superintendent Williams and the ACPS School Board utilized a number of facially neutral classifications that fell disproportionately on African American students. After being ordered to desegregate by Federal District Court Judge Albert Bryan, Williams and the school board adopted a series of criteria by which they would evaluate school transfer requests. One of the most common means to deny a transfer was to cite the academic underachievement of African American students. Indeed, Criterion Number Three, adopted on October 28, 1958, declared that the School Board could take into account the "mental maturity" of those seeking transfer and admission. In order to meet the courts' equal protection requirements, the October 28 resolution declared that *all* students—white and black—seeking admission to the first grade would be tested in order to ascertain their preparedness for the first grade curriculum. This decision to administer the tests "on a racially nondiscriminatory basis" had unsettling consequences for issues beyond race, because it uncovered significant gaps among white children as well.

The district administered the tests of mental maturity to all incoming first graders in the summer of 1959.[2] The alarming results of those citywide tests prompted a special meeting of the School Board on September 2, 1959. At the meeting, Williams related that "a number of applicants for 1st grade enrollment" had "quite low" mental ages. At Williams' urging, the Board first ordered a retest of all students who had not passed the "mental maturity" tests. Also, the School Board approved a program of "readiness classes" for students whose retest in mid-September showed a mental age below 4 ½ years. (The chronological age requirement for enrolling in first grade was a sixth birthday by October 1 of the school year).

Williams recommended that the parents of these underperforming children be notified that their youngsters were "not enough advanced in development for first grade enrollment and cannot be accommodated there."[3] Instead, they would be enrolled in one of four "readiness" centers at schools across the city (with no transportation provided, unless students could take an existing bus route to a school with a readiness class). Two of the centers were at the two all-black elementary schools. Of the 130 students who eventually enrolled in readiness classes, eighty-four attended all-black schools. At the board meeting approving the readiness classes, Williams took pains to claim no one was being denied an education: "It is emphasized that these pupils are not excluded from school but that they would be hopelessly lost in a first grade situation and cannot, with profit to themselves, be accommodated in a first grade."[4] While the effects of delaying entrance of students into first grade fell disproportionately on African American students, white students from a few schools were amply represented in the readiness classes, with over half of the forty-six white students coming from three schools alone.[5]

Part of the motivation behind the requirement of testing all students was clearly an effort to document the education gap between white and black students in Alexandria and thereby find a judicially acceptable, "nonracial" basis upon which the district could prevent blacks from transferring to all-white schools. While the readiness program smacked of a "desegregation containment" policy, the program yielded more than its intended result. Indeed, the readiness program possessed many elements of the progressive, early-intervention models favored by researchers and educators today. At the same time, Williams' rhetoric concerning mental age and underperformance expressed a desire to control and contain a "contagion" in the school district, a "contagion" of underperformance that now extended beyond a defense of segregation. As he stated in a board meeting at the conclusion of the first year of the readiness classes: "In our search for means of reducing the spread of pupils (i.e., achievement levels) in our grades, I am confident that in embracing the readiness classes we have hit upon a most potent factor in exercising a beginning control over the situation. Previously, these weak pupils have been allowed to enter and to accumulate from year to year. If we can now control the trouble at its source, we will eventually make a profound contribution to the school system."[6]

While seeking to limit the enrollment of students deemed unready for schooling, Williams and the Alexandria School Board simultaneously built and expanded a program of special education, composed of psychological testing, remedial classes for "irregular students," and expanded programs for retarded students. These efforts came about, in part, to address the "wide 'spread' of children in various of our school grades,"[7] the salience of which was heightened by the School Board's repeated use of Criteria Three in the six-point school assignment memorandum. The federal courts did not allow the School Board to refuse transfers based upon race, but Williams was nonetheless motivated to identify and contain those students who in his view would disrupt the education of other, higher-achieving pupils.

In order to acquaint the school board with these issues, Williams directed his district staff to write a series of reports "to keep the Board more closely in touch with the various operations of the schools."[8] The reports, covering such topics as remedial reading, the "underachiever," psychological testing, and classes for retarded children, intersected in important ways. They laid the foundations for the expansion of programs that effectively segregated many African American students—particularly low-achieving individuals—from their white peers. At the same time, Williams' studies identified significant numbers of white students who also fell into "underachiever" categories, thereby complicating the issue. In short, race did not correlate perfectly with ACPS's indicators of troublesome behavior, underachievement, and retardation. A system of ostensibly race-neutral testing and assessment identified a significant portion of whites in need of remedial services, and this outcome meant that programs for students with special needs would eventually be rethought, redesigned, improved, and expanded.

Williams seemed particularly distressed by issue of the "slow-learners" and their effects on the classroom. The report on "underachievers" was, in his words,

> probably even more important than the report concerning the [curricular reform in the] high schools as it effects [sic] pupils in a more formative period of their schooling and those who are finding themselves at a loss in the schools as they are conducted at the present time.... We have accumulated these children in the grades largely through, I believe, the admission of many immature children into the first grade simply because they were chronologically six years of age. A combination of this program with the readiness program should go a long way toward solving a problem which has been a thorn in our sides for some time.[9]

The report on underachievers was compiled by a committee of eight principals, along with the district's Director of Special Education. It surveyed all of Alexandria's schools, apparently for the first time, to identify "irregular students," defined as those students who were working at an academic level one or more years below their grade level. Using school records, the report's authors relied upon the "physical symptoms" of underachievement (including, among other things, the students' poor eyesight, deafness, speech impediments, malnutrition, lack of muscular coordination, and emotional disturbance); student academic records (which apparently noted the economic background of students as well as any "lack of drive"); and any previous remedial studies to determine whether students were "underachievers." Of the roughly 14,000 students enrolled in the Alexandria Public School District in 1960, the committee identified 712 elementary students and 317 high school students who were deemed "irregular." Of those, the report suggested that 280 of the "irregular students" be placed in courses for the mentally retarded beginning in the autumn of 1960.[10] Given that enrollment in courses for the mentally retarded had totaled only 115 children in the spring of 1960, this number would have represented a 243 percent increase in students receiving services for mental retardation. While African American students were disproportionately represented among the 280 children slated for enrollment in special classes (114 of whom were white and 166 of whom were African American), the number of white students identified as "mentally retarded" would have jumped more than 175 percent in one year.[11] Dissatisfied with these statistics, Williams had the 280 students "retested" and decided that only twenty-three of them merited referral to courses for the "mentally retarded."[12]

Nonetheless, the authors of the report recommended—and the School Board agreed, with William's concurrence—that 712 elementary students be placed in special "remedial" courses at eleven schools throughout the city. While this purging of underachievers disproportionately affected African Americans, whites constituted the numerical majority of students assigned to the remedial irregular classes. The attention to the academic "spread" between white and black students that the School Board thought could be used to delay or at least defuse court-ordered desegregation had an indirect effect of creating an expanded special education program for both black and white students. Indeed, this new program required the hiring of personnel to work full-time on the "irregular" curriculum and students, under the Supervisor of Special Services.[13]

The "irregular learners" program was devised and put into place over the summer of 1960. While the program was scaled back somewhat from Williams' original projections, it still taught, in the fall of 1960, some 580 students at ten centers in schools throughout the city. Of those 580 pupils, 282 attended all-black schools. In spite of its potential to simply be a warehouse of poorly performing students, the program seems to have captured the imagination of a number of teachers. The twenty-nine teachers in the program, "nearly all of whom...volunteered for this special assignment," were regular members of the teaching staff, and they taught smaller-sized classes than the regular classroom teachers. During the program's orientation in the fall, the teachers exhibited "keen interest" through their "many questions, lively discussion and several provocative suggestions worthy of further consideration."[14]

Nonetheless, the district's official line was that some students were already lost:

> The committee recognizes that within this group [of irregular students] there will be two types of learners: the fami[li]al type (the one who learns very slowly always and will not change)and the child who has made poor progress even though he has the ability. The former type will continue to need special type instruction. [sic] The other type should be able to return to a regular classroom after special instruction. The number of classes will probably decrease after the first year and largely the fami[li]al type will be

left in these classes. This year we need to put special emphasis on rehabili-
tating the child with ability so he may be returned to a regular class.[15]

Teachers' enthusiasm for the program appeared to conflict with the apparent fact
that some of their pupils were to be permanently confined to a program explicitly
designed to uphold modest expectations at best.

These special education innovations—which undoubtedly helped to maintain the segregation of black students from white—came at a time when public
demands for increasing services for students with special needs were being vocally
expressed in Alexandria. In a June 28, 1961 letter to Superintendent Williams, Mrs.
T. Edward Braswell, President of the Alexandria Association for Retarded Children,
presented a resolution by the Association requesting that the School Board provide
public schooling to "trainable" mentally retarded children, defined as children with
IQs of 55 or lower. She included in her note a list of thirteen such students living
in Alexandria who needed such services. The Association's resolution pointed out
that the surrounding jurisdictions of Arlington County and Fairfax County already
provided such classes to trainable mentally retarded students and stressed that the
state would reimburse localities one-half of teachers' salaries (up to $1600) for such
classes.[16]

When discussing the letter at a July meeting, Williams indicated he would
research the surrounding jurisdictions' offerings. Given Williams' penny-pinching
style, his findings were not surprising. He emphasized the limited utility of such
courses for students and lamented the cost of such a program. "It is recognized at
once," he wrote in his monthly Superintendent's Report, "that the retention span
of such pupils is not great and that most of the skills taught must be of a manual
nature." Moreover, he stressed, "[a]ll of the jurisdictions having these classes report
that they are tremendously expensive."[17] At the same meeting, he indicated that he
had received requests for special courses for deaf children "with the claim that there
are a number of children who need such attention." After insisting that his records
identified only seventeen deaf children in Alexandria, he stated that he was "not
impressed with the urgency of the situation," but he did ask principals to make a
survey in their schools.[18]

The strategy of containment and delay that Williams seems to have perfected in
the desegregation struggle worked equally well in the battle over providing additional services to mentally retarded and deaf students. After testing the thirteen
students that the Alexandria Association for Retarded Children claimed were in
need of public schooling, Williams reported to the School Board that no such need
existed. He argued that there were insufficient numbers of potential students, but
only after he eliminated eight children on eligibility grounds. He recalled that of the
thirteen students, "the [testing] appointment was canceled for one child. Another
child, after all the examinations, was found to be eligible for a readiness class and
was so enrolled. Three of the children had moved from the City. One was too young

for the class, being only 4 ½ years old, and two were beyond the usual cut-off age of sixteen for these classes." Among the remaining five, three "were found to be of such a nature that they would not profit at all by being included in a trainable class, as they were not judged to be trainable. Their presence would be one of simply being there." Only two were actually found to be eligible, but "it does not seem that so few would justify a class as it has been found that in all of the [neighboring] areas the smallest number for any such class is seven." He offered to provide homebound instruction for the remaining two.[19]

Williams had less luck making hearing-impaired students disappear. After surveying their schools, district principals had located 150 students that they suspected were hearing-impaired. Nonetheless, "[i]t should be recognized," wrote Williams, "that this is not a definite indication that these pupils have hearing difficulties." A check by the school nurse would "probably eliminate a number of those who have been listed."[20] At the December board meeting, Williams sought to refute the findings of the teachers and principals by introducing a letter from Dr. T.F. McGough, Alexandria's Director of Public Health, who indicated that the Alexandria Health Department (which provided school health services) had identified only sixty-three students with hearing problems. Moreover, Dr. McGough stated "it should be reiterated that only a relatively small percentage of these students will need special attention beyond that which they are already receiving. It is our belief that very few students, therefore, will need any special arrangements such as special classes."[21] At the meeting, Williams was openly challenged—a rare event at the school board meetings. According to the minutes, Mrs. Jacques Kusseling, President of the Alexandria Association for the Hard of Hearing, disputed the medical expertise of Dr. McGough: "It was her opinion that the figures furnished by the Health Department were not representative due to the fact that the screening techniques failed to properly identify the children with hearing defects."[22] She also named doctors willing to support her position.

The struggle between Williams and citizen advocates for better resources for hearing-impaired students continued for several months, until the Board voted to hire an additional speech teacher to work with the deaf children in the school district.[23] By this time, T.C. Williams had decided to retire, effective January 1, 1963.

At the end of his tenure as superintendent, Williams was increasingly besieged by parents and community members seeking transformation of multiple aspects of the school system in Alexandria. They sought, in addition to greater racial integration, the following: more resources for mentally retarded children; better school facilities for African American children; effective measures to reduce dropouts; an end to overt religious celebrations during Christmas and Easter seasons; and the end of segregated and unequal extracurricular and athletic programs across the city. Among the first reports received by the School Board after Williams departed was a request by the Northern Virginia Association for Retarded Children "for adequate educational provisions for the mentally retarded."[24]

The Federal Commitment to Students with Special Needs

Across the nation, the quest for adequate provision for special needs students—and the articulation of a broader right to education for children with special needs— grew, in no small part, out of the activism of the civil rights movement and, more specifically, the use of litigation to desegregate schools. The mobilization of parent groups in the 1960s, groups like the Northern Virginia Association for Retarded Children, brought the issue of "mental retardation" and childhood handicaps into a broader arena. In addition, the visibility of national public officials who spoke frankly about the experiences of handicapped family members helped shift public attitudes toward the needs of children with disabilities or handicaps.[25] Nonetheless, it often took judicial intervention to force localities to accept or pay for the educa- tion of children with special needs. From the 1950s to 1970, Congress created a number of programs to promote research on special education, create schools, and train more special education teachers, but in none of this legislation "was there any suggestion that children with disabilities had rights, and the states were not *required* to take any action at all."[26]

In Virginia, rights for the disabled were no more forthcoming than they were from the federal government, but an unusual confluence of events placed special education on the state agenda, prior to federal action. In 1968, Virginia undertook a constitutional revision process, in part to turn the corner on the 1902 Constitution that had entrenched the Jim Crow institutions struck down by the Supreme Court and federal civil rights legislation. As part of that reform, legislators eventually adopted (and the public ratified) a constitutional amendment that called for a sys- tem of "high quality" education,[27] and charged the State Board of Education with the task of defining the "standards of quality" that school districts shall provide.[28] While these constitutional provisions took some years to be fleshed out in statutory enactments, they committed Virginia to the principle that more than minimal edu- cational offerings were needed to meet Virginia's constitutional obligation in public education.

At roughly the same time that the General Assembly introduced the idea of a constitutional commitment to "high quality" education, a federal three-judge panel struck down the private school tuition vouchers that the state legislature had adopted during Massive Resistance to allow students to attend private schools at public expense.[29] Over the course of the 1960s, however, many parents of handi- capped children in Virginia utilized the private school tuition vouchers not as a way to avoid sending their children to integrated schools, but to help obtain scarce and expensive special education services for their children at private facilities. While the federal court in the *Griffin* decision declared that such use was still acceptable, sup- porters of special education proposed during the Assembly's constitutional delib- erations that the state explicitly convert the existing language concerning vouchers into a means to fund special education, with the grants to be used only for the "education or training of emotionally disturbed, mentally retarded, and mentally or physically handicapped Virginia students, and such other handicapped Virginia students as may be prescribed by law."[30] The proposal enjoyed significant support, and won passage in the first round of constitutional revision. Legislators, however, later added language that allowed parents to use sectarian schools for special education services as well.[31] At that point, church-state objections doomed the special education tuition voucher. Nonetheless, the legislature left the existing Massive Resistance era provisions intact, and, with court approval, parents continued to use the vouchers at private special education facilities.

Meanwhile, several state legislators began a push for an expanded set of services for handicapped persons, including students, throughout Virginia. In 1970, the Virginia State Senate directed the Virginia Advisory Legislative Council to study the needs of handicapped persons in Virginia, both students and adults, in order to devise new legislation promoting the health, education, and rehabilitation of persons with handicaps. The report recommended, among other things, that the Virginia State Board of Education be required to develop "a program of education for handicapped children" that all local districts would then be required to provide.[32] A year after the report, the Virginia legislature put into place a number of special education reforms.

First, the legislature required every school district to survey its special needs students and prepare a plan "for their proper education and training of all handicapped children within its jurisdiction." This was the first statewide requirement that school districts meet the needs of students with handicaps. In addition the State Board of Education, fulfilling its new constitutional charge to create a school system of "high quality," promulgated Standards of Quality that required school districts to "identify exceptional children including the gifted" and develop a plan "to provide appropriate educational opportunities for them."[33] In effect, the state was requiring school districts to either provide parents with a tuition voucher in order to comply with the new compulsory provisions, or to provide within schools an "appropriate" education for handicapped children.

This shift in policy emerged at virtually the same time as two federal court decisions in 1972, *Pennsylvania Association for Retarded Children (PARC) v. Commonwealth of Pennsylvania* and *Mills v. Board of Education of the District of Columbia*. Together these two decisions imposed a federal constitutional burden on schools to provide education for handicapped children and provided a template by which other school districts and states could meet that constitutional burden. In *PARC*, the state of Pennsylvania signed a consent agreement that prevented it from excluding from public schools children with mental retardation. The decree also required that the state "place each mentally retarded child in a free, public program of education and training appropriate to the child's capacity."[34] Moreover, the state agreed that "placement in a regular public school class is preferable to placement in a special public school class"[35] and that the state would, for each child with mental retardation, develop "an annual statement of educational strategy . . . for the coming year and at the close of the year an evaluation of that strategy."[36] These three elements—free and appropriate education, assignment to a regular classroom whenever possible, and an individualized plan for education progress—would, in a few short years, constitute the fundamental principles of the federal strategy to ensure that special education services were provided to all students who needed them.

Because the PARC decision emerged out a consent decree, it did not definitively declare the nature of federal constitutional rights for students with mental retardation, although the judge suggested the plaintiffs would have prevailed absent the consent decree. The Mills decision, however, squarely located the constitutional issues: the denial of public education to the special needs plaintiffs violated the Due Process Clause.[37] As a result, "The defendants are required by the Constitution of the United States, the District of Columbia Code, and their own regulations to provide a publicly-supported education for these 'exceptional' children."[38] The conjunction of PARC and Mills meant that states and school districts were on notice that their failure to provide education for handicapped children placed them, at a minimum, in legal jeopardy.

Although Virginia's 1972 steps did not go as far as the PARC and Mills decisions, they nonetheless put Virginia ahead of many other states as the federal judicial mandates hit local schools. The Old Dominion's requirement that school districts 1) conduct a census of all special needs students within their boundaries; 2) devise a plan for providing education to these students and; 3) either enroll or provide tuition vouchers to all special needs students by Fall 1974 represented an early and important effort to meet the educational needs of Virginia's handicapped students.

Within a few years, Virginia received additional guidance from the federal government about just what kind of education it needed to provide special needs students. The enactment of the 1975 Education for All Handicapped Children Act (EAHCA), popularly known by its Public Law number, 94-142, was a watershed moment in American public education. While earlier federal legislation—particularly the 1970 Education of the Handicapped Act[39]—had expanded programs for special education students, the federal government had not directly mandated how states needed to organize their special education programs and curricula. With the EAHCA, however, Congress undertook a major redefinition of the federal role in special education, extending and codifying the protections that were advanced in PARC and Mills. Indeed, the EAHCA borrowed directly from both the PARC and Mills decisions, requiring that states and districts provide "free and appropriate public education," that they ensure due process protections to special education students, and that they develop an individual education plan (IEP) for each special education student and, whenever possible, "mainstream" children with special needs in a regular classroom environment. All these elements were present in the PARC consent decree and have remained central components of US special educational policy through the latest reauthorization in 2007 of what is now called the Individuals with Disabilities Education Act.[40]

Virginia's emergent structure of special education quickly adapted to the federal regulatory scheme. The primary challenge under any program of special education is to balance the benefits a special needs student will receive by virtue of her inclusion in a regular classroom against the benefits she might receive through separate instruction in a special education classroom. Not all disabilities are alike in this regard: some students with severe cognitive handicaps respond better to specialized classroom instruction than a student with a learning disability like dyslexia. In addition, while some disabilities (like blindness or deafness or dyslexia) place obstacles but not limits on the academic achievement of students, others, generally associated with brain injury or neurological disability, impose a meaningful ceiling on the academic achievement of students. Moreover, once a student is assigned to a special education classroom—with, typically, a less ambitious curriculum and slower pace—it often becomes difficult for that student to return to the regular classroom at a later date. For students with borderline diagnoses or misdiagnoses, being assigned to a special education classroom is quite often a prescription for educational failure. For all of these reasons, EAHCA specified that states utilize the "least restrictive environment" to provide a "free and appropriate" education and insisted on an individual education plan to map out a child's progress and to evaluate that progress on a yearly basis.

Special Education and the Emergence of the Grand Compromise

From Refusal to Conditional Acceptance

The challenge of developing this structure of special education in Alexandria was immense. In the mid 1960s, Alexandria did create—after much prodding from groups like the Northern Virginia Association for Retarded Children—facilities for students with what was then termed "trainable mental retardation." These students were housed in the district's "Trainable Center" where they were taught basic life skills and household tasks. In addition, the district operated centers for students with "educable mental retardation" at four elementary schools and at each secondary school. In these segregated classrooms, students learned vocational or occupational skills, with the eventual goal of achieving at a sixth-grade level.[41] These two programs, plus the state-funded tuition vouchers and a speech program, constituted the entire array of Alexandria's special education services until 1973. The district provided no services for students with learning disabilities or who were emotionally disturbed.

The scale of the programs the district did run was not large. A survey of "exceptional students" conducted in the 1972–1973 academic year, by order of the state, found a total of 594 students receiving services in Alexandria schools, although 334 of those were identified as having speech problems.[42] Among students with serious disabilities, the district provided services for sixty-six trainable mentally retarded students in the district, 186 educable mentally retarded students, and eight with impaired vision. Another sixty-six students received tuition vouchers for education at private facilities and twenty-three received homebound instruction, but they were not counted among the students serviced directly by the schools.

By its own admission, however, the district was not coming anywhere close to meeting the special education needs of its students. Setting aside students with speech problems, the district provided special education to a total of 260 students, but it had identified 351 additional students as having special needs. Thus, the district was providing special education services to less than 43 percent of the students who needed them. Factoring in the number of students that the district suspected as needing special education services, but had not yet fully evaluated, the level of unmet need skyrockets: The district reported a total of 3,713 students as either identified or suspected of having special needs, but who were receiving no services. All told, the district's own census found that it provided services to only 16 percent of the students that were either identified or suspected of having some form of handicap.[43]

The largest area of unmet need were in the categories of learning disability and emotionally disturbed students, two disabilities for which the district did not provide any services at all. In its census, the district found that 136 students had been identified as emotionally disturbed and another fifty-five had learning disabilities. More staggeringly, it suspected that another 550 students were emotionally disturbed and 1100 students suffered from a learning disability. The reluctance to serve these students stemmed, in part, from both the district's lack of experience in addressing these needs and their potential costs. After a parent of student with learning disabilities asked the school board to develop a program for addressing learning disabilities, Dr. Edwin Bondareff, a school board member, responded as follows:

> Learning disabilities is a rather diffused category and it is a very difficult one to diagnose and a difficult area to deal with. Other jurisdictions, it is true, have begun [to address learning disabilities] and we are about to also. We have begun by improving on [our treatment] of the more routine disabilities, physical and mental and psychological, that are more easily grouped together, are a more standard type of disability. Moving in the area of the learning disabled is a far greater problem and more difficult to assess.[44]

The reluctance of the district to embark on a new program of student services was not, however, sitting well with activists parents who had long lobbied for improvements to the special education offerings and who saw parallels between their own claims and the claims of African American parents. Some of them even threatened lawsuits. Rose Cassidy, a parent of three school-aged children, (one of whom was learning disabled) testified at a budget hearing that other neighboring communities "have already made considerable strides in their programs for special education, including the learning disabled." Noting that the new Virginia law required all school systems to provide an education for special needs children, Cassidy suggested that "there is more than one type of class action suit which might be brought against the school system in behalf of equal opportunity for education of all children. I would prefer to have the School Board take free action to remedy this real need in our schools."[45]

While the school district may have worried about potential lawsuits, it was busy enough simply complying with the new 1972 Virginia law that required every school district to develop a plan for the provision of special education. To help devise the plan, the law also required each district to appoint a special education advisory committee. In Alexandria, that committee was appointed less than four months before the plan was due in Richmond (and a week after Ms. Cassidy made the veiled threat of litigation). While the Committee's work was rushed, it nonetheless resulted in a detailed thirty-page overview of existing programs and recommendations for future hires and expansion of special education. The Advisory Committee's report was far more detailed than the district's own five-year plan and included a detailed critique of not only the administrative structure of the special education programs, but the ability of the system to identify, assess, and provide adequate instruction for special needs students in Alexandria.

The report drew particular attention to the district's inability to address learning disabilities of many of its students. While the district's own survey highlighted the large number of Alexandria students with either confirmed or suspected learning disabilities, the report found "a general inability of regular classroom teachers to recognize or cope with learning disabled children."[46] In addition, it criticized the district for the absence of programs for emotionally disturbed students and for its persistent misplacement of students, sometimes using racially or culturally biased modes of assessment.

For example, the Advisory Committee found that because there were no programs for emotionally disturbed students the district had transferred some to the Trainable Center at the Lee school, where they "inter-mixed with trainable and educable mentally retarded children, most of them on the elementary level." The report noted that "these children are not being served according to their handicap" and they "are treated as disciplinary problems when they become unusually upset or hyperactive and are punished by being put in closets or made to isolate themselves in the hall."[47]

The report also cited a close connection between special education referrals and disciplinary techniques. According to the committee, most teachers in Alexandria "generally know very little about exceptional children" and "have a disinclination to work with other than the average, conforming child." As a result, teachers "too frequently see disciplinary action as the answer to poor classroom behavior and low academic performance by the student." In fact, the subcommittee investigating the need for services for emotionally disturbed students found that staff at the secondary level used the "so-called Resource Centers" as "merely detention centers for pupils with disciplinary problems, but not necessarily emotionally disturbed." The report questioned the "qualifications and functions of the crisis resource teachers for the emotionally disturbed" at two middle schools and recommended that only "properly trained teachers" be utilized in resource centers.[48]

The Advisory Committee's characterization of the Resource Centers' use as detention centers is confirmed by a 1976 report by the Ad Hoc Committee on the Learning Environment. That committee, responding to growing complaints from the African American community that disciplinary enforcement in Alexandria schools was racially biased, investigated the disciplinary mechanisms employed in Alexandria's schools and the extent to which white and black students were treated differently in the disciplinary process. One of the background briefings given to the committee explained the origins of the Resource Centers. According to Arnold J. Thurmond, coordinator of the district's Resource Centers, the centers were created during the 1969–1970 academic year, in the wake of an increase in suspensions and "alienation [sic] of a large percent of the study body."[49] As designed, the centers added "another dimension to the school and community resources by attempting to help students stay in school longer and avoid suspensions and obtain the individual and professional help that is needed to deal with his or her school problems."[50] According to Thurmond, prior to the creation the Resource Centers, school administrators had "no choice but to suspend or send a student home for any infraction that occurred in single class, however successful the student was in his other classes."

While the Resource Centers initially had a goal of providing additional services to students, the lack of any programs for emotionally disturbed students (or for students who acted out because of a learning disability), transformed the program into simply a form of in-school detention, albeit one managed by the director of Special Education. Harry Burke, director of Special Education for ACPS, told the Ad Hoc Committee on the Learning Environment that the crisis center teachers fell under the purview of special education because "they must be qualified to handle all children in the area of exceptionality and this requires special training."[51]

In many ways, the fusion of disciplinary policy and special education was the byproduct of the district's reluctance to develop programs for emotionally disturbed children or for students with learning disabilities. With norms concerning student-teacher relations sharply changed, racial tensions and misunderstandings heightening (particularly in the midst of the new elementary integration), and no means for teachers to discern and address the causes of behavioral problems among students, Resource Centers and special education assignments became a way to channel disruptive students. Despite the recommendations of the Special Advisory

Committee to provide services for emotionally disturbed and learning-disabled students, the district explicitly made a decision to *not* provide those services. In the fall of 1973, Harold Burke, the new Director of Special Education, provided the School Board with a status update on compliance with new special education laws in Virginia, and offered a "wait and see" reply to the Special Advisory Committee's report from the previous spring. In general, Burke wrote, the "report represents a great deal of effort and thought. The particular recommendations in each category [of disability] will require more work, thought, and cooperation between the committee, staff, and administration."

Burke was particularly hesitant to adopt a program for emotionally disturbed children, writing "the category of emotionally disturbed children presents difficulties. Although we would like to provide support services for children who have problems in the regular classroom we feel it is necessary to be very cautious in categorizing a child as emotionally disturbed."[52] Burke went on to write, "Emotional disturbance because of an exceptionality may be relieved by special education; however, placement in a special education category (e.g., educable) because emotional disturbance inhibits intellectual functioning is a mistake for the particular child and for the other children served in that area." In effect, Burke's language reveals the administration's inability to conceive of emotional disturbance as an independent category of special education that might be addressed within context of mainstreaming. Under his reasoning, emotionally disturbed students necessarily require removal from a regular classroom and assignment to a form of special education (most likely an educable mental retardation classroom). At the same time, he realized that approach is not an appropriate strategy for a student who does not have mental retardation. Thus, the school system persisted in not adopting policies for learning disabilities or emotionally disturbed students and relied on a disciplinary process to resolve the difficult classroom dynamics that ensued.

To be fair, two issues complicated the task Alexandria faced. To create a program for the emotionally disturbed during precisely the same semester that the school system was, for the first time, fully racially integrating all its students at all elementary schools would most likely have produced a hostile reaction from the African American community and, presumably, further investigation by HEW. In this regard, the racial impacts of special education assignments would have collided with the integrating policies that Alexandria had recently adopted. The political fallout and the prospect of further HEW investigation into perceived efforts to maintain racial segregation undoubtedly induced district leaders to slow down special education reforms. In addition, while other neighboring school districts were adopting these programs (Fairfax and Arlington Counties, in particular), the logistics of mainstreaming and providing services to special needs children within a regular classroom environment were still emerging. Most schools relied on the notion of a unitary classroom in which all students of the same age learned the same material at the same rate at the same time. To provide special education services without removing students from the regular classroom required schools and school districts to devise new institutional and organizational routines, changes that took several years to become widespread.

Nonetheless, Alexandria's explicit insistence on not providing these services prior to the federal Education for All Handicapped Children Act in 1975 is remarkable. Even after Burke's memo indicated that it would continue to study the matter, the School Board adopted a special education placement policy that explicitly declined to devise a policy for emotionally disturbed students, gifted students, or students in kindergarten and first grade with learning disabilities. "In these three categories," the policy stated, "we do not yet have enough experience to define the most effective policy for providing services for the student. A policy will be defined in the future."[53] Thus, despite the need under state law to define criteria for assignment to special education, the school district explicitly omitted three categories of exceptional students that encompassed the largest number of students, given its own survey of student needs.

Shortly after the adoption of the policy in December 1973, special education officials presented to the School Board an "Updated Five Year Plan for Special Education Programs," revising what School Board member Connie Ring called a "quite sketchy" initial plan.[54] The revised plan outlined in far greater detail the needs of the system and the steps the district would take to meet those needs. Although the emphasis of the plan was still on educable mental retardation (EMR) and trainable mental retardation (TMR) programs, the district for the first time detailed plans to develop programs for emotionally disturbed students and students with learning disabilities over the coming five years, even though it still had no explicit policy for identifying those students.

Susan Finnell, chair of the Special Education Advisory Committee, lauded the new plan—in particular the addition of nine new special education teachers for the 1974–1975 academic year. Finnell noted, however, that the District's own estimates of the need of special education services and the September 1976 deadline for the provision of special education for *all* students who needed it meant that the District faced a looming staffing shortfall of certified special education teachers in Alexandria. For learning disabled students alone, Finnell estimated that the District would need thirty-five new teachers, but she noted that the current budget proposal called for hiring only one teacher for learning disabled students for the coming year.[55]

In addition, Finnell noted that the statutory obligation to meet the need of special education students was currently being partly met by the provision of special education vouchers to finance private placements for students. These costs, she warned, would soon balloon and the district would be in far better position if it developed the capacity to address special education needs through hiring staff, rather than financing vouchers.

But Finnell reserved her harshest criticism for the continuing neglect of emotionally disturbed students in the revised five-year plan. In this area, she insisted the problem was not budgetary, but how the district conceived of special education for students with emotional problems. She noted that the district's estimate of its emotionally disturbed students was "ridiculously high" and based on the number of students that were referred to the Crisis Resource Centers in the secondary schools. Because teachers routinely sent to the crisis resource centers "any student the teacher may regard as a behavioral or disruptive problem in the classroom" the centers "become little more than detention centers, and crisis resource teachers little more than monitors in the schools."[56] The district's continuing refusal to articulate "precise criteria and procedures for identifying and referring emotionally disturbed children" reflected, Finnell said, a larger reluctance to come to terms with special education. "There remains widespread indication within the Alexandria schools that many principals and teachers do not understand the conditions of exceptionality among their students and, therefore, are prepared neither to help identify or work with them."[57]

Despite this difficulty in understanding the importance of providing special education services in the context of regular classroom instruction, the school district nonetheless, after 1975, began an expansion of its special education services. The federal mandate required the expansion of programs that Alexandria simply had not offered before, so with the assistance of federal matching funds, Alexandria began hiring additional staff and increasing the number of its teachers with special educational credentials. The result of this expansion of services, as we shall see below, was a growing local budget for education, despite shrinking enrollments. Thus even if it did not fundamentally revise its emphasis on providing special education outside of regular classroom instruction—or address the fusion of special education and disciplinary procedures—the growing provision of special education nonetheless built a constituency for the programs, particularly among the teachers and the school board. In fact, by 1985, support for special education was so strong, that the school board held a ceremony to commemorate the tenth anniversary of the enactment of the Education of All Handicapped Children Act.[58] Part of that acceptance hinged, however, on achieving the second half of the grand compromise: placating the key local constituents who might undermine the political commitment to integrate students by race, by class, and now by special needs—parents who were concerned about high academic standards.

The Second Half of the Grand Compromise: Gifted, Talented, and Tracked

In contrast to the district's unwillingness to address the needs of emotionally disturbed and, to a lesser extent, learning-disabled students, the district was very eager to embrace the state's requirement that it identify and address the needs of gifted and talented students. In the fall of 1973, the first year of full elementary school integration, the district submitted a grant application for federal funds under Title III of the Elementary and Secondary Education Act to develop a gifted and talented program. In its statement of need for the proposed program, Richard Hills, director of elementary education in Alexandria, wrote that subsequent to Virginia's enactment of the 1972 Standards of Quality legislation, the "Alexandria City School Board not only accepted the mandate, but endorsed it fully."More than a little disingenuously, Hills wrote that as Alexandria developed its five-year plan for special education, "it became evident that Alexandria had taken long strides toward meeting the needs of eight areas of special education; however, in the area of gifted and talented in special education, there was a need for refinement of the program." Hills went on to assert "six teachers work with pupils in the retarded and learning disability part of special education. There are no teachers to serve the gifted and talented." He then flatly and wrongly claimed "the gifted and talented represent almost a 50 percent larger group."[59] In the state-mandated survey, submitted in June 1973, Alexandria reported that there were *four* identified gifted and talented students not receiving services, one of whom was in a private school.[60] Citing a gross screening of elementary students in the fall of 1973, Hills claims that 139 "academically talented learners" have been identified "without a program to deal with their exceptionality." He added that developing such a program was necessary because "it is an essential part of a state standard to have a program for this group."[61]

While the eagerness to develop the gifted and talented special education program contrasted sharply with the district's unwillingness to provide services for learning-disabled or emotionally disturbed students, it is not clear that the gifted and talented program, as originally designed, was explicitly aimed at segregating white and black students within newly integrated schools. Although Hills did cite the full integration of Alexandria's schools as a rationale for developing the program,[62] the program made a commitment to reach out to the minority community to identify potentially talented students who would not be located via conventional academic metrics. As Hills wrote in the grant application, "The composition of Alexandria's population is diversified. School programs should reflect this diversity."[63] In an earlier section of the grant application, Hills claimed that "this study has great potential in innovation as it seeks to identify giftedness in minority students." He added, however, that it might also serve as a means to "maintain the student composition of the Alexandria school system."[64] At least an implied objective of the program, then, was to reduce the incentives for white flight.

The district's initial commitment to minority outreach was tempered, however, by the structure of the program, which consisted of two parts. The first element— the academic segment—drew students who had been identified through testing and grades as high-achievers in traditional academic subjects. The second element—the talented segment—accepted students whose talents in art or music were noteworthy. A handful of students were identified for both programs. The talented students roughly mirrored the racial profile of the ten elementary schools participating in the program, with 54 percent of them white and 42 percent black and 4 percent classified as "other." In the academic portion, however, whites comprised 68 percent of the groups and blacks 32 percent, with none of the participants classified as "other." Thus, the overall racial tilt was only modestly white, but the academic segment of the program was predominantly white. Eventually, those ratios skewed even further, as the initial commitment to a measure of racial balance faded. By 1981, seven years after its inception, the program had grown to include 14 percent of all students in grades 4 through 6. However, that expanded program was now 83 percent white and only 12 percent African American (and five percent other).[65] Thus, as the program grew, it grew increasingly white.

Even prior to the growing racial imbalance, however, there was evidence that the program might worsen social relations within schools. The federal grant that paid for the gifted program required the school district to assess multiple student outcomes in order to improve understanding about which programs worked best. The Alexandria program did this by assigning students to one of three kinds of gifted and talented instruction (three different forms of regular classroom pullout), and then examining changes in academic achievement, social relations among students, teacher perceptions of the program, and parental satisfaction. While the evaluation did find meaningful differences among the types of gifted and talented instruction, it also uncovered significant opposition to the program among regular classroom teachers because, in their view, it fostered a sense of elitism among participating students *vis à vis* the regular classroom. As the report summarized the classroom teachers' views, they "reported a substantial amount of elitism which took the form of the G & T pupils exhibiting attitudes of superiority."[66] Although the report discounted the teachers' views because of a "self-reported lack of contact with and information about the program,"[67] it is not clear why teachers' exposure to their own classrooms was an incomplete window on the behavior of students within the program.

In addition, the evaluation's own assessment of the social relations among students, using the Fundamental Interpersonal Relation Orientation (FIRO) inventory devised by William Schutz in 1958, showed that program participants in the academic segment (the predominantly white program) scored high on attributes which, taken together, " might be considered 'elitism' by some." The reported quickly noted, however, that these scores " *are not of a magnitude that would be considered abnormal.*"[68] Among the evaluation's ten conclusions was the observation that "the student testing data and the teacher data imply that 'elitism' in the form of G & T pupils exhibiting attitudes of 'superiority' may be in a nascent state. The data, however, are far from conclusive, but do require careful inquiry during Year 3."[69] It is important to note that this finding most likely understated the total effect on social relations because the study never assessed changes in regular classroom students' perceptions of inferiority or superiority. In other words, the district had no idea what the effects of the gifted and talented program were on those students *not* chosen to participate in the program, only some indication of the effects on those who were chosen.[70]

The follow-up evaluation of "nascent" elitism in Year 3 confirmed that teachers saw further growth of elitism among students assigned to the gifted and talented program, but the study also found that "program's effects in the area of social relations are minimal, and indicated that the gifted program has not contributed to problems in this area."[71] The study based this conclusion on the behavioral and attitudinal evaluations of the students, which compared students to a baseline norm. In the first year of the study, the authors had set a "performance standard" to measure how closely Alexandria students tracked the norm, establishing that if 85 percent of the students fell within one standard error of measurement above or below the norm, they would be deemed to have "passed" the performance standard. In the second year of the program, students in the gifted and talented pilot study "passed" twenty-five out of fifty-four measures of social relations, giving rise to concern about the "nascent elitism," although the students were in the statistically normal range for their ages.

In Year 3, however, the evaluators of the program redefined what constituted "passing" score on social relations. In short, district officials concluded that because in prior years, the student's social relations scores had not "shown any consistent departure from statistical norms," the "best interests of the pupils would be served" by lowering the performance standard from 85 percent to 75 percent. In other words, the "careful inquiry" into the dynamics of elitism called for in the second report was ignored, even explicitly rejected. The third year of evaluation lowered the bar for students in the gifted and talented program: By reducing the "performance standard" from 85 percent of participants to 75 percent of participants falling within one standard error of measurement, the project management (presumably not the author) increased the number of categories in which students "passed" the performance standard. If the criteria in effect in Years 1 and 2 of the study had remained in place, the students in Year 3 would have "passed" only nine out of fifty-four categories, a clear worsening of social relations, if FIRO scores have any validity.[72]

By virtue of this "improved" performance in social relations scores among program participants in Year 3, the author of the study could then discount the teachers' perceptions of worsening social relations. As the report noted, "Teacher ratings of the effect of the program on social relations of pupils were not favorable to the program," adding that the ratings of the teachers "were lower than average during Year 2 and showed an overall decline during Year 3." The cause of the unfavorable ratings in the area of social relations, the report indicated, "seem to be closely related to feelings that the program is fostering 'elitism.'" The report then dismisses these concerns in a single, factually incorrect, sentence: "These unfavorable ratings by the teachers are, however, not supported by other sources of data."[73]

Other constituencies, however, strongly supported the program, according to the report. In particular, parents expressed growing satisfaction with the program. In Year 3 of the survey, the authors concluded "the parents are quite satisfied with the academic progress of their children."[74] As children progressed through the program, the parents' interest shifted from obtaining more knowledge about how the program functioned to "a desire for more information about the *individual progress* of the child." The authors noted that after the first year parents had "a desire to closely monitor their children's performance."[75] Parental satisfaction seemed to be a key element of the program's success, along with the evidence of the increasing test scores of the students who participated in the program. The report from year three of the program concluded that "Overall, the Program for the Gifted and Talented appears to produce sizeable and marked gains in academic achievement."[76]

In light of the study's conclusions that the program boosted academic scores, was popular with parents, and did not exacerbate social relations in the classroom, its expansion over the next few years was not surprising. As federal funds ran out, the School Board opted to continue funding the gifted and talented program with local funds, despite the misgivings that teachers expressed in their evaluation of the program. Within five years of the end of the federal grant, enrollment in gifted and talented programs had grown to 14 percent of students in grades four through six, and by 1986, the program enrolled 25 percent of Alexandria's students, the vast majority of which were white.[77] (The initial 1973 application for federal funds for a gifted and talented program had estimated that three to five percent of Alexandria's students were gifted.) At this point, even the school district admitted that the gifted and talented program was too much of a good thing, with Superintendent Robert Peebles proposing a consolidation of the program. Alexandria Education Association President Pam Walkup told a reporter that "much stricter guidelines are needed," noting that many students [in the program] are highly motivated, but not necessarily gifted.[78]

Tracking and Segregation by Expectation

The bifurcation of Alexandria students—gifted vs. non-gifted, special needs vs. non-special needs—exacerbated further the separation of students that had been achieved through tracking. In the early 1970s, the school system had moved away from formalized tracks to a more amorphous "ability grouping" within classrooms. According to press reports, ability grouping in Alexandria left teachers "free to teach them [students] as more or less separate groups within the class."[79] Combined with the newly adopted gifted and talented program, the informal tracking system enabled the district "narrow the range in the classes,"[80] as Donald Dearborn, director of elementary education, phrased it.

Although the School Board did not explicitly formalize the policy, it was allowed—despite some opposition—to become de facto policy. As the elementary school desegregation plan was implemented in the fall of 1973, the Northern Virginia office of the Urban League protested in a letter to the School Board that "it is obvious that ability grouping is taking place again." Urban League Director Harold Pollard described the experiences of the students: "In the first seven weeks of this school year, students (and particularly Black ones[sic]) have been transferred and rescheduled two or more time, and in some instances, we find almost all Black [sic] classes at George Washington and Hammond."[81]

By the late 1970s, both school officials and many members of the African American community accepted tracking as a legitimate practice. T.C. Williams Principal Robert Hanley told a reporter "We want to keep racially balanced as closely as possible, but we have to take students where we find them. I think it's a much fairer system for the students rather than throwing them all together."[82] The result, however, was that advanced courses in math, science, and English at T.C. Williams enrolled few or no African Americans. Despite the racial disparities in high schools, Ulysses Calhoun, president of the Alexandria NAACP, remarked that while his organization had received a few complaints about the practice, the organization was reserving judgment: "[W]e can't make a decision now," he told a reporter, "on whether it's equitable or not."[83] Other black leaders, however, were more forceful in their denunciations of ability grouping. Angella Current, director of the Northern Virginia Urban League, stated flatly, "Superintendent Bristol has yet to address the problems of black students in Alexandria."[84]

The local NAACP's reluctance to challenge the academic offerings presented to African American students may have stemmed, in part, from the group's continuing efforts to address the burdens of desegregation. In 1978, the Alexandria NAACP filed a new lawsuit against the school district, claiming that recent school closures—brought about by declining enrollments—disproportionately affected black students. The suit alleged that ACPS unfairly targeted schools located in predominantly black neighborhoods or closed schools that forced black children to undertake longer bus rides. The suit was unsuccessful, although the school district did later reopen Cora Kelly Elementary School in the Lynhaven neighborhood.

The African American community's focus on the racial geography of schooling rather than the academic quality of the classes for African American students emerged, in part, because of increasing tension between new Superintendent John Bristol and Alexandria's black residents. Bristol's style was far less politic than that of John Albohm, whom he replaced in July, 1977. Within seven months of his arrival, Bristol had proposed the closure of two elementary schools in predominantly black neighborhoods at the end of the school year.[85] The 6-3 vote to close the schools saw all three African American board members vote against Bristol's proposal and sparked a testy exchange between Board member Shirley Tyler and Bristol. One School Board member later complained to a reporter, "I don't think he understands the complexity of the community. I don't think he understands the needs of the black community, the needs of the foreign-born community."[86]

Bristol further revealed his tin ear when he proposed additional consolidation of Alexandria schools, this time scrapping the 6-2-2-2 plan pushed through by Albohm only eight years earlier. Bristol's plan would have reverted back to two conventional four-year high schools, abandoning the notion of a single, unifying high school for the city. Many members of the community were appalled by his suggestion: "The plan he proposed shocked the community," one activist told a reporter. "It showed a disregard for the history of the community."[87] The Board ultimately rejected Bristol's plan and moved the tenth grade into T.C. Williams, and made two traditional junior highs of seventh through ninth grade. In the course of doing so, however, the Board also closed Parker-Gray Middle School—the last remaining connection to the all-black high school in Alexandria.

Within a year of Bristol's proposal to move away from a single, unified high school, he announced his resignation from ACPS. Bill Euille, an African American member of the school board (and later Mayor of Alexandria), commented at the time, "I suspect he was not cut out for the pressures of Alexandria." Euille added "he never understood why blacks objected to two schools in black neighborhoods being closed at the same time. He can be a personable man, and not a racist, but he could be insensitive at times."[88]

Given these symbolic and real contests over the schools, communities, and neighborhoods, it is not surprising that the prevalence of tracking and the continuing segregation of educational expectations were left unaddressed. But the effects of a racialized special education system, a predominantly white gifted and talented program, and de facto tracking of all children beginning in elementary school were clearly apparent when, in 1985, Superintendent Robert Peebles announced, for the first time in Alexandria's history, the results of standardized tests by race: White eleventh-graders scored at the 75th percentile nationally on tests for reading, math, and language arts, while black eleventh-graders scored at the 27th percentile.[89] While the eleventh grade figures showed the greatest disparities, across all grades tested white Alexandria students averaged thirty-seven points higher than black Alexandria students. School officials admitted they had known about the disparities for quite some time, but Peebles decided to release the figures to spark a public debate on the matter: "It's unfortunate we still have vestiges of the old days and the old ways in Alexandria. Some Alexandrians, both black and white, still assume that poor kids—black poor kids, specifically—cannot learn; that they cannot succeed in school. This must change . . . We must assume that every child can learn."[90] Black leaders in the community contended however that more than an attitude shift was needed: "Because of political pressures," said Urban League member Melvin Miller, "Alexandria public schools are designed to educate white students. The board responds to the needs of white, upper-class students."[91] Board Member Lou Cook took offense at Miller's claim, calling his comments "insulting." Cook did acknowledge, however, that some teachers did not hold the same expectations for black students as they did for white students: "It is wrong to expect any less from blacks. But because this is not a perfect world, yes, some [teachers] do."[92]

Two weeks after Miller and Cook's exchange, Alexandria City Public Schools announced an expansion of its gifted and talented program. This program would, for the first time, start in kindergarten, providing enriched instruction for selected children in kindergarten through third grade in all ten elementary schools. According to news reports, "Final selection [for the program] will be based on such factors as high SRA test scores in reading and math, class work, teacher and parent evaluations and IQ."[93] No mention was made of racial diversity.

Conclusion: Growing Budgets, Declining Enrollments, Happy Constituents

The creation and growth of special education in Alexandria cannot be examined without reference to race. Whether one examines the origins of the program, the creation of gifted and talented programs, or the district's continuing racial disparities in special needs identification, race has played a central role in the Alexandria's implementation of the federal mandate to educate all children. At the same time, however, the receptivity of local officials to the array of programs needed to meet that mandate emerged, in significant part, because of growing local demand in Alexandria for more social services. Special education appealed to two constituencies in particular: an increasingly liberal electorate who wanted more social spending on children who needed additional services, and parents anxious about the effects that integration would have on lowered academic standards. The latter group was, in particular, appeased by a rapid growth in a gifted and talented program and the maintenance of significant tracking within Alexandria schools.

By the mid-1980s, Alexandria's reluctance to adopt programs of special education was overcome by two factors: a growing local political support for the programs and continuing federal pressure to provide these programs. Local school officials used that federal pressure to create a bifurcated system that provided more assistance to students with special needs, but increasingly exposed students to profoundly different educational expectations and experiences. Because holding on to parents who could either move or send their children to private school was a constant concern of school officials, special education—both "gifted" programs and programs for learning disabilities—offered school officials a way to reconcile those conflicting pressures.

The result was a kind of grand compromise that reconciled federal mandates to provide services to special needs children and local demands to ensure high-achieving students received demanding courses and enrichment. A few charts illustrate these trends and their connection to changes in locale electorate, described in Chapter Four. Figure 5.1 shows the percentage of Alexandria students who were identified as special needs students between 1983 and 2009. Although numbers of special needs students are not readily available until 1983, we see that for the first five years of data, the percentage hovers around 12 to 13 percent of all students. Beginning in 1988, however, there is an enormous spike in the percentage of students identified as special needs, jumping from 13 percent in 1988 to 21 percent in 1990. This increase was, apparently, not related to federal reauthorization of

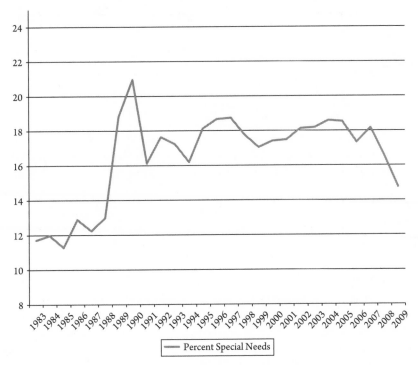

Figure 5.1 Percentage of enrollment indentified as special needs, Alexandria, 1983–2009.
Source: City of Alexandria, Virginia. Department of Finance and U.S. Department of Education,
Common Core of Data

the Education for All Handicapped Children Act in 1990 (redubbed the Individuals with Disabilities Education Act (IDEA)), as the Alexandria spike begins in 1989 and the percentage of special needs students actually drops in 1991, the first year of the IDEA's implementation. And the increase is large: this 1988–1990 change represents nearly a 60 percent increase in the number of students identified with special needs in Alexandria over a two-year period.

Just prior to this jump in the number of special needs students, the per pupil expenditures in Alexandria started to take off. Between 1986 and 1990, the per pupil expenditures in Alexandria increased from $10,673 to $13,607 (in constant dollars), a real growth of over 27 percent in four years. This increase was not the result of state funding increases, as Virginia's formula for school funding provided little money to affluent districts in Northern Virginia. Instead, it appears that the liberalization of Alexandria's politics in the early 1980s, detailed in Chapter 4, was starting to change the local regime's spending patterns.

So, with declining enrollments, per pupil expenditures were rising and special needs populations were growing, at times dramatically. Yet there was little political outcry over this additional expenditure. Part of the answer lies in the changing nature of education within Alexandria's budgetary politics. Figure 5.3 shows the percentage of Alexandria's budget that is devoted to local schools. This percentage

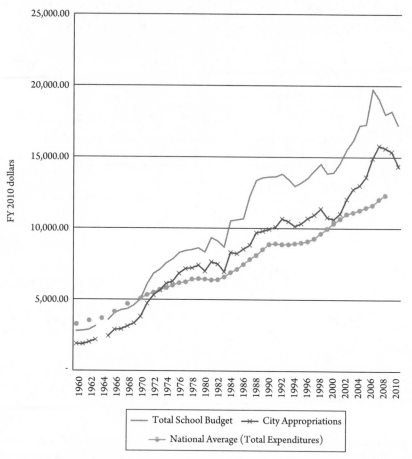

Figure 5.2 Per pupil expenditures in Alexandria, 1960–2010. Source: City of Alexandria. Office of Management and Budget. Annual Budget. (enrollment data missing for 1964) and National Center for Education Statistics, Digest of Education Statistics, Table 190.

peaked in 1970, when the fullest effects of the baby boom were felt. As enrollments declined from their peak in 1970, we see a corresponding decline in the percentage of local educational expenditures within the city's total budget, dropping from 40 percent to around 27 percent. In the mid-1980s that figure jumps around a bit before climbing steadily in the 1990s, back up to around 33 percent. Thus, at the time that per pupil expenditures were rising, public education was increasingly making less of a claim, on a percentage basis, on Alexandria's coffers.

This suggests two things: First, Alexandria was expanding its other local services at a relatively fast clip during the late 1970s and 1980s and education was in an unusual position of having more per pupil resources available even as its share of the city budget dropped. Second, this relative decline in the overall importance of

Figure 5.3 Percentage of Alexandria's general fund to schools. Source: City of Alexandria, Office of Management and Budget. Annual Report.

education in the city's budget gave officials more political space to be more generous to public education. Since the mid-1970s, Alexandria has consistently been either the highest or second-highest spending district in the Washington, DC metropolitan area. Yet at the same time, the City of Alexandria has increasingly been able to bear that cost without sacrificing other city services.

From a purely fiscal perspective, the federal demand that schools provide more resources to special needs students came at a time of fiscal stress for many school districts, particularly since the additional federal dollars under IDEA often did not cover the cost of additional services. In Alexandria, however, the local regime's increasingly liberal views after 1980 meant that the attention to special needs students found a receptive home, even if the district was unable to overcome its race-based practices of using special education as a disciplinary device and often exacerbated a black-white test score gap by providing unequal opportunities to learn to white and minority students.

In sum, Alexandria's struggle to adopt a program of special education was marked initially by both racial resistance and financial resistance. Not until the local regime incorporated African Americans into the governing coalition, becoming more liberal in the process, was there widespread local acceptance of the federal imperative to extend special education services to all students who needed them. Even then, the persistence of a racial divide within Alexandria's curricular offerings and learning environments was pronounced, despite the additional resources that special education afforded some students. The intersection of the federal drive to integrate schools with local perceptions of school quality and educational standards held radiating implications for other forms of educational opportunity for all kinds of students across the local landscape. The next chapter turns to an examination of how immigrant students fared within a similar context—one in which the federal demand for better schooling was far weaker, even contradictory.

6

From Arlandria to
Chirilagua: English-Learners and the
Catch-22 Education State

Introduction: Making Room to Be Brown

In the preface to his book *White Scourge: Mexican, Blacks and Poor Whites in Texas Cotton Culture*, historian Neil Foley reflects on his upbringing in Alexandria: "Growing up in Alexandria, Virginia, in the suburbs of Washington, DC, during the 1950s and 1960s, I realized that however one might characterize the federal city, it was not then a multiracial city. Like the rest of the South, its culture was black and white." He adds that his Mexican mother, witnessing the treatment of African Americans in Virginia and DC, had to convince shopkeepers and neighbors that she was white, "not exactly Anglo, of course, but white nonetheless." The racial polarity of Washington, DC and Virginia—its racial lens of blackness and whiteness—made Foley's mother keenly aware that she was unable to be who she had been in the Southwest, a *mexicana*: "There simply was no room to be brown in a black-and-white city."[1]

This chapter is about the invisibility of being brown in Alexandria and how that invisibility has affected the educational outcomes for immigrant youth, who are predominantly, but not exclusively, Latino. The absence of political and social incorporation of immigrant interests into the local political structure has roots in both the immigration patterns into the Washington, DC area and the politically debilitating effects of federal immigration policy. Both local and national political contexts of immigration pose significant obstacles for the incorporation of newly arrived immigrants into US society, particularly for undocumented students, and both local and national political practices impose barriers to immigrant youth that have a direct bearing on their educational achievement. The federal education policies that most affect immigrant youth emerge from the federal government's modest commitment to provide additional resources for districts with English-learners. Scholars who study educational policy about English-learners typically focus on classroom and school-level issues because those are the things that education officials most directly control. But what happens in classrooms and in schools is mediated by the processes of inclusion and incorporation within the broader community. Without paying attention to the political and social incorporation of English-learners and their families into local communities, scholars and educational policy analysts often miss important features of the education state.

This chapter seeks to redress that gap by examining the implementation of federal policies regarding English-learners in Alexandria and how the political incorporation (or lack thereof) of immigrants within the local political regime delimits the effectiveness of those federal educational policies. Simultaneously, the chapter will explore how immigrants' political and educational engagement highlights the inadequacies of federal policies relating to the education of English-learners.

The argument is that the educational experiences of immigrant students are the product of a contradictory commitment to building an education state that can address the needs of immigrant children and English-learners.[2] Despite the growing numbers of immigrant students needing English language services, both local and federal actors have insufficiently developed administrative or institutional routines to address their needs, but for different reasons. At the federal level, the policy demands on locals to devise effective educational strategies for English-learners have been weak and tepid, primarily because a deep federal ambivalence over language policies in the United States. At the local level, the insecure political status of the undocumented has suppressed their local political expression and their ability to make political demands on local school officials. To the extent that Alexandria has responded to the educational needs of immigrant students it has done so because school-level accountability requirements under No Child Left Behind ignore the legal status of English language learners. All students—whether documented or undocumented, English-learner or English-proficient—must meet a common definition of proficiency. Yet the same federal policies that arose under the move toward greater "accountability" (described in further detail in Chapter 8) have created a punitive educational environment that inhibits the kinds of relationships necessary for successful education outcomes for English-learners and immigrant students, more broadly.

The result is a kind of catch-22 educational state: federal educational accountability policies regarding students who do not speak English demand results, but they do not provide structure or meaningful resources. At the same time, many of those same English-learners and their families confront a precarious immigration status that renders it difficult for them to make meaningful demands on the local regime, demands for resources and inclusion that are integral to achieving educational results. The nonincorporation of immigrants into the local regime—despite their numerical presence in Alexandria—makes them politically invisible, but their educational underachievement defines them as a policy problem, a problem hard to resolve without a local political incorporation. The challenges of becoming part of the local governing regime means, educationally, that the ability of immigrants and English-learner families to secure policies that aid their children is highly attenuated.

The lens of English-learners offers a particularly rich perspective on the development of the education state because the concerns of the nation-state are so clearly implicated in the incorporation of new immigrants. In addition, the symbolic and practical dimensions of English language skills tap directly into debates over US immigration and educational policies. Despite the clear connections between the English language and state concerns, the federal government has relied overwhelmingly on local districts (probably more so than with any other federal education initiative) to identify, assess, and teach new immigrants both language and civic skills, simply assuming that school districts have the administrative capacity—and political willingness—to do so. As the demographics of US schools have changed, and the percentage of English-learners has increased, the federal government has been unable to devise either immigration or educational policies that will successfully address the educational needs of these students, highlighting the very partial nature of the education state in the age of accountability. Indeed, among the four policy domains examined in this book—racial integration, special education, English-learners, and accountability policies—it is in the development and delivery of schooling for English-learners that we see the education state in its most fragmented and ineffective form. The level of government that ought to be most concerned about processes of inclusion of immigrant children (the federal government), for a variety of reasons, has not adequately addressed the issue. At the same time, the level of government that has the greatest understanding of the needs of these children lacks the political incentives to meet those needs. The result is fragmentation, incoherence, and a joint failure to educate.

This chapter explores these issues in five sections. The first section, "The Historical Place of Bilingualism in American Education and Federal Policies for English-Learners," recounts the historical development of bilingual education in the United States and the limited nature of federal involvement in bilingual education. The second section, "Washington, DC as an Immigration Gateway and the Emergence of Arlandria-Chirilagua", examines Washington, DC's emergence as a gateway for recent immigrants, particularly the influx of Central American political refugees in the mid-1980s. The section focuses on transformation of a northern slice of Alexandria, formerly known as Arlandria, into what many now call Chirilagua, a predominantly Salvadoran and Latino neighborhood. In "English-Learners and the Challenges of Inclusion" the chapter explores the educational challenges these new immigrants and their children confronted, both nationally and in Alexandria, as well as the history of local mobilization efforts to overcome the invisibility of Alexandria's English-learners. The next section, "English-Learners and the Policy Legacies of Jim Crow" turns to the early twenty-first century condition of Alexandria's programs for English-learners, examining the school district's efforts to devise programs for these students, policies that often tap into long-standing community complaints about racial isolation of Latino and African American students.

A few words about terminology: In this chapter, I refer to "English as a second language" (ESL) programs and bilingual programs. There are many variations of both, but the primary distinction between the two is whether a program uses a child's first language as the foundation for instruction, both for academic content and English language. ESL programs generally do not do this, relying either on immersion within the regular, English-speaking classroom and additional "pull-out" or "push-in" services, or using a "sheltered immersion" approach which separates non-English speakers for a portion of the day to provide them both with English language instruction and, typically, watered-down content instruction. In contrast, bilingual instruction relies on first language skills to teach or bolster literacy and also to teach English and academic content. The use of first language may be short-term or long-term or it may involve a dual-language immersion in which children are taught in two languages (typically Spanish and English). This latter approach also has the virtue of enriching the education of native English speakers by teaching a second language at an early age.[3] No matter what kind of program a child is in, I refer to the child as an English-learner.

The Historical Place of Bilingualism in American Education and Federal Policies for English-Learners

Bilingual education has rich and long social and policy history in the United States. The local organization of public education beginning in the mid-nineteenth century and the regional concentrations of immigrant groups often ensured that schools would provide instruction in children's native language. Bilingualism as a means of facilitating the "Americanization" of immigrants was a widely accepted educational practice; the mid-nineteenth century American Midwest was, in the words of one author, "a virtual heyday of dual-language instruction."[4] In Texas, public funds paid for "bilingual education for Tejanos from the advent of the public school system until the nativist hysteria of World War I."[5] Across the Midwest, cities like Cincinnati, St. Louis, Milwaukee, and Indianapolis—all with large immigrant populations and strong traditions of local rule—emerged as centers of public bilingual schooling in nineteenth century America. These city schools enrolled thousands of immigrant students in both German language elementary schools and dual-language programs. In rural Wisconsin, Iowa, and Minnesota, Norwegians created schools that preserved their heritage language and cultural legacies.

The emergence of these schools—and the favorable legal and regulatory frameworks allowing their spread—frequently hinged on the political acceptance of new immigrants. Indeed, the simultaneous development of public schooling and the arrival of German immigrants across the Midwest meant that immigrants were "cofounders and partners" of the emergent school system.[6] Immigrants' role in the development of local institutions "facilitated the emergence of numerous state school laws that actually encouraged bilingual instruction."[7] In many cities, educationally progressive German immigrants felt that without dual-language instruction, US schools would be inferior to schools in Germany and they insisted on bilingual schools to ensure a high-quality public education. Other cities, such as St. Louis, with established school systems, offered German language instruction as way to lure immigrant families out of parochial schools. Thus, in the mid-nineteenth century United States, bilingual education assured immigrants that their children would receive a form of schooling that resonated with their linguistic and cultural practices, but also signaled to new immigrants that their participation in public life was welcome and needed.[8]

The localist orientation of schooling also meant that as attitudes toward the political and social desirability of immigrants and immigration changed, local public schools would be the sites of new, frequently hostile, and intolerant forms of "Americanization." In the more reactionary and hostile environment of the post-World War I era, many states and cities imposed "English-Only" requirements on teachers and school officials in an effort to strip out residual "un-American" traits of new immigrants. Political support for German language, in particular, or dual-language programs collapsed rapidly. Indeed, many states emulated Nebraska's example, which went so far as to ban any instruction using foreign languages, in both public and private schools.[9] (Nebraska also limited the teaching of foreign languages to children beyond the eighth grade). This effort was only put to a stop by the U.S. Supreme Court in 1923 when it declared in *Meyer v. Nebraska* that Nebraska's ban on German language instruction at all private schools violated the due process rights of students and school officials alike.[10]

Despite *Meyer v. Nebraska*, the growth of English-only practices reflected more explicit and intolerant forms of Americanization in schools that treated the speaking of a foreign language as a threat to American identity and the full inclusion of immigrants within US political institutions and society. Schools throughout the United States turned to an idea of assimilation premised on the eradication of foreign traits, practices, and attitudes that were "un-American." In their place, students would be exposed to norms of democratic participation, patriotic loyalty, anti-Communism, hard work, and the value of a common language (English) as a marker of a common intellectual and sociolegal tradition. In Texas, at the height of anti-German sentiment during World War I, one state legislator argued that "all immigrants, citizen or not, should be made to speak English to prove their Americanism." Indeed, he urged local officials that "Americanism should be taught in public schools, the same as arithmetic or geography."[11] The ethos of the early twentieth century attitude toward the need to use public education as a process of Americanization is encapsulated in the comments of a speaker at the National Education Association meeting in 1903: "The kindergarten age marks our earliest opportunity to catch the little Italian, the little German, Pole, Syrian, and the rest, and begin to make good American citizens of them."[12]

The most robust versions of Americanization urged the adoption of an "English-only" pedagogy, a curricular development that had long-lasting effects on the teaching of languages in US schools, even as overt hostility to particular immigrant groups faded. This pedagogy, according to historian Kevin Carlos Blanton, was premised on the notion that translation weakened the ability of children to learn a new language, so that simultaneous exposure to two languages only delayed or, worse, prevented the acquisition of English. The result was an emphasis on linguistic isolation to foster the ability to "think in English." Writes Blanton, "One teacher from San Marcos wrote that inability to think in English would always render Mexican Americans mentally handicapped.... Another teacher put it succinctly: 'Never give the Spanish word first for we do not wish the children to translate from Spanish to English, but to think in English.'"[13]

The pedagogical need to control exposure to languages other than English had a radiating effect outside the classroom. Blanton quotes an El Paso superintendent who sought to limit all student expressions in Spanish during school hours: "English must be used not only in the classrooms but also in the corridors and on the premises." Any Mexican American student who neglects "or is willfully indifferent or is defiant in the observation of this rule ... should be suspended from school." All this was done to help "Spanish-speaking students become acquainted with English."[14] When the strict English-only pedagogy intersected with both cultural disapproval of Mexican American students and a clear articulation of racial and ethnic hierarchies, the effects were devastating. According to Blanton, in the 1940s, the annual enrollments of Mexican American students across Texas dropped precipitously between first and second grade, with the second grade population of Mexican American students roughly half the size of the first grade population. Blanton calls this reduction "a staggering statistical anomaly that can only suggest a shocking failure or dropout rate. Most Tejano children were not getting past the first grade in one year."[15] The resulting retention of first graders confirmed existing stereotypes of Mexican Americans, and gave school officials an excuse to segregate Mexican Americans in separate schools for ostensibly pedagogical, rather than racial or ethnic, reasons.

Not until the 1960s did the United States see an official reconceptualization of the value of bilingual classrooms. Building on a wave of research that highlighted the gross inadequacies of English-only approaches to language acquisition, federal officials funded projects to train teachers in new methods of language instruction. These efforts gained a significant boost under President Lyndon Johnson, who himself had taught an English-only pedagogy at a segregated, Mexican American elementary school in Cotulla, Texas in the late 1920s.[16] With Johnson's encouragement, Senator Ralph Yarborough from Texas introduced the Bilingual Education Act in January 1967. Signed into law by President Johnson a year later, the law provided financial assistance to school districts that provided language instruction to poor, non-English-speaking students. While it was the first federal legislation directly aimed at bilingual education, the act was not an ambitious one. Instead, it simply declared that it was "the policy of the United States to provide financial assistance to local educational agencies to develop and carry out new and imaginative programs" for students with limited English-speaking ability.[17] The federal legislation did not, however, require any school district to provide any particular level of assistance or even to devise programs to meet the needs of these students. Indeed, "no particular program, approach or methodology was recommended."[18] Instead, the law simply extended money to districts if they sought to develop programs.

Another ambiguity, however, hampered the Bilingual Education Act of 1968 from its inception. Beyond the limited nature of its funding and the absence of any means to compel school districts to offer services to English-learners, a more fundamental question about the goal of these services was unaddressed.[19] Left unresolved was the tension between the goals of rapid acquisition of English and the maintenance and development of a student's native language. These two contrasting perspectives are important because they reveal sharply different views on the nature of inclusion, assimilation, and incorporation of new immigrants into the United States. For some, a student's learning and use of English, particularly in a public sphere such as a school, is a necessary task for successful assimilation into contemporary US society. For others, the shift to the English language means the loss of linguistic diversity and, along with it, the loss of cultural identity and the ability to navigate a bicultural or multicultural world. The goal of most bilingual programs is to sustain and develop a child's ability to speak, write, and read in her or his native language, while also teaching English. Opponents of bilingual programs see this goal as problematic, even illegitimate; for them, to maintain a native language is to delay or even prevent a child's incorporation into "real" American society, which they explicitly define as English-speaking. Left out of this debate, initially, was the central question of whether either approach better contributed to the educational success of students.[20] In short, the Bilingual Education Act—and its checkered history—reflected a fundamental tension over the federal role in the education of English language-learners: "an unresolved conflict between bilingual education as a means of smoothing children's transition into English language instruction or as a vehicle for the maintenance of their native language and culture."[21]

The lack of any compulsory element to the Bilingual Act of 1968, combined with the limited amount of funding available, allowed this fundamental conflict to simmer for a few years among educational professionals and policymakers, without sparking much public controversy.[22] That quiet phase ended in 1974 when the U.S. Supreme Court handed down the landmark decision of *Lau v. Nichols*. Prior to *Lau*, the 1968 Bilingual Education Act had enabled local districts to apply for federal funds, but the law provided no mechanism by which the federal government could *require* states or districts to provide bilingual instruction.[23] The *Lau* decision, however, imposed on school districts a legal obligation to provide educational services to meet the needs of language minority students.

The case emerged out of San Francisco, where school officials had provided no additional services to over 1,800 students who spoke only Chinese. Ruling that failure to take into account the linguistic abilities of students amounted to unlawful discrimination on the basis of national origin, Justice Douglas wrote that "there is no equality of treatment merely by providing students with the same facilities, textbooks, teachers, and curriculum; for students who do not understand English are effectively foreclosed from any meaningful education."[24] Although the U.S. Supreme Court did not impose any particular remedy, the ruling nonetheless declared that not providing services to students who did not speak English violated Title VI of the Civil Rights Act. Neither the ruling nor the earlier 1970 Office of Civil Rights memorandum that *Lau* upheld required claimants to show intentional discrimination, only that the impact of the existing district policies harmed non-English-speaking students.

With the *Lau* decision, two tracks now existed for the federal government to foster, encourage, even require programs for English learners. The statutory track—exemplified by the Bilingual Education Act—offered resources to school districts that created bilingual programs, while the civil rights track—based on *Lau* and Title VI of the Civil Rights Act of 1964—compelled local districts to provide services.[25] Within a year, the Office of Civil Rights in the Department of Health, Education and Welfare had promulgated a set of guidelines to help the hundreds of school districts that offered no services to English-learners comply with the *Lau* decision. These "*Lau* Remedies," as they came to be known, specified a set of practices that, if school districts adopted them, would meet the requirements of *Lau* and the 1964 Civil Rights Act. Importantly, the *Lau* Remedies required districts that had violated the rights of linguistic minorities to provide bilingual instruction for elementary students who speak little or no English.[26] Between 1975 and 1980, the *Lau* Remedies formed the basis for negotiating consent decrees with nearly 500 school districts across the country that previously had not offered services to English-learners.[27]

At roughly the same time, Congress set about reauthorizing the Bilingual Education Act. This time, the supporters of bilingual education secured language that placed the federal government more firmly behind the promotion of bilingual programs to address the needs of English-learners. The 1974 reauthorization emphasized that native language and heritage were important, even essential, to the learning of English, and, for the first time, restricted federal funds to programs that used a bilingual approach. In addition, Congress substantially increased both the authorization and appropriations for the Bilingual Education Act.[28] Both *Lau* and the 1974 reauthorization of the Bilingual Education Act marked, however, the high water mark for federal support for programs that used a student's native language as a primary means of teaching English.

Part of the backlash against bilingual programs emerged, ironically, from the civil rights community, which saw native language programs less as a culturally responsive mode of teaching English than as a means of segregating students—frequently Latino or students of color—from white, English-speaking students. In the 1977 Congressional hearings over the reauthorization of the Bilingual Education Act, political scientist Gary Orfield testified that "In a society where Spanish-surname children are now more segregated than blacks . . . a program that tends to increase separation raises serious questions."[29] Combined with a scholarly dispute over the effectiveness of bilingual programs to hasten the acquisition of English, concerns about segregation and "separatism" (particularly among Latino students) led Congress in 1978 to emphasize that federally funded programs should use native language instruction "to the extent necessary to allow a child to achieve competence in the English language."[30] The focus on the acquisition of English, as opposed the maintenance of a native language, marked an important turn in US policy toward English-learners.

The *Lau* Remedies soon took a similar, but more precipitous, fall from grace. After being challenged by the state of Alaska for failing to be in compliance with the Administrative Procedures Act, the newly created Department of Education agreed to issue the *Lau* Remedies as a formal regulation. After revising the guidelines, the Department offered a proposed regulation in August 1980, holding hearings and inviting written comments. The reaction was hostile from all sides: Hispanic groups opposed what they saw as a watered-down bilingual commitment, while education groups and local districts chafed under the mandated native-language instruction. In the Washington, DC area, all the local districts formally expressed opposition to the regulations and the *Washington Post* prominently editorialized against the proposed regulation. In the end, the Department of Education pulled the regulation back, and, eventually, the newly inaugurated Reagan administration spiked the proposed regulation entirely and even abandoned the 1974 informal guidelines as well.

In their place, the Reagan Administration issued a few years later a new memorandum for language minority compliance under Title VI of the 1964 Civil Rights Act. This 1985 memo essentially allowed local districts to pursue *any* program that provides additional services to English-learners: "Any educational approach that ensures effective participation of language minority students in the district's educational program is accepted as a means of complying with Title VI requirements."[31] The memo stressed that in making the determination as to whether a district's program would be effective, the Office of Civil Rights avoided "making educational judgments or second-guessing decisions made by local educational officials." It would consider, however, "whether the program has been determined to be a sound educational program by *at least some experts* in the field."[32] Given the academic controversies raging in the mid-1980s over the effectiveness of bilingual and ESL modes of instruction for English-learners, virtually any program could secure the support of at least some experts.

By this time, the political climate over bilingual education and immigration more broadly was increasingly fractious, even hostile. In 1985, newly installed Secretary of Education William Bennett termed the Bilingual Education Act a "failure."[33] The 1984 and 1988 reauthorizations of the Bilingual Education Act limited the duration of grants for funding for bilingual programs to three years and slashed funds from the bill. Real spending under the Bilingual Education Act dropped by 47 percent between 1980 and 1988.[34] The 1988 reauthorization also saw the creation of a new category of programs that relied solely on monolingual English instruction to deliver services to some English-learners. Combined with the growth of the English-only movement, and state-level attacks against bilingual education in the 1990s, the climate for using native language to not only learn English but to maintain an existing language was dismal at best.[35]

NCLB and English-Learners

With the enactment of No Child Left Behind in 2001, federal policy moved substantially away from supporting bilingual education programs, even though, on its face, NCLB seemed to assure greater attention to the needs of English-learners. With annual assessments in math and reading, schools had to demonstrate that students with "limited English proficiency" (along with other designated subgroups) were making annual progress toward statewide proficiency benchmarks. This accountability mechanism, supporters argued, would force schools to pay attention to a group that they had long ignored. Moreover, under NCLB the federal funding mechanism for English-learner programs completely changed.[36] No longer would districts seek support to fund particular programs through a grant-in-aid process, but money would be allocated to states through a formula based on the percentage of English-learners within a state's school-age population. States would then pass this on to local districts, based on the numbers of English-learners within a district.[37] Additionally, Title III of NCLB required states, for the first time, to set standards for the development of English language proficiency aligned to the standards in reading and language arts that native English speakers had to meet in order to be deemed proficient. That is, the measurement of an English learner's proficiency in English had to be aligned to the academic skills and tasks in reading and English language arts that NCLB required all students to demonstrate.

These three elements of NCLB, at first glance, seemed to improve the educational environments of English-learners, providing districts with more resources and striving to ensure that the English language instruction that they were receiving was the kind of "academic English" they needed to succeed in school. Unfortunately, the accountability framework of NCLB itself created a whole series of perverse incentives that effectively removed bilingual programs—particularly those aimed at native language supports—from the nation's schools and fostered the growth of more English-only or "structured immersion" strategies that did little to maintain a student's native language.

These effects emerged, in short, because NCLB required that all students take a common set of state-level assessments, even if they had not yet mastered the language in which the test was given. The law then held schools accountable for the inability of a non-native English speaker to pass a test given in English. Typically, English-learners are allowed one year of English services before being subject to NCLB-mandated assessments. But from that point forward, all English-learners had to take the same content tests as native English-speaking students. Then, if a school did not meet the "percent proficient" targets for Limited English Proficient (LEP) students (or any other subgroup) for two consecutive years, it had to undergo a series of "corrective actions," which were progressively intrusive. The school could eventually be closed.

Given these high-stakes outcomes on NCLB-mandated tests, the incentives to maintain native languages among English learners are virtually nonexistent. Bilingual programs do not always show the same short-term growth in English skills that ESL programs do, but their long-term effects can be impressive, particularly for dual-language immersion programs that split instructional time between English and another language during the school day or week.[38] As one review of NCLB's effects on language policies in schools concluded, "Because NCLB does not permit the time required for bilingual programs to reach fruitful outcomes, many schools respond to testing pressures by eliminating their bilingual programs and replacing them with ESL programs in which instruction is solely in English."[39] For example, in New York City between 2003 and 2011, the percentage of students enrolled in transitional bilingual programs dropped from 37.4 percent of English learners to 18.5 percent, while the percentage of students in English as a Second Language programs increased from 53.4 percent to 70.2 percent.[40]

Beyond its effects on bilingual programs, the accountability structure of NCLB effectively made it nearly impossible for schools with high percentages of English-learners to make "Adequate Yearly Progress" (AYP). By definition, the category of "English-learner" is unstable: once a student gains mastery of English, he or she is no longer classified as an English-*learner*, and is moved into the general student population, for NCLB purposes.[41] At the same time, as new English-learners enter the school system, either as new immigrants to the United States or in kindergarten, they will, generally, be at lower levels of English proficiency than those who have moved out of the category because schools successfully taught them English. Thus, to expect a school to demonstrate yearly growth in the proficiency rates for a subgroup which is, by nature, annually repopulated by students at lower levels of achievement is to set that school up for failure. As one scholar put it, "even with the best resources, there is not much chance for improving the AYP indicator of the LEP subgroup over time."[42]

In short, the accountability framework of NCLB has magnified the challenges of assessing English-learners.[43] The implications of NCLB-accountability for English-learners is not lost on front-line administrators. In a U.S. Department of Education-funded study of the implementation of NCLB's Title III, the report's authors highlighted the concerns of educational officials that testing English-learners was actually impeding their ability to teach these students English. The report found that two-thirds of the officials charged with implementing Title III "expressed concern about the burden placed on teachers and staff and the loss of instruction time" due to the sheer number of proficiency and content tests imposed on English-learners. Over half of those respondents also "raised concerns about the validity of administering content-area tests in English" to English-learners before they were proficient in English.[44]

The implementation study also noted that many officials at the state and local level wanted and needed more information about the best strategies for helping English-learners succeed in the classroom, with over 40 percent of officials in the study's Title III districts reporting that the "lack of proven curricula and programs" for English-learners was a "moderate or major challenge." The focus groups convened by the report authors found that many district leaders and school staff "felt they had limited information about the effectiveness of their programs."[45]

Finally, it is important to note the meager funding the federal government contributes to the language services for English-learners. While English-learners account for roughly 10 percent of the total enrollment in US schools, the federal government pays states less than $150 per English-learner to meet the statutory obligations under Title III.[46] Given this low level of funding, it is in state and local districts' interests to either minimize the number of relatively "expensive" English-learners or to provide only the minimal additional services needed to meet the federal obligation. As the U.S. Department of Education's own implementation study noted, while district officials "appreciated the [federal] Title III funds," they described them as "a rather small supplement" to the state and local funds that paid for the vast majority of services for English-learners.[47]

Taken together, these effects of NCLB on programs for English-learners have been profound. While Title III offers a more reliable funding stream, the accountability framework imposes serious sanctions on school districts for a failure to ensure that English-learners are achieving at the same level as the general student population. At the same time, the structure of that framework makes it almost a certainty that English-learners *won't* achieve at the same level as the general student population, primarily by annually recomposing the subgroup and by insisting that all content tests be administered in English. The combination of NCLB, limited federal financial assistance, and limited or no guidance regarding the best practices for the instruction of non-English-speaking students[48] produces a false sense of rigor, one in which the federal government imposes punitive sanctions for failing to meet an assessment target that grows more and more remote every year and for which it has no advice or recommendation on how that target can be met.

As these federal policies hit the ground in particular locales, they must contend with a dizzying array of circumstances: different languages, concentrations of immigrants, local tolerances for immigrants, and local practices of political incorporation of new groups. In Alexandria, the issue of English-learners in public schools was not on the radar until the 1980s, when a rapidly growing DC metropolitan area saw a large influx of Central American, Asian and African immigrants. Those local patterns of settlement and reception were key to how the Alexandria City Public Schools advanced the federal aims of improving education for English-learners.

Washington, DC as an Immigration Gateway and the Emergence of Arlandria-Chirilagua

The 1980s brought many things to Washington: Ronald Reagan to the White House, rising fame for Chuck Brown's go-go music, and hundreds of thousands of immigrants to the Washington, DC metropolitan area. All left their imprint on the city, but the influx of immigration was perhaps the most dramatic. Because it lacked an industrial base that provided jobs to low-skilled workers, Washington, DC historically had never been a major gateway for new immigrants to the United States. In the 1980s, however, undocumented migrants fleeing civil wars in Central America, and legal migrants from across the world seeking reunification with their families drove DC area immigration to unprecedented heights. Between 1980 and 2000, the immigrant population in the metro area grew threefold, from 256,000 in 1980 to over 830,000 in 2000; during the same years, the overall population in the DC area grew 42 percent.[49]

The bulk of this immigration took place in the suburbs as lower-cost housing, a booming service sector, and plentiful construction jobs drew in thousands of residents born abroad. New suburban gateway locales emerged as the patterns of immigrant settlement changed. Metrowide, this new population hailed from over 193 countries, with 75 percent coming from thirty nations. In particular, Fairfax and Arlington Counties in Virginia, along with Alexandria, saw an amazingly diverse set of immigrants arrive within a few short years. In Alexandria alone, the foreign-born share of the population grew by 200 percent between 1980 and 2000, jumping from 10,868 to 32,600 according to U.S. Census figures,[50] with El Salvador and Ethiopia as the two single largest sending nations, at 18.0 and 7.5 percent of new Alexandria immigrants in 2000, respectively.

While not all of these new suburban immigrants settled into geographic enclaves, in Alexandria many of the newly arriving Salvadorans took up residence in the affordable garden apartment complexes on the northern edge of Alexandria, a portion of the city known as Arlandria. Many of those residents hailed from a single Salvadoran

village, Chirilagua, an area deeply contested by rebel and government forces during the Salvadoran civil war. Within a few short years, Arlandria was transformed
from a predominantly African American neighborhood— which had experienced
rapid white, working-class flight in the early 1970s—to a largely Latino neighborhood populated by Salvadorans, Hondurans, Guatemalans, and Nicaraguans. One
press account described the neighborhood as 80 percent Latino by 1986, with over
5,000 natives of Chirilagua, El Salvador living in Arlandria-Chirilagua by 1999.[51]
Even after they had moved on to other parts of the DC area, many Salvadorans
regarded Arlandria-Chirilagua as part of "back home." According to Jorge Chicas,
head chef at DC's high-end Zaytinya restaurant, Arlandria-Chirilagua is "where so
many [Salvadorans] land when they come to this country. And no matter if they
move on to Woodbridge or Rockville, they come back here to shop. They say, 'Hey,
I'm dealing with my people.' "[52]

While a strong sense of community can serve as a resource and a comfort
for new migrants, it could also reflect the isolation many Salvadorans felt in the
United States. In part, the tight-knit feel of Arlandria-Chirilagua emerged because
so many of the Salvadoran immigrants to DC were undocumented. Fleeing a brutal civil war, these residents were, for the most part, denied official refugee status
by the US government; indeed, only 3 percent of Salvadorans immigrants were
granted political refugee status.[53] The rest were left in legal limbo, a status complicated by the granting of "Temporary Protected Status" (TPS) in 1991 to civil war
refugees that temporarily allowed undocumented Salvadorans to live and work
in the United States, but not to sponsor the immigration of family members. This
halfway legal status for many Salvadorans in the United States, combined with
high rates of poverty and low levels of education, meant that they confronted
real obstacles to both political and civic membership within the United States.
Indeed, for many Salvadorans, the creation and maintenance of transnational
ties to communities in El Salvador served as a replacement to a fuller civic incorporation here in the United States. According to Raúl Sánchez Molina, "Being
excluded from refugee status has made it more and more difficult for Salvadorans
to incorporate into the host society, forcing them to develop strategies for hid-
ing in order to adapt to the social exclusions that they have to face."[54] Moreover,
Sánchez Molina writes, their "social exclusion has propelled Salvadorans settled
in Washington to deploy transnational strategies in order to overcome structural
barriers faced in the host societies."

These transnational strategies frequently involved the sending of remittances to
family members back in Central America. While this capital flow certainly provided
material benefit to family members who remained at home, it also perpetuated immigrants' poverty here in the United States. For female migrants, separated from their
children, the sense of isolation and disempowerment could be acute. One ethnogra-
pher who interviewed Honduran women living in Arlandria-Chirilagua found that
many women felt isolated in their jobs (frequently domestic or night-shift janitorial

work) and burdened by household duties, which fell to them because of traditional gender roles, even if both spouses worked. Moreover, many of these women often went years without seeing their children (who remained in Honduras), sending home remittances to help support them—payments that meant they were generally unable to save any money for retirement or emergencies.[55]

This isolation often is not always overcome if or when their children are able to join them. Children might resent having been left behind while parents migrated or feel a closer attachment to grandparents or other family members who raised them through childhood. At the same time, these children must navigate a new country and new language, often with both parents working. The result is that family dynamics, even when reunification occurs, can be complex and tense, particularly if the immigration status of family members is not regularized.

Immigrants, particularly those with children, contend with multiple forces of adjustment as they navigate their new communities. If they—or members of their families—must also worry about deportation and/or harassment by legal authorities, they are more likely to build tighter bonds within their co-ethnic community. These bonds, however, also render it more difficult for city and education officials to gain trust within these communities. In addition, new arrivals—whether documented or not—are far less likely to place demands on local officials for fear of triggering retaliatory arrests or deportation within their neighborhood (whether that fear is grounded in reality or not).

Compounding the reluctance of new migrant communities to engage public officials are the challenges they face working with other fellow immigrants. The diversity of immigrant groups that arrived in the 1980s and 1990s was staggering. A few miles west of Arlandria-Chirilagua, in the Landmark section of Alexandria, East Africans—both Ethopians and Eritreans, nations that were formerly at war—settled in large numbers. According to one tally of the U.S. 2000 Census, Alexandria, had, at 3 percent of the local population, the highest percentage of Amharic speakers of any municipality in the United States.[56] In addition, migrants from West Africa made the languages of Krio and Twi not unusual in the Alexandria Public School System. This linguistic diversity—combined with religious, cultural, and existing political divisions across immigrant communities—has made it exceptionally difficult for immigrants to band together to work for their common interests in Alexandria schools and politics.

The rapid transformation of suburban Washington, DC into an international gateway has brought into schools languages and cultures virtually unknown to area educators just a few years ago. Alexandria's Arlandria-Chirilagua is just one vivid example of a neighborhood undergoing a transformation not unlike the racial transformation of the early 1970s. This time, however, the combined efforts of federal and state authorities have not begun to address the needs of these students. The educational challenges of immigration are profound, but generally not high on the political agenda in Alexandria.

English-Learners and the Challenges of Inclusion

It must be stressed that these concerns are faced by school officials outside the Washington, DC metropolitan area, as well. Today, nationwide, one out of every five public school children in the United States was born in another country. Most of these students arrived in the United States without knowing English and often from households with low incomes and low levels of formal education. In a recent study of educational achievement among immigrant children, only one-third of the students had a mother with a high school degree or higher, and less than a quarter had a father with those educational levels.[57] The average father of a student from Mexico in the study had roughly *six* years of formal schooling.[58] In contrast, over 88 percent of the US population over the age of twenty-five in 2012 held a high school degree or higher.[59] These disparities yield an enormous gulf in parental educational expectations and even in a parent's capacity to help a child learn, placing immigrant children at a profound disadvantage relative to the rest of the school age population.

In addition, the challenges of learning a second language, while simultaneously staying on grade level in educational content, pose significant difficulties, particularly for students who arrive in middle school or high school years. Scholars of second-language acquisition in the United States estimate that it takes roughly five to seven years of concerted effort by students and schools to teach a child a second language to a fluency level that places her or him on par with native speakers.[60] Thus, depending on their age at arrival, English-learners must spend at least *one-half* of their time within US public schools simply seeking language mastery that would enable them to stay on grade level.

Compounding their challenges, immigrant students often begin their schooling below grade level, and as they devote time to acquiring English they frequently fall further behind native English speakers. In addition, the ability to acquire a second language generally hinges on the fluency and language skills a child has in his or her first language. For many immigrant children, their own schooling has been disrupted or has not provided them with the fundamentals of literacy or language skills in their native language. In many ways, the limited literacy these children possess in their native language acts as a multiplier on other obstacles they and their families confront: low levels of educational attainment within their families, the challenges of poverty and insecure employment, the social and familial dislocations that accompany crossing international borders, whether documented or undocumented—all these circumstances place many immigrant children at enormous risk for leaving school early.

For students who were not born abroad, but born in the United States, growing up in a household in which English is not spoken poses a similar set of obstacles. Many non-English-speaking households confront similar poverty and insecure work options, and while students born in the United States do not personally face insecurity because of undocumented status, many in their families frequently do.

This fact, combined with their parents' limited English skills, often places students in the awkward position of being family representatives for official encounters with school officials. The result is that family involvement in the schooling of English-learners—even among the most concerned and devoted parents—is often limited or constrained, by language, by poverty, by undocumented status, or by an inflexible employer's labor demands.

In the mid-1980s, as immigration into the DC area surged, the Alexandria school system seemed unable to recognize the changes going on around it, or at least unwilling to acknowledge that these changes required new procedures or routines for the school system. The School Board had in 1980 officially opposed the Carter Administration's efforts to formalize the *Lau* Remedies, writing to the U.S. Department of Education that its efforts to require the bilingual programs for English-learners would "be most unwise and in violation of [federal laws] which prohibit the Department from establishing a national curriculum." Moreover, the Board claimed that its existing ESL program was meeting the needs of its students, within existing budget constraints: "Limited resources demand creativity on the part of local school districts in meeting the needs of all students," according to the letter. "This creativity will be stifled or eliminated by expensive and rigid mandated programs that have unproven results."[61] Added School Board member Claudia Waller, "I am not so sure that teaching kids for years in their own language would improve their mainstreaming."[62]

Beyond the classroom, however, the School Board seemed caught unaware that a growing portion of its constituency was not fluent in English. In the midst of a 1984 effort to redraw school attendance zones, one parent, who did not speak English, asked another woman to speak on his behalf at a board meeting. According to the *Washington Post*, "It was the first time some school officials can remember that a non-English-speaking parent had made his views known to the board at public meeting."[63] During the course of the boundary reconfiguration, said James Akin, the system's acting director of elementary education, it became "obvious that many parents were having difficulty receiving [school] services and we were kind of appalled."[64]

In Alexandria, the timing of increased immigration coincided with the federal government's move toward accepting *any* program of services for English-learners. Thus, just as increasing numbers of English-learners were entering the school system, the federal government began to back off its emphasis on bilingual programs, and to encourage greater adoption of English as a Second Language programs. So while the absolute number of English-learners doubled in Alexandria between 1980 and 1990 (and the percentage of English-learners jumped from 4.5 percent to 12 percent of total enrollment), the U.S. Department of Education effectively mandated no particular program of instruction for these students, backing off its earlier use of the *Lau* Remedies. Similarly, the Bilingual Education Act increasingly encouraged, over the course the 1980s, the use of ESL programs designed to quickly mainstream English-learners. Accordingly, the stated goal of Alexandria's ESL program was "to help students develop as quickly as possible the English language and content area skills that are prerequisite to successful transition to mainstream classes."[65] To achieve this goal, ACPS employed pull-out or sheltered ESL instruction at the elementary level, and "selectively institutionalized sheltered instruction" at the secondary level.[66] The district, however, did not adopt an explicit curriculum for English-learners or any program standards for progress through ESL instruction.

A jumble of approaches, curricula, and teaching strategies resulted, all absent any clear criteria for ESL placement levels or exit levels. According to a 1999 evaluation of ESL services, "Many teachers indicated that there were not curriculum guidelines for different ESL levels and no clearly specified exit guidelines at the district level. Schools differed greatly in their instructional resources. In some schools, there were not enough materials, textbooks, teachers, and assistants. In others, there was not enough classroom space for the ESL program . . ."[67]

The report also surveyed ESL teachers and students, revealing a number of concerns about the program, particularly its marginality within the Alexandria school system. As the report's findings blandly stated, "the survey data suggests that many ESL teachers perceive the ESL program to be a low priority in the system. Other observations are that, in some schools, ESL teachers are not granted the same professional courtesy as other teachers and ESL students are not treated as equally as other American students."[68] The teacher's written comments were far more colorful. In the section of the report detailing teachers' comments, the authors clustered together two pages of comments under the heading "Program Marginality."[69] These comments expressed sharp and highly critical complaints about the organization and delivery of services to English-learners. Several teachers commented on the low regard that school and district leadership held for ESL teachers. One wrote, I "feel ESL is a marginal part of the ACPS. ESL is not a priority in ACPS," while another commented that "ESL teachers are not considered real teachers and not extended professional courtesy." Another contended that the district held "little respect for the ESL professionals," and another teacher wrote that "administrators and others consider ESL to be babysitting service and pass off problems to ESL teachers." One teacher was particularly stinging: "We are not even the least priority. We are like stepchildren."

Another set of comments focused on the differential treatment that ESL students received in Alexandria's schools, treatment that further limited their progress: "Let's not treat ESL students differently," wrote one teacher. Another commented, "Treat them like Americans, call parents, involve the guidance counselor.... ESL students should be treated with the same dignity as everyone else." Yet another stated that "ESL students should feel welcomed, receive excellent education, and be treated with the same dignity as everyone else." Some teachers also recounted episodes of personal bias against them for either being nonwhite or speaking Spanish. Wrote one teacher, "I, myself as an ESL teacher of (certain ethnic group), have always felt unwanted in the (specific) school. I don't even have a phone to communicate with parents." Another commented "In some schools, Hispanic parents have to wait for hours for somebody to talk to them. Because I communicate with students and help them understand English through their native language, I have received negative evaluations. No career for Hispanic ESL teachers here."

A number of comments explicitly invoked the political status of Latinos and immigrants within Alexandria as the rationale for the district's seeming inability to organize a coherent program for English-learners: "Students, parents and teachers [should] not be regarded as second-rate or expendable merely because majority of the population does not vote." Another teacher invoked the existing racial lenses of Alexandria officials: "Administrators do not care about the Hispanic population, everything is either black or white. You have a sense of not [being] wanted." This lack of caring, according to another speaker, spread across both students and teachers: "ACPS have no sensitivity [to]ESL population, no opportunity to [attend]professional conference[s]." The result was, to another teacher, a significant inequality in educational opportunity for English-learners: "In intermediate and advance level of ESL, students are not receiving the same quality of literature that mainstream students are offered."

These comments reveal a system in which the needs of English-learners were largely an afterthought, to be scheduled or accommodated around other needs and priorities. Lacking a coherent curriculum and standards for entry and exit into the ESL program, the services that ACPS provided to English-learners were a hodgepodge of approaches that frequently made it impossible for English-learners to receive substantive academic content while they learned English. By the time they learned sufficient English to enter the mainstream classroom they were behind grade levels and, as a result, assigned to unchallenging or remedial courses, courses that often made them ineligible for college admission.

Jon Liss, founder of Alexandria's Tenants and Workers United, a community organizing group that works with immigrants to address community needs in Northern Virginia, contended that this attitude in the mid-1980s and 1990s centered around a "politics of impermanence." According to Liss, the school system "was not really focusing" on the issues that confronted immigrant students. "They thought they were doing their jobs," but paying attention to immigrant students "was not an urgent need." According to Liss, school leaders did not see the immigrant community as a permanent element of Alexandria's landscape: "They were still operating within a black-white paradigm and that's how they conceived the world."[70] The black-white divide that structured the politics of Alexandria during those years, Liss said, left little room for immigrants and Latinos in particular. "We needed disproportionate strength to get anything done," said Liss. Patrick Welsh, a long-time T.C. Williams English teacher, described the "politics of impermanence" in a more direct way, in his profile of Latino students at T.C. Williams, written in 1991:

> The kids who scream 'go home' are merely voicing what many adults not only hope, but believe: that the Central American 'problem' in the

Washington area will disappear, that 'these people' will go home to their countries and their friends and relatives will stop coming.[71]

To contest the "politics of impermanence," Tenants and Workers United fought City Hall on a number of issues: affordable housing, labor rights, and educational opportunities for Latino and immigrant youth. One of the first organizing efforts Tenants and Workers United undertook in the schools was a student-led effort to hire bilingual counselors. Evelin Urrutia, who graduated from T.C. Williams High School in the 1990s, was one of the founders of *Grupo Juvenil de Arlandria,* a student group sponsored by Tenants and Workers United. Pressuring the school leadership and the School Board for a year-and-a-half finally led to an agreement in 1993 to hire the first bilingual counselor at T.C. Williams. Urrutia described the environment that led students to organize: The Latino students "were all in one hallway" set apart from the rest of the school, in sheltered immersion courses. She remembered filling out worksheets that were "designed for kindergartners" and not getting any meaningful advice from school counselors on course selections or even college opportunities. "No one knew we were there," she said.[72]

Comments from other ESL students interviewed as part of the 1999 ESL evaluation report echoed her sentiments. Many of these comments expressed a clear sense that students knew they were not receiving a challenging education that was comparable to other students.[73] Said one student: "I have been in the ESL program for a year.... Some stuff they are teaching, I learned in my country. It is like repeating what I have already learned. It is wasting my time. I need more. They have to challenge me." Another student stated "I learned a lot in the ESL classes. But I want to get out of ESL class next year. Because if I want to be a doctor, I have to learn more." A third commented, "The teacher said she had been teaching for twenty-five years. I couldn't believe that. As an experienced teacher, you don't just read definitions from books. That class is not useful. We went to it just because we had to."

Other students' description of the ESL program indicated just how far the gap was between immigrant students and the regular classroom: "The ESL teachers did their best jobs [sic]. It is me. I never went to school in my country. If I fail the test, they give me makeups." Another student stated, "My ESL teacher always gives us more than we can handle. That is a big challenge for us. Once you learn more, she always has some more for you." And another commented on the environment within the ESL program and the limited ability of teachers to reach some students: "The teacher just try to keep students quiet. She is nice, but I don't think she has effective ways to deal with students. The teacher has no authority over these students. She just said 'be quiet' and the class went on." Another set of comments stressed the gulf—social and academic—between mainstream and ESL courses. Wrote one student, "School shouldn't separate ESL students really from mainstream students. I don't like to be called ESL students. Because it is like you are not part of their community. When they ask what course you take, you said ESL, then they changed the subject or not talk to you any more."

The ESL student comments were unanimous in their frustration with the guidance counselors, who either did not provide accurate information or had difficulty communicating with students. Stated one T.C. Williams ESL student, "I don't think she is very helpful. She is not listening to me. I wish I knew I had to get good grades, to take courses colleges are looking for in admission. I only realized this last year. It was too late for me. I want to be a dentist, but I know I cannot get into any college except NoVA (Northern Virginia Community College)." Another student expressed similar frustrations, "I think my counselor can do a better job to help me. She told me I had to fill out papers only a few months ago if I want to go to college, which I guess is too late.... There are too many things that I found out too late to do anything about it.... As an ESL student you don't know how the school system in the US works." Yet another stated, "I talked to her. But I don't have full information from her.... I wish the counselor could tell me how many credits I need to graduate and how to apply for college."

For immigrant high school students who were unfamiliar with the system of higher education in the United States, the combination of an ESL system that offered no organized curriculum and a counseling system that was literally unable to communicate with ESL students and their families was a debilitating one. Evelin Urrutia, who successfully organized students to secure bilingual counselors, said the Latino students' frustrations with their isolation led them to demand more from school officials. "We got to a point where we said, 'we need more' from the schools." The biggest difficulty for ESL students at T.C. Williams, she claimed, was the limited number of bilingual staff. In fact, she said, many of the ESL teachers were taking on the ESL assignments "to improve their own Spanish." After a year and half of a "forceful letter-writing and lobbying campaign" district officials found the money to hire a bilingual counselor at T.C. Williams. "The students make an enormous amount of sense," Superintendent Paul Masem told a reporter. "I was very impressed with the way they prepared the case and brought it to the Board. They were organized, respectful, composed, and very articulate."[74] The condescending tone, notwithstanding, this was the first official effort to provide additional resources beyond ESL to Latino youth, which now constituted nearly a fifth of T.C. William's enrollment.

Student leaders, however, continued their organizing efforts, next securing an agreement with Northern Virginia Community College to allow any person with a legal work permit to pay in-state tuition rates. Urrutia stated, "Most of our parents were thinking that we needed to get a job." But "we wanted to go to college." She added that "a lot of us were undocumented at that point" and the precarious immigration standing of Salvadoran students in particular limited many options for higher education. In 1991, however, the federal government created a "temporary protected status" for Salvadoran refugees, many of whom had been denied traditional asylum relief. Although limited, the TPS status enabled Salvadorans who arrived prior to October 19, 1990 the ability to work lawfully in the United States.[75] This, in turn, was sufficient to obtain in-state tuition at NoVA, although the State of Virginia later reversed that policy.[76]

The challenge of pursuing higher education, however, proved daunting to many Latino students in Alexandria. Many students experienced pressures from family members to earn money; others felt little connection to school or were so far behind academically that staying in school meant little sense, particularly if they were not on course to earn a diploma. Compounding the individual circumstances of hardship was a larger structural problem in Alexandria schools: the combination of a tracked mainstream curriculum and curricular incoherence within the ESL program. In short, because academic content was not the primary focus of the ESL program, students who required two to three years to learn English in the ESL program were one or more grade levels behind by the time they exited ESL. Upon exit, they confronted a tracking program that, in many cases, made it difficult to earn an Advanced Studies diploma or to take AP and honors courses necessary for college admission. In 2007, the Advancement Project, in conjunction with Alexandria United Teens, a project of Tenants and Workers United, documented the extent of this problem in a report entitled "Obstacles to Opportunity: Alexandria Students Speak Out." Undertaking a survey of nearly 400 T.C. Williams students, the report found that comparable rates of white and minority students hoped to attend college. The report concluded, however, that minority and immigrant students were far less likely to do so, because they lacked the necessary coursework to be eligible for college admission.

Importantly, the report found that strong majorities of African American, Latino, Asian, and ESL students wanted to take more AP and honors courses but that there were few opportunities for them to do so. In fact, 81 percent of ESL students surveyed expressed a desire to take these courses.[77] The report found, however, that while 50 percent of all white students were enrolled in at least one AP or Honors course in the 2006–2007 academic year, only 6 percent of Latinos were.[78] The disparity stemmed, in part, from advisors and counselors urging them to enroll in the less demanding courses,[79] but it also stemmed from a tracking system that often limited exposure to college preparatory courses to students enrolled in the gifted and talented program. As the report concluded, "the ACPS curriculum is structured so that the chances of a child receiving a college preparatory education are dictated by whether he or she is selected for the [gifted and talented] program by the time they reach sixth grade."[80] Thus, the report found, "in a district in which the students are majority black and Latino, only a small number of mostly white students are positioned starting in elementary school to benefit from the primary college preparatory track."[81]

The school district itself resisted both the production and the findings of the report, according to Liss. With the district blocking access to information, Tenants and Workers United was forced to file Freedom of Information Act (FOIA) requests against the district to obtain data on the racial composition of AP and Honors courses. The district even took to leafleting against the report at community meetings where Alexandria Teens United was announcing its findings. For its, part, the district contended that the data in the report were outdated and did not reflect the current state of affairs in Alexandria schools. In short, according to Liss, Superintendent Rebecca Perry "was not a friend of ours."[82]

Perry's contentious relationship with the Latino community could, in part, be traced back to a dispute in 2004, when the leadership and some families of the Mount Vernon Community School sought to adopt a year-round calendar for the elementary school. At the end of Herb Berg's tenure as superintendent, Mount Vernon had become a dual-language bilingual immersion school, with Dr. Lulu López as principal. In 1999, Mount Vernon enrolled the highest percentage of English-learners within the school system,[83] but López had by 2003 achieved full accreditation for the bilingual school. Seeking to build on those successes, many parents and the school leadership felt that a year-round calendar would increase the opportunities for English-learners. The Perry administration, along with the school board, resisted the effort, insisting that 75 percent of teachers and parents had to approve the plan in a plebiscite before it could be implemented. Tenants and Workers United geared up for the effort by hiring a parent organizer to rally the vote, which was, according to Liss, "a hell of a fight." The conflict hinged between the desires of middle-class families to hold on to summer break traditions for their children, on one hand, and the educational benefits that a year-round calendar could confer on English-learners, on the other[84] The "battle royale" culminated in a victory for the parents of English-learners who voted overwhelmingly for the year-round calendar.[85]

With Superintendent Perry's departure in 2008, however, the time was ripe for a new relationship between the Latino community and school district leadership. Incoming Superintendent Morton Sherman seized on the "Obstacles to Opportunity Report" to build his case for a new effort to reach underperforming students. While many in Alexandria later criticized Sherman for being too removed from the realities of teaching practices and for introducing unworkable pedagogical strategies, Liss contended that Sherman was the first superintendent truly to understand the educational circumstances of Latino and immigrant youth. According to Liss, Sherman had all his senior staff read the Obstacles to Opportunity report. Liss stated in an interview he felt that Sherman's efforts to circulate the report "opened the eyes for a lot of people in Alexandria."

The outreach effort by Sherman was formalized in 2009 in a memorandum of understanding between Tenants and Workers United and the school district in which the two parties agreed to pursue three strategies to improve the educational outcomes of Latinos and students of color in Alexandria. ACPS and Tenants and Workers United agreed to "improve cultural competency" within the school district in order to ensure that school and district personnel truly understood the contexts and circumstances of these students' lives. In addition, both parties agreed to "develop and implement individualized Student Education Plans" at the secondary level. Building on Alexandria Teens United's long-term complaints about the advising and counseling process at T.C. Williams, this effort would, according to the agreement, provide "individualized roadmaps" for student success. As we will see in Chapter 8, these individualized plans would prove to be a central, if problematic, element of T.C. Williams's response to its designation as a persistently lowest-achieving school in 2010. Finally, both the district and Tenants and Workers United agreed to foster a culture of parent and youth involvement. With a single document, Sherman had, at least on paper, recognized the permanence of Latino and immigrant youth in Alexandria and committed the district to devising new strategies to explicitly address their educational needs. The challenges of doing so, however, were only apparent when the federal government in 2010 demanded that Sherman live up to what he promised Tenants and Workers United six months earlier.

English-Learners and the Policy Legacies of Jim Crow

In the spring of 2010, the U.S. Department of Education deemed T.C. Williams High School "a persistently lowest-achieving" school because it scored in the bottom five percent of all Title 1- eligible high schools in Virginia in math and language arts tests and had not sufficiently reduced its failure rate in the past two years. The efforts of school and district officials to reverse that designation is the subject of Chapter 8, but one element of those efforts intersects with the district's efforts to educate English-learners. Because English-learners were consistently among the lowest performers at T.C. Williams, addressing their educational needs soon became a central part of what was known at the "transformation effort." The challenge school officials faced, however, as they planned ways to improve their ESL offerings was the policy legacy of past practices of segregation among Alexandria students, either segregation through tracking or the older practices of Jim Crow.

The school transformation plan, developed and funded through a "School Improvement Grant" funded by the U.S. Department of Education, consisted of multiple components, but the two pieces that most directly affected English learners were the Individual Academic Plans and the new "International Academy" teachers and staff wanted to develop at T.C. Williams. As school officials undertook the implementation of the transformation plan, they encountered challenges that, for some reason, they had not anticipated as they written the plan. Most prominent among those challenges was the academic future of English-learners at T.C. Williams. The school transformation plan that Alexandria City Schools adopted required the counseling and teaching staff to devise—in conjunction with students and family members—an Individual Academic Plan (IAP), a road map through high school and on to a career or college. Similar to the individualized Student Education Plans that were described in the memorandum of understanding signed with Tenants and Workers United, these plans laid out in concrete detail the courses, skills, and requirements a student had master in order to realize their college or career goals.

The process of writing these IAPs, however, drove home to many teachers and counselors the extent to which, for many students, support at home was lacking in their lives, particularly among new immigrant households. After hearing accounts of successful and unsuccessful IAP meetings, some of which were "unbelievably meaningful because the parent and the child were fully invested" in the IAP process,[86] and others which were less successful because that engagement did not exist, Superintendent Mort Sherman remarked that it appeared to him that "there's still a portion of our community who are ... not coming to the table, and that's a piece we still need to focus on in some way."[87] He was referring to English-learners, who composed nearly a quarter of Alexandria public school students. Indeed, after hearing reports that nearly 50 percent of English learners at T.C. Williams failed a course in the first quarter of Fall 2010, and that the 9th-12th grade dropout rate was approximately 25 percent for Latino students,[88] Sherman stressed the importance of reaching English-learners: "It seems at least to me that the success of our transformation is right here. All the other pieces that we've talked about are essential, but if we don't make it for our ELL kids ... we're not going to make it as a school division."[89]

T.C. Williams Principal Suzanne Maxey also made it clear that English-learners needed greater attention in the transformation process. Stating that T.C. Williams was not meeting the needs of students with low levels of English skills, she also asserted that the social and emotional aspects of new immigrant students (many of whom may be undocumented) needed to be addressed in order to make any headway on the achievement gap and promoting the aspirations of students:

> If a student is not documented and doesn't have a social security number, it's very, very difficult for them to get into a college, because of required documentation. So you say to Latino kids, as you say to all of our children, we expect you to be college ready, we expect you to be da-da-da. And they realize that no matter how hard they work in high school, it's almost like [their] future is [limited to] working at McDonald's. [As a result], they're much more susceptible to [participation in] gangs, because they're not sure they have a future beyond high school.[90]

While these broader contexts were currently not on T.C. William's agenda, Maxey said, they needed to be. As she said, merely putting these students "into a classroom and giving them more instruction" will not address the complex contexts of their education that limit both their motivation and their incentives.[91] She added later "I think this problem [of English-learners' achievement] is one of the keys to our success. We're going after it and I don't think we can just hope things work out.... [For] this particular group, we are going to have to zero right down to every child and really go after it."[92] She promised to return to the next meeting with a school-wide plan to address the challenges facing English-learners.

At the same time that T.C. Williams's leadership was realizing the extent to which the school was not well-equipped to address the educational needs of English learners, the district was preparing plans for a district-wide response to these students. While that plan addressed issues particular to elementary students as well, much of it was devoted to the creation of an International Academy at T.C. Williams, a program designed to offer additional services to Alexandria's high school English-learners in order to improve their chances of success at T.C. Williams. As the Transformation Committee discussed the idea of the International Academy, however, concerns grew about perceptions in the community concerning the segregation of English-learners. After being briefed by the ELL Planning Committee on the plan, Superintendent Sherman expressed concerns about how a separate program for largely Spanish-speaking high schoolers would be perceived in the community. As T.C. Williams's Principal Suzanne Maxey told the Transformation Committee, Sherman instructed her "to revisit this whole plan, because the criticism is, or the concern is, that we are isolating those kids into a certain part of the building and that will have negative consequences."[93]

When staff pushed back and indicated the dire situation of many of these students and that this program would better serve their needs, Maxey responded, "So when the Campagna Center or the Building Better Futures[94] say to us: you're making those kids isolated ... how are we answering [them], [telling them] it best meets their needs?"[95] What ensued was a lengthy conversation in which the staff proposing the International Academy stressed that the social supports that the program would provide—along with the language and subject matter instruction—would actually promote closer ties between high school English-learners and the broader T.C. Williams community. For many staff members, the problem was that there were few mechanisms by which the school could effectively reach these students. They argued that a smaller, more close-knit International Academy offered a better chance to provide counseling and establish the relationships that these students needed to stay in school and to overcome their academic obstacles.

Maxey then urged the planners to bring key members of the community into the process to head off any objections, stressing that the meeting shouldn't be just an update: "I wouldn't make it informal, I'd make it formal. I'd have a formal meeting inviting them and so that they are part of this.... I think they'll be pleased, if we sell it the right way, they'll be pleased that their children are no longer invisible, and that's the word that I keep using, I think our kids are invisible."[96]

Later on, Amy Yamashiro, an Accountability Analyst, cautioned that other groups—beyond the Latino or immigrant communities—might object to the perceived segregation of the International Academy, saying "I think you'll get backlash from ... well, like you know, the NAACP.... It could be any group that says, why are you isolating these kids who are mainly kids of color?" She added that "it's going to happen, and so you just need to be prepared for that."[97] Peter Balas, executive associate principal at T.C. Williams, then informed the Steering Committee that "it has happened in the past," stating that "this concept has been tried before, and [it] became very explosive and controversial."[98] Long-time Alexandria City Public Schools administrator Tammy Ignacio explained:

> The issue in the past wasn't necessarily with an ELL academy, it was more with an alternative setting ... for kids, a therapeutic setting. We talked about [placing it at] Jefferson Houston ... and the community went ballistic. [They claimed] it will be full of Hispanic and African American males, it will be a watered-down program, that's where all the ... bad kids will go, where you won't have the best teachers, and it really just took this community and went PSHHT.[99]

Suzanne Maxey then responded by invoking both the logic of accountability, but also the imperative of the federal obligation Alexandria was now under to respond, in some fashion, to the low test scores.

> I think one of the differences between what happened ten years ago or whatever and now is that we are no longer hiding data and not talking about it, because we don't want to insult any group. We are very clear, this is the data of the school system. The school system has to react to it. We can't just say well, we don't want to hurt anybody's feelings. This is what it is.[100]

The continuing presence of past educational policies were the source of potential community objections to the International Academy, but the language of accountability and transparency also gave Maxey and Alexandria's school leadership an ability to navigate those treacherous waters. By invoking both the constraints that the Federal government was imposing on Alexandria and a perceived moral need to address the educational performance of this large and growing segment of Alexandria's student body, Maxey could align Alexandria City Public Schools' obligations to the political expectations and needs of the community, even if that community was made somewhat uneasy by the appearance of segregation.

In short, the federal government's demand that T.C. Williams transform its school culture was pitted against localist memories of isolation and invisibility for both black and brown students. While the federal government may have demanded that T.C. Williams no longer ignore its English-learners, the lack of guidance from the federal government about how, exactly, to meet the needs of these students meant that T.C. Williams's efforts to isolate Latino students for "good" reasons rather than

"bad" reasons raised the specter of Jim Crow. This time, however, the racial coalitional regime that had been in place in the early 1990s no longer had the same powers to object, partly because the federal government now afforded them no space in
which to make an objection, but also because the political order in Alexandria has
shifted, making their concerns about racial isolation less salient. In other words, as
the lines of authority shifted, the existing local political institutions were less and
less relevant venues in which to voice complaints. Compounding that shift was the
persistent but widely acknowledged marginalization of immigrant communities
from local channels of influence.

Conclusion: Political Efficacy and Educational Efficacy

Arlandria-Chirilagua in 2013 is on the cusp of yet another transformation. Having
undergone a white exodus in the 1970s and a Latino in-migration in the 1980s
and 1990s, it now is at the heart of a debate within Alexandria over the economic
diversity of both Alexandria and the inner Virginia suburbs of Washington, DC.
The growing affluence—and whitening—of Arlington County is extending to
Alexandria as well. Gentrification and redevelopment have been the central political issues affecting Arlandria-Chirilagua most recently. New projects aim to tear
down existing garden apartments and replace them with higher density multistory
buildings. Controversy has also stirred over the city's commitment to maintain
affordable housing.

Between 2010 and 2013, a pro-growth coalition on the City Council has
approved three major projects in Arlandria-Chirilagua, adding over 900 housing
units, only eighty-seven of which would be affordable housing.[101] In the Landmark
section of Alexandria, new redevelopment projects promise a facelift for a suburban neighborhood and commercial district that was built out in the 1960s, but
now houses a large percentage of Alexandria's East African immigrant population. The new construction and commercial development bring with it the reality
of higher rents and the displacement of low-income households, predominantly
immigrant. The traditional urban political battles over development agendas, housing, and linkages to transportation networks are familiar ground, the regular politics of urban redevelopment. At the same time, they place immigrants and families
of English-learners at a political disadvantage—largely for the same reasons that
these students are at disadvantage within the educational system. The unwillingness or inability to participate, the lack of familiarity with mechanisms of power
and influence, and, for many families with undocumented members, a fear of detec-
tion and detention—all these factors limit the influence of immigrant households
in both schools and politics. The underfunded and somewhat incoherent federal
attention to the needs of these English-learners and their families has—apart from
imposing greater accountability pressures on teachers and principals—done little

to ensure them an equal opportunity to succeed. For its part, the political regime in Alexandria has been slow to respond to the educational needs of these students, relying on their relative invisibility to pursue other priorities. While there may be more room to be brown in Alexandria than two generations ago, being heard and being brown continues to be a challenge.

PART THREE

THE POLITICS OF ACCOUNTABILITY

From Equality of Inputs to Equality of Outputs

A funny thing happened on the way to equal opportunity: reformers—at all levels—redefined the concept of equal schooling. The federal goal of assuring that all students, whether racial minorities, special needs, or English-learners, had an equal access to a public education morphed into something completely different. Beginning in the early 1980s and through the 1990s, the advocates of "accountability" in education began to argue that the provision of equality could no longer focus solely on the inputs to the educational equation. Instead, they argued, results mattered.

Too many students—whether poor, black, white or middle class—were receiving lousy educations, they argued, because no one was being held accountable for their learning. Accountability supporters contended that district, state, and federal officials were mistakenly focusing solely on the inputs to public education: the racial demographics of schools, the money spent on schools, the compliance requirements of special education, etc. Inputs alone were not doing enough to produce what really mattered: demonstrable learning. And the easiest way to demonstrate learning was through standardized tests.

The accountability coalition was built out of a number of groups frustrated with the direction of US education, but most drew their inspiration from the *Nation at Risk* report released in 1983.[1] Business leaders thought that a more results-oriented, concrete bottom line was needed to impose discipline on an inefficient bureaucracy. Some civil rights leaders felt that ignoring test scores was allowing school leaders to get away with educational malpractice, particularly for minority and poor students. Similarly, many minority parents lost their enthusiasm for the integrationist project and felt that the improvement of educational outcomes mattered far more than whether their child sat next to a white child in school. There were back-to-basics parents and activists who felt that fuzzy-minded, progressive education was not focusing sufficiently on content, facts, and substantive knowledge and that testing would was impose some objective rigor on a school system smitten with "feel good" exercises that promoted a false sense of self-esteem. Meanwhile, enterprising politicians—particularly governors—sought to capitalize on growing political support for improving education and advocated for holding schools and students accountable through standardized tests to achieve systemic reforms.

The standards and accountability movements have a long history and their prominence has prompted an extensive literature, addressing both their origins and their effectiveness. The rejoinder against high-stakes accountability and the reliance of standards-based assessment typically pivots on a few key points. Many opponents argue that high-stakes, standards-based assessments crowd other subjects out of the curriculum (such as art, music, history, or physical education), subjects that are untested or for which there are no consequences. Second, many contend that an overwhelming focus on assessment creates innumerable perverse incentives for teachers and students alike, ranging from cheating, teaching to the tests, and adopting "drill and kill" techniques to boost test scores, to pushing underperforming students to drop out, etc. These objections frequently exemplify Campbell's Law, a principle advanced by Donald T. Campbell in a conference paper in 1976: "The more any quantitative social indicator is used for social decision making, the more subject it will be to corruption pressures and the more apt it will be to distort and corrupt the social processes it is intended to monitor."[2] While Campbell was speaking broadly of evaluation research, he drew particular attention to educational testing, writing that "when test scores become the goal of the teaching process, they both lose their value as indicators of educational status and distort the educational process in undesirable ways."[3] Finally, many teachers, parents and administrators contend that schools ought to be more than the collection of their test scores. That is, because they're social institutions many unmeasured factors contribute to the health and vitality of schools as learning organizations and that an overemphasis on standards proficiency and accountability robs students of school experiences that will teach them important lessons beyond the formal curriculum.

In Virginia, both sides were advanced, but the proponents of standards and accountability prevailed. Indeed, the state was a leader in the 1980s and 1990s in the development of these reforms. For Alexandria, the ideas of greater rigor and more accountability held particular resonance, especially after Superintendent Robert Peebles's 1985 decision to release district test scores by racial group publicly highlighted the large black-white test score gap in the city. But just as the fact that many of Alexandria's students have not been meeting performance expectations is not new, so, too, the calls for accountability in Alexandria are not new, with some dating back to the early 1970s. Part Three of this book examines the local origins and implementation of these accountability policies in close detail. Chapter 7 explores a grassroots effort in Alexandria in the early 1990s to demand electoral accountability at the local level, as well as the expansion and implementation of Virginia's Standards of Learning accountability regime. Chapter Eight turns to the federal version of the accountability and standards movements, focusing on No Child Left Behind and the more recent School Improvement Grant, a program significantly expanded under the American Recovery and Reinvestment Act, President Obama's stimulus bill. As a result of being dubbed a "persistently lowest-achieving school" T.C. Williams High School was subjected to federally mandated "transformation" under the School Improvement Grant program. Chapter 8 explores in close detail the issues that school staff had to confront as they grappled with federally mandated "transformation."

All these articulations of a need for greater accountability—at the local, state, and federal level—have been sustained by two transformative, but conflicting, sentiments. The first sentiment—rooted in a growing dismay with existing educational elites—holds that schools can and must improve their efficiency as public bureaucracies. Since the early 1990s, Alexandria schools have seen accountability policies enacted at the local, state, and federal level, all of them adopted in an effort to improve the performance of schools and to sharpen schools' focus on educational achievement of students. By seeking to hold schools "accountable," advocates for more stringent accountability provisions argue that schools have ventured too far from their central task of simply educating children. The second sentiment holds that educational equity is best advanced not by changing the inputs to education, but by a relentless focus on outputs. This shift in focus has been perhaps the greatest change in federal educational policy of the past generation. Advocates of accountability policies see these two sentiments as intrinsically and fundamentally fused: the inequality of educational outcomes in the United States, many claim, are not the product of unequal inputs, but the inadequate efforts of the existing school authorities to appropriately design and implement a quality education.

In Alexandria, the effects of these twin sentiments—articulated through policies at the local, state, and federal level—were complex, but resulted in a profoundly altered governance landscape in Alexandria's schools. All three forms of accountability policies moved away from a focus on representational equality in school governance or an equitable distribution of resources and curricula in schools. In their place, these policies focused simply on achievement outcomes, and imposed punitive sanctions on teachers and schools if those outcomes were not meeting policymakers' understanding of efficiency or equity.

As these twin sentiments were reflected in policies enacted at further and further remove from local authorities in education, they left Alexandria authorities with an increasingly small space in which to articulate and defend locally defined priorities for schooling. In their fullest expression at the federal level, these accountability policies significantly decoupled local governing commitments from school operations, to a far greater degree than either local or state efforts at ensuring accountability. The result was an arguably liberal attention to the test-score gap, but one that forced school officials to ignore, or at least discount, the inputs that generated educational inequalities in the first place. The resulting test-driven attention to racial and class divides flattened the notion of equal opportunity in Alexandria's schools, forcing schools to impose greater burdens on underperforming students, ironically constricting their educational horizons in an effort to foster greater equality.

7

Local Activism and Accountability Politics

Introduction

In July 1971, at the height of Superintendent John Albohm's efforts to restructure Alexandria's high schools, newly appointed School Board member Dr. Jack Carlson introduced, at his first School Board meeting, a proposal to require "quantitative performance measures in the Alexandria School System," in order "to improve measurement of the results achieved for the dollars and programs provided." These tests also aimed to "improve internal management (e.g., evaluation of teachers, department heads, and principals) to enhance accountability of the administration to the School Board and to increase accountability of the School System to the public."[1] The proposal was, in effect, an embryonic form of No Child Left Behind: it sought to quantitatively document the results of teaching through a system of testing. These "performance measures" would in turn reveal the economic efficiency (or inefficiency) of a school system, as well as enable the public to hold the leaders of the school system accountable for academic performance. The School Board's reaction to the motion? The matter was referred to committee for consideration and never saw the light of day again.[2]

The impulses behind Carlson's motion, however, did not go away. Efforts to "hold accountable" teachers, school officials and politicians for the performance of students and schools dominated both Alexandria and Virginia school reforms from the late 1980s through the mid-1990s. Significantly, the efforts in Virginia both echoed and anticipated efforts in other states. While schools have always been accountable to someone (parents, school board members, mayors, etc.), it was between the mid-1980s and the mid-1990s that many reformers and policymakers throughout the country concluded that "efforts to hold schools accountable should focus on performance—specifically, what students actually learn and what they can do."[3] Importantly, this focus on outputs of education also held an egalitarian appeal: to the extent that all students could gain a level of mastery of subject matter, and could demonstrate an ability to cross a threshold of proficiency on complex skills and rigorous content, their educations could be deemed equal. Utilizing this threshold conception of equity, advocates for test-based accountability could argue that this approach was a better response to the civil rights demands of disadvantaged students than focusing on inputs to education.[4]

The emergence of accountability politics in Alexandria began in the 1990s with a local effort to shift from a City Council-appointed School Board to an elected School Board. This campaign stemmed from a growing frustration on the part of some parents about the direction of Alexandria schools. As that frustration grew, calls for a more "accountable" School Board grew increasingly insistent and eventually produced a significant shift in the governance structure of Alexandria's schools and in its educational priorities. These changing priorities emerged at roughly the same time Virginia was revising its existing statewide assessments. A major expansion of testing and the imposition of a high-stakes accountability regime, the Virginia Standards of Learning (SOLs) represented both an incursion into local control and a national model that other states soon emulated. Fresh off a campaign to impose electoral accountability on Alexandria schools, the local school leadership in Alexandria, unlike many school districts across Northern Virginia, endorsed the SOLs with enthusiasm. The local acceptance of Virginia's accountability model stemmed, I argue, from the concerted efforts of local activists to impose a norm of accountability on Alexandria's schools and students alike. Nonetheless, the shift from inputs to outputs required the local leadership to navigate with care race-based claims about diminished representation and equity within the system.

This chapter explores these issues in two sections. The first section, "Local Activism and Electoral Accountability" examines the local pressures to remove the authority to appoint school board members from the city council and move to an elected board. Central to that debate were concerns among some parents that the school district's efforts to reduce academic tracking were lowering Alexandria's academic standards. At the same time, African Americans in Alexandria felt that the turn to an elected school board was an effort to diminish their representation and to deprive their community access to resources. The second section, "An Accountability of Proficiency: From Inputs to Outputs" details the local push for greater test-based accountability in the wake of the newly-elected school board's selection of a new superintendent.

Local Activism and Electoral Accountability

The drive for elected school boards in Virginia began with litigation in the late 1980s. On behalf of black plaintiffs, the American Civil Liberties Union filed suit against the Virginia State Board of Elections, claiming that Virginia's method of selecting school board members in school districts throughout the state violated the

14th Amendment's equal protection clause, as well as the 15th Amendment and the Voting Rights Act of 1965. Virginia's unique system of selecting school board members did not allow for the direct election of school boards, but instead vested the authority to appoint school board members in either city councils, county boards of supervisors, or a county-wide school trustee selection commission, depending on the local governing authority.[5] The system dated back to the original 1870 statute creating a statewide public education system in Virginia,[6] and was further entrenched by the 1902 Constitution, which effectively disenfranchised African Americans (and poor whites) in Virginia. In 1947, the state legislature allowed one jurisdiction, Arlington County in Northern Virginia, to elect its school board, but it later stripped the county of its electoral independence after the Arlington County School Board in 1956 voted to comply with *Brown v. Board of Education*.[7] Since that time, no school board in Virginia was directly elected. Between 1973 and 1988, at least forty-seven bills were introduced in the Virginia legislature to alter the selection system, and both the Virginia House of Delegates and Virginia Senate commissioned legislative studies of the issue, but all efforts to reform the process failed.[8]

In 1988, the ACLU's lawsuit also failed. The federal court in Richmond ruled that while the original aim of the selection system—and of the 1956 reversal of Arlington's right of election—was to discriminate against African American voters and office-seekers, there was no evidence that African Americans were currently disenfranchised by the selection process. After reviewing evidence that the percentages of African Americans in Virginia and the percentage of African American school board members in 1987 were equal at 18 percent, the court concluded that "the plaintiffs have not demonstrated that the appointive system is presently maintained for racially discriminatory reasons."[9] Appeals to the Fourth Circuit Court of Appeals and the U.S. Supreme Court subsequently failed, and in 1990 reformers were left with the challenge of pushing the reform though the Virginia state legislature.

While support for elected school boards was very strong in Northern Virginia, representatives from across the state were less enthusiastic. In part, the opposition stemmed from an unwillingness to fracture existing authority at the local level. City council members and county supervisors in Virginia wield the local taxation authority that funds a large percentage of school budgets, along with the power to appoint school boards. If school board members were directly elected by voters, detractors argued, the political incentives of board members could conflict with the financial responsibilities of cities and counties. In short, by cutting the ties of school board members to city councils or county boards of supervisors, the direct election of school boards could, absent taxation authority, pit the political representation of schooling against the financial responsibility to fund schools.[10] This situation could encourage school board members to create new, politically popular programs that other actors would have to fund. Supporters of the reform contended, however, that the prevailing arrangement already divided the loyalties of school board members—between the parents who seek reforms and the politicians who appoint them. James Murphy, a Fairfax County parent and longtime school board election activist, argued that "we want to ensure that the constituency most affected by the school board's decisions can talk directly to someone who is accountable to them."[11]

The theme of accountability resonated strongly among some voters in Alexandria, particularly those parents who had tussled with the School Board (and City Council) over the leadership and direction of local elementary schools. In one such episode, parents and teachers had clashed repeatedly with the recently hired principal at George Mason Elementary School. George Mason enrolled a largely white and upper middle-class population from the surrounding neighborhood, but also saw a significant number of African American students bused in from the Berg, a historically black neighborhood in Old Town that was, at the time, also the site of Samuel Madden Homes, a public housing project.[12] According to some disgruntled parents, the principal had failed to enforce discipline at the school, leading to classrooms that were plagued with disruptions and, in a few instances, to injured children. Parents of third-graders from the neighborhood also bitterly complained that the school's academic expectations had been lowered because of the learning and behavioral difficulties of some students and that the academic progress of their children was compromised because the school adjusted its curriculum to accommodate the lowest-achieving students at the school. One teacher allegedly explained to a parent that tests or written work had not been assigned in science and social studies because "half the kids cannot read, and it would not be fair to them."[13] Eventually fifteen families with children in the third grade withdrew them from the school, with thirteen of the families enrolling them in private school.[14]

Before they left the school, however, the parents had lobbied the City Council extensively to replace School Board members who had not been responsive to their complaints about George Mason. In June of 1990, as the terms of three School Board members were expiring, George Mason parents vigorously sought the removal of all three board members. As City Councilwoman Redella S. "Del" Pepper stated after the council vote, "The pressure to remove all, or at least one [of the incumbents], was unprecedented."[15] At the time, Vice Mayor Patricia Ticer stated in an interview with a reporter "There is a perception in the community that maybe the School Board has not been as strong ... as it should be." In the end, however, the City Council returned all three members to the Board. For some parents at George Mason, this reappointment was the final straw. Carol LaSasso, a professor of education and George Mason parent, cited the City Council's actions in an article describing her family's decision to remove their nine-year-old from the school, stating that the responsibility for the problems at George Mason went beyond the individual actions of the principal: "Many of us involved would ascribe equal responsibility to the Superintendent of Schools, the School Board, and the City Council, which reappointed three School Board members, despite considerable public opposition.... Had there been an elected school board, school administrators might have been more responsive".[16]

The conflicts at George Mason touched on a broader conflict within Alexandria on what, exactly, the goals of the school system were, and the ability of its governance structure to reconcile the demands of politically influential parents with the academic needs of students who most needed educational assistance. For many, the school district had gone too far in its efforts to boost the educational fortunes of minority students. Superintendent Paul Masem had made improving minority achievement a priority of the school district, but many white and middle-class parents saw those efforts as coming at the expense of their own children's success in school. As Masem stated in an interview with the *Washington Post*, many students in Alexandria faced poverty and domestic issues that created enormous obstacles to learning. Nonetheless, "I have a hard time getting what I call my electorate to identify with that."[17]

These concerns about the priorities of the school system cut across the Democratic establishment that governed Alexandria, but they echoed many of the academic quality debates from the early 1970s. Alexandria's Democratic Mayor Jim Moran (newly-elected to the House of Representatives in 1990)characterized Masem's challenge as one centered on limiting middle-class flight from Alexandria's schools, and the cascading difficulties such flight would entail. If Masem's programs "tilt too much" toward aiding minority students, Moran told the *Washington Post*, "then the parents of the more advantaged children are going to take their children out of the school system. If that happens then you're going to lose the leadership of that community and ultimately the financial leadership." In a similar vein, former chair of the Alexandria Democratic Committee and Alexandria City Councilmember Lonnie Rich said in an interview in 2011, "We need to run the school system so that those who have a choice decide to stay in the system."[18] That attitude, according to Rich, was precisely what was missing from Alexandria City Public Schools under Paul Masem. According to Rich, at one point in the George Mason controversy, the principal at George Mason told the parents who complained of disciplinary and curricular problems that "if they didn't like [the school's policies] they should send their kids to private schools."[19]

From the perspective of white, affluent parents at George Mason, this under appreciation of the needs of their children emerged from both the superintendent's overt efforts to boost minority achievement and the nature of School Board representation of interests within the city. Carol LaSasso stated that parents and children at George Mason Elementary "became victims of a political philosophy that wants kids in the same classroom regardless of motivation, ability, interest, or self-control." She added that "we were being asked to accept a watered-down curriculum and double standards of discipline for the sake of social engineering."[20] Rich argued that "our concerns [at George Mason] were not exotic, just discipline and higher standards," adding that "there never could be accountability on an appointed school board" because the connection between City Council elections and schools was far too attenuated: "The reason you vote for City Council never had anything to do with schools." As a result, the governance of Alexandria City Public Schools was "in a political rut" and parents at George Mason "wanted School Board members with a different attitude."[21]

These views on the School Board had become fixed, according to Rich, because the City Council "kept appointing the same type of people from the same groups." According to Rich, these School Board members supported a "civil rights estab-lishment" view in Alexandria that equated the language of discipline and standards with harming the interests of black students. "Any time you talked about discipline problems" in schools, said Rich, "you were seen as talking about regulating black males."[22]

The fused themes of academic standards and school discipline had come full circle between 1970 and 1990. While the federally compelled integration of schools in the early 1970s had prompted political fights that eventually had produced an expanded representation of African American interests on the Alexandria School Board and had also produced a more or less racially integrated school system, it had not overcome the continuing and robust conflicts over how best to educate the students, as racially and economically diverse as they were, within those integrated schools. The political repercussions of integration within Alexandria and the accom-panying liberalization of its politics, detailed in Chapter 4, had produced a govern-ing regime premised on a racial partnership among liberal Democrats. When the concerns of affluent parents about the quality of schooling *for their children*—never far from the surface in Alexandria—were not sufficiently well handled by school administrators and the Superintendent, it produced an attack on the governing ide-ology of the local regime. That, in turn, produced a sharp attack on the nature of the governing coalition that promoted minority achievement as a primary mission of the schools. The local turn to electoral accountability in Alexandria was certainly in keeping with broader demands across Virginia and the nation for better perfor-mance in schools, but the particular nature of the politics of electoral accountability in Alexandria stemmed from the ongoing divisions about the local priorities of edu-cational governance.

Those priorities were, in large part, established by the Superintendent and sup-ported by the School Board, a creature appointed by the City Council. According to Rich and former Superintendent Herb Berg, the City Council at this time had been operating under an informal agreement that at least four members of the nine-member School Board be African Americans.[23] As a result, efforts to move to an elected school board were viewed by many within the local civil rights establish-ment as an attack on black students in Alexandria. Noting that "black children make up almost one-half" of the Alexandria school system, but "black voters make up just slightly less than one-fourth of the electorate in Alexandria," Alexandria NAACP President Emmitt Carlton contended that it would be "very difficult to elect as many blacks to the School Board as currently are appointed" by the City Council.[24] Carlton went on to add that representation was a crucial element of equitable schooling, arguing "African Americans must continue helping to make the tough decisions on policies that will affect all of our children. This involvement is important if sayings such as 'we're all in this together' are to mean anything."[25]

Diminished black influence over the educational policymaking process was not simply a hypothetical concern on the part of Alexandria's African American community. State legislation enabling local districts to put the issue of elected school boards before local voters was finally enacted in spring of 1992 just as substantive policy issues with clear racial implications were confronting Alexandria. The issues—the expansion of all-day kindergarten, the conversion of junior high schools to middle schools, and a move away from academic tracking—are all standard educational policy issues debated and adopted throughout the country. But the intersection of these issues with existing racial and class cleavages in Alexandra, at precisely the time an elected school board became a possibility in Virginia, ultimately produced a sweeping change in Alexandria's educational governance, a change fueled and sustained by the political rhetoric of "accountability."

While some in the African American community saw the attack on appointed school boards as simply part of a broader assault on educational interests held by African Americans, others in Alexandria—predominantly white—saw the move to an elected school board as a kind of Progressive-era reform that would reduce what they saw as a politically illegitimate, interest-driven relationship between City Council members and School Board cronies. In truth, both views were correct. The political incorporation of African American interests into the governing regime of Alexandria in the late 1970s and 1980s—driven in large part by processes of school integration—had created mechanisms of constituent service that delivered benefits to the African American community. In the 1990s, the continued (or expanded) delivery of these benefits to African Americans and attention to their needs were seen as now threatening the educational interests of middle-class white students.

Kindergarten Seats and Resource Allocation

In February 1992, just as the Virginia state legislature was finally approving legislation that would allow localities to vote on the adoption of an elected school board, black parents in Alexandria were irate over the distribution of seats to an all-day kindergarten program. Created in 1990, the all-day kindergarten program allocated half the all-day seats to white children and half the seats to African American and minority children, in an effort to ensure that the program was fully integrated. The program proved very popular with minority parents, but the original allocation of seats did not change to reflect the much larger numbers of minority applicants. Given the number of white and minority applicants, the 50/50 split meant minority parents had only a one in nine chance of winning an all-day kindergarten slot for their child, while white parents had a one in four chance of gaining entrance to the all-day program. Under pressure from the City Council, and after being sued by

African American and Latino parents, the School Board increased the number of seats for minority children to better reflect the applicant pool.[26]

Tensions flared further, however, when the City Council pushed the School Board to create more space for minority applicants to kindergarten. The Council exercised its budgetary authority and moved nearly $80,000 from the school district's administrative budget to its instructional account in order to fund two additional kindergarten classes. When the School Board balked at the additional classes and used some of the new instructional funds for school supplies and field trips, the issue of accountability flared again, but this time over the Board's lack of responsiveness to the Council's agenda. Council member Kerry Donley stated that because the School Board is appointed by the City Council, the "Board needs to show some accountability." City Councilmember Redella S. "Del" Pepper echoed, "We are the ones who take the heat in the community," adding, "It's outrageous for the board to say they know better."[27] From the perspective of some African Americans, preserving an appointed school board would preserve the ability of African Americans to advance their interests in the school system, in part because of the strong ties of the local civil rights community to the City Council.

Middle School Reforms and the Loss of Allies

For all the sniping, however, the dispute over all-day kindergarten was, fundamentally, largely a resource question, one in which all participants agreed on the ultimate goal, but differed on the pace of implementation. Larger disputes—with less obvious means of resolution, and which touched on long-standing racial and class tensions—arose when Masem and the School Board adopted structural and curricular changes in junior high schools, prompting a debate about the rigor of academic offerings and the academic tracking of students. In December 1991, Masem put forward a plan to move ninth-graders from the city's two junior high schools into a single, all-city ninth-grade school, and shift sixth-graders from elementary schools into newly created middle schools that would include sixth-, seventh-, and eighth-graders. With student enrollments projected to grow again, elementary schools faced greater crowding, and moving sixth-graders to middle school would open up space for more all-day kindergartens, a clear priority of city voters.[28] Masem also contended that an all-city ninth-grade school would offer educational benefits that would enable the district to attend to the special needs of ninth-graders. "We don't want students to get lost [in the transition to high school]," Masem told a reporter.[29]

While Masem had proposed that the new scheme begin in the fall of 1994, School Board members opted to accelerate the program, voting to launch the middle schools and the new ninth-grade-only school in the fall of 1993. According to former School Board Member Bill Purdy, the push to move sixth-graders into middle schools stemmed from the Board's desire to free up space for more full-day kindergarten and early childhood education. The idea, he said "was pushed by the early childhood advocates on the board who wanted to bring at-risk preschoolers into the elementary schools".[30] As a result, the school district "had to clear sixth-graders out of elementary schools to make space for the kids that the preschool lobby on the board wanted to put in," according to one school administrator.[31] This rushed schedule alienated more than a few parents, one of whom told the School Board, "The parents of Alexandria will support change. But we will not support restructuring if it is jammed down our throats."[32]

Beyond the timing issues, City Council members also grew concerned as the costs of creating a new ninth-grade-only school grew. To reduce costs, Masem proposed moving ninth-graders into the existing Minnie Howard building, a former school now utilized by the district administration, but the move also required central administration to relocate into leased space, adding to the expense. More importantly, however, the new school required over thirty-five new full-time employees to staff the facility.[33] Thus, the new school would add roughly $1.5 million to the $66 million annual budget of the school system, plus a one-time renovation expense of over $800,000—all in a year when the City of Alexandria faced a $16 million deficit due to declining real estate values.[34] Compounding the City Council's frustration was Masem's uncooperative position over reducing the education budget in the face of fiscal distress. When the city's budget office asked all city offices to prepare fiscal year 1994 budgets that pared expenditures back by five percent, Masem delivered a budget that increased his spending by two percent. In reaction to Masem's move, Councilmember Redella S. "Del" Pepper stated "I was just stunned." Council member David Speck added, "It wasn't particularly subtle."[35] While the City Council eventually approved both the ninth-grade center and a hold-steady 1994 budget, Masem's lack of tact in budget negotiations—over both the center and also the 1994 budget—won him no allies on the City Council, just at the time when he and the School Board would need them.

Tracking and the Fight to Preserve "Honors"

As preparations for the ninth-grade center continued, the district developed a new student grouping to be implemented at the new school. Adopted at roughly the same time that the School Board decided to forge ahead with the middle-school reform plan, the new policy aimed to phase out academic grouping of students. This new policy catalyzed a growing opposition against the School Board and Masem. A vocal group of parents—largely, but not exclusively white—contended that the anti-tracking plan would only further water down the rigor of Alexandria's academic program, hastening the flight of parents who felt that the quality of school system was declining.

The fight began as a group of students in honors classes appealed to the school board to not eliminate a ninth-grade Honors Western Civilization course. The administration had been planning to offer only one world civilization course (required of all ninth-graders) but the common course prompted outcry that the lack of differentiation would produce less learning. Speaking before the school board, Ben Adams, a ninth-grader at George Washington Junior High, claimed, "The future students of Alexandria are going to be deprived of opportunities.... This is a threat to the very foundation of our educational system." Clare Stackhouse, a tenth-grade T.C. Williams student, questioned, "What credible high school does not have an honors program?"[36]

In response, the School Board backpedaled, indicating that it was not eliminating honors courses, and modified the proposal to keep the existing Honors Western Civilization course, but stated that any student would be allowed to enroll in the course.[37] Despite the concession on the Western Civilization class, the broader policy of reducing academic grouping of students remained in effect and continued to prompt controversy and conflict. As both the ninth-grade center and the middle-school reorganization proceeded, activist parents, particularly among white, upper middle-class neighborhoods, appealed to the City Council to force the School Board to reverse the policy. For his part, Masem contended that academic grouping hurt low-achieving students and did not provide any particular benefit for high-achieving students, claiming that a fundamental issue of fairness in the delivery of public education was at stake: "The issue is whether the way we are organized [as a school district] permits us to provide equity in education," he said. "Research shows that traditional grouping hurts poor and minority students, as do traditional remedial programs. The gap widens and self-esteem drops."[38]

Masem's plan, however, directly challenged a long-term implicit understanding at T.C. Williams: tracking kept the peace. The threat to that peace emerged, in part, because Masem took seriously the task of focusing on minority student achievement, and, in part, because all students enrolled in public school in Alexandria attended one high school. For some parents, tracking was the glue that kept them attached to an economically diverse school; it enabled them to reconcile the wide class and racial cleavages within Alexandria to the idea of academic preparation for an Ivy League college. From Masem's perspective, however, tracking generated the very cleavages that a public education aimed to alleviate: "We have a mission to make this multicultural society work," Masem stated. "We ought to give every kid who comes through the doors a fair shot at earning a place in society."[39]

The most strident foes of the plan replied that Masem's effort amounted to little more than "social engineering"[40] and was an illegitimate compromise of the interests of higher-achieving households, seen largely in racial terms. Walter Diercks, a leader of the parent group opposing the new policy, predicted that the conflict was "going to get real ugly.... You just don't mess with people's kids. It reaches basic emotions—'I'll protect my children at all cost.'"[41] The proposed mixing of students of differing abilities—even in elementary school—was untenable for some teachers as well. One teacher at Cora Kelly Magnet School commented that "there are not enough good students to go around. We have too many leftovers who are not ready to learn and will pull everyone down." With divisions in the city quickly hardening, City Councilmember Lonnie Rich told a newspaper reporter, "There's brewing a fairly serious political/education crisis in the city.... If it's not resolved, there will be widespread flight" from Alexandria's public schools.[42] He added that "the [school] system is not going to survive if middle-class blacks and whites are not vested in it."[43]

In reaction to the public pressure, Mayor Patricia Ticer requested that the School Board hold a public meeting to address questions about the policy in an effort to defuse tensions. School Board Chair Angie Godfrey agreed, admitting, "There are a lot of racial issues we need to confront."[44] The public meeting did little to resolve the racial issues, however. At times, parents and school officials engaged in "shouting matches" during the public forum. Parent Hal Alterman called the administrators' statements at the meeting "gobbledygook" and told a reporter that he was "pulling my daughter out" of public school and placing her in a private school.[45] On the other side, many black parents complained that their children were not sufficiently challenged in class, with low teacher expectations and a Gifted and Talented program that overenrolled white students.[46] Nolan Dawkins, a black judge in town, told a reporter, "There's no way I can be convinced that 18.5 percent of all students belong in the talented and gifted program."[47] In the end, John Haines expressed the views of many parents when he invoked the upcoming local referendum on whether the School Board should be elected, telling an administrator, "We [parents] should sit down ... and come up with some excellent candidates for School Board.... That should be our next move."[48]

Some School Board members did themselves no favors during this struggle by labeling all opposition to the grouping policy as racially motivated. One African American School Board member called honors courses themselves "racist" and another told the *Alexandria Gazette*, "The bottom line is not curriculum changes. It's about my big, black son sitting next to someone's little white daughter."[49] In many ways, the divergent views over whether tracking was necessary to ensure a quality education for higher-achieving students or was simply a way to preserve segregation within integrated schools mapped onto one's view about whether Alexandria had really changed as a community. One administrator in the school system expressed sympathy for African American school board members working to end tracking. Many black leaders "project their own experiences onto this scene. They see a situation where lots of bright black kids are being systematically excluded from honors courses—the way they may have been when they were growing up."[50] For these leaders, veterans of the conflicts under Superintendents T.C. Williams and John Albohm, to fight for the equal treatment of white and black students was to fight the continuing effects of Jim Crow Virginia, to battle long-standing and entrenched prejudices. These prejudices, from their point of view, might no longer be expressed as directly as they once were, but they still drove the division of resources in Alexandria schools. From their perspective, a teacher who regarded academic low-achieving elementary children as "leftovers" who might bring down other students simply reflected a systemic bias against children in poverty, who were disproportionately black in Alexandria.

Others, even some within the black community, were more critical of the civil rights establishment in Alexandria. One black teacher expressed frustration over the quality of black leadership, claiming that "The black leadership [in Alexandria] is afraid that they will look bad if they face what horrible shape so many of these students are in."[51] A white parent expressed sympathy for the black community, saying that black students in Alexandria "are being sold down the river again, [but] this time it's by their leadership in Alexandria [which] insists on seeing their kids as victims."[52]

Perceptions of Cronyism and the Resort to Direct Election

The perception that the school board and Masem were less concerned with educating children and more concerned with appeasing the interests of particular constituencies also informed the backlash against the School Board. Author and T.C. Williams English teacher Patrick Welsh recounted an encounter he had with a City Councilmember, in which he asked why the Council reappointed a school board member widely regarded as inept: "A few years ago when I asked why a notoriously ineffective and factious School Board member was reappointed, a City Council member told me 'there was no way' they could get rid of the member because it was an election year and the member delivered Democratic votes."[53] In an interview, former Superintendent Herb Berg (who followed Masem) described the appointed School Board as "almost a patronage system" in which the "School Board members deferred slavishly to the City Council."[54] In turn, according to Welsh, School Board members expected to derive benefits for either themselves or for their own constituents. Welsh cited instances of School Board members orchestrating the reassignments of principals, determining what courses a teacher would teach, and intervening in disciplinary matters. Berg characterized the Board's approach as "ward-based politics" that had influence "down to teacher hiring," in which nepotism or "hiring on the basis of personal connections" was common.[55] A school district administrator commented that some of the Board members "have a very narrow focus. As long as they get what they want they are happy, but the whole suffers."[56]

The upshot of the reciprocal relationship between the City Council and the School Board was a sense among community members, particularly parents, that they had little influence over school district policy or direction. Citywide PTA President Patricia Moran told Welsh, "Nothing the community says affects what [board members] do.... They renewed Masem's contract when parents wanted him out. People are moving to other districts and putting kids in private school because of them. Potential home purchasers think twice about moving here because of the image this Board has created. It's time they were held accountable."[57]

That time came in the fall of 1993, when the voters of Alexandria passed by an overwhelming margin the local referendum on elected school boards. With Democratic City Councilman Lonnie Rich organizing a slate of candidates endorsed by the group Alexandrians for Better Community Schools (ABCs), the supporters of elected school boards won in every precinct in the city, garnering nearly 74 percent of the vote.[58] The result was a resounding victory for the notion of electoral accountability and launched a campaign for nine new School Board members in the spring of 1994. After some debates over at-large versus ward-based elections, the City Council approved a three-district election format, in which each district would elect three board members. While the NAACP made efforts to halt the election, the U.S. Justice Department approved the election format, a review required under the Voting Rights Act.

The May 1994 election yielded an outpouring of candidates, with seventeen candidates joining the race. Only four of the nine appointed school board members chose to run in the election, and three of the four won election, with Vice Chair Leslie Barnes Hagan losing, and Vernon Collins, Rodger Digilio, and Stephen Kenealy winning. Two other former School Board members lost their bids to rejoin the board. Only one African American, newcomer Bernadette Johnson-Green, won election, confirming the Alexandria NAACP's fears that an elected body would shrink the pool of African American officeholders in the city. A week after the election, newspaper reports indicated that Masem was a finalist for a superintendent's position in University Heights, Ohio, although rumors of his departure had been circulating for weeks. In early June, Masem accepted the Ohio post.[59]

With elections bringing in six new Board members and the appointment of a new superintendent, the electoral accountability movement in Alexandria produced a sweeping change of governance and personnel within a short period of time. Herb Berg, the man hired to replace Masem, characterized the new Board as "wild revolutionaries" with no ties to the old Board and no ties to the City Council: "They were coming in to change things. It was a sea-change in this place."[60]

After the new Board came into office, it made an explicit effort to reach out to community members, in an effort to capitalize on the newfound reform energy. Conducting community meetings, surveying community residents about the characteristics they would like to see in a superintendent, and forming a citizens' advisory committee to aid their search, the new Board went out of its way to incorporate public views into the superintendent search process. The Board settled on Herb Berg, a dynamic and politically savvy superintendent from Puyallup, Washington. While Masem may have had difficult relations with some members of the Alexandria community, Berg threw himself into community outreach and engagement: "At one point," Berg said in an interview, "I had twenty-seven consecutive nights out at meetings or events."[61]

Despite the fact that the City Council no longer appointed School Board members, Berg was keenly aware that it held the purse strings for the school district.

"The people with the gold rule," he said. "You've got to work with them to accomplish what you want to accomplish." In an effort to build better bridges between the Superintendent's Office, the City Council and the School Board (something lacking during Masem's tenure) Berg instituted a monthly meeting among all the key players: the Mayor, the Vice Mayor, the Chair of the School Board, the Vice-Chair, the Superintendent, and City Manager Vola Lawson. "We met on their turf, on their grounds, and I tried not to do things without telling them in advance." But, Berg added, these were not all easy meetings, "there were tensions in those meetings." The "wild revolutionaries" who had been elected, Berg said, "wanted stuff."[62]

An Accountability of Proficiency: From Inputs to Outputs

The stuff that Berg and the School Board wanted was not insignificant. Berg's plans for the school district included a complete technology upgrade for the entire school system, as well as a major capital spending plan that would revamp several school facilities and build the first new elementary school in the district in forty-seven years. Berg also started began a Primary Years Initiative that focused on K-2 students, with the aim of getting all students on grade level in math and reading by the end of second grade. Importantly, he also created a program designed to comply with the accountability provisions of Virginia's newly adopted Standards of Learning program.

While many of the other Superintendents in Northern Virginia were opposed to test-based accountability, Berg embraced it. "If you've got high [socioeconomic status] students, you don't need standards. If you've got a district with troubled kids, you can use the standards to push past" the obstacles those kids face.[63] In many ways, Berg's acceptance of the statewide accountability effort emerged from the contexts of his own appointment by a newly elected School Board committed to the idea of greater accountability in Alexandria's schools. While the statewide effort to develop an accountability regime had a more "back to basics" element, its local reception in Alexandria was conditioned by a growing frustration with the persistent underperformance of poor and minority students and a sense among reformers that the local school system was not attending to the fundamentals of instruction. In short, the political forces that produced a local accountability movement meant that the statewide effort would find a more or less welcome reception in Alexandria.

Virginia has long been at the forefront of the accountability movement. The origins of its accountability regime date back to the 1968 state constitution, which mandated a "high quality" system of public education and required the state Board of Education to devise "standards of quality" by which to judge the public schools. Later, in the midst of the 1970s competency movement, the state Board of Education devised "standards of learning" for students. These efforts were amplified in 1986 when Democratic Governor Gerard Baliles appointed an eighteen-member

Commission on Excellence in Education, urging the commissioners to propose bold reforms in Virginia's public school system.[64] The commission's recommendations resulted in new Standards of Quality that required an assessment of all sixth graders in reading, writing, and arithmetic. These tests comprised the "Passport to Literacy" which all students had to pass (in either the sixth, seventh, or eighth grades) before being promoted to ninth grade, marking the first time the state linked a mandatory assessment to grade promotion.[65]

In Alexandria, the Passport to Literacy did not go well: In 1990, the first administration of the test, only 52 percent of Alexandria's sixth graders passed, compared with the statewide pass rate of 65 percent.[66] Among major school systems in Northern Virginia, Alexandria's student performance on Passport to Literacy tests was the lowest: 74 percent of neighboring Arlington's sixth-graders passed; 81 percent of Fairfax County's and 79 percent of Falls Church's sixth-graders passed.[67] These results, which emerged during Superintendent Paul Masem's efforts to close the minority achievement gap, fueled parental concern that Alexandria was not keeping up with neighboring jurisdictions. It also reinforced the growing awareness of a black-white test score gap that had been made explicit by Superintendent Robert Peeble's release of test score data by racial groups in 1985. The relative underperformance of Alexandria students, compared to neighboring jurisdictions, led to more vocal demands for academic rigor and a sense that Masem's strategy of eliminating tracking and honors classes was the wrong approach to beefing up Alexandria's academic expectations.

The enthusiasm across Virginia for accountability and standards grew significantly in the early to mid-1990s. While Democratic Governor Douglas Wilder's efforts to adopt a "Common Core of Learning" ran afoul of religious conservative objections that his administration was seeking to impose secular beliefs on students,[68] his successor, Republican Governor George Allen, nonetheless forged ahead with a plan to both revise the state standards and also to increase the scope of state testing based on those standards. In 1994, his Champion Schools Commission undertook an effort to revise the state's educational standards, pursuing a more "back-to-basics" understanding of educational performance standards.[69] A year later, the state Board of Education adopted revised standards for language arts, math, and science in every grade of Virginia's schools. The state expected local districts to incorporate these revised "Standards of Learning" into their curricula.[70]

In 1996, the state Board of Education fused those Standards of Learning (SOLs) to a statewide testing regimen that required annual assessments for students in grades three, five, eight, and high school. As criterion-referenced assessments, keyed to the new SOLs, these tests would drive the state accreditation process for schools, as well as serve as mandatory high school graduation requirements for students.[71] All told, the state required twenty-seven tests to be administered annually in five subject areas (math, science, language arts, social studies, and computer technology).[72] While no consequences fell on elementary school children for failing to pass SOLs, a Virginia high school student would not be able to earn a high school diploma without passing at least six "end-of-course" SOLs during high school. (Nine passing SOL scores were needed for the more rigorous "advanced" diploma.)

The tests also held consequences for schools as well. In order for a school to earn state accreditation, 70 percent of its students had to pass the SOLs in the four core assessments (English, Math, Science, and History/Social Studies). In addition, the schoolwide SOL test results would be distributed to all parents in an annual School Performance Report Card. While many educators complained that these assessments (all standardized multiple-choice tests, except in English) paid little attention to critical thinking skills or social contexts, their supporters contended that these assessments were "content-rich" and forced students to master clear and objective knowledge in order to graduate from high school.[73]

All told, the SOL revisions and the creation of a formal accountability system represented a major consolidation of state authority over education in Virginia. While both the graduation requirements and the school-level accreditation process would be phased in over several years, many districts in Northern Virginia were deeply opposed to the incursion into local control of curricula and assessment. The state had long established graduation requirements, but the imposition of multiple high-stakes tests in order to graduate from high school was seen by many critics as unfair, particularly to students in poverty. As Lawrence Cross, a professor of educational research and evaluation at Virginia Tech, contended, "The deeply rooted social and economic problems associated with poor test performance cannot be resolved by shaming the victim or the schools."[74]

In Alexandria, however, the newly elected School Board—along with its newly chosen Superintendent—endorsed many of the elements of the standards and accountability efforts of the state Board of Education, at times even carrying the reforms further than the state Board was willing to go. In fact, in 1999, one year after the first administration of the new SOL tests, the Alexandria School Board decided to incorporate the results of the high school SOL "end-of-course" exams into each student's grade for the course. The idea, according to Board members, was to focus students' attention on the tests, even though passing the SOLs would not be required for graduation until 2004. School Board member Rodger Digilio told a *Washington* Post reporter, "The only way you can assure an accurate appreciation of the situation on the part of students is to make the tests count."[75] Alexandria was the first district in Northern Virginia to adopt the policy of incorporating test results into students' final grades, but the Board endorsed the proposal unanimously. Vice Chair Claire Eberwein stated, "We are moving our entire system toward the higher standard, and so whatever we do to improve student attitude toward the test will ultimately decide if our schools will be accredited. We don't have the luxury of fooling around."[76]

A few weeks later, the School Board again took measures to expand the accountability regime, this time approving cash bonuses to principals whose schools raised their SOL scores significantly. The Board allocated $34,000 for the bonuses and authorized Superintendent Berg to determine the size of the individual awards and the testing targets each principal would have to meet. The School Board had promised Berg himself a $30,000 bonus in the fall of 1998 if the school system hit specified achievement levels within four years,[77] but the principal bonus plan was the first one approved in the Washington, DC area. The Board's enthusiasm for the idea of incentives was not limited to principals either: At the time of its adoption, "several Alexandria School Board members said they may eventually extend the bonuses to teachers..."[78] Other members of community were less enthusiastic. In fact, Alexandria's principals themselves vetoed their own bonus plan, arguing that teachers and other staff were just as responsible for any test score boost.

The Superintendent's office was as supportive of the new accountability scheme as the School Board, and also took actions that signaled the new get-tough attitude. In the fall of 1998, Superintendent Herb Berg announced that Alexandria was ending the policy of social promotion: "Beginning with this school year," Berg told a reporter, "we are putting an end to social promotion in Alexandria,... Students have to meet the grade-level standard to be promoted." While he acknowledged there would be complaints and a "disproportionate number of retentions" in the first year, he reasoned "once the children and their families realize that we are serious about learning, the students will rise to the new standard."[79]

An indication of the district's support for the accountability regime could also be seen in 2001, as the Alexandria PTA Council sought more information from schools about how SOL test preparation was influencing classroom instruction. Members of the PTA Council had formed a Standards of Learning Awareness Committee (SOLAC) and sought permission from the ACPS to survey teachers and principals about the effects of SOLs on what was taught and the amount of time devoted to arts, music, and other non-tested subjects. Monte Dawson, director of monitoring and evaluation services for ACPS, refused SOLAC's request, indicating that the survey would take up too much staff time and duplicate an existing state survey. In response to Dawson, PTA Council President Christopher Colligan wrote that "you must be aware that a sizeable portion of the ACPS community continues to be concerned about the effects of the SOLs and the culture of all-or-nothing end-of-the-year tests on our student body," adding that SOLAC's goal was simply one of fact-finding. SOLAC member Allen Flanigan told a reporter, "I cannot imagine a responsible educator who would not want to receive feedback from the frontlines about such a sweeping reform effort."[80]

Part of Alexandria's increasing defensiveness may have stemmed from the continuing poor performance of the district's students on statewide tests. Despite the increased attention to accreditation and allocating more resources to schools with higher percentages of children in poverty, Alexandria's SOL results between 1998 and 2005 were invariably the worst in Northern Virginia. Figures 7.1 through 7.6 show the percentage of students in grades 3, 5, and 8 that passed their SOLs in Math

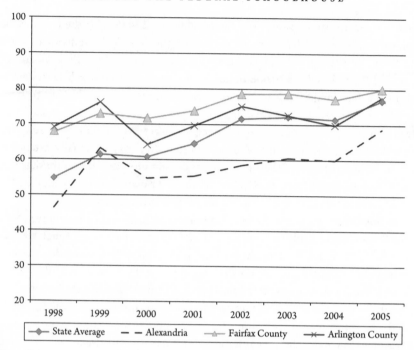

Figure 7.1 Alexandria and environs, percentage of 3rd graders passing English SOL, 1998–2005.
Source: Virginia Department of Education

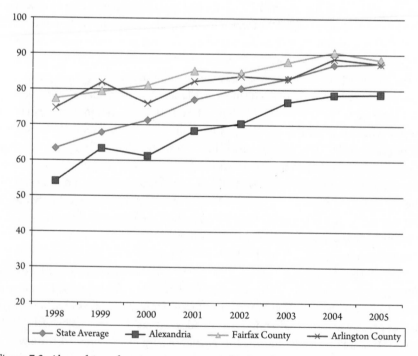

Figure 7.2 Alexandria and environs, percentage of 3rd graders passing Math SOL,
1998–2005. Source: Virginia Department of Education

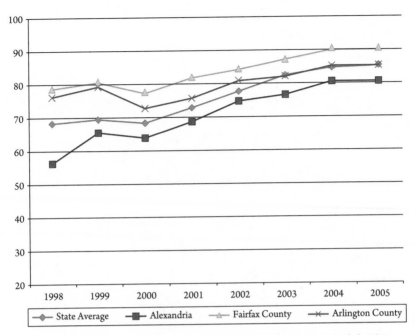

Figure 7.3 Alexandria and environs, percentage of 5th graders passing English SOL, 1998–2005. Source: Virginia Department of Education

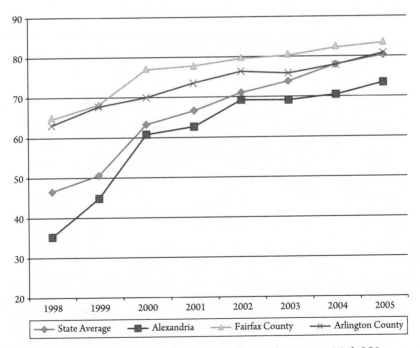

Figure 7.4 Alexandria and environs, percentage of 5th graders passing Math SOL, 1998–2005. Source: Virginia Department of Education

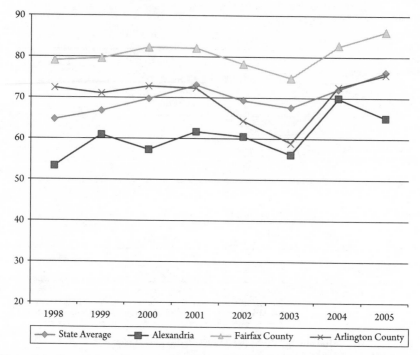

Figure 7.5 Alexandria and environs, percentage of 8th graders passing English SOL, 1998–2005. Source: Virginia Department of Education

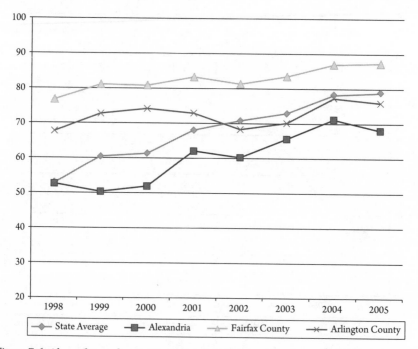

Figure 7.6 Alexandria and environs, percentage of 8th graders passing Math SOL, 1998–2005. Source: Virginia Department of Education

and English during this time period. While the trend lines generally show steadily increasing percentages of students passing the SOLs over time, Alexandria students, in comparison to their neighboring jurisdiction, performed significantly worse on the SOLs. Of course, Alexandria enrolled higher percentages of poor and minority students during this time than these other districts, but aside from third grade math in 1999, Alexandria never exceeded the statewide averages for these assessments over this eight-year period.

These comparatively low pass rates held consequences for the accreditation process in Alexandria as well. In the first three years of the SOL administration, only two of Alexandria's seventeen schools earned full accreditation.[81] While virtually all Alexandria's schools were either fully or provisionally accredited by 2004, their success in the accreditation process was, in significant part, more a product of acclimation to the tests and lowered state requirements than demonstrably higher achievement. Indeed, the frustration of school officials and a growing backlash throughout Virginia against both the newly designed SOLs and the low rates of school accreditation led state authorities to lower the cut scores for students on the history SOLs as well as allow districts to omit the test scores of students with limited English proficiency who had been in Virginia schools for less than five years.[82] As a result, SOL pass rates increased substantially across the state after the first two years of SOL administration. As one analysis of the history of SOLs concluded, "The revised standards and the lower cut scores, in conjunction with a teaching force growing increasingly more adept at test preparation, contributed to the sharp rise in scores."[83]

But the initial wave of citywide low test scores were not the only concerns of local residents as state-level accountability overtook local electoral accountability as the primary vehicle of school reform in Alexandria. Among African Americans in Alexandria, concerns about the impact of high-stakes testing on graduation rates intersected with growing apprehension about a lack of representation on the now-elected School Board. The first elected School Board saw only one African American candidate elected in 1994, and the second elected Board in 1997 had no African American members. After Bernadette Johnson, the sole African American Board member, lost her reelection bid in 1997, Antoine Cobb, chair of the Alexandria NAACP Education Committee, told a reporter, "Our worst fears have come true."[84] School Board Chair Claire Eberwein obliquely addressed the legitimating function of African American representation on the School Board when she commented to a reporter that she was personally "very disappointed we don't have more minority representation on the board.... It makes it more difficult to govern," she said, "because it makes one's actions suspect, no matter how fair" they may seem to be to the Board.[85]

The Board certainly did not win over supporters within the African American community when it passed over Acting Superintendent Maxine Wood in 1994 in order to select Herb Berg as Superintendent. Wood, an African American, had arrived in Alexandria in 1988 after a twenty-year career in Baltimore City schools and enjoyed considerable support in the African American community. But, according to former School Board member and chair Rodger Digilio, Wood was too much of an incrementalist reformer, not one to undertake the rapid changes within the school system that the School Board envisioned.[86]

Superintendent Berg, however, recognized that unless he addressed those potential tensions, his endorsement of a performance-based accountability model amidst the persistence of a white-black test score gap could potentially exacerbate the political fallout over low test scores. Berg was able to manage those reactions, partially by working with a new generation of black leadership, particularly former School Board member and future Mayor Bill Euille, whom Berg characterized as a political "star on the way." Euille understood, according to Berg, the need to raise expectations for students, and gave Berg his political support: "Mr. Euille knew that I was trying to improve learning for black kids. Because of that he was incredibly supportive and helpful. He gave me cover that I appreciate to this day."[87] In particular, Berg singled out his Primary Years Initiative as the program that won Euille over: "This was the program," Berg said, "that caused Euille to be on my side."[88]

Conclusion

Berg left Alexandria's schools in 2001, a few months before No Child Left Behind required all school districts to disaggregate student test results by race, class, English-language proficiency, special needs status, and gender. But the movement to NCLB was, in administrative terms, relatively painless for Virginia, as its own accountability model looked similar to the one required by NCLB. As SOL scores increased in the early 2000s, whether because of growing student and teacher familiarity, or less stringent standards, test-based accountability eventually achieved a grudging acceptance within Virginia. Even so, Alexandria's early endorsement of test-based accountability was remarkable, an acceptance that both ran counter to the general trend in Northern Virginia and at times asked even more accountability from students and staff than what the state was willing to ask. Given the racial demographics in Alexandria and its past performance on other forms of standardized assessments, this eager reception seems particularly odd, especially since it was clear early on that Alexandria would not necessarily do well under the SOL regime. The answer lies in the fact that political support for the idea of accountability—initially cast as electoral accountability—was fused during the late 1990s to the notion of test-based accountability. Both efforts were seen, at the local level, as mechanisms to improve the rigor of education and to produce rapid change within an educational establishment seen as unwilling to change and unresponsive to calls for change.

In short, Berg's own personal views in favor of accountability and standards were reinforced by both the reformist Board that hired him and the hundreds of vocal parents who voted for an elected School Board in order to pursue higher standards and greater accountability in Alexandria's schools. The combination meant that political fallout over the racial disparities in academic performance was somewhat muted by the broad support for increased rigor in Alexandria's schools and the perception that Virginia's Standards of Learning could help enforce that rigor. In this way, the local politics of accountability in Alexandria—first launched by the effort to create elected school boards and to move away from what was perceived as a patronage-based system of educational governance—helped lay the foundations for both a local acceptance of Virginia's Standards of Learning and later, No Child Left Behind.

As the acronyms shifted from SOLs to NCLB and AYP, however, the tenor of the conversation shifted, as we will see in the next chapter. As the federally required attention to race and class reasserted itself, the school system became more focused on meeting a formulaic notion of proficiency, rather than systemic reform. Objections over the initial implementation of NCLB were drowned out by a local scandal and growing School Board infighting. In the midst of this conflict, old tensions surrounding the test score gap resurfaced and shaped the school system's ability to respond to the demands of federally imposed school transformation.

8

The Titans Meet the State: Federal Accountability and School Transformation

Introduction

On the stage of the John C. Albohm Auditorium at T.C. Williams High School, it was a remarkable gathering: The U.S. Secretary of Education Arne Duncan; former Washington Redskins star Darrell Green; Bill Euille, the first African American mayor of Alexandria; and Ferdinand Day, Alexandria's first African American School Board Member and Chair. The event was the 2010 Alexandria City Public Schools Convocation, in which the entire faculty and staff of the school system gathered for a back-to-school celebration prior to the start of the school year.

Mayor Euille awarded Day with a commendation for his devoted service to his community, citing his integration of Alexandria's secondary system, nearly forty years earlier. ACPS Superintendent Morton Sherman honored Day with a gift from Alexandria's Congressman Jim Moran: a US flag that had flown over the US Capitol building on the day of President Obama's inauguration.[1] Secretary Duncan spoke of the continuing need to challenge students for the realities of work and higher education: "We have to, as a country, raise our expectations of what we can do for every single child."[2]

The gathering seemed to fuse the symbols of dramatic transformation and progress in two eras of American educational and political history: a local civil rights leader from the 1960s, honored by an African American mayor (who got his start in politics on the Alexandria City School Board) and presented with a flag celebrating the inauguration of the first African American U.S. President. And all of them urged on to greater success by a Secretary of Education committed to the notion of educational achievement as this generation's civil rights struggle. The day could not have been more celebratory of the achievements of a civil rights agenda.

Except for one thing: The venue for the event, T.C. Williams High School, had been labeled a few months earlier as a "persistently lowest-achieving" school, according to the metrics established by the U.S. Department of Education, under the School Improvement Grant program, a Department of Education program significantly expanded under the 2008 America Recovery and Reinvestment Act. Because T.C. Williams's students scored in the bottom five percent of all Title I-eligible high schools in Virginia on language arts and math tests and because it had not reduced its failure rate by 10–15 percent per year over the past two years, it was one of six high schools in Virginia (and the only one in Northern Virginia) to be dubbed as a "persistently lowest- achieving" school.[3] While this status made T.C. Williams eligible for $6 million dollars over three years in new federal aid, it also required that the school undergo major federally imposed reforms. Perhaps of equal importance, the designation sharply affected the city's and the school district's self-perception. With local newspapers bearing the headlines "T.C. in Crisis" and "Wake-Up Slap for T.C. Williams" the news jolted many in the community who thought that, while the school had some problems, it was a generally well-regarded institution.[4]

Indeed, the school, in many ways, was not the "dropout factory" that many schools on the "persistently lowest-achieving" list were. Its graduation rate averaged 77 percent in 2008 and 2009.[5] Of those graduates, over 50 percent went to some form of higher education.[6] In addition, between 2005 and 2009, the percentage of students taking at least one AP exam averaged 24 percent of the student body, with the number of total AP tests administered increasing 23 percent over that time.[7] Even more remarkably, T.C. Williams students were earning higher scores while taking more AP tests: Between 2005 and 2009, the percentage of AP exams taken by T.C. Williams students who earned a score of three or higher climbed from 39 percent to 54 percent.[8] In short, during the time period that the U.S. Department of Education found T.C. Williams to be a persistently lowest-achieving school, over half of its students were heading off to higher education and more students were taking more AP exams and scoring higher on the tests.

That being said, however, T.C. Williams's performance on state and federally mandated assessments has been, at best, uneven. In 2008–2009, one out of four eleventh-graders failed their end-of-course assessments in mathematics and one out of six failed their reading assessments.[9] Importantly, these relatively high failure rates were not distributed evenly across demographic groups: In the 2008–2009 reading assessments, 33 percent of all students at T.C. Williams scored at the "Advanced" level in Reading, but for white students that figure was 71 percent, but only 18 and 20 percent for African American and Hispanic students, respectively. Among economically disadvantaged students, only 16 percent scored at the Advanced level. At the other end of the testing distribution, 13 percent of African American and 12 percent of Hispanic and economically disadvantaged students failed the End-of-Course reading test, while only 3 percent of whites failed.[10] Among T.C. Williams's students, whites were clustered at the high end of achievement test scale, while African Americans, Hispanics, and poor students were overrepresented at the low end of the test score distribution. These racially skewed figures have remained stubbornly consistent at T.C. Williams for quite a few years. As the school system indicated in its 2011 response to its "persistently lowest-achieving" designation, "The reality that some students are not meeting state performance guidelines is not new.... These results are ones we have seen over the course of many years ... ."[11]

This chapter continues the examination of accountability politics in Alexandria, with a focus on federal efforts to improve the educational achievement of Alexandria's students, first through No Child Left Behind and then through the process of school transformation at T.C. Williams High School under the School Improvement Grant. Both these federal efforts yielded a local push for proficiency—particularly at T.C. Williams—that has placed enormous professional strain on education officials in Alexandria, and prompted significant reforms at a number of underperforming schools. Indeed, efforts to remove Alexandria's flagship high school from the U.S. Department of Education's list of "persistently lowest-achieving" schools have, since 2009, been a consuming passion for the staff of both T.C. Williams and the school district. Their efforts to respond to the demands of federal accountability policies are constrained, however, by poor federal guidance, poverty, and language barriers confronting their students—as well as the community expectations of what T.C. Williams represents: a common public high school for all Alexandria's youth. The reality is that the decision to unite all high-schoolers in Alexandria—a decision made in the early 1970s and one, for political reasons, unlikely to be undone—helped create a school system in which the civil rights rhetoric of No Child Left Behind could actually gain political traction. With all the city's youth anchored to one high school the commitment to ensure that the education at T.C. Williams was first rate was strong. At the same time, the racial and economic diversity of T.C. Williams also meant that the local political support for the school leadership hinged on its ability to manage divergent parental expectations about schooling and post-high school plans. Because T.C. Williams (and Alexandria's schools as a whole) have educated upper middle-class, Ivy League-bound students, as well as students from housing projects—and now immigrant students from Central America, East Africa and other far-flung locales—its school leadership must frequently navigate among the competing pressures that arise from these diverse constituencies. At the same time, however, federal accountability policies have begun to narrow the political space in which Alexandria schools must navigate those concerns and demands. The federal insistence on proficiency—and its willingness to label anything short of full proficiency as failure—has thwarted the ability of T.C. Williams's staff and district leaders to create robust and rich schooling for kids who are teetering on the edge of failure or success.

Indeed, this chapter argues, in three sections, that the inflexible accountability mechanisms built into NCLB and the school transformation process made it more difficult for T.C. Williams—and schools throughout the nation—to address the real causes of the achievement gap. In short, the steps necessary to confront unequal learning do not, in the short run, produce the test score changes that NCLB requires. As a result, there are continual tradeoffs made between long-run lasting changes and short-term "fixes" that simply patch over the problem. The first section, "From Standards of Learning to No Child Left Behind," offers a brief overview of NCLB's requirements. In "NCLB in Alexandria: Initial Results and Local Scandal," the chapter explores NCLB's effects in Alexandria, as well as recounts an episode of School Board infighting that caused the district to lose focus on the ever-increasing demands of NCLB. The third section, "T.C. Williams in Transformation," turns to T.C. Williams's experiences under "school transformation," an extension of NCLB's accountability regime created under the School Improvement Grant program. The chapter concludes with some thoughts on the consequences of the accountability movement's turn away from inputs and its relentless focus on outputs of schooling.

From Standards of Learning to No Child Left Behind

The No Child Left Behind Act of 2001 sought to expand a modest federal accountability structure first enacted in the 1994 reauthorization of the Elementary and Secondary Education Act (ESEA). NCLB's structure requires that states and districts adopt a combination of federal- and state-defined requirements in order to receive federal education money. The requirements fall into four general categories: testing, setting goals, performance reporting, and sanctions for failing schools.[12] The testing is annual in grades three through eight in both reading and math and must be aligned with state-level curricular standards; every state must report annually which schools made their performance goals. Those performance reports are disaggregated into multiple subgroups encompassing major demographic divisions: race, class, language proficiency, special education students, as well as the entire school population. If any *one* of those subgroups fails to meet the performance goals established by the state, the entire school is deemed to have failed to meet its Adequate Yearly Progress (AYP) goals. Those goals are ratcheted up every year so that, in theory, all students in each state will have achieved "proficient" status in all testing areas by the year 2014. This ratcheting means, in effect, that if a subgroup or school falls behind in one year, it must redouble its efforts to meet next year's *higher* AYP goal. The law does provide a school a "safe harbor" if it fails to meet its proficiency target for a particular subgroup but is able to reduce the failure rate for that group by at least 10 percent.[13] Finally, 95 percent of students within a school must take the tests and the state AYP must also include at least one other indicator of academic attainment (typically graduation rates).

NCLB sanctions begin after a school has not met AYP for two consecutive years. At that time, a school is designated as "in need of improvement," a stage that lasts two years if a school does not meet AYP. While "in need of improvement," Title

I schools must offer all students at the school (not just Title I students) the option of attending another school within the district, with transportation provided; both Title I and non-Title I schools must develop school plans for improving test scores for subgroups that did not meet AYP. In addition, students who remain at a Title I school "in improvement" will be offered supplemental services, such as tutoring, provided either by the district or outside vendors, and approved by the district or state. If a school (Title I or not) does not meet AYP for all subgroups for two additional years, it enters "corrective action." Title I schools must still continue to provide school choice and supplemental services and all schools must undergo significant changes, including the adoption of a new curriculum, the replacement of school personnel, and extending the school day or year. If test scores are not increased during this one year of "corrective action," a school enters the most drastic phase of the sanctions, "restructuring," which involves one or more of the following: replacing all or most of the school staff, contracting the operation of the school to an outside management company, the conversion of the school to a charter school, or even the closure of the school. Title I schools in restructuring must still provide school choice and supplemental services.

These policies seek to leverage the federal government's spending on education by creating a hybrid federal-state standards-based accountability system that does not impose the consequences of high-stakes testing on students, but on school and district officials. But in order to put this system of accountability in place, federal lawmakers had to tread onto political and institutional turfs that had previously been largely the domain of state and local educational leaders. NCLB, in dramatic fashion, placed the federal government in the position of demanding that states, districts, and schools engage in a process of continuous improvement or otherwise face federally mandated sanctions that directly intruded on traditional prerogatives of local and state education officials. David Tyack and Larry Cuban have written of the "institutional grammar" of public education, in which the basic building blocks of schooling (classes, elementary schools, high schools, districts) appear remarkably constant across dramatically different demographic and geographic landscapes.[14] The changes wrought by NCLB challenge not so much the institutional grammar of education, but its "political grammar," with the federal government playing a much sharper coercive role than it has in the past.

Despite this intrusion, however, there has been little local organized effort in Alexandria—or anywhere, really—to halt the implementation of NCLB. While thirty-eight states have considered legislation opposing No Child Left Behind (and five states, including Virginia, have enacted laws expressing in some fashion opposition to NCLB) all states have effectively complied with at least the letter of the law.[15]

Instead, there has been growing dismay over NCLB's effects on at-risk students (who are more likely to drop out under a high-stakes accountability system) and its effects on school curricula and the narrowing of the educational ambitions of public schools. In the early years of implementation, states did engage in significant evasion of NCLB sanctions though state-level gamesmanship of cut scores and the manipulation of the size of subgroup categories in schools in order to exempt them from review. In recent years, however, NCLB's AYP targets have been increasingly out of reach even for high-performing schools, producing "failure" rates that approach 100 percent. Yet there has been little movement to reform NCLB in Congress, largely because of political stalemate on federal educational issues. With no movement from Congress and as proficiency targets have reached nearly absurd levels, the U.S. Department of Education has engaged in a wholesale strategy of offering states waivers from NCLB, with the condition that states adopt other federal educational objectives. In effect, the U.S. Department of Education has utilized waivers from a law that is essentially impossible to comply with in order to extract further education reforms from states, particularly reforms concerning the use of value-added measures for teacher evaluations and the opening of school systems to charter schools.

The transformative ambitions of NCLB's authors fueled little organized resistance, in part because the law's framework fragmented potential opponents. The policy, in effect, pursued ends that appealed to liberals, using mechanisms that were lauded by conservatives. In addition, the law's national scope meant that, if the states accepted federal money, the exit costs were enormously high for states and impossible for districts. As a result, most districts—and many states—simply tried to game the NCLB system in order to avoid its worst penalties rather than confront the underlying problem of achievement gaps. As Paul Manna has described the effects of No Child Left Behind, "By and large, NCLB's implementation tended to produce practices that decreased academic quality and expectations in the nations schools. Furthermore, it expanded bureaucratic rules that often led policy implementers to focus their efforts on meeting technical rules. As a result, substantively important outcomes for schools and students suffered."[16]

NCLB in Alexandria: Initial Results and Local Scandal

In Alexandria, NCLB's required subgroup breakdowns sharply revealed familiar patterns of racial and class disparities in test scores. While Virginia's SOL regime did not require schools to show that all student demographic groups were meeting the 70 percent proficiency target to achieve accreditation, NCLB's new Adequate Yearly Progress benchmark did. As a result, NCLB imposed a new category of inadequacy on schools that had only just achieved accreditation by the Virginia Department of Education. Indeed, in the first year of NCLB implementation less than 40 percent of Alexandria's elementary schools made Adequate Yearly Progress.

At the same time, these NCLB results do not indicate by any means a wholesale failure of Alexandria's elementary educational system. Because of the diversity within Alexandria's schooling system, the elementary schools had to meet proficiency

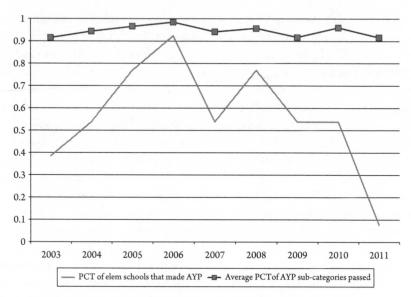

Figure 8.1 Alexandria elementary school AYP performance under No Child Left Behind, 2003–2011.
Source: Virginia Department of Education

targets in twenty-nine separate subcategories. Despite those obstacles, in the first four years of NCLB's implementation, Alexandria's elementary schools were on a rising AYP trajectory, with increasing numbers of schools satisfying proficiency targets in all twenty-nine subcategories. In 2006, all but one of the city's elementary schools made their AYP targets. In addition, Alexandria's elementary schools met the AYP proficiency targets in over 90 percent of the subcategories between 2003 and 2011, meaning that among those schools that were not making AYP, this shortfall was usually only in only a few categories, typically English-learners, African American students, and special needs students. After 2006, however, the trajectory of improvement changed and fewer Alexandria schools hit the AYP benchmarks in the succeeding six years.

But that trajectory change had little to do with declining test score performance. It's important to remember that the AYP percent proficiency targets were increasing by four points every year between 2003 and 2010: the math benchmark jumped from 59 percent to 83 percent during that time, while English increased from 61 to 85 percent. Thus the story of declining numbers of schools to make AYP in Alexandria after 2006 is less of a story about declining educational performance than it is about an ever higher federal bar of proficiency that eventually tripped up all Alexandria schools. Alexandria was by no means alone: By 2011, 61 percent of all schools in Virginia failed to make AYP, and 97 percent of all school districts in the state failed to make AYP.[17] In June 2012, the U.S. Department of Education granted Virginia a waiver from the "unrealistic and arbitrary" NCLB benchmarks, as the Virginia Department of Education press release described them.[18]

The political reaction in Alexandria to the decline in the numbers of schools meeting NCLB's AYP was, for the most part, muted. On one hand, the success in meeting Virginia's accreditation standards suggested that by one metric Alexandria's schools were doing better and voters could discount the federal indicators of "failure." On the other hand, there was growing concern that some of the district's actions taken under NCLB to address the failure to make AYP in some schools were disruptive to other successful schools. In fact, at a meeting between parents and Superintendent Rebecca Perry in April 2004 precisely those complaints were made. While the meeting itself was not politically momentous, the events in the immediate aftermath of the meeting set the stage for some of the most acrimonious moments in Alexandria's recent school history.

Local Scandal and School Board Dysfunction

The central item on the agenda of the PTA meeting at Lyles-Crouch Traditional Academy on April 22, 2004 was the recently announced transfer of highly popular and effective principal Lucretia Jackson from Lyles-Crouch to Maury Elementary, effective at the end of the school year. Although Maury Elementary had, as part of an elementary integration plan, been "paired" with Lyles-Crouch until the late 1990s, the performance of the two schools had recently been on very different trajectories. In 1999, during a controversial school boundary change, Lyles-Crouch and Maury were unpaired and Maury's boundaries were changed to include many of the students who lived in the housing projects near the Charles Houston Recreation Center and who were currently attending George Mason Elementary. The combination of the unpairing and the boundary shift produced a school population at Maury that was significantly poorer.

The academic results quickly showed. In 2003, Maury was the only school in Northern Virginia to be placed on NCLB's "needs improvement" list. In response, Superintendent Rebecca Perry had required all teachers at Maury to reapply for their jobs and offered rehired teachers a $3000 bonus if they hit performance targets on Maury's SOLs.[19] Despite these changes, Perry felt a need for new leadership at the school and decided to assign Lyles-Crouch principal Lucretia Jackson to Maury. The parents at Lyles-Crouch were informed of the change in a letter sent home with students, but many were outraged that they had not been consulted earlier about the change and sought to reverse Perry's decision at the meeting on April 22nd. According to Kate Watters, the incoming PTA President at Lyles-Crouch, "We were hoping that they would listen to us and reconsider this decision. The superintendent wasn't interested in our opinion and the Board members were condescending and dismissive. There was a lot of chest-thumping and very little listening. I was very disappointed."

Originally, according to press reports, Perry had not planned on attending the meeting, but decided to do so after receiving numerous emails from parents at

Lyles-Crouch concerned about the transfer.[20] The meeting was, by all accounts, fraught with tension, and attracted roughly one-hundred parents at a school that enrolled (at the time) under 250 students.[21] Later, School Board member Mark Eaton stated that Perry was subjected to "some of the most emotional and at times hostile questioning." According to Eaton, one parent remarked to Perry, "Get a clue…. You work for us."[22] Another parent told a reporter, "I have just come back from Liberia where I have been teaching an emerging democracy about transparency in government…. Perhaps I should have stayed home and given the seminar to this Board."[23]

After the meeting ended around 9:45p.m., Perry, a staff member, and School Board member Melissa Luby headed off to a nearby restaurant and had a few drinks. Perry and Luby left the restaurant about three hours later. A few blocks away, Alexandria police officer Seth Weinstein pulled Perry over for driving erratically.[24] Suspecting that Perry had been drinking, the officer administered a field sobriety test and a breathalyzer test, which registered 0.12 blood alcohol content, exceeding Virginia's legal limit of 0.08.[25] Perry claimed later that she had been "tired and stressed" after the Lyles-Crouch meeting, but that she only had a single glass of wine.[26] She was nonetheless charged with driving while intoxicated, and later pleaded guilty to the charge, receiving a $300 fine, a thirty-day suspended jail sentence, and a one year driver's license suspension. She was also ordered to enroll in an alcohol treatment program.[27]

The arrest put the School Board in an awkward position. Alexandria, like many school districts, had adopted a zero tolerance policy toward drugs and underage drinking and there was considerable public outcry over the School Board's hypocrisy when it simply placed Perry on one week's paid leave, while it deliberated her fate. A week after the arrest, the school board voted 7 to 1 to keep Perry, but it demanded that she make a public apology and shortened her contract by one year. (School Board Member Melissa Luby, who had been drinking with Perry, recused herself from the deliberations and vote.) Many members valued the progress Perry had made on earning accreditation for Alexandria's elementary schools and there was strong support for her instructional leadership. In addition, many Board members felt that hiring a new superintendent at this juncture—just as construction was beginning on the new T.C. Williams High School and as the district sought to comply with No Child Left Behind—would be too disruptive.

The public outcry grew more heated, however, when the School Board announced, shortly after her plea bargain, that Perry would be receiving a raise on her annual $168,000 salary. School Board Chair Mark Wilkoff defended the raise, saying Perry was contractually entitled to an annual pay increase comparable to the average wage increase of all ACPS employees. "It is a provision that has been in the contract from the very beginning," he said. "It is a non-performance-based adjustment."[28] The contractual commitment notwithstanding, many activist parents continued to fight Perry's retention, particularly a group of Lyles-Crouch parents who still smarted from the reassignment of Principal Lucretia Jackson to Maury Elementary. James Boissonnault, a Lyles-Crouch parent, started a recall petition against School Boardmember Melissa Luby, who had been drinking with Perry and was in the car when Perry was pulled over.

The School Board also took a beating in the local media: *Washington Post* columnist Marc Fisher ran a series of columns berating the board's hypocrisy on its zero tolerance standards. (The headline of one column read: "3 R's for Today: Rigid, Regressive and Unresponsive.").[29] Events turned personal when the School Board demoted Vice Chair Gwendolyn H. Lewis, who cast the sole vote against retaining Perry, and named a strong Perry supporter as vice chair in her place.[30] Events took something of a comic turn when Melissa Luby's nineteen-year-old son and a son of a City Councilmember were arrested and convicted of egging the house of James Boissonnault, Luby's recall antagonist.[31]

Even efforts on the Board to repair relations went poorly. In the midst of a two-day retreat in August, Board members traded accusations of personal attacks and inflammatory emails. Prior to the retreat, Board member Gwendolyn Lewis had sent her constituents an email alleging that the Board had "little or no leadership" and that the "Superintendent's arrogance and disrespect is the results [sic] of her employer, the Board, allowing her unbridled power to do whatever she wants to in the wake of her inexcusable behavior." At the retreat, Board member Sally Ann Baynard circulated a copy of the email to her fellow board members, arguing that it was "part of a pattern of distortion that is unacceptable.... Covert attacks on the Board and its members by its members should stop." In response, Lewis called upon her fellow Board members to halt their "mean-spirited, tyrannical behavior." At the conclusion of the retreat, School Board Chair Mark Wilkoff called for a second retreat, this one closed to the public and run by a trained facilitator.[32]

The Board sought to put an end to all this turmoil in November, when it voted 7-2 to renew Perry's contract for three more years. Board Chair Wilkoff indicated that there was broad support for Perry on the Board and that she had been a "real change agent" in the school district. "There's a tremendous amount of support for what Rebecca Perry has done for the school system," Wilkoff told a reporter.[33] Board member Charles Wilson estimated that public opinion ran about 70–30 percent in favor of keeping Perry, "But the 30 percent that says no, they make more noise than the rest."[34]

While the renewal of Perry's contract more or less resolved the matter for the Board, it did not remove opposition in the community. Views had hardened and a committed group of activists viewed the Board's contract renewal as a sign of its disengagement from community wishes.[35] When, in the fall of 2005, news emerged that most, if not all, of the School Board members would not be seeking reelection in Spring of 2006, many committed anti-Perry parents and community members saw a chance to reverse what they considered to be a fundamentally flawed decision.

Thirteen newcomers vied for eight seats in Spring 2006, with only incumbent Charles Wilson seeking to retain his seat. According to press reports, the battles of the past two years had taken their toll: while some outgoing members cited work or family reasons for their inability to stand for reelection, others "alluded to the difficulty and stress of being on a Board whose disagreements often deteriorated into personal attacks."[36] Shortly before the election, three outgoing members wrote an open letter to candidates seeking election to the Board, offering "a word of advice." They wrote "Personnel matters are explosive," and that "as a Board member your most sensitive (and some say only) employee relationship, of course, will be with the Superintendent." They added their own views on Perry's performance: "Based on the increase in the number of schools accredited under the SOLs, improved standardized test results, increased participation and success in Advanced Placement courses, and effective hiring and significant improvements in school facilities and programs, we think that position is very capably staffed in Alexandria."[37] Many of the candidates disagreed, however, and campaigned with an explicit commitment to begin a search for a new superintendent.

Eight new members were elected to the Board in spring of 2006 and Arthur Peabody, a clear opponent of Perry's, was selected chair as the Board assumed office in July. While the Board made a concerted effort at greater civility and vowed to operate with greater transparency than its predecessor, many of its members nonetheless made it clear that they were willing to push back against Perry's programs and administration. Newly elected board member Scott Newsham described a lack of transparency from officials in the central administration: "They're very defensive," he told a reporter. "You don't feel like you can approach them and really engage."[38] Other Board members cited the Superintendent's lack of specificity on the budget details as the Board negotiated with the City Council and her "top-down" administrative style, as well as her seeming detachment from community concerns, as reasons to watch Perry closely.[39]

The watching ended shortly enough. In May 2007, Board Chair Arthur Peabody told Perry in a private meeting that five Board members were ready to open the search for a new superintendent rather than renew her contract. Peabody failed, however, to inform the other four members of the Board of the sentiments of the "Backroom Five," as news accounts referred to them.[40] Nonetheless, after a closed session of the full Board on May 21 to discuss Perry's superintendency, the Board emerged and, without public debate or full comment, publicly voted 5-4 to not renew Perry's contract when it expired in June of 2008. Board members indicated that a confidentiality clause in Perry's contract prevented them from divulging their reasons for sacking Perry, but many in the community—who had found the educational progress under Perry to be remarkable—were upset by the sudden and secretive decision. Deputy Superintendent Cathy David told Board member Claire Eberwein in an email that "I strongly believe that change in the leadership of this school division will negatively impact the gains in student achievement that have been made over the past six years."[41] She also told a reporter that the school system had "the wind taken out of our sails."[42] Others worded their opposition to the Board's action more strongly: "The politics of hate and revenge have won.... And the children of Alexandria are the losers," said former Chair of the School Board Mark Wilkoff.[43]

When opponents challenged the Board's action because the Board had failed to provide the required thirty-day notice of a meeting to decide a superintendent's fate and that it had also failed to provide the statutorily required performance evaluation of the Superintendent, Board members indicated that their review process began long ago. Board Chair Peabody commented that "each member of the Board has been evaluating her since they took office."[44] As for the lack of public comment allowed at the May 21st meeting, Board member Claire Eberwein quipped, "I believe the citizens of Alexandria commented during the last election."[45]

Other citizens of Alexandria, however, saw the Board's actions as hasty and divisive. In particular, the African American leadership rallied around Perry. Chair of the Alexandria chapter of the NAACP, S. Howard Woodson (whose son was involved in the egging of a Perry opponent in 2004) commented that the decision was "based on personal vendettas and political agendas."[46] He added that "If this superintendent has been effective in helping minorities improve their achievement ... why is it that she's not wanted any longer?"[47] The first African American chair of the Alexandria School Board, Ferdinand Day—at age eighty-eight—made a rare appearance at a School Board meeting, coming out to testify "because," he said, "my city is in trouble.... There is a ... growing split, not only in the administration but among the citizenry of Alexandria."[48] He told the Board that the dismissal of Perry was poorly handled and would have lasting consequences. "The process was wrong," he said "And the ability of the public to understand the process was deliberately undermined" by the Board.[49]

Relations between the Board and Perry soured even more during the last few months of her contract. Eventually the two sides reached an agreement that would enable Perry to leave in January of 2008, five months ahead of schedule, but even this agreement ran aground in a last minute tiff between Perry and Eberwien, who was now School Board chair. The announced plan was that Perry's final day would be on Friday January 19, and she would be allowed to move her personal effects over the weekend. But when Eberwein and Perry clashed at the signing of the departure agreement on Thursday, she was told to clear everything out by Friday at 5p.m. At 5:05 Friday afternoon, the locksmith arrived to change the locks on the door.[50] Perry supporter and Board member Eileen Cassidy Rivera told a reporter "It was as if she were being treated as a criminal or a thief." Another supporter, Board member Sheryl Gorsuch commented that "It's unfortunate.... How we treat the Superintendent reflects on morale throughout the system." When asked if she had any advice for Alexandria superintendent candidates, Perry simply commented, "Don't come. At least not until after the next School Board election."[51]

On the surface, these internecine battles over a superintendent appear to have little relation to federal educational accountability policies. Instead they come off as the product of an excessively localized politics of personality. In many ways, they reflect the numerous critiques of school boards made over the past 30 years: Because of small electoral turnouts, school boards are not broadly representative, they are not always well-managed institutions, and they are often driven by the intense interests of a political minority.[52] At the same time, if we look at both the impetus and the consequences of the deteriorating performance of the Alexandria School Board we see that federal accountability policies played a key role in both generating the pressures imposed on Superintendent Perry and raising the stakes for the inability of the Board to provide effective leadership at both the district and school level.

The hostility that Perry confronted on that spring evening at Lyles-Crouch emerged because parents who felt a sense of entitlement over "their" principal were being told that her talents were needed in another, lower-performing school. The individual who told Perry to "get a clue, you work for us" was in fact chafing against the federally imposed obligation to ensure that *all schools* perform at higher levels of achievement. Truth be told, Rebecca Perry was not, in fact, working for Lyles-Crouch parents, but was instead responding to the federal frame of accountability, which in this instance collided with the local frame. Similarly, the frustration that some on the School Board felt about Perry's "top-down" style of management no doubt partially emerged from Perry's obligation to implement federal, not local, policies. The federal frame of accountability imposed on both ACPS and Perry, as its chief operating officer, the need to focus relentlessly on the outputs of education, not on the inputs that localist perspectives are so keen to adjust and regulate. Perry knew that moving Principal Jackson to Maury would probably enable that school to avoid federally required restructuring, and she moved her despite the intense pressures of Lyles-Crouch parents. Certainly, Perry did not need to drink and drive in order to manage those competing pressures; her lapse in judgment was acute. Nonetheless, the scandal of her arrest—and the subsequent political infighting among Board members—arose in part because of a federal imperative to govern Alexandria schools through a focus on the outputs of an Alexandria education, not its inputs.

For its part, the Alexandria School Board could have risen to this federal challenge in a far more graceful and effective way. Indeed, its inability (or unwillingness) to respond adequately proved to have further dire consequences, this time at T.C. Williams High School. The political catfights plaguing Alexandria's School Board between 2004 and 2007 came at a very bad time. Precisely when the school system needed to develop rigorous and focused strategies to satisfy the ever-increasing requirements of No Child Left Behind, it was frittering its institutional energies on the politics of succession. The result was profound institutional drift, as well as internal dissension, both in the school system and at T.C. Williams. An external audit of the school system's efficiency—a so-called "efficiency review," conducted by an external consultant, under Virginia Department of Education supervision—found a deep lack of confidence in the School Board among district administrators, as well as a profound lack of vision and focus from the Board. This voluntary review of the district's operations focused on its organizational management, budgeting and fiscal controls, facilities use, and transportation systems, as well as its human resource and technology management, and was undertaken primarily to ensure "educational dollars are being utilized to the fullest extent possible."[53] The report, while not primarily focused on the political features of the system, nonetheless found, in part, that the political dysfunction of the School Board was inhibiting the school system's efficiency. As the authors of the report wrote, "The School Board lacks a clearly articulated vision, mission, and goals that will guide the future of the school division," adding the Board "has been sidetracked from its traditional role of establishing a vision, mission, and goals...."[54]

The report also surveyed senior district administrators and principals about their perceptions of the School Board. The results showed a profound lack of confidence in the Board members among administrators: 3 percent of central office administrators considered the board members' knowledge of the operations of the school division to be good or excellent; 88 percent considered their knowledge to be fair or poor. Similarly, only 6 percent of central office administrators rated the School Board members' knowledge of the educational needs of Alexandria's students as good or excellent, while 85 percent thought they had fair or poor knowledge of student educational needs. Out in the schools, the perception was not much better: Only 25 percent of principals viewed School Board members' knowledge of student needs as good or excellent; 67 percent of principals rated them poor or fair. These ratings were substantially worse than similar rankings in other Virginia school districts.[55]

In another era, this underperformance of the School Board might have gone unnoticed, or the Board might have, over time, defined its vision and become more knowledgeable about school district operations and student needs. But as the federal accountability expectations grew, the lack of direction was made manifest at the school level, particularly at T.C. Williams. John Porter, the long-serving principal at T.C Williams, stepped down in 2006 after serving at the school for twenty-seven years, twenty-two as principal. In the next three-and-a half-years, two more principals came and left in rapid succession.[56] The rapid turnover of leadership at T.C. Williams, combined with the firing of Perry and ongoing School Board conflict, all meant an inconsistent response to the significant challenges that NCLB posed for T.C. Williams and the district as a whole.

That lack of focus and accompanying inconsistent leadership at T.C. Williams coincided with robust expansion of the federal accountability regime, this time through the School Improvement Grant. The Spring 2008 and 2009 SOL tests showed poor results for key subgroups at T.C. Williams, particularly in Math, and, as a result, the school was named one of Virginia's "persistently lowest-achieving schools." While that entitled the school to significant new federal revenues, the designation also cut to the core of some fundamental divisions within both T.C.

Williams and ACPS as a whole. The response of the school and the community to that designation reveals, however, the limitations of a federal accountability regime focused solely on educational outputs.

T.C. Williams in Transformation

In the spring of 2010, the leadership of Alexandria City Public Schools confronted a challenge that in many ways resembled the school desegregation battles of the 1960s and 1970s. An unwanted federal presence, forcing a school system to confront its inability to provide an equitable education to minority students, prompted complaints that the federal government's ham-handed and intrusive micromanagement of schools was unfair and unwarranted. As recentlyhired Superintendent Mort Sherman told a gathering of T.C. Williams faculty on April 4, 2010, "I don't know of one person who likes this new state designation. I don't think it's fair, you've heard me say that to you [before] ... The 'persistently lowest-achieving' school designation is something that is off the mark, it's wrongheaded. But it is reality."[57]

What differed, and differed substantially, from the earlier eras of federal intrusion was that the political stakes of federal intervention for local officials were not nearly as high. The entire power structure of the local regime was in no way predicated on the maintenance of the achievement gap in Alexandria's schools. Instead, Alexandria's sense of itself as a generous, well-intentioned liberal city that provided ample resources for the education of its youth was challenged by the federal (and state) insistence that it was not doing enough for poor, minority, and special needs students. The struggle to ensure that these children received the same education as their white, affluent peers was a long-standing one in Alexandria, and upon his arrival in the fall of 2008 Superintendent Sherman had called attention to the city's unsuccessful effort to chose achievement gaps among students.[58] So while the pride of Alexandria may have been wounded by the persistently lowest-achieving designation (PLA), the aptness of the label was not fundamentally questioned.

At the April 2010 faculty meeting, Sherman noted the PLA designation had engendered a new urgency, even a crisis in the school district, noting that "it is, in a sense, a crisis when you have the state and federal government paying attention to the level they are." Nonetheless, he hoped that this designation could provide a renewed commitment to the district's collective mission of educating all the children of Alexandria. Addressing teachers directly, he said, "What I'd ask you to do is what our School Board has asked me to do, which is to turn this crisis" into an opportunity. He continued,

> So, although we didn't ask for this designation, it is now ours to deal with.... The anger that we might have toward any one person or one organization needs to be put aside. We need to move ahead. So I hope all of you

have gotten over those initial shocks and initial reactions about 'how could this be?' So put that aside; the numbers are real, the facts are facts. Other schools outperform us. We can and we must do better.[59]

Thus, while federal intervention in the era of accountability prompted both outrage and frustration from local officials, the rapid acceptance of the necessity for local change by Alexandria school and public officials signaled a far greater alignment between federal and local goals than had existed thirty or forty years prior.

The link between the two episodes, however, can be found in the complex response of ACPS to the federal mandate. The transformation response sought to address the federal mandate, but did so in a way closely tailored to the local political realities of Alexandria's demographics and the unique position of T.C. Williams as the community's only public high school. Because the student population at T.C. Williams encompassed a far broader range of students than that of most schools undergoing state-ordered transformation, a transformation plan that only addressed the academic needs of the bottom third of T.C. Williams students would not garner the kind of political and parental support needed. Moreover, because Albohm, forty years prior, had made the all-important decision to merge three high schools into one, Alexandria confronted the full range of its diversity within one school, unlike many high schools in the Washington metropolitan area. The context of a single, all-city high school and the enormous range of the students contained within that high school meant that the project of T.C. Williams's transformation had to address issues not present in many other school transformations. In a sense, the relative success of Alexandria's desegregation (at least at the secondary level) in an earlier generation made its efforts to comply with the federally mandated school transformation far more difficult.

Under the School Improvement Grant program, significantly expanded under the American Recovery and Reinvestment Act of 2008, a school designated as a "persistently lowest-achieving" school must adopt one of four reform models: Restart, in which the local school district converts the school to a charter school, or turns it over to an educational management organization; Closure, in which the school is closed; Turnaround, in which the principal and at least 50 percent of the staff are fired; and Transformation, which requires the dismissal of the existing principal, a redefined program of professional development for teachers that is directly linked to student achievement, and the use of student growth models to evaluate teachers and staff, among other requirements. Two of the four options—Restart and Closure—would have meant that that Alexandria City Public Schools would not be operating a high school, clearly an untenable situation. Confronted with the choice of firing half the teaching force at T.C. Williams or adopting a robust set of professional development plans and a student growth model to guide the evaluation and retention of teachers, Sherman opted for the Transformation model.

The plan to guide T.C. William's transformation plan was adopted in late spring of 2010 and Principal Suzanne Maxey was hired to implement it.[60] Over the course of the next two academic years, school leaders and staff, district officials, outside consultants, and state and federal officials, as well as community members, met monthly for a full day to assess the implementation of the plan. A court reporter transcribed verbatim these "transformation meetings" and transcripts of them were made available on the T.C. Williams website, running over hundreds of pages. The documents provide a fine-grained account of the difficulties confronting the transformation team. In particular, the documents reveal a struggle to reconcile two contradictory goals: boosting test scores enough to move off the PLA list and building a sustainable transformation that would change the school's culture and narrow the achievement gap. The PLA designation was a punch in the shoulder for the teachers and staff at T.C. Williams and Alexandria City Public Schools generally, and it is abundantly evident from the transcripts that there was an enormous desire and effort to both close the achievement gap among the students at T.C. Williams and to get off the PLA list. There also was profound frustration, and, often, a sense of fatigue, as the teachers, staff, and leadership realized the enormity of those two tasks.

The immediate challenge confronting the leadership at T.C. Williams was to remove the school from the "persistently lowest-achieving" list. The only way to do that was to boost the Standards of Learning (SOL) test results scores within a three-year window, relative to other high schools in Virginia. Given the bifurcated nature of the test scores at T.C. Williams, however, a schoolwide focus on test-taking and SOL remediation would simply alienate high-achieving students (and their parents) seeking a rigorous college preparatory program in order to gain admission to highly competitive colleges. True schoolwide transformation would require a much broader cultural transformation of educational expectations and skills. It would require that teachers, students, and parents foster and create relationships in order to raise student ambitions and expectations, as well as create a sense of responsibility and ownership about a student's academic performance. While building that culture would certainly hold appeal to higher-achieving students and their parents, it would not necessarily have a clear and direct connection to increased SOL scores. Thus, school and district officials faced something of a conundrum: the quick and dirty test score boost that would most likely remove the PLA school designation would, at the same time, alienate other major constituencies within the community. On the other hand, building a broader, more ambitious reform effort to change school culture among low-achieving students at T.C. Williams might not produce the test score boost needed to move the school off the PLA list.

Two central features of the transformation plan at T.C. Williams—the Professional Learning Plan (PLP) and the Individual Academic Plan (IAP) — sought to reconcile this central tension. Through the PLP, every teacher at the school—together with his or her supervisor—was to devise a set of goals and professional development activities directly linked to a proven strategy of boosting test scores. Through the IAP, every student, in conjunction with an individualized IAP committee, was to develop personally relevant educational goals and identify the skills needed to attain those goals, both long- and short-term. Together, the PLPs and IAPs sought to reconcile the deep tension between immediate test score boosts and changing the culture of T.C. Williams.

As the school leadership implemented the transformation plan, a number of themes emerged in the transcripts of their meetings with the Transformation Committee. These themes revolved, fundamentally, around the difficulty of balancing the federal need to focus on educational outputs against the local need to make school decisions based on the inputs to the educational process: teachers, resources, students, and curricula. These inputs emerged out of a political context, and an exclusive focus on outputs, at times, meant a difficult negotiation of those political realities. Primary among these themes was the staff's task of generating a culture of high-quality teaching and learning while simultaneously meeting the obligation to generate metrics that would accurately document the learning of T.C. Williams's students. In short, changing the culture of T.C. Williams was seen as a prerequisite to boosting test scores, but there were few or no useful metrics to document a changing culture. A second theme was the replication of the "skill vs. will" tension among teachers that the school confronted in its students. In other words, as school leaders sought to increase the skills of teachers in order to raise the achievement of students, not all the administrative staff was convinced all teachers had the necessary ability to develop those skills. Third, both the staff and the leadership resorted frequently to a language of "professional love" to reconcile the necessity of focusing only on outputs while recognizing the profound input constraints that shaped the abilities of students to meet those output thresholds. The seeming rigor of "accountability" had to be softened by the expression of "love" in order to maintain effective and important relationships with students who were on the brink of failure or exit. Together these three themes constructed the accountability culture that has permeated T.C. Williams throughout the transformation process.

Changing a Culture vs. Meeting the Metric

The "culture vs. metric" contradiction confronting the transformation team was evident early on in the process. Dr. Marty Brooks, an outside consultant hired to help evaluate the reform efforts, commented in early November 2010, in the first few weeks of the transformation model's implementation:

> [U]ltimately, there are two efforts going on simultaneously. One is the transformation of the school and the second is to get the school off of the PLA list. Theoretically those two goals are linked. But it is conceivable that you would transform the culture of the school but not move a sufficient number of students to AYP in order to get the school off of the PLA list.[61]

Similarly, the school system's Director of Accountability, Monte Dawson, when asked what benchmarks the district was using to track T.C. Williams's transformation, noted the tenuous linkage between changing an academic culture and boosting test scores: "If I look with a narrow lens, yes, we're talking about SOLs. We're talking about what got us to this table in the first place in terms of persistently lowest achievers. The goal and the hope is as we look at curriculum, infuse it with richer tasks, that multiple choice tests will follow behind that as an artifact. We don't know that yet, but all the research seems to suggest that should be the case."[62]

From an organizational standpoint, the simultaneity of those two efforts raised questions about which effort was a higher priority for the school leadership and how should both staff and leadership address situations in which the pursuit of one goal rendered the other goal more remote. As the reforms proceeded through the spring of 2011 and the first set of assessments loomed, both staff and leadership seemed torn about which goal of transformation was a priority. Susan Kaput, head of T.C. Williams's math department, addressed this issue in an April 2011 meeting:

> We're kind of between two worlds. We're trying to build and develop the understanding and the knowledge, and have the kids be successful with math.... [B]ut at the same time we're trying to plug all these holes [in their knowledge] because many of them are eleventh or twelfth graders who need to pass an SOL test, which may be a very unrealistic expectation.... We want to get out of [PLA designation] as quickly as possible, but we also want to build a program that allows us to not return to it.... [W]e could use smoke and mirrors immediately and maybe get out of it [PLA designation], but the math center should be something that supports the school.[63]

Despite these tensions and ambiguities, the coherence in the Transformation Plan lay in the supposed linkage between the Individual Academic Plans (IAP) and the Professional Learning Plans (PLP). The IAPs were labor-intensive documents prepared by the counseling staff through meetings with individual students together with teachers, parents, and a counselor. The meetings brought together all the academic actors in a student's life and sought to surface both short-term and long-term goals of the students as well as identify the obstacles that hindered the realization of those goals, including very specific academic skills, content knowledge, and personal habits. In addition, during IAP meetings, counselors and social workers identified specific social or even household issues that hindered a student's academic progress. With the money that came through the School Improvement Grant, the school created time within teachers' schedules to allow them to participate in the IAP meetings by reducing the teaching load of English and math teachers. In addition, the school used SIG funds to hire additional counselors to help craft the IAPs.

Cathy David, Deputy Superintendent for Curriculum and Instruction, explained to the Transformation Steering Committee the way district leadership hoped the IAP process would work:

> So we will bring together everyone, at a bare minimum the student, the parent or guardian, the counselor, the math teacher, the current English teacher, [academic] dean if necessary, social worker if necessary, and anybody else the student would like to have there.... If there's a pastor, if there's a mentor in the community, even to the point if there's a proba-tion officer that should be part of the conversation, and the parent and the student want that person there, we will have them there to help us develop the plan.[64]

As part of the IAP process, this team would review the student's interests and moti-vations, specific test scores, grades, academic strengths, as well as attendance data, using them to identify not only short-term goals (such as pass Algebra I with at least a C grade), but also lay out a post-high school, college, or career trajectory for each student. In addition, the data review would, hopefully, also identify specific skills and tasks that a student needed to attain or complete in order to achieve those goals, (such as passing an English 9 grade SOL, for example, or mastering polyno-mial factoring through additional instruction in the math center). The hope was that that these goals would be clear, measurable, and trackable over time, enabling both teachers and counselors to see readily if the established benchmarks were being met on time, through the existing student information systems.

Despite the ambitious plans to inspire students to take ownership of their learn-ing and to devise a personalized path to college or career success, the IAP process quickly bogged down. Producing the IAPs proved to be burdensome, awkward, and, in the eyes of some, unproductive. For the counselors, undertaking such an intense, individualized review of academic and personal goals for roughly 2800 students was a laborious process. Employing a triage method that identified the 25 percent of T.C. Williams students most likely to not graduate on time, counselors first targeted those most in need of academic intervention. In addition, counselors received training on facilitating communication with parents and students. They also held pre-conferences with students to learn their aspirations and goals and then assembled the IAP teams to meet with students. While the initial goal was to complete the first 25 percent of the IAPs within the first quarter of the 2010–2011 school year, by April 2011 just under a third of them were completed.[65] The push to complete all the IAPs by the close of the 2010–2011 academic year often ren-dered the process more of a pro forma review than the mutual, collaborative pro-duction of a personal mission statement and five-year plan. As Mr. Michael Cohen, a T.C. Williams math teacher and chair of the school's AYP Action Committee, told the Steering Committee, "Whenever we have IAP meetings that really are tailored toward the individual student, or the student sees that it's been tailored toward him or her, whether it is for the long-term goals or the short-term needs of the student, those are the most successful meetings. When we are rushed, pressured, whatever the reason is, and that meeting becomes less individualized, less personalized, those are the IAP meetings that are less fruitful."[66]

For Principal Maxey, whether rushed or fruitful, the academic payoff for the IAPs was too remote. As the year wore on and she saw the amount of staff time required to write an IAP for each student, she became less convinced it would produce a meaningful effect on achievement scores:

> I think when I'm looking at all of our reforms … we have to decide, are we getting the most bang for our buck? I think with the IAPs we're not. What we're doing is creating another plan that, if it's not implemented, it doesn't mean anything. And I think we've put a lot of energy into IAPs. I would question whether or not they're effective.[67]

Maxey's eyes were on three-year window to remove T.C. Williams from the persistently lowest-achieving list. This ticking clock meant that the school's need to demonstrate immediate results on SOL tests collided with a careful and thoughtful process to provide individual attention to students who lacked direction or needed specific remediation. At times documenting the number of IAPs conducted within a month or semester—in order to show "results" to state and federal authorities—seemed more important than creating an effective institutional mechanism to advance the academic progress of students.

The IAP process did, however, reveal some important dynamics at the school. As school officials conducted the IAP conferences, many teachers and administrators came to a better understanding of the obstacles confronting student academic and career success. This realization that not all the relationships in a student's life promoted greater academic success confirmed a set of expectations about student ambitions, but also drove home how difficult changing the culture of T.C. Williams would be for a particular set of students. Jasmine Jennings, a twelfth-grader at T.C. Williams, made this point to the transformation committee as she described her understanding of teacher-student relations:

> I know a lot of people who have sat down with their parents and their teachers and had this [IAP] meeting about their situation. I know, ideally, we think that if we talk to the parents then that will create this change. But [for] a lot of kids … it only matters for that meeting. And then afterwards, it's just nothing.… [I]t's only going to be good if that relationship with that parent and child [is good].… [E]verybody's family isn't like that.[68]

Just as Ms. Jennings was making this point, Susan Kaput, the head of T.C. Williams's Math Department, chimed in: "A cultural change."[69]

The conversation then shifted toward whether students who need math remediation should be required to attend sessions at the math center, and Ms. Kaput reminded the group that only 45 percent of those students assigned to special in-school pull-out sessions to work on math actually attended those sessions. At this point the nature of the relationships teachers had with students and their ability to overcome student or family indifference became the central issue of the conversation. Outside consultant Bena Kallick stressed that the IAPs were key to promoting that kind of relationship and motivation: "That's the question of the IAP. If it's going to have any meaning ... it has to be transactional, relational, and it has to give that person a base.... Somehow we've got to figure out how to make that strong and that goes to some of your questions about the [role of] the IAP."[70]

At this juncture, Maxey revealed a central limitation of the IAP—the factors that lead students to simply not care:

> [T]here's so many pieces to this whole transformation process, from teachers being willing to build relationships with kids, and getting teachers involved and [getting] students to understand the importance of their education. That's a huge issue at the school, isn't it? And I mean I heard that when I came in [to T.C. Williams]. Student apathy about education was very high here.[71]

Maxey then added, "We have a huge road ahead of us, because we are fighting against so many forces that are ingrained in the community, the parents, and the staff and in the students."[72]

As the leadership of T.C. Williams grappled with getting off the PLA list it had to focus relentlessly on outputs—the SOL scores of predominantly poor and minority students. Yet the ability to boost those scores hinged on teachers and staff contending with the inputs to the educational process—the motivations of students, the ability of teachers to bond with students and encourage them, the support of parents, and the career or college expectations of students. Accountability policies argued those factors should be irrelevant to student success, but the transformation process increasingly confirmed their salience.

Teacher Learning and the "Skill vs. Will" Dilemma

The second "pillar" of the transformation model were the Professional Learning Plans. These plans were to be developed by each individual teacher in conjunction with their department chair and principal to improve specific skills of teachers or develop a substantive knowledge base that would help their students achieve at a higher level. The PLP process asked teachers to assess where their own teaching needed improvement and to devise a specific series of professional development activities that would address those weaknesses. Ideally, these improved teaching strategies would translate into higher test scores. As Cathy David, Deputy Superintendent for Curriculum and Instruction, told the Transformation Steering Committee,

> the thinking is this: we have some very ambitious goals and targets and metrics based on student achievement, so the professional learning should be aligned with those goals, and if I [as a teacher] learn that and implement it in my classroom room, then the evidence should be in improved student achievement."[73]

According to Superintendent Mort Sherman, he conceptualized the transformation model as a whole to be sustained "by a direct line from the PLP to the IAP."[74] His hope, along with others in the school district, was that teacher learning and skill improvement would be manifest in improved achievement scores of students.

Part of Sherman's enthusiasm for Professional Learning Plans as a pillar of the transformation process lay in his overall enthusiasm for foisting instructional reforms on teachers, which many saw as an administrative failing, not a virtue. In an interview, former T.C. Williams English teacher Patrick Welsh indicated that many teachers in Alexandria felt inundated with reforms during Sherman's tenure and that he relied heavily on external consultants to advance his reform practices, many of which were seen as operating at cross-purposes.[75] Welsh reiterated the point in an article he wrote for the *Washington Post*: "Sherman brought in a parade of highly paid consultants and introduced so many educational philosophies that he sowed massive confusion among administrators, teachers, and students."[76] The professional development models that the school district was employing alongside the transformation of T.C. Williams were proliferating amidst the consultants: At the same time that teachers and counselors at T.C. Williams were developing IAPs and PLPs, they were being urged to become (and given instruction in becoming) "Skillful Teachers" in the classroom and "Skillful Leaders" in their schools, and being told to help students develop "Five College Competencies."

The crush of reforms led some, even the consultants, to question whether the PLPs had any direct relevance to getting T.C. Williams off the persistently lowest-achieving list. When Dr. Marty Brooks, one of the required external consultants, pushed Sherman on whether professional development would have any connection to student achievement, Sherman replied that even if the research did not show much of a relationship, he nonetheless held it as an article of faith: "We've got to believe that there is a connection, otherwise why would we do it?. . .. So for me, there is that connection, and that's the purpose for [it] existing."[77] He went on to argue that in addition to the "very close connection between the professional learning and our student learning" the district's new Professional Learning Plans would bolster the professionalism of teachers in the district, inspiring them to be more proactive and assertive in addressing student underachievement.[78]

The reality, of course, proved different than the goal. As the Transformation Steering Committee, particularly consultants Brooks and Kallick, evaluated the implementation of both PLPs and IAPs over the course of the first year, it began to question the linkage between the two, or at least question how the school system might show empirically the existence of a relationship. Because the U.S. Department of Education demanded, as part of the transformation process, data that demonstrated the results of schoolwide interventions, there was a persistent concern from the consultants about metrics and how the school system could document its progress. Simultaneously, staff in the school district's Center for Professional Learning developed programs that they hoped would more closely link professional learning to student outcomes.

While the Professional Learning Plans were quickly put in place in the fall of 2010, the IAP process took considerably longer, far into the spring of 2011. As a result, initially there was little systematic thinking about the relationships between teacher PLPs and student IAPs. Moreover, student test scores, broken down by teacher, were not available when the PLPs were developed. Accordingly, there was little explicit linkage between the data on student performance and teacher professional development plans. Partly as a result of this weak connection, the tenor of the Transformation Committees discussion of the PLPs shifted somewhat over the first year from being a teacher-identified set of learning goals to a specific set of skills that the school system needed the teachers to demonstrate (in part because those skills were necessary to teach central competencies desired by the school system.) As Chris Gutierrez, staff member at the ACPS Professional Learning Center, commented to the Steering Committee:

> There's just a lot swirling around, and I think we have to help the teachers narrow [their PLP] down and pinpoint specifically, [asking them] what are you going to do to help [for example] a kid's reading comprehension? And here are some things, let's work on them, let's try them, let's learn about them, and bring back the data from your classroom so that we can see how it's working or not. And if it's not working, how come?[79]

Gutierrez's model of guiding teachers toward the development of specific testing-relevant teaching skills conflicted considerably with Sherman's professed ideals of teacher learning and increasing professionalism. To ask teachers what they would like to learn is very different from asking them to acquire and use skills that are known to boost a student's test scores. More importantly, the implication of the follow-on question—"if it's not working, how come?"—held an implicit threat of becoming a supervisory tool and a teacher performance metric. As Gutierrez wound up her presentation, external consultant Brooks recommended that the school leadership remain aware of the potential faculty backlash from such a shift, urging school leadership to "keep your thumb on the pulse of how the faculty is feeling about this, because they're going to respond basically in one of three ways. Their going to be supportive, they're going to be confused, or they're going to resist." At which point, Superintendent Sherman chimed in: "All of that."[80]

Nonetheless by the end of the first transformation year, T.C. Williams Principal Suzanne Maxey cautiously endorsed the PLP process for its ability to make teachers more reflective of their craft as teachers and their role in improving student achievement. In addressing consultant Marty Brooks' persistent question of the PLP's relationship to student achievement, Maxey said:

> When we ask that question, Marty, did it impact on student achievement, that was the one question that's hard to answer. For the most part, my folks said, "I don't know" or "no, it didn't." I don't know that I saw any kind of provable student achievement relationship. But I did see reflective people, who were truly doing things, and had done things, and so I think it was definitely an upgrade for us.[81]

Immediately following Maxey's comment, Peter Balas, Executive Associate Principal for Curriculum and Instruction at T.C. Williams, endorsed her view, saying that "one of the big wins we'll get out this [the PLPs] is starting that culture of accountability for student learning."[82]

At the close of this session, Kathy Taylor, T.C. Williams's Academic Principal for Social Studies and English, related a story about an end-of-year classroom observation of a twelfth-grade AP literature teacher. The teacher told Taylor at the beginning of the meeting that he was nervous about receiving his review "because in the past when we've been observed it hasn't meant anything for us and so things feel different to me now."[83] Maxey's reaction to this story highlights her sense of the culture shift that was only slowly coming to T.C. Williams and causing some difficult adjustment among some teachers at the school:

> [I]t's a paradigm shift when the [teaching] observations would mean something. I mean that to me kind of boggles my mind.... [S]o when you ask them [the teachers] why they're so frustrated and intense, it's because they haven't done things that everybody else in the nation has been doing forever, you know what I mean? So there's some real issues here that we're having to counteract.[84]

At this juncture, Kathy Taylor, rejoined, "Well, I don't think [before] they were held as accountable."[85] Here the focus of accountability shifted from students to teachers, one of several instances in the transcripts of the Transformation Steering Committee meetings in which participants equated the challenges of designing and implementing a PLP with developing an IAP. As Brooks opened the final Transformation Steering Committee meeting of the 2010–2011 academic year, he noted the parallel challenges of transforming both student and professional learning: both required that school systems identify learning needs of teachers and students, design appropriate interventions to meet those needs, and then accurately measure whether those interventions produced the desired outcomes and report that data. As Brooks put it, "we think the same model applies to students and adults."[86] In many ways, the challenges of accountability and of school transformation that utilizes a student growth model to inform its teacher evaluations replicate within teaching staffs the issues that are present in student achievement: What do you do with an underperformer? Is it a question of individual will or of system resources and designing appropriate interventions?

This issue of will versus skill development was something of a philosophical divide between Principal Maxey and Superintendent Sherman throughout the year. Maxey, who bore the responsibility of dealing with recalcitrant teachers, claimed that there were some on her staff who simply no longer had the energy to make the needed connections with students. In the April 28, 2011 Transformation Steering Committee meeting, she summed up her disagreement with Sherman:

> Mort [Sherman] and I, we discuss this back and forth, argue back and forth whether . . . they need more skills, professional development, [or] whether it's a matter of will. I'm arguing that it's a matter of will, and Mort thinks we need, they need more development and things, and. . . I contend it's will. You have to believe that children can do it, even when they smell funny and disrespect you, and wear their hats backwards and everything else. You have to love them, and you have to believe in them.[87]

While the school and district leadership never came to an agreement about the relative importance of a teacher's skill development versus a teacher's will to make connections with students, the issue remained a latent source of conflict between teachers and administrators as they sought to define whether responsibility for low SOL scores lay with students or with teachers. Within an accountability frame, there is no way to limit performance questions solely to students, once one makes the assumption that all students can and must achieve proficiency. Moreover, this accountability frame, set within a "proficiency for all" context, imposes an obligation—fairly or not—on teachers to reform or improve teaching strategies in order to demonstrate the required scores.

Professional "Love" as a Response to Accountability

Maxey's assertion that "you have to love them" reflects another important consequence of an accountability frame on relationships among teachers, administrators, and students: the need to simultaneously express concern for students while administering a public policy that—for some students—holds damaging consequences. Indeed, the language of love, passion, and will emerged frequently in the Transformation Committee's discussions of overcoming the challenges of student achievement and of identifying teachers who had the ability to do so. Shortly after identifying her disagreement with Sherman in the skill vs. will debate, Maxey expressed concern about inspiring her teaching staff: "How do I communicate all this passion that we feel when we have these [Transformation] meetings to teachers? And I am afraid there are teachers on our staff who understand it intellectually and know it's the right thing to do, and simply, they're done. They don't have the will, you know?"[88]

The rhetoric of love as the hallmark of an effective teacher was a persistent theme in the Steering Committee's conversations about both how to reach students and improve the school's climate. For example, the notion of love emerged in context of developing the IAPs with students and the efforts of teachers and counselors to find connections with students, to motivate them to expect more from themselves. Cathy David, at the initial Transformation Steering Committee, introduced the IAP plan to the Committee as not merely a way to map out a student's academic trajectory, but a way of expressing the school system's concern and, indeed, its love for its students. As she explained the process to the committee, she stepped through a mock encounter with a student at a pre-IAP conference:

> [W]e realized we needed to step back and do a little precursor conference with the counselor and the student, spend about ten to fifteen minutes together at some point in time before the big conference to say "Hi, I'm Cathy David, I'm your counselor, we're going to be working together for the next few years."... [Find out] what are you interested in, what are your hopes, your dreams, your ambitions. What's good about school for you, what's not so good....[And explain] that we're going to be having this bigger meeting, because you're worth the time of a lot of people, and you're capable of success and so we're going to bring a lot people around the table, all who know and love you, to sit down and... build a plan for your success.[89]

Maxey also used the language of love to explain why she thought students who need additional math instruction should be required within their IAP to attend sessions at the newly created math center:

> In terms of the mandatory thing, I think you don't do that until you've built up a climate in the school of "we're not going to let you fail," and "we're going to push you and shove you and nurture you." That's what I'm talking about in terms of mandatory. And you have to do that once you've built up the sense that this is an academic atmosphere, this is a school-house where they come to learn, and we do it because we love you, not because we're being dictatorial.[90]

The tensions between "accountability" and "love" as rhetoric of school transformation are obvious. Accountability demands that performance be the single criterion for success—as either a teacher or a student. Failure to meet a benchmark means that either some reward will be withheld or some punishment imposed. Love, on the other hand, requires a capacity for forgiveness and a willingness to overlook faults, to make allowances because of the individual characteristics or talents of an individual because of the reciprocal bonds of love. Moreover, love as a justification for public policy reforms is just plain odd.

In using the language of love, these school officials were, I argue, striving for a way to preserve the relationships between youths and adults that are essential when schools must use accountability policies to bridge the academic gaps between students in poverty and students of affluence. Affluent students enable school officials to assume that students have expectations about their futures, to assume that students have familial resources to address issues that affect their academic performance (money, time, social networks, even transportation). Unable to make those expectations for students in poverty, school officials instead draw on a language of love to fight through barriers of mistrust and alienation that school-level accountability generates among students of poverty. Because accountability policies assume that failure is a necessary element of ensuring quality schooling, students who are on the boundary of persistent failure have little reason to expect that schools have anything to offer them. The language of love, expressed in the midst of proliferating accountability policies, allows teachers, principals, and counselors to conform to the mandates of accountability while simultaneously preserving the fragile relationships that can make an enormous difference in a student's life.[91]

Conclusion

The application of federal accountability policies to Alexandria City Public Schools looks in some ways like a confirmation of past disagreements and disputes within Alexandria over its public schools. The test score gap—first formally articulated in the mid-1980s, but known since the days of desegregation—continues to structure many of the conflicts over how to reform Alexandria's schools. But the redefinition of "equal schooling" under the federal accountability framework—from an effort to ensure that all students receive comparable inputs to a mandate that all student demographic groups perform at the same level—has had a profound effect on Alexandria and schools throughout the nation. Although Alexandria was perhaps more receptive to the ideas of educational accountability than many school districts (because of its move to an elected school board), federally-imposed, output-based accountability has, ironically, made Alexandria's schools less responsive to local demands and local needs. The notion of "governance by outputs," or the structuring of educational processes with an exclusive focus on meeting testing thresholds, will invariably render other issues less salient and important. To the extent that students will not or cannot learn without such an unrelenting focus, such an orientation may be defensible. Yet that focus also has an important institutional effect: it makes the local system less robust by rendering the mistakes or missteps of local schools to be fatal, or nearly so. The normal mode of institutional operations is to muddle through difficulties. Federal accountability politics transforms local educational governance by removing the ability of local institutions to muddle through long-standing local conflicts. High stakes accountability politics may make public schools less governable and less effective because it leaves less room for local actors to accommodate a variety of interests and demands. Without that ability to accommodate multiple demands for multiple kinds of schooling and education, public schools run the risk of losing support of important and influential local constituencies. Rebecca Perry faced that challenge directly and lost, largely because of a lapse of personal judgment one evening. T.C. Williams High School still confronts that challenge, but faces increased public skepticism about its ability to respond to the challenge because of both the federal label of failure (persistently lowest-achieving school) and the narrow federal definition of what educational success looks like: meeting arbitrary benchmark indicators of math and reading accomplishments.

Fortunately, T.C. Williams has responded well to the challenge: after an enormous investment of energy, money, time, and talent, it met all but one of the federal subgroup benchmarks in the spring of 2011.[92] In 2012, it passed all the benchmarks, although its scores dipped. In 2013, T.C. Williams came off the persistently lowest achieving list. Its removal came about, however, not because it achieved the required test scores, but because the waiver of NCLB-requirements that Virginia negotiated with the U.S. Department of Education substituted new metrics. These new, less stringent measures, meant that T.C. Williams's push to boost test scores was, more or less, irrelevant to whether the school was on or off the PLA list.

This did not mean, however, that Alexandria was no longer under the scrutiny of state and federal officials. In summer 2013, the Virginia legislature created the "Opportunity Educational Institution," a state-run entity that would take over any school that had been denied accreditation by the state. Six schools in Virginia met the criteria for takeover, including Alexandria's Jefferson-Houston Elementary School. Jefferson-Houston had never made AYP under No Child Left Behind and over 50 percent of the families within its attendance zone had opted for another school, under NCLB's school choice provisions.[93] The state takeover attempt came in response to that persistent underachievement.

The takeover effort, however, was not the first time that forces outside Alexandria were urging the city to make major changes at Jefferson-Houston: In 1971, HEW officials singled out Jefferson-Houston as a continuation of a *de jure* segregated school that under the *Swann* ruling justified busing. Indeed, it was Jefferson-Houston's opening as a new building in 1971 that had prompted the full integration of Alexandria's elementary schools, under federal pressure. The school's recent academic decline can be traced, in part, to a 1999 vote by the Alexandria City School Board to change the city's school boundaries, reversing the school pairings that had desegregated Alexandria's elementary schools. Those boundary changes produced a greater concentration of poor students at Jefferson-Houston, leading to declining academic fortunes.

In Spring 2013, at the time that Virginia Governor Robert McDonnell was pushing the takeover bill through the state legislature, the Alexandria City School Board had just broken ground on a new building for Jefferson-Houston. Many on the school board and city council were adamantly opposed to the state takeover. As School Board chair Karen Graf stated while the legislature debated the bill, "I would say that Thomas Jefferson himself would be opposed to that [bill]. . . [H]e wrote a lot about education and he felt that place where education should be decided was at the local level."[94] Whatever Jefferson-Houston's fate and whatever the wishes of Graf and her colleagues, it is clear that the education state's accountability measures mean that these decisions will not be entirely local.

Conclusion: Learning from the Education State

If you look at countries today that are outperforming us, they have done some really creative things around teaching. [In] South Korea, which is doing an amazing job, their teachers are known as "Nation Builders." That's what they're called: Nation Builders. And that's a really interesting term to me.

U.S. Secretary of Education Arne Duncan,
speaking at Alexandria City Public Schools Fall Convocation,
September 2010, T.C. Williams High School

A year and a half ago we started this process of writing regulations around the school improvement grant, and we've always wondered how it was going to play out.

Carlas L. McCauley,
Office of Elementary and Secondary Education,
U.S. Department of Education
speaking at a meeting of the
T.C. Williams High School Transformation Committee,
Alexandria, VA, October 8, 2010.

These two quotes, spoken a few weeks apart in the same building by two federal officials, highlight the central ambiguity of the federal schoolhouse: the grand aspiration to achieve a more egalitarian and national system of education and the persistent reliance on local officials to define the content and reality of that system. Efforts to build a new kind of educational system—the federal schoolhouse—has required federal officials and policymakers to rely on local administrators to achieve ends that are both ill-defined and, at times, corrosive of the mechanisms by which educational policies are legitimated at the local level. Education Secretary Arne Duncan's admiration of "nation builders" collides with the uncertainty of federal officials about how, precisely, to construct that educational system. The federal incorporation of operational localism into the federal schoolhouse has resulted in a hybrid and complex education state, one that simultaneously seeks to transform local schools, while remaining dependent on the locals' established institutional contexts and routines to achieve that transformation.

The creative aspirations of the federal schoolhouse—building an educational system that offers more equal educational opportunity—has, at the same time, required federal officials to undermine local mechanisms that generate inequality. The challenge in the school desegregation and integration eras was the centrality of racial inequality to the very operation of the local regime. The persistent federal intervention in the racial patterns of schooling led to a reconfiguration of the local regime, which, in turn, generated new problems for the education state. As locals responded to federal pressures, they abandoned policies that had been central to many white residents' perceptions of what made for good schools. The result was a loss of faith in Alexandria's public schools, at least among some constituents. As the local regime incorporated new interests and concerns into school practices it sought legitimation from taxpayers and voters for its new policies.

What is clear from this examination of the relationship between federal educational ambitions and local school practices is that operational localism is not merely the administration or implementation of policies defined elsewhere. Indeed, operational localism is dependent on the construction of local coalitions and regimes to support the taxation upon which most school systems heavily rely. When the political needs and goals of that regime are in conflict with federal aspirations, the political landscape of the locality becomes a limiting condition on the federal schoolhouse. At times, the federal government's pressure breaks down the local regime as a way to overcome the limiting condition. At other times, the federal authorities accept the limited implementation or redefinition of federal goals and their ambitions for schools are subordinated to the political needs of locals.

Whether the federal aspirations or the local contexts are more legitimate depends, ultimately, on which actor is best situated to expand the range of educational opportunity for citizens. Unfortunately, this is not always clear. Part of the challenge is that new aspirations for policy at the federal level frequently highlight failures of practice at the local level.[1] That is, as the federal government demands that local schools undertake new tasks—requiring *all* students to meet "proficiency" benchmarks in reading and math, for example—it reveals the inability of local schools to accomplish those tasks. As Cohen and Moffitt write, "[P]olicies can create incompetence in practice. The further they depart from extant practice, the more difficult are the entailed changes in practice, the more incompetence the policy creates, and the more such policies require the acquisition of new capability. . ."[2] But if the new capabilities that the feds are demanding from the locals run counter to the political priorities of the local regime, then local constituents see the worst of both worlds: federal creation of local failure and local inability to overcome that failure, both of which erode the legitimacy of the institutions that are tasked with educating children: local schools. In these contexts, the federal policy prescription diminishes public support for schools, while seeking to improve them. Studying one school district over a period of roughly fifty years enables us to see how the local characteristics of a school system align or do not align with the evolving federal expectations and requirements for public education. While the particularities of the experiences of Alexandria may produce a distinctive or unusual accommodation between local governing needs and federal educational ambitions, the process of reconciling those two forms of governing authority is common across the United States. Localities may vary, but they generally share features of operational localism, which, in turn, structures the nature of the accommodation between local governance needs and federal policy demands. In some places, the accommodation may be simple and easy, given the nature of local politics; in other places (like Alexandria) it may be, at times, a painful and difficult process. But in all places, the characteristics of the local governing relationships will structure the federal schoolhouse.

This conclusion will first recap the efforts of federal educational policy in Alexandria, looking across policy domains, to sketch out how the construction of the education state relates to the alignment of local regime characteristics to the demands of federal policy innovation. The second half of the chapter will then turn to some of the implications of the arguments made within these chapters, as well as the implication of the cross-policy comparison. The findings in Alexandria hold implications for several audiences, but I will focus on three: those within the educational policy field; political scientists who study the nature of the both education politics and the nature of state development in the United States; and, third, the students, families, teachers, and officials in Alexandria.

Alexandria's Reception of Federal Educational Policies Across Policy Domains

The federal government did not begin its interventions in Alexandria schools in order to change how students learn. It began its interventions in order to dismantle an educational system premised on the unequal treatment of white and black students. The reversal of Jim Crow in Alexandria (and Virginia and the South) was the first stage in the construction of the federal schoolhouse. That clash between localist assumptions about the unequal distribution of educational opportunities to black and white students and the federal mandate of equal treatment both broke down the existing local regime and laid the foundation for future policy interventions within public education. The long story of partial accommodation through desegregation and then grudging incorporation through integration forced the governing white elites of Alexandria—and hundreds of other Southern communities—to reconfigure their political relationship with black citizens. How Alexandrians established the terms of that new relationship within their schools has held long-term consequences for policy innovations beyond integration. Integrating Alexandria's schools did not eliminate racial conflict or racism or diminish racial politics—far from it. It did, however, establish a norm that African Americans would play a key role in the governance of the institutions of the city.

Moreover, the crucial decision to unify the city, in some fashion, by means of a single high school has come to represent more than simply a real-life Hollywood moment of racial progress. It represents to thousands of Alexandrians the identity of a city that is still divided on racial and class lines. That decision came about, however, not because of federal pressure or even out of a federal inclination; it came about because the local politics of order trumped the federal call for elementary integration. School discipline and the perception of a school system in crisis were more urgent matters than HEW compliance. Chapters 2 and 3 seek to tell the story of that struggle in a way that honors the ambitions and contradictions of Alexandrians, black and white, in their efforts to realize and administer the dreams of the civil rights generation. At key moments in that story, the federal government's concerns about removing all vestiges of a segregated system collided with local understandings of how neighborhoods related to school attendance zones and how far a school district needed to go to address the economic inequalities of schooling in Alexandria.

That struggle between federal aspirations and local commitments did not come without cost, however. Both the explosive conflicts of the 1960s and 1970s and intersections of race and class in Alexandria's schools meant that white Alexandrians could not ignore the educational challenges of children in poverty (particularly poor black children) in a way they could in earlier generations. For many, the challenge was not worth staying in Alexandria. The declining population of Alexandria in the 1970s—at a time of a population boom across Northern Virginia—meant that public education was, increasingly, a less central concern to the political authorities of Alexandria. Simultaneously, school officials' efforts to preserve a middle-class white presence in Alexandria schools meant that race figured indirectly in hundreds of decisions about curriculum, pupil assignment, disciplinary practices, and provision of services to students. Concurrently, the exodus of political conservatives from Alexandria meant that the city was increasingly out of step with a Virginia that was a central player in the Southern Republican realignment of the Reagan era. Instead, the political forces in Alexandria fashioned a racial coalitional regime that hewed a more liberal line.

The federal demand to provide services to students with special needs coincided with both these trends, and, as a result, Alexandria schools moved from a position of profound reluctance to provide additional services to an enthusiastic endorsement of more generous services, in alignment with the new regime's priorities. Unlike desegregation and integration, the federal effort to increase educational opportunities to children with special needs was, within a relatively short period of time, locally endorsed. The key elements in this local adjustment were an increasingly liberal local citizenry and the expansion of services to gifted and talented students, in addition to students with physical handicaps, emotional disturbances, or learning disabilities. The inclusion of gifted and talented students within special education offered assurances to white parents that the "rigor" of Alexandria schools would not be diminished because of racial integration, a concern that drove a significant portion of the white flight from Alexandria's schools. So, the ready adoption of federal special needs mandates—although done in a racially skewed fashion—served the local regime's interests and furthered its aims to deliver more services to its constituents. In addition, the differentiation of services for special education populations entrenched and expanded an academic tracking system that largely maintained segregated classrooms within Alexandria's comprehensive high school. In many ways, the segregation battles of the 1960s and 1970s—largely fought at the level of school buildings—were successful, in part, because Alexandria's classrooms resegregated along economic and special education lines. The policy legacy of both integration and white flight sharply informed the delivery of special education within Alexandria, even as more and more services were provided.

In contrast to special education, the federal effort to provide greater educational equality to students who did not speak English largely foundered in Alexandria—in large part because both the federal ambition was modest and the local capacity and interest were lacking. Despite enormous changes in the demographics of Alexandria in the 1980s and 1990s—a transformation that saw the Washington, DC metropolitan area become one of the nation's immigration gateways—Alexandria did little to provide a substantive, academically rigorous program of study to students—particularly secondary students—who did not speak English. While providing English language services may have enabled them to learn English, many English-learners fell further behind their age cohort, with many of them tracked into courses that either would not enable them to gain admission to college or, in some instances, to even graduate from high school, under Virginia's increasingly demanding accountability system. The relative invisibility of Alexandria's English-learners—many of whom were and are undocumented—meant that there was little local political pressure to provide services for these students. Even hiring a single bilingual high school counselor—at a time when Spanish-speaking students were 12 percent of the enrollment—required an organizing campaign by T.C. Williams's English-learners, an effort aided by Tenants and Workers United, a local community organizing group.

After the federal government adopted NCLB's accountability structure, which required greater attention to the academic needs of English-learners (and others), Alexandria began to rethink its English-learner program, but that planning effort was constrained, somewhat, by concerns that Alexandria was simply once again engaging in segregation or racial tracking. The limited federal ambition for English-learners meant that there was no guidance on *how* to provide services for these students, only an inflexible demand that these students produce test scores comparable to the rest of the student population. Thus, the accountability mechanism that currently structures federal educational policy, as applied to English-learners, exists largely to establish a procedure to define students and schools as failures rather than ensuring schools have the resources, capacities, or knowledge to provide a high-quality education to English-learners. With the repeal of the Bilingual Act of 1968 under No Child Left Behind, the federal policy toward English-learners is fundamentally a punitive one, both for students and schools, punishing students for not speaking English and punishing districts for enrolling them, which they are required to do under federal law. Among the four policy domains examined in this book, the education state's efforts to provide services for English-learners is the most contradictory.

Ironically, the accountability philosophy that undergirds No Child Left Behind initially found a receptive home in Alexandria in the 1990s. With Virginia staking out a leadership role in the early accountability movement, and Alexandria's mobilized constituents pursuing an electoral accountability for the School Board, the policy shift toward accountability aligned well with the change in local governance of schools. Long before No Child Left Behind, Virginia's Standards of Learning and high-stakes assessments combined with Alexandria's adoption of an elected school board to place heightened administrative and political emphasis on "results" in Alexandria's schools. This move toward outputs and away from inputs meant, of course, that political representation and opportunities to learn were increasingly less important than hitting student achievement benchmarks. Growing frustration with a persistent black-white test score gap and a perception of declining rigor in Alexandria's schools had fostered this greater emphasis on accountability, but it was not until No Child Left Behind enveloped the local and state accountability structures that Alexandrians saw accountability policy as ceding authority to the federal government. Amidst a local scandal and a resulting loss of administrative focus on student performance at T.C. Williams, the accountability structure identified Alexandria's sole high school as a "persistently lowest-achieving" high school— even though its performance was largely within the bounds of past performance. T.C. Williams's combination of upper middle-class, college-aspirant students and its poor, increasingly immigrant, and minority population meant that rising proficiency benchmarks were increasingly difficult to achieve across all student groups. As a result, tightening federal policies defined T.C. Williams, effectively, as a failure.

The resulting school-level effort to reverse the "persistently lowest-achieving" designation highlighted, however, the limits of a relentless focus on student outputs. The strategies adopted by school and district level leadership sought simultaneously to boost test scores in the short run and create a culture of higher expectations in the long run. The two were often at odds with each other: The intensive counseling and advising efforts devised to alter student expectations and behaviors revealed that many students in poverty or English-learners did not have the family supports, resources, or academic preparation to sustain the culture shift the school leadership was striving for. As a result, the efforts fell back on short-term, intensive strategies of test prep to meet score targets. Compounding this tension between long-term and short-term change, district leadership rapidly spun out numerous pedagogical and classroom reforms in an effort to boost teacher skills. The resulting cacophony of reforms left teachers less clear about effective strategies and diverted energies away from a substantive engagement with the challenges of teaching T.C. Williams's very diverse student body. It also contributed to Superintendent Mort Sherman's dismissal in August 2013.

Let's step back and consider what this story of Alexandria across the past fifty or so years looks like from the vantage point of a federal reformer. Looking across these four domains and federal efforts to reshape local educational enterprises, this story reveals a jointly constructed educational state that is both robust and strangely ineffectual. The feds demanded and ultimately achieved school racial integration. Federal insistence that students with special needs received additional resources was, after an initial resistance, met with alacrity. A modest effort to teach English to students who do not speak English was given modest attention (despite growing local need), and a federally imposed delineation of student test score performance yielded a focused and serious response from Alexandria's schools, but one that only marginally changed student performance. And the overall goal of equal educational opportunity remains elusive: by most measures (of outputs and inputs) the inequalities confronting racial minorities, special needs students, and English-learners remain large, and in some instances are growing. In short, the ability of Alexandria schools to provide more equitable educational opportunities is greater, but still highly constrained.

We are then faced with a conundrum: Federal engagements with race, special education, English-learners, and educational accountability have profoundly shaped American education. The withholding of educational resources from minorities, students with disabilities, or English-learners is no longer normatively defended as it once was, and it is now commonplace to expect students to meet proficiency benchmarks. At the same time, the ongoing press to organize, fund, and administer public schools by local entities often means that federal imperatives are recast into a local idiom, one that is consonant with the needs of local regimes. This process of patterned reconciliation of federal demands and local needs defines the construction of the education state. The federal schoolhouse exists as complex state structure that, despite federal ambitions, cannot be uniform across geographical boundaries because its legitimacy rests on the ability of locals to place the federal schoolhouse in the service of local needs. As they currently operate in the United States—for good or for ill—public schools exist for the benefit of local communities and they are legitimated by the participation of locals in their operation and by the taxes of locals in their funding. This necessarily generates inequalities among schools and school districts, but until federal authorities wholly fund and operate their own public schools, operational localism is a defining characteristic of the American education state. I do not make this argument to defend localism, only to draw attention to its current functions within the education state.

The Implications of the Education State

Recognizing the dynamics of how the education state has been constructed holds implications—both for policymakers and for scholars of the American state. For policymakers, two lessons stand out. The first is a simple admonition: Education state-building should not be confused with making education better. Just because education state-building is happening does not mean education is improving. While many improvements in the American educational system have occurred through building the federal schoolhouse—particularly the rapid reduction of the test score gap during the era of vigorous school integration—there is not an automatic linkage between the two processes. The construction of the federal schoolhouse has done much good, but we need to be open to the notion that local resistance and modification of the federal schoolhouse blueprint can also improve education for children. The construction of the federal schoolhouse reveals numerous examples of school officials "seeing like a state"—pursuing practices or policies that diminish rather than enhance the ability of a school district, principal, or teacher to help a child learn.[3] At the same time, distinguishing between improving education and constructing the education state enables us to see when ensuring educational opportunity requires fundamental reorganizations of local schools and regimes, changes that are prerequisites for overcoming class and racial inequities in education.

Second, examining education through the lens of the education state enables reformers and policy practitioners to understand better the limits of their policy reforms and their potential consequences. Understanding how the federal schoolhouse is built is essential if policymakers are to fully grasp the kinds of state authority that are being deployed within the educational realm and the limits and characteristics of that state authority. A key element of this self-understanding of reformer limitations is recognition that policy domains are interconnected at the local level, both over time and at particular moments. In other words, the functional division of educational policy into distinct domains ignores the fact that these policies operate simultaneously within the federal schoolhouse, though not always harmoniously.[4] Moreover, the historical choices made in the implementation in one policy domain constrain the policy options at a later time in another domain. Understanding how those connections emerge requires being attentive to developments and implementation across policy domains, a skill too often lacking among education reformers.

For scholars interested in the nature of the American state, the construction of the federal schoolhouse holds a number of implications. First, for scholars of education politics, the idea of the education state provides an important analytical construct for understanding the immense complexity of the US educational system. The politics of education has been largely peripheral to the study of American politics and, to a lesser extent, to the study of educational policymaking, in large part because the politics of education encompasses multiple subfields: urban politics, federalism, political socialization, public policy, judicial politics, bureaucratic politics, interest groups, and state and local politics. Cutting across all these fields, however, is the entity that conjointly funds, organizes, regulates, and delivers schooling: the education state. By seeing how this complex of services and bureaucratic routines is organized, sustained, and legitimated, scholars interested in the politics of education can link up these diverse and divergent fields into a more coherent assessment of how power is gained, used, and deployed and how resources are allocated, two essential questions to the study of politics in any field.

Second, to the extent that the construction of the education state is an important feature of American political development, this book reveals that political development in the United States is not invariably a top-down reconfiguration of state and local authority. The growth of the American state, for most scholars, has been accompanied by increasing standardization and centralization at the federal level. Yet public education reveals that while those tendencies exist, they are not always successful. The historical examination of changes in the organization of public education in the United States shows rather clearly that some components of American political development are defined by a "bottom up" component of state-building that needs to be accounted for in our understanding of the American state. Indeed, the study of public education clearly reveals that the smaller geographic unit often has the far greater administrative capacity—simply by virtue of the fact that such units are largely responsible for operating schools. Thus, legal and formal authority of states or the federal government may pale in comparison to the operational or administrative authority—the sheer ability to get things done—of cities or counties or school districts. Similarly, the power of the American state may be most clearly and effectively exercised not by the federal government but by a local school district. Understanding how the federal schoolhouse is part of the American state helps us understand better its complexity.

In a related fashion, the construction of the federal schoolhouse reveals an American state in which the vertical integration of local, state, and federal actors varies substantially by policy domain. This ability of some policy domains to resist federal centralization and coordination suggests a need to revisit the theories of state-building in the United States. The variation of state capacity across policy domains—health care, education, welfare, and national security—indicates that the distinguishing characteristic of American state-building is its unevenness. The American state is organized not only by its formal design (Constitutional or legal) but also by its policies and by the mechanisms utilized to deliver those policies. That the American education state looks very different from the American welfare state or the American national security state raises important issues about the normative legitimacy of state-building and the capacity of reformers to enact policies that respond to changing circumstances in our economy, society, and technology. A full development of this "multiple-states" theory of American state-building would need to relate the degree of federal centralization and standardization across policy sectors to the political economy of those policy domains, paying close attention to the sequencing of institution building and the ability of federal actors to displace existing sources of authority within those domains. While the development of this theory is beyond the scope of this book, I hope that this investigation into this historical development of federal–local relations in public education would inform this kind of comparative policy analysis. Given the importance of education as a social policy, the education state merits inclusion into the growing scholarship on the dynamics of state-building.

Finally, as current and future reformers look to transform public education, both the challenges of the existing education state and its assets need to be kept in clear view. Recent structural and governance reforms in public education have sought to remove political geography from the delivery of public education. Through increasing use of charters, school choice, and vouchers, many reformers have, for very good reasons, sought to use market mechanisms to increase opportunity to students constrained by the geographic monopoly on schooling that school districts enjoy. Some reformers have also utilized these mechanisms to undermine existing school regimes that (because of organizational incompetence) are unable to provide quality schooling. Similarly, growth of "portfolio" districts and the increasing tendency of officials to shift school operations into general-purpose governance (rather than special purpose, geographically defined school districts) highlights the declining salience of place in American schooling.[5] The loss of place, however, is not without a price, given that the current educational state relies so heavily on operational localism. Indeed, in its fullest expression, with its wholesale adoption of charters, vouchers, and choice, the "new educational state" deigns local districts as entities not to be reformed or reconstructed, but to be utterly evaded or even destroyed, and replaced with alternative governance mechanisms. The legitimacy of these new actors rests not on a foundation of operational localism, but on the market-based validation of consumers.

But the logic of decoupling the education state from geography is potentially faulty, if the aim is to improve equality of educational opportunity. Untethered from the constraints of operational localism, the proliferation of governance models results in an even more complex schooling environment, one that drops any semblance of uniformity or equality and is instead only an institutional patchwork of schooling options—one that is not universal, not accountable, and not subject to democratic controls at the federal, state, or local level. And it is not even clear that these actors produce better educational outcomes as part of the bargain. The current wave of efforts to dismantle existing educational governance arrangements is—in some places—building an educational state that is more unregulated and unaccountable to political actors. In charters and voucher-based schooling, the efforts to reshape school governance will, in the end, make schools less subject to national-level reform efforts. If we look at the effects of these new governance models on English-learners and special education, we see that the transfer of authority over public education to private, nonprofit, or for-profit providers has already produced significant evasions of previous landmark federal reforms, particularly the Individuals with Disabilities Education Act. Recent studies show that charter networks, utilizing public funds, are less likely to enroll special needs students or English-learners.[6]

A Final Note

At some point in the writing of this project, a colleague asked me the gut-check question of school reform: Would I send my own children to T.C. Williams? My initial answer at the time was no, but that was before I had written the chapter on the school transformation process at T.C. Williams. In the course of researching and writing that chapter, my view changed. Middle-class parents may worry about the blending of student populations across socioeconomic lines and its effects on student achievement, but there is also a tremendous value that students and communities gain by being part of a larger collective enterprise of learning together and from each other. The effort and determination of the leadership at T.C. Williams to ensure that the entire range of academic abilities among the youth in Alexandria was developed to its fullest was remarkable. Equally impressive was their sense that Alexandria as a city would be unimaginable without a common high school. The city's identity—and future—is bound up in the success or failure of that school. Increasingly, that kind of relationship is rare in the American educational landscape, but the expectation of a clear relationship between a place and the governance of its schools is not wholly gone. The federal schoolhouse—when run well and provided with sufficient talent and resources—is a remarkable institution. It is a blended institution of state power that seeks to advance a contradiction: the notion that very unequal places can, with federal support and insistence, produce educational opportunity for all. The federal schoolhouse does not always succeed and, indeed, it has failed many. But if there is to be a future for places like Alexandria and T.C. Williams, it will grow out of the education that takes place there. The task of the education state is, as it always has been, to foster within our nation's communities a greater sense of promise.

NOTES

Preface

1. President John Kennedy, "Letter to Gorman Ridgely," July 12, 1963, Folder "Work Sessions," *School Board Minutes, July 12*, Alexandria City Pubic Schools Records Center, Alexandria, Virginia.
2. Ibid.
3. For his part, Ridgely politely replied with a letter to the President in which he indicated that the school board received a monthly report on dropouts and had increased the number of guidance counselors. The district also was beefing up its vocational education at its African American high school. He briefly reported that the School Board had approved the enrollment of forty-five black students at formerly all-white schools. Gorman Ridgeley, "Letter to President John Kennedy," July 12, 1963, Folder "Work Sessions," *School Board Minutes, July 12*, Alexandria City Pubic Schools Records Center, Alexandria, Virginia.
4. One example of a non-local, non-state, and non-federal entity that helps comprise the education state would be a publicly funded charter school, or charter network.
5. See, in particular, Richardson Dilworth, ed., *The City in American Political Development* (New York: Routledge, 2009).
6. Adam Nelson's rich book *The Elusive Ideal: Equal Educational Opportunity and the Federal Role in Boston's Public Schools, 1950–1985* (Chicago: University of Chicago Press, 2005) is a model for engaging simultaneously local and federal policy decisions, and I learned much from his approach. My undertaking differs from his, however, in that I am less concerned with a precise chronological framing of events and focused more on the connections between local educational policy and the nature of the local political regime, which Nelson takes as more or less fixed, or at least exogenous to school policies. In my view, federal educational policies—and their local implementation—have deep effects on local politics that need to be better understood.

1 The Local Politics of Federal Education Reform

1. The data for 8th and 4th grade reading and math NAEP assessments, broken down by year, national sample and public school student sample, is most readily obtained using the National Center for Education Statistics NAEP Data Explorer website at http://nces.ed.gov/nationsreportcard/naepdata/. The score results reported here were generated from that site. Accessed February 13, 2014. For the full reports see, National Center for Educational Statistics, *The*

Nation's Report Card: Reading, 2013 (Washington, DC: Institute of Education Sciences, 2013) and National Center for Educational Statistics, *The Nation's Report Card: Mathematics, 2013* (Washington, DC: Institute of Education Sciences, 2013).

2. NAEP Data Explorer, http://nces.ed.gov/nationsreportcard/naepdata/. Access date February 13, 2014.

3. Jaekyung Lee and Todd Reeves, "Revisiting the Impact of NCLB High-Stakes School Accountability, Capacity and Resources," *Educational Evaluation and Policy Analysis* 34, no. 2 (2012): 209–231; Bruce Fuller, et al., "Gauging Growth: How to Judge No Child Left Behind?" *Educational Researcher* 36, no. 5 (2007): 268–278.

4. Kelly, D., Xie, H., Nord, C.W., Jenkins, F., Chan, J.Y., and Kastberg, D. (2013). *Performance of U.S. 15-Year-Old Students in Mathematics, Science, and Reading Literacy in an International Context: First Look at PISA 2012* (NCES 2014-024). U.S. Department of Education. Washington, DC: National Center for Education Statistics, http://nces.ed.gov/pubs2014/2014024.pdf. Accessed February 13, 2014, p. 10.

5. Ibid., p. 9.

6. Ibid., p. 20.

7. National Center for Educational Statistics, *The Nation's Report Card: Mathematics, 2013.*

8. Linda Darling-Hammond, *The Flat World and Education* (New York: Teachers College Press, 2010).

9. National Center for Education Statistics, *Digest of Education Statistics* (Washington, DC: U.S. Department of Education, 2011), Table 181.

10. According to the Center on Budget and Policy Priorities, the federal government spent $773 billion on Social Security and $689 billion on national defense in fiscal year 2012, making them the top two budgetary line items. Medicare spending was $472 billion. Center on Budget and Policy Priorities, "Policy Basics: Where Do Our Federal Tax Dollars Go?" April 12, 2013. Available at http://www.cbpp.org/files/4-14-08tax.pdf. Accessed January 26, 2014. The US Department of Education's *Digest of Education Statistics* estimates that in fiscal year 2012 all levels of government spent $650 billion on public education. U.S. Department of Education *Digest of Education Statistics*, "Table 29: Expenditures of Educational Institutions, by level and control of institution." Available at http://nces.ed.gov/programs/digest/d12/tables/dt12_029.asp. Accessed January 26, 2014. If public education were a wholly federal responsibility, the total expenditures would be comparable to defense spending.

11. While the book as a whole will focus primarily on federal-local interactions, I understand and recognize that state politics and administrative capacities are changing over this time period as well, often in response to federal educational initiatives. There are episodes in the book, particularly during the development of special education mandates and the rise of accountability policies, when developments within the Virginia state government are relevant to Alexandria and I provide an overview of those changes. I do not, however, provide a full accounting of the parallel story of the institutional and political development within educational policy that occurs within Virginia within this 50 year period. To do so, while focusing on the political dimensions of the interaction of operational localism and federal policy, would simply be too much to attempt. There is another book to be written on the development of state level administrative structures and their relevance to local and federal educational politics, but I do not provide it here. Instead, I must bracket that history while I focus on the local narrative.

12. Richard Briffault, "The Local School District in American Law," in *Besieged: School Boards and the Future of Education Politics*, ed. William G. Howell (Washington, DC: Brookings Institution Press, 2005), 28.

13. Ibid., 24.

14. U.S. Department of Education, *Digest of Education Statistics*, Table 235.10: Revenues for public elementary and secondary schools, by source of funds. Available at http://nces.ed.gov/programs/digest/d13/tables/dt13_235.10.asp. Accessed January 27, 2014.

15. There are two exceptions: schools run by the U.S. Department of Defense for children residing on U.S. military bases, both in the U.S and overseas and school districts that have been taken

over by the state, under state legislation, generally because of long histories of educational failure and or corruption. Both are atypical circumstances.

16. As Clarence Stone has written, "Sustained effort for [educational] change rests ultimately on some form of local support. The local political context is thus a matter of utmost importance. It is at the local level that crucial support for reform is built, resistance is mounted, and conflicts over education worked out." Clarence Stone, "Introduction: Urban Education in Political Context," in *Changing Urban Education*, ed. Clarence Stone (Lawrence: University Press of Kansas, 1998), 2.

17. Douglas S. Reed, *On Equal Terms: The Constitutional Politics of Educational Opportunity* (Princeton, NJ: Princeton University Press, 2001).

18. Frank J. Munger and Richard F. Fenno, Jr., *National Politics and Federal Aid to Education* (Syracuse, NY: Syracuse University Press, 1962), 2–9. During the Great Depression, Congress authorized the Reconstruction Finance Corporation to loan money to distressed school districts unable to meet payrolls, or to provide unemployment relief to unpaid teachers. These loans and unemployment relief generally do not meet a definition of federal aid to education.

19. Harvey Kantor, "Education, Social Reform, and the State: ESEA and Federal Education Policy in the 1960s," *American Journal of Education* 100, no. 1 (1991): 47–83; Julie Roy Jeffrey, *Education for Children of the Poor: A Study of the Origins and Implementation of the Elementary and Secondary Education Act of 1965* (Columbus: Ohio State University Press, 1978); Hugh Davis Graham, *The Uncertain Triumph* (Chapel Hill: University of North Carolina Press, 1984).

20. Kantor, "Education, Social Reform, and the State," 51.

21. Jeffrey, *Education for Children of the Poor*, 51. Because Title I represented, in the mid-1960s, a comparatively weak intervention into local schools, I do not address it separately as a federal policy initiative aimed at challenging operational localism. In fact, Title I explicitly and overtly accepted the primary of localim, in the early years. As Cohen and Moffitt write, Title I "did not require major changes in practice or organization: poor students would get better education by way of expanded conventional services. Teachers would do the same sort of work;.... There would be no revolution in practice, and educators would make nearly all of the key educational decisions. Here, too, it meant no new infrastructure would be needed." David K. Cohen and Susan L. Moffitt, *The Ordeal of Equality: Did Federal Regulation Fix the Schools?* (Cambridge, MA: Harvard University Press, 2009), p50. Later, beginning in the mid-1990s, Congress began to demand more results for its educational money and required school districts to show improvement in student learning as a condition of receiving federal Title I money. This accountability-based intervention is closely examined in Part III of this book, but I do not directly address the early effects of Title I in Alexandria because, in effect, none were sought, beyond the desegregation of schools.

22. Gary Orfield, *The Reconstruction of Southern Education: The Schools and the 1964 Civil Rights Act* (New York: John Wiley & Sons, 1968).

23. Gary Orfield, Susan E. Eaton, and Harvard Project on School Desegregation, *Dismantling Desegregation* (New York: New Press, 1996).

24. The federal government began offering funds to operate bilingual and bicultural educational programs under the Bilingual Education Act of 1968, which became Title VII of ESEA. The 1974 Supreme Court decision *Lau v. Nichols* held that providing instruction only in English violated the 1964 Civil Rights Act for students who did not speak English. The Bilingual Education Act of 1974 was meant, in part, to provide resources for school districts to meet this new requirement to provide instruction—whether transitional or for language maintenance—in a child's home language. See Susan Gilbert Schneider, *Revolution, Reaction or Reform: The 1974 Bilingual Education Act* (New York: Las Americas, 1976).

25. For the best treatments of NCLB see, Elizabeth Debray, *Politics, Ideology and Education; Federal Policy during the Clinton and Bush Administrations* (New York: Teachers College Press, 2006); Patrick McGuinn, *No Child Left Behind and the Transformation of Federal Education Policy, 1965–2005* (Lawrence, KS: University Press of Kansas, 2006); Paul Manna, *Collision*

Course: Federal and Education Policy Meets State and Local Realities (Washington, DC: CQ Press, 2011); Jesse Rhodes, *An Education in Politics: The Origins and Evolution of No Child Left Behind* (Ithaca: Cornell University Press, 2012).

26. Desmond King and Marc Stears, "How the U.S. State Works: A Theory of Standardization," *Perspectives on Politics* 9, no. 3 (2011): 508.

27. King and Stears, "How the U.S. State Works," 506.

28. Bill Turque, "New WTU Pres Nathan Saunders: 'It's Been All Teacher Blood' on the Floor." In *D.C. Schools Insider*. (Washington, DC: Washington Post, 2010), December 2. Available at http://voices.washingtonpost.com/dcschools/2010/12/saunders_its_been_all_teacher. html. Access date January 27, 2014.

29. Clarence Stone, "Systemic Power in Community Decision-Making: A Restatement of Stratification Theory," *American Political Science Review* 74, no. 4 (1980): 978–990.

30. Clarence Stone, *Regime Politics: Governing Atlanta: 1946–1988* (Lawrence: University Press of Kansas, 1989), 3.

31. Ibid., 6.

32. Stone, "Introduction: Urban Education in Political Context," 8.

33. Ibid., 9, italics omitted.

34. Ibid., 9, italics omitted.

35. Ibid.,14.

36. Moreover, as we think about regimes in general, many business actors within a particular regime may not have the kind of employment ties to the local community that will place education high on their list of concerns. Capital-intensive businesses, with little demand for large numbers of locally based workers, for example, will care little about the quality of high school graduates in the areas where they do business; they will most likely find it more efficient to import (i.e., transfer in) the skilled employees they need in a particular community. Likewise, manufacturing firms that are moving their operations overseas will have little need for skilled vocational workers in the local community, and will, most likely, seek lower local property taxes on their existing property holdings, acting as a restraint on increasing revenues for public education. Thus, the local political economy of any particular community (and the changes in that political economy over time) will play a significant role in defining the nature of regime actors' interest in the reform of public education.

37. Jeffrey Henig, *The End of Exceptionalism in American Education* (Cambridge, MA: Harvard Education Press, 2013), 18.

38. Importantly, for the case study that this book develops, the state of Virginia requires school systems to be financially dependent on either the local city or county; they have no independent taxation authority. In this sense, the experiences of Alexandria perhaps foreshadow the future of educational politicking if Henig's observation bears out nationally.

39. Karen Orren and Stephen Skowronek, *The Search for American Political Development* (Cambridge, MA: Cambridge University Press, 2004), 22.

40. Orren and Skowronek, *The Search for American Political Development*, 25.

41. See, generally, Patrick J. McGuinn, *No Child Left Behind and the Transformation of Federal Education Policy, 1965–2005* (Lawrence, KS: University Press of Kansas).

42. This notion of path dependence is not new in political science, but it has not been extensively applied to the politics of education reform. Indeed, there is some disagreement about how best to define and use the notion of path dependence in the analysis of politics. For the purposes of this book, path dependence refers to the policy inertia that stems from the political or financial costs that local regime actors must confront when they seek to change policy directions. As Pierson describes the calculus, path dependence exists when "the relative benefits of the current activity compared with other possible options increase over time. To put it a different way, the costs of exit—of switching to some previously plausible alternative—rise." Paul Pierson, "Increasing Returns, Path Dependency and the Study of Politics," *American Political Science Review* 94, no. 2 (2000): 251–267, p252. In many analyses of education policy, the benefits or costs that are tallied are frequently only those that are associated directly with the

policy itself, and not those that accrue to the political supporters of a particular policy. My analysis expands that calculus to include the broader range of costs and benefits.

43. Stephen Skowronek, *Building a New American State: The Expansion of National Administrative Capacities, 1877–1920* (New York: Cambridge University Press, 1982), p166.

44. Suzanne Mettler, *From Soldiers to Citizens: The G.I. Bill and the Making of the Greatest Generation* (New York: Oxford University Press, 2005).

45. The classic account of the origins of public schooling and its relationship to notions of nation-building is Carl Kaestle's *Pillars of the Republic: Common Schools and American Society, 1780–1860* (New York: Hill and Wang, 1983).

46. Martha Derthick, *The Influence of Federal Grants: Public Assistance in Massachusetts* (Cambridge: Harvard University Press, 1970), p216.

47. While Arlington County, Virginia was also a candidate, I excluded it on the grounds that my children attended school there, giving rise to possible conflicts of interests, particularly as I sought out interviews.

48. As we will see in Chapter 7, the shift to an elected school board represented a significant shift in the nature of the local regime.

49. Indeed one of those legacies is that Alexandria was, at one time, within the boundaries of the District of Columbia and directly governed by Congress. For an overview of the political tensions over slavery that led to its retrocession back to Virginia, see A. Glenn Crothers, "The 1846 Retrocession of Alexandria: Protecting Slavery and the Slave Trade in the District of Columbia," in *In the Shadow of Freedom: The Politics of Slavery in the National Capital*, ed. Paul Finkelman and Donald R. Kennon, 141–168. (Athens, OH: Ohio University Press, 2011). For a more popular account of life in Alexandria, DC, see Michael Lee Pope, *Hidden History of Alexandria, DC* (Charleston, SC: The History Press, 2011).

50. In one way, Alexandria is significantly different from other districts in the country. In 1993, under Governor Doug Wilder, the state of Virginia banned collective bargaining by public sector unions, including teacher unions. In Alexandria, the school district and the Education Association of Alexandria (which is affiliated with both the Virginia Education Association and the National Education Association) hold "meet and confer" sessions in which both sides engage in what amounts to "interest-based bargaining," according to Lisa Staib of the Education Association of Alexandria. That language is then incorporated into school district policies (which are voted on by the School Board) or school district regulations (which are issued by the Superintendent). Through this process, the district establishes common pay scales and workplace regulations outside of a collective bargaining agreement. According to Staib, the lack of a collective bargaining agreement process makes for a "huge difference" between collective bargaining and non-bargaining districts. "There's a real difference in culture," she said (Lisa Staib, Phone interview, September 9, 2013). Additionally, Virginia is a right-to-work state, meaning that union membership cannot be required for employment, and strikes by public employees are also banned. In Virginia teachers are tenurable after a probationary period of three years. In effect, these differences, for our purposes, mean that teachers—since 1993—have been less powerful members of the local regime. Their interests and concerns are still manifest, but as we shall see in Chapter 8, they have less of a footing to challenge the Superintendent's policy directions. This, in turn, would strengthen the hand of federal reform efforts to enforce a robust accountability mechanism.

51. I am indebted to an anonymous reviewer at Oxford University Press for very helpful comments that clarified the presentation of the research design of this book.

Part One: Race and Regime

1. For an overview of this episode, see Mark Howard, "An Historical Study of the Desegregation of the Alexandria, Virginia, City Public School" (PhD diss., George Washington University, 1976), 161–163.

2. "School Board Won't Reinstate Cook Fired for Role in Desegregation," *Washington Post*, September 11, 1958, B1.

3. Ibid.

4. Susanna McBee, "Negro Alexandria Cook Fired after She Joined Bias Suit Is Rehired," *Washington Post*, October 3, 1958, B1.

5. The standard account is Richard Kluger's *Simple Justice* (New York: Vintage Books, 1975). A more recent re-appraisal is James Patterson's *Brown v. Board of Education: A Civil Rights Milestone and its Troubled Legacy* (New York: Oxford University Press, 2001). For examinations of events in Virginia, see Robert Pratt's *The Color of Their Skin: Education and Race in Richmond, Virginia, 1954-1989* (Charlottesville: University of Virginia Press, 1992) and Jill Ogline Titus's *Brown's Battleground: Students, Segregationists and the Struggle for Justice in Prince Edward County, Virginia* (Chapel Hill: University of North Carolina Press, 2011).

6. "Williams Elected Schools' Director," *Washington Post*, April 13, 1933.

2 Race and the End of a Regime

1. The lawsuit that desegregated Alexandria schools is *Jones v. School Board of City of Alexandria, Virginia*. Although officially an unreported ruling, the text of Judge Albert Bryan's decision can be found at *Race Relations Law Reporter* 4, no. 1 (1959): 29–36.

2. Mechlin Moore, "Smoot-Thomson Race Turns into Debate over School Integration Issue," *Washington Post*, April 13, 1957, B1.

3. Gray Commission, *Report of the Commission on Public Education to the Governor of Virginia*, (1955), 7 (hereinafter, Gray Commission Report).

4. Ibid., 9.

5. Ibid., 7.

6. *Almond v. Day*, 89 S.E.2d 851(1955).

7. Robbins L. Gates, *The Making of Massive Resistance* (Chapel Hill: University of North Carolina Press, 1962), 85.

8. James W. Ely, *The Crisis of Conservative Virginia: The Byrd Organization and the Politics of Massive Resistance* (Knoxville: University of Tennessee Press, 1976), 74.

9. Under then-prevailing state law (enacted as part of the Massive Resistance campaign), all requests for African American transfers to or enrollment in traditionally all-white schools required the approval of a state Pupil Placement Board created to thwart the efforts of any desegregation-minded local board. While the state placement board was struck down in 1957 in *School Board of City of Newport News v. Atkins*, the Alexandria School Board adopted its own six-point criteria in October of 1958, as the *Jones* case was proceeding. When the state Pupil Placement Board was reenacted by the state legislature, the state continued its oversight of placement decisions. I have found no instance in which the School Board's recommendation was overturned by state authorities. For an overview of how pupil placement boards functioned in Virginia, see Daniel J. Meador, "The Constitution and Assignment of Pupils to Public Schools," *Virginia Law Review* 45, no. 4 (1959): 517–571.

10. All the key court rulings and school board resolutions in the case of *Jones v. School Board of City of Alexandria, Virginia* can be most conveniently found at *Race Relations Law Reporter* 4, no. 1 (1959): 29–36.

11. Ibid., 30–31.

12. Alexandria City School Board, *Executive Session Minutes*, Alexandria City Public Schools Records Center, Alexandria, Virginia, February 4, 1959.

13. *Session Minutes*, February 4, 1959.

14. Douglas J. Smith, "'When Reason Collides with Prejudice': Armistead Lloyd Boothe and the Politics of Moderation," in *The Moderates' Dilemma: Massive Resistance to School Desegregation in Virginia*, ed. M.D. Lassiter and A.B. Lewis (Charlottesville: University Press of Virginia, 1998), 45–50

15. Ibid., 38.

16. Ibid., 47.

17. John Lawson, "Parent Advised State Deals with All Placements," *Washington Post*, August 16, 1958, D1.

18. Howard, "An Historical Study of the Desegregation of the Alexandria, Virginia, City Public School," 167

19. Susanna McBee, "Bogle Gets Moeller's School Post," *Washington Post*, June 24, 1959, B1. The move was apparently orchestrated by State Delegate James M. Thomson, arch-segregationist and brother-in-law to Harry S. Byrd, Jr., who had handily defeated Boothe's good friend and fellow moderate Albert A. Smoot in the 1957 Democratic primary race for the General Assembly. Thomson, at the time the campaign manager for former Alexandria Mayor Marshall J. Beverley's effort to unseat Boothe from the State Senate, led a successful effort to replace Moeller with Ralph H. Bogle, a ward chairman for Beverley's election bid. Typically, incumbent School Board members were reappointed by the City Council as long as they expressed a continued willingness to serve. But when Moeller's term was up, City Council member James T. Luckett (brother to School Board member Frank Luckett) nominated Bogle to replace him, and Council members Josiah S. Everly (the prior School Board chair) and Joseph Pancoast and F. Clinton Knight joined with Luckett to outnumber Mayor Leroy Bendheim and Council members John Ewald and James Duncan, who sided with Moeller.

20. Susanna McBee, "Schools Post, Politics Linked," *Washington Post*, June 12, 1959, B4.

21. Alexandria City School Board, *Exective Session Minutes*, Alexandria City Public Schools Records Center, Alexandria, Virginia, October 19, 1959, Case Nos. 2 and 4.

22. Ibid., Case Nos. 6, 10, 9, 13.

23. Ibid., Case Nos. 2 and 3.

24. This commitment to segregation came at a high monetary price. As late as June 1960, the School Board authorized payments totaling $5,000 (over $36,000 in 2009 dollars) to the attorneys representing the school district in what were, by now, hopeless appeals. Two payments—$4,000 to John Barton Phillips and $1,000 to Earl F. Wagner—were authorized by the School Board for their work on the *Jones* v. *School Board of the City of Alexandria* case. "Checks Presented for Payment at School Board Meeting," *School Board Minutes*, June 16, Alexandria City Public Schools Records Center, Alexandria, Virginia, June 16, 1960.

25. Alexandria City School Board, *Executive Session Minutes*, Alexandria City Public Schools Records Center, Alexandria, Virginia, September 8, 1960.

26 Under existing state law, these transfers had to be formally approved by the state Pupil Placement Board, but by the early 1960s, this board rubber-stamped Alexandria's submissions.

27. The figure of seventy-five students is obtained from totaling all petitions from African American students to attend a white (or formerly white) school. The actions taken on these petitions are found in the *School Board Minutes, Executive Sessions* from the following dates: January 22, 1959; April 28, 1959; October 19, 1959; September 8, 1960; September 14, 1960; July 12, 1961; September 13, 1961 and June 13, 1962. The total of 2442 African American students for the 1962–1963 school year is from a memo entitled "Racial Composition of Schools—Students and Faculty," *Desegregation File Cabinet*, Alexandria City Public Schools Records Center, Alexandria, Virginia, July 19, 1966 (copy in author's possession).

28. Alexandria City School Board, *Executive Session Minutes*, Alexandria City Public Schools Records Center, Alexandria, Virginia, June 13, 1962, 2.

29. "Superintendent's Report," *School Board Minutes, December 19*, Alexandria City Public Schools Records Center, Alexandria, Virginia, December 19, 1962, 9.

30. John C. Albohm, "Integration: Constructive Steps Taken since March 11, 1963," *Folder, Leonard S. Brown Conference,* Alexandria City Public Schools Records Center, Alexandria, Virginia, April 25, 1963. Upon his arrival in early March 1963, Superintendent Albohm was confronted with requests by African American leaders to both improve conditions at the city's black schools and to accelerate desegregation. Leonard Brown was the chairman of a group

called the Alexandria Citizens Committee for Colored Voters. Two copies of Albohm's memo regarding integration are in the files. One is marked "Confidential."

31. "Letter from Alexandria Nonviolent Action Group," *Executive Session Minutes*, Alexandria City Public Schools Records Center, Alexandria, Virginia, April 16, 1962; "Letter from Alexandria Council on Human Relations," *School Board Minutes, July 18*, Alexandria City Public Schools Records Center, Alexandria, Virginia, July 18, 1962; "Resolutions Adopted by the Alexandria Citizens Committee for Colored Voters," *School Board Minutes, November 21*, Alexandria City Public Schools Records Center, Alexandria, Virginia, November 21, 1962.

32. Ibid., April 25, 1963.

33. "Letter from Alexandria Citizens Committee for Colored Voters," *School Board Minutes, April 16*, Alexandria City Public Schools Records Center, Alexandria, Virginia, April 16, 1962.

34. "Agenda for Work Session," *Folder, Work Session*, Alexandria City Public Schools Records Center, Alexandria, Virginia, September 12, 1963, 3–4.

35. Ibid., 4.

36. Ibid.

37. "Memorandum to High School Principals," *Folder, Work Session*, Alexandria City Public Schools Records Center, Alexandria, Virginia, November 23, 1963.

38. "Special Staff Meeting—Agenda for December 16, 1963," *Folder, Work Session*, Alexandria City Public Schools Records Center, Alexandria, Virginia, February 12, 1964, 1–2.

39. John C. Albohm, "Letter to Walter H. Rogers, Jr.," *Folder, School Board Roundtable Meeting*, Alexandria City Public Schools Records Center, Alexandria, Virginia, January 3, 1964, 1.

40. Ibid., 1.

41. Alexandria City Public Schools, Psychological Services, "An Inquiry into the Assimilation of Students Transferred to Nearby Schools in the City of Alexandria, 1963-1964," *Folder, Work Session*, Alexandria City Public Schools Records Center, Alexandria, Virginia, February 1, 1964, 2.

42. Ibid., 8.

43. Ibid., 14.

44. Alexandria Schools Psychological Services, "An Analysis of the Intellectual Strengths and Weaknesses of an Educationally Deprived 8th Grade Class," *School Board Minutes, February 12*, Alexandria City Public Schools Records Center, Alexandria, Virginia, February 12, 1964, 8.

45. Ibid., 2.

46. Ibid.

47. Ibid., 1.

48. Ibid.

49. Alexandria Schools Psychological Services, "Description of a Project for Upgrading Education in One Section of the City of Alexandria, Virginia," *Folder, Work Sessions*, Alexandria City Public Schools Records Center, Alexandria, Virginia, July 8, 1964, 2.

50. Susanna McBee, "U.S. To Aid Alexandria Slum Fight," *Washington Post*, September 28 1957, D1; Everard Munsey, "Slum Residents Suffer with Cold, Filth, Vermin," *Washington Post*, October 24, 1960, B1; "Council to Review Anti-Slum Plan," *Washington Post*, October 26, 1960, 20; Everard Munsey, "Slum Dwellers Face Choice: Risk Fire or Freeze," *Washington Post*, December 16, 1960, A3.

51. Alexandria Schools Psychological Services, "Description of a Project for Upgrading Education in One Section of the City of Alexandria, Virginia," 4.

52. Ibid., 5.

53. Ibid., 6.

54. "Superintendent's Report," *School Board Minutes, November 18*, Alexandria City Public Schools Records Center, Alexandria, Virginia, November 18, 1964, 6.

55. Howard, "An Historical Study of the Desegregation of the Alexandria, Virginia, City Public School," 185.

56. Gary Orfield provides a fascinating account of the birth of the bureaucracy charged with ensuring compliance with Title VI. See Gary Orfield, *The Reconstruction of Southern Education: The Schools and the 1964 Civil Rights Act* (New York: Wiley-Interscience, 1968), 76–85.

57. Orfield, *Reconstruction of Southern Education*, 79–80. Ultimately, Professor G.W. Foster, Jr., of the University of Wisconsin, synthesized in a single document the basic criteria and techniques of desegregation that federal District and Circuit Courts had approved in desegregation court orders across the South. This memo, first written to an Arkansas school superintendent, circulated informally, and then, after some revision, was published, of all places, in the *Saturday Review* in March of 1965. Orfield explains that the promulgation of these guidelines was delayed, in part, because of internal disagreements at HEW over whether the distribution of minimum requirements to meet Title VI would prevent the Department from seeking greater desegregation from Southern school districts. Professor G.W. Foster, Jr., provided an overview of guidelines to the *Saturday Review* in an effort to spur HEW's release of official regulations concerning Title VI compliance. See *The Reconstruction of Southern Education*, 87–92.

58. Compliance with a court order would suffice as Title VI compliance only if the court order mandated specific actions to eliminate a dual school system.

59. Orfield, *Reconstruction*, 98.

60. "Receipts," *School Board Minutes, December 16*, Alexandria City Public Schools Records Center, Alexandria, Virginia, December 16, 1964.

61. "Assurance of Compliance with Department of Health, Education and Welfare Regulation under Title VI of the Civil Rights Act of 1964 (Hew Form 441)," *Desegregation File Cabinet Folder, "Compliance—Rules, Regulations,"* Alexandria City Public Schools Records Center, Alexandria, Virginia, January 8, 1965.

62. "Letter to Harry R. Elmore, Assistant Superintendent of Public Instruction," *Desegregation File Cabinet Folder, "Compliance—Rules, Regulations"* Alexandria City Public Schools Records Center, Alexandria, Virginia, January 29, 1965. Albohm's list of actions taken since he took office included the impending conversion of formerly all-black Parker-Gray High School to a middle school; the desegregation of fourteen schools (of twenty-two schools) within the district; the partial integration of school district faculty; the expansion of the School Board from six to nine members and the selection of the city's first African American school board member; and the full integration of summer schools, adult education, auditoriums, recreational facilities, and libraries.

63. Albohm, John C. "Letter to R. Worth Peters, Regional Representative, Office of Education, Region 3," *Desegregation File Cabinet, Folder "Compliance—Rules, Regulations,"* Alexandria City Public Schools Records Center, Alexandria, Virginia, April 2, 1965.

64. Howard, "An Historical Study of the Desegregation of the Alexandria, Virginia, City Public School," 195–196.

65. Ibid., 191

66. "Statement of Policies for School Desegregation Plans Under Title VI of the Civil Rights Act of 1964," 45 Code of Federal Regulations Sec. 181.54. (1967 Supp), 407.

67. Howard, "An Historical Study of the Desegregation of the Alexandria, Virginia, City Public School," 205.

68. Historically, Alexandria had operated Grades 1–7 elementary schools and housed eighth-graders either in separate schools or in high schools. As part of its desegregation plan, Albohm proposed a new alignment of schools, a 6-2-4 plan, with grades 1–6 in elementary school, grades 7 and 8 in separate middle schools and grades 9–12 in traditional high schools. The four proposed middle schools involved both the conversion of existing schools and new construction: Parker-Gray Middle School had been created out of the formerly all-African American Parker-Gray High School the previous year; Minnie Howard Middle School was a converted elementary school; Thomas Jefferson Middle School was currently an eighth-grade-only school; and John Adams Middle School was a brand new school in the far west of the city, slated to open in January 1967.

69. Maurine Hoffman, "Alexandria School Plans under Fire," *Washington Post*, May 1, 1966, 8.

70. Susan Filson, "Integated Schools Want 'the Best'," *Washington Post*, April 17, 1966, 10.

71. Maurine Hoffman, "Albohm Views School Busing as Real Issue," *Washington Post*, May 12, 1966, B3.

72. Ibid.

73. Maurine McLaughlin, "Alexandria to Improve Urban Grade Schools," *Washington Post*, June 25, 1966, A7. The district did, however, lower the student-teacher ratio from 25 to 1 to 22 to 1, and created a "continuous progress" curriculum within ungraded primary classrooms, which would allow students to learn at their own pace. If needed, students would be allowed four years to complete the first three years of primary school. In addition, the district increased resource teachers in reading, art, music, physical education, French, and speech therapy. Maurine McLaughlin, "Grade School Licks Desegregation Fears," *Washington Post*, October 10, 1966, B1.

74. Howard, "An Historical Study of the Desegregation of the Alexandria, Virginia, City Public Schools," 215.

75. "A Proposal for an In-Service Training Program in the Alexandria City Public Schools under Title VI of the Civil Rights Act of 1964," Alexandria City Public Schools Records Center, Alexandria, Virginia, July 18, 1966, 4.

76. Ibid., 4.

3 Racial Change, Conflict, and the Incorporation of Interests

1. Joseph D. Whitaker, "Black Youth Tells of Chase: 'Then He Took out His Gun'," *Washington Post*, October 10, 1969, C1.

2. Ibid.

3. Ibid.

4. Maurine McLaughlin, "Controversial Policeman: 'I'm Paid to Defend Citizens'." *Washington Post*, October 10, 1969, C1.

5. Whitaker, "Black Youth Tells of Chase: 'Then He Took out His Gun'."

6. Hank Burchard and Carl W. Sims, "2 Police Firings Demanded," *Washington Post*, October 12, 1969, 31.

7. *Washington Post*, "Alexandria Blacks Protest," *Washington Post*, October 15, 1969, E4.

8. Maurine McLaughlin, "Alexandria Acts on Race Tension," *Washington Post*, October 21, 1969, C1.

9. Maurine McLaughlin, "Pvt. Callahan Is Honored in Alexandria," *Washington Post*, October 30, 1969, B1.

10. Maurine McLaughlin, "Arlandia's Dilemma: Floods, Buck-Passing," *Washington Post*, August 21, 1969, E1.

11. Maurine McLaughlin, "Alexandria Lifts 'Emergency' Bans," *Washington Post*, June 7, 1970, A1.

12. Flemming, son of former HEW Secretary Arthur Flemming, himself left the Council a year later, when he resigned because, as Flemming put it, his position as Special Counsel to President-Elect Richard Nixon left him with a "practical conflict of interest" between his job in the White House and as City Council member (*Washington Post*, "Nixon Aide Flemming Resigns from Alexandria City Council," January 15, 1969, 41.

13. Washington Post. "Melee Shakes Alexandria." *Washington Post*, October 10 1969, C1.

14. E. J. Bachinski and Michael Hodge, "Youth Slain, Disorder Hits Alexandria," *Washington Post*, May 30, 1970, 17.

15. E. J. Bachinski, "Knife Planted in Killing, Alexandria Court Told," ibid., June 13, 1970, A1.

16. Jim Mann, "Municipal Candidates Cite Disorder," ibid., June 2, 1970, B1.

17. Joseph D. Whitaker, "Mayor, Blacks Give Views on City's Unrest," ibid., June 2, 1970, B1.

18. Maurine McLaughlin, "Alexandria Lifts 'Emergency' Bans," ibid., June 7, 1970.

19. Ibid.

20. Maurine McLaughlin, "Alexandria Has 6th Night of Disorder," *Washington Post*, June 4, 1970, A1.

21. Maurine McLaughlin, "Alexandria Vote Puts Negro on City Council," *Washington Post*, June 10, 1970, A1.

22. Paul G. Edwards, "Jury Splits 11 to 1, Ends Hanna Trial," ibid., November 29, 1970, 1.

23 "Jury Splits 11 to 1, Ends Hanna Trial." Six weeks later, Judge Franklin Backus ordered the framed Confederate flag removed from the courtroom, telling a Post reporter, "I ordered it taken down, so you would never write about it again in the Washington Post." *Washington Post*, "Hanna Judge Ousts Confederate Flag," ibid., January 20, 1971, B2.

24. Paul G. Edwards, "Youths Express Outrage in Memorial to Gibson," ibid., January 22, 1971, C1.

25. Ibid.

26. Ibid.

27. Washington Post, "Cross Burned at Va. School," *Washington Post*, November 3, 1970, C20.

28. Alexandria Gazette, "School Cross-Burning Incidents under Investigation by Police," *Alexandria Gazette*, November 2, 1970, 1.

29. Washington Post, "Youths Scatter as Cross Burns," *Washington Post*, October 25, 1970, 48.

30. Ibid., "Nazis Picket at Home of School Head," *Washington Post*, November 9, 1970, C6.

31. Paul G. Edwards, "Discipline Is Made Issue in Alexandria," *Washington Post*, November 26, 1970.

32. Along with his statement, Haynes circulated an excerpt from Federal District Court Judge Sidney Mize's opinion in *Evers v. Jackson Municipal Separate School District*, a Mississippi desegregation case in which Mize stated that "differences between Caucasians and Negroes are genetically determined and cannot be changed materially by environment" and that " separate classes with teachers of the same race are academically superior and maintain a better disciplinary status." The full excerpt, circulated at the School Board meeting, is as follows: "Here plaintiffs have conceded, by their unwillingness or inability to contest the issues of which they had been seasonably informed, first, that the learning traits which are characteristic of Negro children do differ to an educationally significant degree from those which are typical of white pupils; second, that separate classes with teachers of the same race are academically superior and maintain a better disciplinary status; third, that such classes substantially diminish the number of delinquents and dropouts in the schools; fourth, that such separate classes alone can be adapted to the difference in instruction which is necessary to realize for the learning patterns of both groups the equality of educational opportunity which the Constitution requires; fifth, that differences between Caucasians and Negroes are genetically determined and cannot be changed materially by environment; and, sixth, that integration—not segregation—injures the Negro school child." *Evers v. Jackson Municipal Separate School District*357 F.2d 653 (5th Cir. 1966), 251.

33. Edwards, "Discipline Is Made Issue in Alexandria."

34. Edwards, "Discipline Urged in Schools."

35. Ibid.

36. Maurine McLaughlin, "Broad Vote Base Elected Kennahan," ibid., November 6, 1969, B4.

37. Richard M. Cohen and Maurine McLaughlin, "Alexandria Turmoil Strains Old School Ties," ibid., March 2, 1969, 45.

38. Edwards, "Discipline Is Made Issue in Alexandria," November 26, 1970; Julie Parker, "Parents Complain About GW Scuffle," *Alexandria Gazette*, October 22, 1970, 1; "Lin Robinson Is Elected GW Senior Class President," *Alexandria Gazette*, October 31, 1970, 14.

39. Doug Poretz, "School Officials, Students Meet on School Discipline," ibid., November 30, 1970, 1.

40. Doug Poretz, "Student Violence Increases," *Alexandria Gazette*, October 28, 1970, 1.

41. Edwards, "Discipline Is Made Issue in Alexandria," November 26, 1970; Alexandria City School Board, "George Washington High School—Incident of December 10, 1970," Box # 030113, *School Board Minutes*, December 16, 1970.

42. Edwards, "Discipline Is Made Issue in Alexandria," November 26, 1970.

43. Poretz, "Student Violence Increases."

44. According to an accounting of the incident by school officials, the students spelled out the word POOL before igniting the roofing tar, a possible reference to a City Council decision to not build a School Board-recommended, Olympic-sized swimming pool at Parker-Gray Middle School, formerly the all-black high school. The Council opted, instead, to build multiple small wading pools in the city (see McLaughlin, "Alexandria Lifts 'Emergency' Bans"). The principal of George Washington believed, however, it referred to a nearby pool hall (see Alexandria City School Board, December 12, 1970).

45. Cohen and McLaughlin, "Alexandria Turmoil Strains Old School Ties."

46. Ibid.

47. Ken Ringle, "Teachers Get Right to Expel in Alexandria," *Washington Post*, January 22, 1971, A1.

48. Ken Ringle, "Fire Alexandria Superintendent, Alexandria Councilman Asks," *Washington Post*, April 26, 1971.

49. As Sanger stated in a radio interview with Albohm broadcast on November 7, 1970 (later reprinted in the internal district-wide newsletter), "This [student] militancy that we are faced with today is coming from the colleges. It started out in the colleges and universities a few years ago and... we were fearful that it would permeate down into the high schools, and of course this is what is happening right now." Albohm, meanwhile, insisted that the schools alone should not be held responsible for the changing behavior of youth: "And the other institutions of this society, whether they be the courts or the churches or the marriage institutions, are just as faltering.... [W]e are not the one agency that should bear the blame for the collapse of American society." See John C. Albohm and Raymond F. Sanger, "Disruption and Discipline," in *Internal: For the Teachers and Administrators of the Alexandria Public Schools* (Alexandria City Public Schools, 1970), copy available in *School Board Minutes*, December 12, 1970, Box #030113.

50. Ibid.

51. Paul G. Edwards, "Fires Set at Alexandria's GW High as Black Students List Demands," *Washington Post*, March 26, 1971, B6.

52. See Chapter 2, 44–46.

53. Table 3.1 clusters the elementary schools into East Side, Central, and West Side attendance areas, showing a distinct pattern in the rate of growth of the African American student population during this time period. The citywide African American enrollment was roughly 30 percent, but those students were overwhelming concentrated in schools on the East Side. While one of the elementary schools previously designated for African Americans (Lyles-Crouch) had gained some white students, several other elementary schools saw white enrollments decline as black enrollments increased substantially. As a result, Alexandria had three previously all-white elementary schools that by the early 1970s were roughly 70–80 percent African American (Ficklin, Cora Kelly, and Robert E. Lee). In addition, Charles Houston, one of the formerly all-black schools, was still above 95 percent African American, while the other, Lyles-Crouch, was still at 70 percent African American. In contrast, on the West Side of town, no elementary school had more than 10 percent African American students and most had one to two percent African American enrollment.

54. *Green v. County School Board of New Kent County*, 391 U.S. 430 (1968), at 437–438. *Brown I* was the initial decision in 1954 that declared segregated schools unconstitutional. *Brown II* in 1955 sought to identify a remedy for the constitutional violation and was the source of the infamous "all deliberate speed" language that many scholars contend inspired the South to delay compliance with *Brown I*. See *Brown v. Board of Education of Topeka, Kansas* 347 U.S. 483 (1954) (*Brown I*) and *Brown v. Board of Education of Topeka, Kansas* 349 U.S. 294 (1955) (*Brown II*).

55. Ibid., 442.

56. Eloise Severinson, Regional Civil Rights Director, HEW, "Letter to Dr. John C. Albohm," *Box # 030113, School Board Minutes April 7,* January 19, 1971.

57. Paul G. Edwards, "Fires Set at Alexandria's GW High as Black Students List Demands," *Washington Post,* March 26, 1971, B6.

58. Paul G. Edwards, "Eleven Black Students Suspended after Protest," *Washington Post,* March 28, 1971, 57.

59 Paul G. Edwards. "GW Principal Hit in New Racial Unrest," *Washington Post,* March 31, 1971, C2.

60. Ibid.

61. Paul G. Edwards. "Alexandria School Talk Set Today," *Washington Post,* April 1, 1971, A30.

62. Ibid.

63. Mark Howard, "An Historical Study of the Desegregation of the Alexandria, Virginia, City Public School" (Phd Dissertation, George Washington University, 1976), p. 237.

64. John C. Albohm, "Memorandum Re: Alternate Plan for Pupil Distribution, Grades 7 through 12," *Box #030113, School Board Minutes,* April 15, 1971.

65. Susan Samson, "Proposed Plan for Central City High School," *Box 030113, Alexandria City School Board Minutes,* May 5, 1971.

66. John R. Stubbings, "Reorganization of the Secondary Schools in Alexandria," *Box 030113, School Board Minutes,* May 5, 1971.

67. William Blair, "Implications of the Central High School Plan in Its Relationship of the Athletic Program in Alexandria," *School Board Minutes—May 5,* May 5, 1971.

68 Alexandria City School Board, *School Board Minutes—May 19, 1971,* Box 030113, May 19, 1971, 29.

69. Kennahan's public disagreement with both Albohm and the School Board no doubt widened the rift that had opened during disputes over school discipline. In late July 1971, Kennahan announced that he would no longer serve as the School Board's attorney, following an opinion by the Virginia Attorney General that Commonwealth Attorneys were under no duty to represent school boards in the state. *Washington Post,* "Va. Attorney Won't Serve School Unit," *Washington Post,* July 30, 1971, D3.

70. Alexandria City School Board, *School Board Minutes—May 19, 1971,* Box 030113, May 19, 1971, 17–18.

71. Samuel E. NeSmith, "Statement on Education and Secondary Reorganization in Alexandria," Box 030113, *School Board Minutes—May 19,* May 19, 1971.

72. Alexandria City School Board, *School Board Minutes—May 19, 1971,* Box 030113, May 19, 1971, 26.

73. Ibid., 27.

74. Ibid., 30.

75. Eloise Severinson, Regional Civil Rights Director, HEW, "Letter to Dr. John C. Albohm, June 24, 1971," *Box # 030114, School Board Minutes—July 7, 1971,* July 7, 1971.

76. John C. Albohm, "Letter to Eloise Severinson, Regional Civil Rights Director, HEW," *School Board Minutes—July 7, 1971,* July 8, 1971.

77. William J. Sando, father of two Hammond High School students, sought a court order to block the 6-2-2-2 plan and its move away from neighborhood-based secondary schools. In August 1971, Federal District Court Judge Oren R. Lewis found the School Board to be under an obligation to desegregate and that the 6-2-2-2 restructuring was a legitimate means to meet that obligation. Pointedly Lewis wrote "this Court knows of no constitutional provision, federal or state—and none has been cited—requiring the City of Alexandria to maintain neighborhood secondary schools for the use and benefit of the plaintiff's children." *Sando v. Alexandria City School Board,* 330 F. Supp. 773(1971).

78. Office of the Superintendent Alexandria City Public Schools, "Minutes of Conference Held in Dr. Albohm's Office on July 20, 1971—2:15pm," *Desegregation Cabinet, Alexandria City Schools Record Center, July 20, 1971,* pp. 1–2.

79. July 20, 1971, p. 2.

80. Ibid., p. 2.

81. Ibid., p. 3.

82. Ibid., pp. 3–4.

83. Ibid., p. 4.

84. Ibid., p. 5.

85. Ibid., p. 5–6.

86. Ibid., p. 9.

87. Ibid., p. 10.

88. Ibid., pp. 10–11.

89. Ibid., p. 11.

90. Ibid., p. 12.

91. Ibid., p. 12.

92. John C. Albohm, "Letter to Eloise Severinson, Regional Civil Rights Director, HEW," *Box 030114, School Board Minutes—August 4, 1971,* July 30, 1971.

93. Jay Mathews, "Aide Says U.S. Won't Push Alexandria School Mixing," *Washington Post,* August 13, 1971, A14.

94. Paul G. Edwards, "Melee Disrupts School," ibid., September 9, 1971, B1.

95. Ibid.

96. Kevin Klose, "Alexandria Secretly Drafts Plan to Meet Most of Negro Demands," ibid., October 19, 1969, 1.

97. O.U. Johansen, "Letter to William C. Pace, February 12," Box 030113, *School Board Minutes, February 17,* February 12, 1971;Virginia High School League, "Alexandria Warned by VHSL," *Box 030113, School Board Mintues, February 17,* February 18, 1971.

98. Leonard Shapiro, "Williams' Success Is Seen in Black and White," *Washington Post,* October 24, 1971, D4.

99. Lawrence Feinberg, "Alexandria Makes Little Progress toward School Balance," ibid., March 5, 1972, B1.

100. J. Stanley Pottinger, "Letter to John C. Albohm," Box 15-556, *School Board Minutes, February 23, 1973,* February 3, 1972

101. Alexandria City School Board, *School Board Minutes—February 23, 1972,* Box 15-556, February 23, 1972, p. 9.

102. Nancy Scannell, "U.S. Prods Alexandria on Schools," *Washington Post,* February 24, 1972, E2.

103. J. Stanley Pottinger, "Letter to John C. Albohm," Box 15-209, *School Board Minutes, March 1,* Alexandria City Public Schools Records Center, Alexandria, Virginia, February 28, 1972. The quick reversal by HEW was, it seems, the result of high-level pressure applied by local figures who had close ties to the Nixon Administration and, particularly, Secretary of Health, Education and Welfare Eliot Richardson. According to press reports, Pottinger explained the reversal as the result of a phone call from a "representative" of Albohm and the School Board, who requested that integration not affect three elementary schools that had formerly been all-white, but were now about 70 percent black, due to neighborhood transformation. At the same time, Donald Baldwin, a lobbyist for several trade associations and a major Republican fundraiser with strong ties to the Nixon Administration and also the head of the Alexandria Committee for Quality Education (which helped bring the Sando lawsuit), sent a letter to Secretary Richardson, asking that he clarify that HEW was not requiring busing to achieve racial balance in Alexandria schools. Baldwin also persuaded Representative Joel Broyhill and Senator William Spong to send telegrams to Richardson urging him to reverse HEW's demands for elementary integration. The mobilization efforts paid quick returns. Richardson replied to Baldwin's letter on February 29th by enclosing Pottinger's February 28th letter to Albohm and noted that "As you can see, the [Alexandria] school system is not currently under an obligation to prepare a school desegregation plan." See Feinberg, "Alexandria Makes Little Progress toward School Balance."

104. Feinberg, "Alexandria Makes Little Progress toward School Balance."

105. Alexandria City School Board, "Transcript of Regular Meeting," *Box 15-709, School Board Minutes, March 1*, Alexandria City Public Schools Records Center, Alexandria, Virginia, March 1, 1972, p. 44.

106. Donald Baldwin, "Letters to the Editor: Busing and School Discipline," *Washington Post*, June 4, 1972, B7.

107. Jim Thomas, "Statement of Jim Thomas, George Mason School PTA," *Box 15-709, School Board Minutes, March 1*, Alexandria City Public Schools Records Center, Alexandria, Virginia, March 1, 1972.

108. Archie R. Sabin, "Statement by Archie R. Sabin," *Box 15-709, School Board Minutes, March 1*.

109. Alexandria City School Board, "Transcript of Regular Meeting," March 1, 1972, pp. 45–46.

110. Ibid., p. 67

111. Alexandria City School Board, "Agenda—Regular Meeting," Box 15-709, *School Board Minutes--March 1, 1972*, March 1, 1972, 2.

112. Paul G. Edwards, "Alexandria Blacks Criticize Schools," *Washington Post*, June 8, 1972, C2.

113. "Two Top Alexandria Officials Back Putting Black on Board," *Washington Post*, January 11, 1973, D2.

114. "Busing Foe Named to School Board," *Washington Post*, October 11, 1972, B1.

115. The opponents of busing, however, countered NeSmith's candidacy with some vigorous arm-twisting of their own, particularly squeezing Republican City Council member H. Winfield McConchie, generally regarded as a liberal Republican. According to press reports, a conservative caucus of the Alexandria Republican Central Committee sent Hugh Mulligan, a former chair of the Alexandria Republican Committee, to meet with McConchie and persuade him to back Johnson. *Washington Post* reporter Paul Edwards wrote that "The day before the Council vote, McConchie had an animated, lengthy lunch with Hugh Mulligan, the conservative former city Republican chairman, and Mulligan's wife at the Warehouse restaurant [in Alexandria]. They gave McConchie the message from the conservative party leaders: Switch to Johnson." ("Lobbying a Key to Victory for Alexandria Busing Foe," *Washington Post*, October 16, 1972, C1.) McConchie's vote gave Johnson a 4-3 victory, with three Republicans and a conservative Democrat pitted against two liberal Democrats and a Black Independent.

116. Alexandria City School Board, "Transcript of Regular Meeting," *Box 17-665, School Board Minutes—November 15*, November 15, 1972, p. 64.

117. Ibid., November 15, 1972, pp. 64–65.

118. Ibid., p. 73.

119. *Adams v. Richardson*, 51 Supp. 636 (US District Court DC 1972).

120. *Adams v. Richardson*, p. 97.

121. Joanne Omang, "Grade School Race Balance Plan Ordered," *Washington Post*, March 22, 1973, B1.

122. Marguerite Wallace, "Items Carried over from the Board Meeting of February 21, 1973," *Box 17-2087, School Board Minutes, February 21*, February 22, 1973.

123. Alexandria City School Board, "School Board Minutes—Executive Session—Proceedings," *Box 18-674, School Board Minutes, March 21*, March 21, 1973, p. 20.

124. "School Board Minutes—Executive Session—Proceedings," pp. 21–22.

125. "School Board Minutes—Executive Session—Proceedings," pp. 68–69.

126. Joanne Omang, "Alexandria Schools Get HEW Deadline," *Washington Post*, March 30, 1973, A33.

127. Alexandria City School Board, "Regular Meeting—April 18—Transcription," *Box 18-1074, School Board Minutes, April 18*, 1973, p. 19.

128. Dick Warden, "Statement of Dick Warden," *Box 18-1074, School Board Minutes, April 18*, Alexandria City Public Schools Records Center, Alexandria, Virginia, n.d., 1973, pp. 1–3. In Warden's written statement, he identifies himself as Dick Warden. In the transcript and minutes of the meeting, he is identified as Dick Ward. The quotes here are taken from the written

statement, although similarly worded statements can be found in the transcripts of the April 18 School Board meeting.

129. Alexandria City School Board, "Regular Meeting—April 18—Transcription," April 18, 1973, p. 52.

130. Joanne Omang, "Alexandria Race Is a Drag; 16 Candidates Complain of Scanty Audiences," *Washington Post*, April 19, 1973, C1.

131. Joanne Omang, "Alexandria School Mix Plans Scored," *Washington Post*, May 3, 1973, C1.

132. Joanne Omang, " 'Moral Issue' Decides Busing Plan," *Washington Post*, May 16, 1973, B1.

133. Joanne Omang, "Board Official Removes Children from Schools," *Washington Post*, June 14, 1973, C1.

134. Joanne Omang, "Action on Seat Was in Doubt," *Washington Post*, June 30, 1973, B1.

135. Ibid.

136. Ibid.

137. Ibid.

4 The Politics of Exit

1. "Audio History," Burgundy Farm Country Day School, www.burgundyfarm.org/gallery/Integration_at_Burgundy.mp3. For further details on the history of Burgundy Farms see www.burgundyfarm.org. [Access date: January 29, 2014].

2. Kevin Kruse, *White Flight: Atlanta and the Making of Modern Conservatism* (Princeton, NJ: Princeton University Press, 2005), 9.

3. The program paid $125 out of state funds and $125 out of local funds, for a total of $250 per year. If a locality refused the pay the tuition grant, the state deducted the locality's share from other state educational funds distributed to the locality.

4. Statewide, the program lasted until 1969 when a federal court decision ended the voucher scheme, although Alexandria officials ended their involvement in the program in December 1964 after a Fourth Circuit ruling declared the voucher program unconstitutional in Prince Edward County, Virginia, which had closed all its public schools rather than desegregate (*Griffin v. Board of Supervisors of Prince Edward County*, 339 F.2d 486 (4th Cir. 1964)). In March 1965, a three-judge U.S. District Court panel ruled the tuition grants unconstitutional if the private schools discriminated on the basis of race, but upheld the grants if no discrimination existed (*Griffin v. State Board of Education*, 239 F. Supp. 560 (1965)). Litigation in the matter continued until 1969 when the District Court reversed itself and declared the tuition assistance program unconstitutional, based on the U.S. Supreme Court's invalidation of similar tuition grant programs in Louisiana and South Carolina (*Griffin v. State Board of Education*, 296 F. Supp. 1178, 1181 (1969)).

5. James W. Ely, *The Crisis of Conservative Virginia* (Knoxville: University of Tennessee Press, 1976).

6. Previously, black students were required to petition the School Board if they wanted to attend a non-black neighborhood school under the district's freedom of choice plan. See Chapter 2.

7. Bart Barnes, "Court Ruling Imperils Virginia Tuition Grants," *Washington Post*, December 6 1964, A18.

8. Burgundy Farm Country Day School, "Audio History."

9. Barnes, "Court Ruling Imperils Virginia Tuition Grants."

10. John C. Albohm, "Tuition Grant Study Committee," *Work Session October 2*, Alexandria City Public Schools Records Center, Alexandria, Virginia, October 2, 1964.

11. Beyond the use of tuition vouchers to provide an integrated education, another set of children used the vouchers to enroll in schools that specialized in special education or programs for children with handicaps. In the fall of 1964, the Northern Virginia Association of Retarded Citizens Day Center and the School for the Handicapped enrolled seventeen Alexandria students who received a tuition voucher to subsidize their enrollment. See "Changes in List

of Approved Scholarship Applications First Semester 1964–1965," *School Board Minutes, December 16,* Alexandria City Public Schools Records Center, Alexandria, Virginia, December 16, 1964. Because Alexandria offered no schooling for students with profound mental or cognitive impairment at this time, the Massive Resistance tuition voucher was the sole means by which Alexandria publicly supported the education of children with such pronounced special needs. (See Chapter 5 for more details).

12. It is possible to answer this question by combining four sources of individual and geographical data available in the Alexandria City Public School archives and the U.S. Census: Individual records of voucher recipients from 1959 to 64, including their home address; petitions from African American students (including their home address) to attend white schools; a precise description of school attendance zone boundaries in effect during this period; and block-level Census data from the 1960 U.S. Census. The voucher recipients are detailed in the following documents: "Approved Applications for Tuition Grants," *School Board Minutes, Executive Session, October 20,* Alexandria City Public Schools Records Center, Alexandria, Virginia, October 20, 1959; "Scholarship Applications, First Semester 1959–1960," *School Board Minutes, December 10,* December 10, 1959; Vera Vinogradoff, "Scholarship Applications Ready for School Board Action, First Semester," *School Board Minutes, January 14,* Alexandria City Public Schools Records Center, Alexandria, Virginia, January 14, 1960; "Scholarship Applications, Second Semester 1959–1960," *School Board Minutes, May 12,* Alexandria City Public Schools Records Center, Alexandria, Virginia, May 12, 1960; "List of Approved Scholarship Applications for Second Semester 1960–1961," *School Board Minutes, May 10,* Alexandria City Public Schools Records Center, Alexandria, Virginia, May 10, 1961; "List of Approved Scholarship Applications for First Semester 1961–1962," *School Board Minutes, January 13,* Alexandria City Public Schools Records Center, Alexandria, Virginia, January 13, 1961; "List of Approved Scholarship Applications for First Semester 1962–1963," *School Board Minutes, December 19,* Alexandria City Public Schools Records Center, Alexandria, Virginia, December 19, 1962; "List of Approved Scholarship Applications for Second Semester 1961–1962," *School Board Minutes, June 13,* Alexandria City Public Schools Records Center, Alexandria, Virginia, June 13, 1962; "List of Approved Scholarship Applications for First Semester 1963–1964," *School Board Minutes, December 18,* Alexandria City Public Schools Records Center, Alexandria, Virginia, December 18, 1963; "List of Approved Scholarship Applications for Second Semester 1962–1963," *School Board Minutes, May 15,* Alexandria City Public Schools Records Center, Alexandria, Virginia, May 15, 1963; "List of Approved Scholarship Applications for Second Semester 1963–1964," *School Board Minutes, May 20,* Alexandria City Public Schools Records Center, Alexandria, Virginia, May 20, 1964; "Changes in List of Approved Scholarship Applications First Semester 1964–1965," *School Board Minutes, December 16,* Alexandria City Public Schools Records Center, Alexandria, Virginia, December 16, 1964. The School Board decisions on requests to attend formerly all-white schools can be found in the following Executive Session minutes: *School Board Minutes, Executive Sessions* of January 22, 1959; April 28, 1959; October 19, 1959; September 8, 1960; September 14, 1960; July 12, 1961; September 13, 1961 and June 13, 1962.

The precise, street-by-street description of school attendance boundaries extant between 1959 and 1965 for Alexandria Public Schools is available in "School Zones 1959–60—1964–1965," *Alexandria City Public Schools Records Center,* Alexandria, Virginia, 1959–1965. The 1960 block-level Census of Housing data is available in Wayne F. Daughtery, "City Blocks Alexandria, Va.," in *U.S. Census of Housing: 1960* (Washington, DC, 1961). This data was merged into a digitized version of this map, using ArcGIS: "City of Alexandria, Virginia," *The Department of Planning, Alexandria, Virginia,* (Reproduced from the Collections of The Library of Congress, 1958). By combining these four sources of data into a geographical analysis of the residential distribution of voucher recipients and also the African American students engaged in the process of desegregating Alexandria's schools, it is possible to explore the relative geographical proximity of desegregation students to voucher students, and, in turn, their relationship to racial and economic composition of Alexandria's neighborhoods.

13. The four were Ficklin, Minnie Howard, William Ramsey, and Cora Kelly. A fourth school, Patrick Henry, was desegregated although the African American students who attended Patrick Henry lived within the William Ramsey attendance zone, in the Lincolnia neighborhood. It is unclear why the school board assigned them to Patrick Henry, even though William Ramsey was their home school.

14. Note that this is not strictly a measure of residential integration. As the percentage of nonwhites increases, the neighborhood becomes less segregated, but then becomes more segregated as that figure continues to increase. In other words, a measure of segregation within a census block is U-shaped with respect to the percentage of nonwhites within that same block.

15. C. Peter Schumaier, "Letter to Gorman Ridgely," *School Board Minutes, July 17*, Alexandria City Public Schools Records Center, Alexandria, Virginia, July 17, 1963.

16. This figure is compiled from *Annual Report*, Office of City Manager (City of Alexandria, 1971–1976).

17. Engelhardt and Engelhardt, Inc., "Public Elementary School Needs—City of Alexandria, Virginia," *Box 17-1410, School Board Minutes—January 17*, January, 1973, Tables 17 and 18, p. 164.

18. January, 1973, Tables 17 and 18, p.164; Alexandria City Public Schools, "Enrollment, Membership, Racial Breakdown," *Box 17-084, School Board Minutes—October 18*, September 29, 1972.

19. Ibid., September 29, 1972.

20. Paul G. Edwards, "Schools Proposal Attacked," *Washington Post*, January 25, 1973, B1.

21. We can replicate the school districts' undercounting of quality of education by counting up those survey responses that *only* indicated that quality of education was their rationale for choosing private school. Among the extant survey returns eighteen respondents indicated that quality of education (and *only* that issue) was the reason; this figure is precisely the number that the school district reported among the 113 parents who enrolled their children in private school.

22. While ACPS reported that 171 families who moved within the metropolitan region replied to the survey, only eighty-three of those returns could be located in the archives.

23. The underreporting is even more evident when we simply look at the absolute numbers: Of 171 respondents who moved within the metropolitan area and sent their children to public schools, the school district reported that twenty-two cited busing as a concern. Among the eighty-three surveys found in the archives, twenty-six cited busing as a concern. The most probable explanation for the discrepancy is that the school district counted busing when it was the *only* rationale cited, ignoring surveys that contained multiple responses.

24 Alexandria City Public Schools. "Total Number of Students Who Entered and Left the Public School System during the Summer of 1974," in *Pre-Akin Files–Desegregation–Parent Survey, 1974*. School Desegregation Cabinet.

25 Calculated from U.S. Bureau of the Census, U.S. Census of Population and Housing, for years 1970 and 1980: *General Population Characteristics*. Table 23: Race by Sex, for Areas and Places: 1970, Virginia (pt. 48-61) and Table 15: Persons by Race: 1980, Virginia (pt. 48-13).

26 Ibid.

27 Ibid. Table 16. Summary of General Characteristics: 1970, Virginia (pt. 48-43) and Ibid. Table 14: Summary of General Characteristics: 1980, Virginia (pt. 48-8).

28 Ibid. Table 26: Persons by Age for Areas and Places: 1980 and 1970, Virginia (pt. 48-64)

29 U.S. Bureau of the Census. U.S. Census of Population and Housing: 1970 and 1980. Vol. I, Characteristics of the Population. Part XX, Virginia (Washington, DC: U.S. Government Printing Office).

30 Enrollment figures are tabulated from *Annual Report*, Office of City Manager (City of Alexandria, 1970–80).

31 Dunbar, Denise. "Monthly Chat: Interview with David Speck." *Alexandria Times*, November 1 2012. Available at http://alextimes.com/2012/11/monthly-chat-interview-with-david-speck/ Accessed January 29, 2014.

32 City of Alexandria, Office of Historic Alexandria. Alexandria Legacies—City Employees Oral History Project, "Interview with Vola Lawson, Retired City Manager." May 21, 2009. Available at: http://alexandriava.gov/uploadedFiles/historic/info/history/OHAOralHistoryLawson. pdf. Accessed February 15, 2014, p. 12.

33 Alexandria's physical and economic growth over the first half of the twentieth century came about largely through the unique mechanisms of Virginia's annexation process, in which jurisdictions file lawsuits in state court against neighboring jurisdictions. A three-judge panel—specially convened for annexation suits—then determines whether the annexation is "necessary and expedient," according to the language of the statute. See, generally, Bain, Chester W. *Annexation in Virginia: The Use of the Judicial Process for Readjusting City-County Boundaries.* Charlottesville: University Press of Virginia, 1966. In effect, the three-judge panel determines whether the proposed annexation would benefit the residents of both jurisdictions, primarily examining the benefits delivered to the area and the taxes imposed. In 1903, Alexandria first broke beyond its colonial area boundaries, absorbing the adjacent towns of Potomac and Rosemont. Then, through a series of annexations, the city grew westward and northward, with a major expansion in 1952 that nearly doubled the area of the city. This addition of largely undeveloped land on the western and northern boundaries of the city fueled much of the city's economic growth in the 1950s and 1960s.

    As that land gained density in the mid- to late 1960s, however, the city's business community sought to replicate the success of the 1952 expansion, this time seeking to annex land south of the city, down as far to Mt. Vernon and as far west as Springfield. At its most ambitious formulation, this annexation would have created a city geographically larger than Washington, DC, and positioned Alexandria to be a rival to not only an emergent Fairfax County but potentially to the District itself. Although the size of the proposed annexation was significantly scaled back by the time of the court filing, the 1967 annexation bid still would have significantly whitened the school-age population of Alexandria and added a swath of affluent neighborhoods to city tax rolls and schools. The annexation court's ruling against Alexandria in 1970 was, in many ways, a turning point for the future development of the city of Alexandria. The Virginia Supreme Court later upheld the annexation court's ruling in favor of Fairfax County and subsequent state-imposed limitations on annexation, caused in part by Richmond's efforts to prevent white flight by annexing portions of neighboring Henrico County, effectively fixed Alexandria's boundaries and made the addition of whiter, richer households through geographic expansion politically untenable in both the state and the region. See *City of Alexandria v. County of Fairfax,* 212 Va. 437 (1971). City leaders were forced to accept the geographically bounded future of Alexandria and white residents who opposed desegregation began to take flight, inducing a cascading set of demographics changes in the city.

5 Special Education and the Politics of Services

1. Peter E. Holmes, "Letter to John C. Albohm, June 13," *Box 19-636, School Board Minutes, June 20,* Alexandria City Public Schools Records Center, Alexandria, Virginia, 1973.

2. The district claimed to have used the "Lorge-Thorndike Test of Mental Maturity," which may be a conflation of the "Lorge-Thorndike Intelligence Test" and the "California Test of Mental Maturity." I could find no reference to the name that Alexandria school officials used for the test in several academic databases, but the other two tests appeared with regularity. See "Test Results of City Testing Program, May 1959 through Sept. 1959," *School Board Minutes,* November 16, 1960. Alexandria City Public Schools Records Center, Alexandria, Virginia.

3. Alexandria City School Board, "Regular Meeting Minutes," *School Board Minutes, September 2,* Alexandria City Public Schools Records Center, Alexandria, Virginia, September 2, 1959.

4. School Board Minutes, September 2, 1959.

5. "Test Results of City Testing Program, May 1959 through Sept. 1959."

6. Thomas Chambliss Williams, "Superintendent's Report, April, 1960," *School Board Minutes, April 20*, Alexandria City Public Schools Records Center, Alexandria, Virginia, April 20, 1960, p. 12.

7. "Superintendent's Report, February, 1960," *School Board Minutes, Regular Meeting February 10*, Alexandria City Public Schools Records Center, Alexandria, Virginia, February 10, 1960, p. 14.

8. "Superintendent's Report, February, 1960," p. 13.

9. "Superintendent's Report, May, 1960," *School Board Minutes, Regular Meeting, May 12*, Alexandria City Public Schools Records Center, Alexandria, Virginia, May 12, 1960, p. 16.

10. "Report of the Child Study Committee on the Underacheiver in the City Schools of Alexandria Virginia," p. 6. *School Board Minutes, Regular Meeting, May 12, 1960*.

11. Ibid.

12. "Superintendent's Report, May, 1960," ibid., May 12, p. 14.

13. Alexandria City School Board, "School Board Minutes, Regular Meeting," *School Board Minutes, August 9*, Alexandria City Public Schools Records Center, Alexandria, Virginia, August 9, 1960, p. 9.

14. "Program for Irregular Classes or Underachievers," *School Board Minutes, September 14*, Alexandria City Public Schools Records Center, Alexandria, Virginia, September 14, 1960, p. 1.

15. "Program for Irregular Classes or Underachievers," September 14, 1960, p. 4.

16. Alexandria Association for Retarded Children, Mrs. T. Edward Braswell, "Letter to T.C. Williams, June 28," *School Board Minutes, Regular Meeting*, July 21, 1961, Alexandria City Public Schools Records Center, Alexandria, Virginia,.

17. T.C. Williams, "Superintendent's Report, September 1961," pp. 18–19, *School Board Minutes, Regular Meeting, September 13, 1961*.

18. Ibid., 19

19. T.C. Williams, "Superintendent's Report, October 1961," pp. 15–16; *School Board Minutes, Regular Meeting, October 11, 1961*.

20. Ibid., 16.

21. "Letter from T.F. McGough, M.D., Director of Public Health, to T.C. Williams, Dated December 13, 1961;" *School Board Minutes, Regular Meeting, December 12, 1961*. (The photocopy of the letter in the minutes is legible, but decaying due to paper acidity. Williams read portions of the letter aloud at the meeting and the quoted portions here can also be found in the minutes of the meeting itself.)

22. School Board Minutes, Regular Meeting, December 13, 1961, pp. 3–4.

23. School Board Minutes, Executive Session, April 16, 1962, p. 1.

24. "Request of the Northern Virginia Association for Retarded Children for Adequate Educational Provisions for the Mentally Retarded," presented by Dr. Nap C. DuFault; *School Board Minutes, February 20, 1963*.

25. For example, President John Kennedy's sister Rosemary Kennedy was cognitively impaired and underwent a lobotomy in her early twenties to alleviate her behavioral and cognitive disorders. Sadly, the procedure severely worsened her condition. Her sister, Eunice Kennedy Shriver, became a champion for rights of the disabled, helping to launch the Special Olympics. In addition, the President's Panel on Mental Retardation, formed by President Kennedy, raised the profile of the issue substantially. Edward D. Berkowitz, "Politics of Mental Retardation During the Kennedy Administration," *Social Science Quarterly* 61, no. 1 (1980): 135–136.

26. Gareth Davies, *See Government Grow: Education Politics from Johnson to Reagan* (Lawrence: University Press of Kansas, 2007), 171.

27. Virginia Constitution Article VIII, Sec. 1.

28. Virginia Constitution, Article VIII, Sec. 2. For an overview of these changes see, Hullihen W. Moore, "In Aid of Public Education: An Analysis of the Education Article of the Virginia Constitution of 1971," *University of Richmond Law Review* 5, no. 2 (1971): 263–318.

29. *Griffin v. State Board of Education*, 296 F. Supp. 1178 (E.D. Va. 1969).

30. Moore, "In Aid of Public Education: An Analysis of the Education Article of the Virginia Constitution of 1971," 301.

31. See "In Aid of Public Education: An Analysis of the Education Article of the Virginia Constitution of 1971," 300–302, for details.

32. Virginia Advisory Legislative Council, *Needs of the Handicapped*. Virginia. General Assembly, 1972, Senate. Document [no.] 4 (Richmond: Commonwealth of Virginia, 1971), 9.

33. Alexandria City Public Schools, "Report of the Alexandria School Board, Five-Year Plan for Special Education," *Box 19-001, School Board Minutes, June 6,* Alexandria City Public Schools Records Center, Alexandria, Virginia, June 6, 1973.

34. *Pennsylvania Association for Retarded Children v. Commonwealth of Pennsylvania* 343 F. Supp. 279 (1972), 307.

35. Ibid.

36. Ibid., 307, 313.

37. *Mills v. District of Columbia* 348 F. Supp. 866 (D DC 1972), 875.

38. Ibid.

39. Despite the enactment of this legislation, appropriations never approached the $500 million authorized for federal programs. R. Shep Melnick, *Between the Lines: Interpreting Welfare Rights* (Washington, DC: The Brookings Institution, 1994), 151.

40. Beyond EAHCA, Congress earlier had protected the rights of handicapped persons by enacting Section 504 of the 1973 Rehabilitation Act. That law, modeled after Title VI of the 1964 Civil Rights Act, made it illegal for any entity receiving federal funds to discriminate against an otherwise qualified person on the basis of a handicap. Persons could no longer be excluded from participation in governmental programs simply because of the existence of a disability or handicap. While EAHCA (later IDEA) established the ground rules for special education that states must follow if they accept federal special education funding, Section 504 bans discrimination against disabled persons in all programs that receive federal funding, not just schools.

41. "Preliminary Report of the Special Education Advisory Committee, May 1973," *Box 19-001, School Board Minutes, June 6,* Alexandria City Public Schools Records Center, Alexandria, Virginia, 1973, p. 9.

42. Alexandria City Public Schools, "Report of the Alexandria School Board, Five-Year Plan for Special Education," ibid., June 6, 1973, p. 10.

43. Ibid.

44. "Alexandria City School Board Public Hearing, March 14," *Box 18-285, School Board Minutes, March 14,* Alexandria City Public Schools Records Center, Alexandria, Virginia, June 6, 1973, p. 32.

45. Ibid., 16.

46. "Preliminary Report of the Special Education Advisory Committee, May 1973," p. 20.

47. Ibid., p.17.

48. Ibid.

49. Arnold J. Thurmond, "Justification and How Students Benefit from the Resource Center," Addendum for Report on Resource Centers Submitted to Alexandria School Board on June 4, *Ad Hoc Committee on the Learning Environment Folder, Desegregation Cabinet,* Alexandria City Public Schools Records Center, Alexandria, Virginia, June 4, 1975.

50. Ibid.

51. "Ad Hoc Committee on Learning Environment, Minutes of October 29, 1975 Meeting," ibid., October 29, p. 2.

52. Harold Burke and J. Thomas Butler, "Memo to Instructional Committee, Alexandria School Board, Re: Special Education Status Report, September 11," *Box 19-1665, School Board Minutes, October 3,* Alexandria City Public Schools Records Center, Alexandria, Virginia, September 11, 1973, pp. 2–3.

53. Alexandria City Public Schools, "Policy for Appraisal and Placement of Students in Special Education," *Box 20-768, School Board Minutes, December 19,* Alexandria City Public Schools Records Center, Alexandria, Virginia, December 19, 1973, p. 3.

54. Alexandria School Board Regular Meeting, "Transcript of February 20 Meeting," *Box 20-1711, School Board Minutes, February 20,* Alexandria City Public Schools Records Center, Alexandria, Virginia, February 20, 1974, p. 8.

55. Ibid., p. 24.

56. Ibid., p. 26.

57. Ibid., p. 27.

58. Michael Specter, "Alexandria Targets Pupil Gap," *Washington Post,* November 21, 1985. B11.

59. "Memorandum to Members of the School Board, Re: Title III Proposal on Exploring Designs for Gifted Students, November 29," *School Board Minutes, December 12,* Alexandria City Public Schools Records Center, Alexandria, Virginia, December 12, 1973, p. 13.

60. Alexandria City Public Schools, June 6, 1973, p. 10. Even if one counts those students that the district *suspected* of being gifted and talented, but had not yet fully evaluated, and compares those to the number of probable learning-disabled students, the numbers do not add up. The district estimated two different numbers for suspected gifted and talented students: 611 (p. 10 of the survey) or 918 (p. 20). Either way, both of those numbers are significantly smaller than the 1,100 students it suspected were learning disabled. Quite simply, given the district's own estimates, there is no possible way of construing the number of gifted and talented students as 50 percent greater than the number of students with retardation and learning disabilities.

61. "Memorandum to Members of the School Board, Re: Title III Proposal on Exploring Designs for Gifted Students, November 29," December 12, 1973, p. 13.

62. Noted Hills, "Since Alexandria Schools had just been reorganized into a system where five primary elementary schools (K-3) were paired with five intermediate elementary schools (4–6), and there were four elementary schools with a conventional organization of K-6, it was felt that the nine intermediate level schools provided the best departure for an organized program for the gifted." "Memorandum to Members of the School Board, Re: Title III Proposal on Exploring Designs for Gifted Students, November 29," December 12, 1973, p. 16.

63. Ibid., p. 27.

64. Ibid., p. 12.

65. Jura Koncius, "Alexandria Studies Increased Class Size," *Washington Post,* October 29, 1981, VA8.

66. Frank Morra, Jr., "Design Exploration for Talented Elementary Students, Evaluation 1975–76 (Microform)," Alexandria Public Schools Program for the Gifted and Talented (Washington, DC: ERIC Clearinghouse, 1976), ED166863, 34.

67. Ibid.

68. Ibid., p. 14. Emphasis in original.

69. Ibid., p. 40.

70. In Year 3 of the evaluation study, Frank Morra did examine a small sample of forty-four students not in the gifted program, but he never examined change over time for this group. Twelve of those forty-four had gone through the gross screening process, but were not selected for the "Gifted And Talented Program." Thirty-two students in the comparison group were in the regular student population. Because these students were only compared to the students in the Gifted and Talented Program at one point in time, there is no way of knowing how the creation of the Gifted And Talented Program changed their sense of self-worth or their relations to other students in the Gifted And Talented Program.

71. Morra, "Design Exploration for Talented Elementary Students, Evaluation 1975–1976," p.17.

72. The change in the performance standards can be found by comparing page 11 of the 1975–1976 report to page 15 of the 1976–1977 report. In the first, we read: "By the end of the 1975–76 school year, the social relations of 85 percent of the Title III ESEA students will not deviate from the norm by more than one standard of measurement on each of the subscales of the Fundamental Interpersonal Relation Orientation Inventory for the Behaviors of Children (FIRO-BC)." In the second, we read: "By the end of the 1976–77 school year, the social relations of 75 percent of the Title III ESEA students will not deviate from the norm by more than one Standard Error of Measurement on each of the subscales of the Fundamental

Interpersonal Relations Orientation Inventory for the Behaviors of Children." The tables indicating the satisfaction of the performance level (including the percentage of students within one SEM) can be found on page 13 of the 1975–1976 report and page 16 of the 1976–1977 report.

73. Frank Jr. Morra, "Design Exploration for Talented Elementary Students, Evaluation 1976–77," Frank Morra, Jr., "Design Exploration for Talented Elementary Students, Evaluation 1975–1976 (Microform)," Alexandria Public Schools Program for the Gifted and Talented(Washington, DC: ERIC Clearinghouse, 1977), p. 32.

74. "Design Exploration for Talented Elementary Students, Evaluation 1976–77," p. 24.

75. "Design Exploration for Talented Elementary Students, Evaluation 1975–76.," p. 19.

76. "Design Exploration for Talented Elementary Students, Evaluation 1976–77," p. 57.

77. Marion C. Pierce, "Alexandria School Budget Focuses on Special Education," *Washington Post*, February 20, 1986, VAC1.

78. Ibid.

79. Paul G. Edwards, "Schools Drop Grouping in Alexandria," *Washington Post*, August 3, 1972, B1.

80. Joanne Omang, "White Pupils Leaving Alexandria Schools," ibid., May 26, 1974, A1. Prior to the adoption of the elementary integration plan, Dearborn had proposed to the School Board a "Policy for Organization for Instruction" which would have codified the existing practice of ability grouping. The Board failed to approve the measure, voting four to four, with the swing vote from Colonel Henry Brooks unavailable, as he was out of the country. "Transcript, Alexandria City School Board—Regular Meeting, August 8, 1972." *School Board Minutes, August 8, 1972*, Box 16-1461, pp. 90–91.

81. Harold G. Pollard, "Letter to Chairman William Hurd and School Board Members," *Box 19-1854, School Board Minutes, October 17, 1973*, October 16, 1973.

82. Lawrence Feinberg, "Alexandria Desegregation: Problems Persist," *Washington Post*, January 22, 1979, A1.

83. "Alexandria Desegregation: Problems Persist." See *Greene v. School Board of the City of Alexandria* 494 F. Supp. 467 (1979).

84. Kerry Dougherty, "Equal Education: Search for Answers," *Washington Post*, December 13, 1978, VA1.

85. Eduardo Cue, "Alexandria Urged to Shut Two Schools," ibid., February 2, 1978, A20.

86. "Alexandria School Chief John Bristol Has Become a Johnny-on-the-Spot," *Washington Post*, March 23, 1978, VA1.

87. Ina Lee Selden, "Handling Crises in the Schools: Bristol's Job," ibid., March 8, 1979, VA1.

88. Robert Meyers, "Alexandria School Superintendent Moving to Illinois," ibid., January 26, 1980, C1.

89. Rick Allen, "Alexandria Plans Push to Help Minority Students in Math, Reading," ibid., August 22, 1985, VA1.

90. Mary Jordan, "Black Leaders Allege Alexandria Schools Focus on Whites' Needs," ibid., August 27, 1985, D3.

91. Ibid.

92. Ibid.

93. Rick Allen, "Program Set for Youngest Gifted," ibid., September 12, 1985, VA1.

6 From Arlandria to Chirilagua: English-Learners and the Catch-22 Education State

1. Neil Foley, *The White Scourge: Mexicans, Blacks, and Poor Whites in Texas Cotton Culture* (Berkeley: University of California Press, 1997), pp. xiii–xiv. I am indebted to Professor John Tutino of Georgetown for Foley's reference to Alexandria.

2. Currently roughly one out of five students in US public schools was not born in the United States. Additionally, roughly 10 percent of students are categorized as English-learners. While there is significant overlap between the two groups, they are distinct. Many English- learners were born in the United States (to immigrants or US citizens), but some students born abroad have mastered English by the time they enter US schools.

3. For an overview of the varieties of approaches, see Rebecca Freeman, "Reviewing the Research on Language Education Programs," in *Bilingual Education: An Introductory Reader,* eds. Ofelia García and Colin Baker. Bilingual Education and Bilingualism. (Clevedon, UK: Multilingual Matters, 2007), 1–19. In the interest of full disclosure, both of my children attended a dual language immersion elementary school in Arlington, Virginia.

4. Paul J. Ramsey, "In the Region of Babel: Public Bilingual Schooling in the Midwest, 1840s-1880s," *History of Education Quarterly* 49, no. 3 (2009): 270.

5. Carlos Kevin Blanton, *The Strange Career of Bilingual Education in Texas, 1836–1981* (College Station: Texas A&M University Press, 2004), p. 27.

6. Ramsey, "In the Region of Babel," 267.

7. Paul J. Ramsey, "A Polyglot Boardinghouse: A History of Public Bilingual Schooling in the United States." (PhD diss., University of Indiana, 2008), 93.

8. "In the Region of Babel: Public Bilingual Schooling in the Midwest, 1840s-1880s,"pp. 270–71.

9. Higham reports that by 1919, fifteen states banned instruction in a language other than English. John Higham, *Strangers in the Land: Patterns of American Nativism, 1860–1925* (New Brunswick, NJ: Rutgers University Press, 2002, 2nd ed), p. 260.

10. Meyer v. Nebraska, 262 U.S. 390 (1923).

11. Blanton, *The Strange Career of Bilingual Education in Texas, 1836–1981,* 65.

12 12. Jeffrey E. Mirel, *Patriotic Pluralism: Americanization Education and European Immigrants* (Cambridge, MA: Harvard University Press, 2010), 54.

13. Blanton, *The Strange Career of Bilingual Education in Texas,* 82.

14. Ibid.

15. Ibid., 85.

16. Ibid., 132.

17. Ofelia García and Jo Anne Kleifgen, *Educating Emergent Bilinguals* (New York: Teachers College Press, 2010), 29.

18. Guadalupe San Miguel, Jr., *Contested Policy: The Rise and Fall of Federal Bilingual Education in the United States, 1960–2001* (Denton, TX: University of North Texas Press, 2004), 30.

19. The ambiguity in the law was, according to Rachel Moran, necessary to win passage. Rachel F. Moran, "The Politics of Discretion: Federal Intervention in Bilingual Education," *California Law Review* 76, no. 6 (1988): 1263.

20. Kenji Hakuta, *Mirror of Language:* The Debate on Bilingualism (New York: Basic Books, 1986).

21. Lorraine M. McDonnell and Paul T. Hill, *Newcomers in American Schools: Meeting the Educational Needs of Immigrant Youths* (Santa Monica, CA: Rand, 1993), 23.

22. The limited funding for the Bilingual Education Act, in particular, restricted the growth of innovative programs. Between 1969 and 1973 annual appropriations always fell far below the amount authorized by Congress. During these years, funding never grew above $35 million, even though Congress authorized up to $135 million. Based on the estimated number of English-learners in US schools, the appropriation never exceeded more than roughly $10 per English-learner, and averaged roughly $5 to $6. (See Moran, "The Politics of Discretion: Federal Intervention in Bilingual Education," 1265.)

23. In 1970, the Office of Civil Rights did issue a memorandum that "authorized administrative and judicial challenges if districts failed to provide assistance" to children with poor or non-existent English language skills (Moran, "The Politics of Discretion: Federal Intervention in Bilingual Education," 1267). That memorandum, based on an interpretation of the Title VI of the 1964 Civil Rights Act, was, however, "largely unforced" until the 1974 Laudecision, according to Moran.

24. Lau v. Nichols, 414 U.S. 563 (1974), at 566.

25. Other statutes and programs provided some additional resources, as well. Because many English-learners are frequently poor, many receive services under Title I of Elementary and Secondary Education Act. Also, programs exist under Title I explicitly for migrant children, many of whom are English-learners, but are simply moving internally in the United States, often because their families work in agricultural labor. Finally, the 1984 Emergency Immigrant Education Act provided limited funds to districts experiencing a sudden influx of immigrants. Until NCLB converted the Bilingual Education Act funding into a formula-based funding stream, Alexandria received funds from the Emergency Immigration Education Act funds appropriation, but those funds covered only about 4 percent of Alexandria's expenditures for its ESL program (Alexandria City Public Schools Montoring and Evaluation Services, "English as a Second Language (ESL) Evaluation Report," (Alexandria, VA: Alexandria City Public Schools, 1999), 38–40.)

26. McDonnell and Hill, *Newcomers in American Schools: Meeting the Educational Needs of Immigrant Youth*, 23; Moran, "The Politics of Discretion: Federal Intervention in Bilingual Education," 1278; See also San Miguel, *Contested Policy: The Rise and Fall of Federal Bilingual Education in the United States, 1960–2001*, 26–34. For secondary students, the *Lau* Remedies allowed English as a Second Language (ESL) programs.

27. Betsy Levin, "An Analysis of the Federal Attempt to Regulate Bilingual Education: Protecting Civil Rights or Controlling Curriculum," *Journal of Law & Education* 12, no. 1 (1983): 37.

28. Moran, "The Politics of Discretion: Federal Intervention in Bilingual Education," 1279.

29. Ibid., 1288.

30. Ibid., 1289.

31. U.S. Department of Education, Office of the Assistant Secretary for Civil Rights, "The Office for Civil Rights' Title VI Language Minority Compliance Procedures," December 3, 1985.

32. Ibid. Emphasis added.

33. James J. Lyons, "The Past and Future Directions of Federal Bilingual-Education Policy," *Annals of the American Academy of Political and Social Science* 508, no. 1 (March 1990): 76.

34 "The Past and Future Directions of Federal Bilingual-Education Policy," 74.

35. The battles in California, Arizona, and elsewhere severely limited state-level efforts to utilize children's first languages in schooling. See, generally, Patricia Gándara and Megan Hopkins, eds., *Forbidden Language: English Learners and Restrictive Language Policies* (New York: Teachers College Press, 2010).

36. No Child Left Behind terminated the Bilingual Education Act, moving its programs from Title VII of ESEA to Title III of NCLB. More symbolically, NCLB expunged all references to the term "bilingual" from ESEA. This involved renaming the Bilingual Education Act the English Language Acquisition, Language Enhancement and Academic Achievement Act. In addition, the programs under this act were now to be administered not by the Office of Bilingual Education and Minority Language Affairs, but by the Office of English Language Acquisition, Language Enhancement and Academic Achievement for Limited English Proficient Students. James Crawford, "The Bilingual Education Act, 1968–2002: An Obituary," in *Advocating for English Learners*, ed. James Crawford (Clevedon, UK: Multilingual Matters, 2008), pp. 124–127.

37. U.S. Department of Education, Office of Planning, Evaluation and Policy Development. *National Evaluation of Title III Implementation – Report on State and Local Implementation.* (Washington, DC, 2012), p. 4.

38. Claude Goldenberg, "Teaching English Language Learners," *American Educator* 32, no. 2 (Summer 2008): 8–18. Goldenberg was particularly clear about the emerging consensus that teaching reading in a child's native language improved reading in a child's second language.

39. Kate Menken, "No Child Left Behind and Its Effects on Language Policy," *Annual Review of Applied Linguistics* 29, no. 1 (2009): 108.

40. Kate Menken and Cristian Solorza, "No Child Left Bilingual: Accountability and the Elimination of Bilingual Education Programs in New York City Schools," *Educational Policy* 28, no. 1 (2014): 96–125.

41. Of course, students in poverty, with special needs, or who are members of racial or ethnic minorities would still be tallied in those subgroups for AYP purposes.

42. Jamal Abedi, "The No Child Left Behind Act and English Language Learners: Assessment and Accountability Issues," *Educational Researcher* 33, no. 1 (2004): 4.

43. For an extensive overview of the challenges confronting the assessment of English-learners, see Ronald W. Solórzano, "High Stakes Testing: Issues, Implications and Remedies for English Language Learners," *Review of Educational Research* 78, no. 2 (2008): 260–329.

44. "National Evaluation of Title III Implementation—Report on State and Local Implementation," (Washington, DC: Office of Planning U.S. Department of Education, Evaluation and Policy Development,2012): xix.

45. "National Evaluation of Title III Implementation," 53.

46. The Title III appropriation for Fiscal Year 2011 was $734 million. The approximate number of English-learners in 2010–11was roughly 4.7 million, resulting in an average Title III appropriation per English-learner of $156.17. See *Digest of Education Statistics,* Center for Education Statistics, U.S. Department of Education. "Table 47: Number and percentage of public school students participating in programs for English language learners, by state" Available at: http://nces.ed.gov/programs/digest/d12/tables/dt12_047.asp. Accessed February 16, 2014 and Committee for Education Funding, "Education Funding History," January 14, 2014, p. 31. Available at: http://cef.org/wp-content/uploads/2011/04/ED-programs-funding-history-FY-14-omnibus.pdf. Accessed February 16, 2014. Although 2011 represents the latest official numbers on English learner enrollments, since that time, Title III budgets have shrunk and English learner enrollments have increased.

47. U.S. Department of Education, "National Evaluation of Title III Implementation—Report on State and Local Implementation," xxiii.

48. Or a refusal to promote practices that actually do improve outcomes, such as greater dual language immersion programs.

49. Audrey Singer, *At Home in the Nation's Capital: Immigrant Trends in Metropolitian Washington* (Washington, DC: Brookings Greater Washington Research Program, 2003), 5.

50. Ibid.

51. Philip P. Pan, "At Home in Chirilagua, Va.," *Washington Post*, December 6, 1999, A1.

52. Walter Nicholls, "Where Do Salvadorans Go for Authentic Tortillas, Tamales and Pupusas? A Neighborhood in Alexandria," ibid., March 24, 2004, F01.

53. Raúl Sánchez Molina, "Modes of Incorporation, Social Exclusion, and Transnationalism: Salvadoran's Adaptation to the Washington, DC Metropolitan Area," *Human Organization* 67, no. 3 (2008): 272.

54. "Modes of Incorporation, Social Exclusion, and Transnationalism,"273

55. Allison Petrozziello, "Feminised Financial Flows: How Gender Affects Remittances in Honduran-US Transnational Families," *Gender and Development* 19, no. 1 (2011): 61.

56. U.S. English Foundation, "Many Languages, One America," (Washington, DC: US English Foundation, Inc., 2005).

57. Carola Suárez-Orozco, Marcelo Suárez-Orozco, and Irina Todorova, *Learning a New Land: Immigrant Students in American Society* (Cambridge, MA: Belknap Press of Harvard University Press, 2008), 11.

58. Ibid., 8.

59. Figures calculated from tables found at http://www.census.gov/hhes/socdemo/education/data/cps/2012/tables.html. Accessed January 28, 2013.

60. Virginia P. Collier, "How Long? A Synthesis of Research on Academic Achievement in a Second Language," *TESOL Quarterly* 23, no. 3 (1989): 509–531.

61. Elsa L. Walsh, "Bilingual Plan Opposed," *Washington Post*, October 23,1980, VA8.

62. Ibid.

63. Lena H. Sun, "Alexandria Schools Climbing a Language Barrier to Parents," *Washington Post*, June 21, 1984, VA1.

64. Ibid.

65. Alexandria City Public Schools, Montoring and Evaluation Services, "English as a Second Language (ESL) Evaluation Report,"Alexandria, VA: Alexandria City Public Schools, February, 1999, 41.

66. "English as a Second Language (ESL) Evaluation Report," 51.

67. "English as a Second Language (ESL) Evaluation Report," 45.

68. "English as a Second Language (ESL) Evaluation Report," 51.

69. "English as a Second Language (ESL) Evaluation Report," 83–84. The report's authors removed potentially identifying information, such as years taught and references to a teacher's school or ethnicity.

70. Jon Liss, in-person interview, October 11, 2013.

71. Patrick Welsh, "Our Classroom Barrios: For Hispanic Students, American Schools Can Be a Nightmare," *Washington Post*, September 8 1991, C1.

72. Evelin Urrutia, in-person interview, October 11, 2013.

73. All the quotations from this section are from Montoring and Evaluation Services, "English as a Second Language (ESL) Evaluation Report," 104–106. The comments are taken verbatim from the report and reflect the speaker's level of English fluency. The comments have not been emended with *sic* to avoid interferring with their own words.

74. Peter Y. Hong, "High School to Hire Counselor for Latinos," *Washington Post*, December 30 1993, VA1.

75. Susan Bibler Coutin, *Nations of Emigrants* (Ithaca, NY: Cornell University Press, 2007), 57–60.

76. Liss, interview.

77. Advancement Project, Alexandria United Teens, and Tony Roshan Samara, "Obstacles to Opportunity: Alexandria Virginia Students Speak Out,"George Mason University, Alexandria, VA: Tenants and Workers United, 2007, 3.

78. "Obstacles to Opportunity: Alexandria Virginia Students Speak Out," 15–16.

79. Importantly, 73 percent of Latino students and 70 percent of ESL students reported not having spoken with their guidance counselor about the college admissions process ("Obstacles to Opportunity: Alexandria Virginia Students Speak Out," 4).

80. "Obstacles to Opportunity: Alexandria Virginia Students Speak Out," 3.

81. "Obstacles to Opportunity: Alexandria Virginia Students Speak Out," 3.

82. Liss, interview.

83. Montoring and Evaluation Services, "English as a Second Language (ESL) Evaluation Report," 16.

84. Brigid Schulte, "Year-Round School? My Kids Love It. Yours Will, Too," *Washington Post*, June 7, 2009, B1.

85. Ibid.

86. T.C. Williams Transformation Committee, *In the Matter of Transformation Meeting*, December 8, 2010, 12.

87. Ibid., 15.

88. Ibid., 155.

89. Ibid., pp. 156–57.

90. T.C. Williams Transformation Committee, *In the Matter of Transformation Meeting*, November 8, 2010, 15.

91. Ibid.,16.

92. Ibid., 29–30.

93. T.C. Williams Transformation Committee, *In the Matter of Transformation Meeting*, April 28, 2011, 144.

94 Campagna Center is an Alexandria social service agency that works with children and youth, particularly children in poverty. Building Better Futures is program within the Campagna Center that focuses on Latino youth, particularly of high-school age.

95. *In the Matter of Transformation Meeting, April 28, 2011*, 145.

96. Ibid., 151–52.

97. Ibid., 171.

98. Ibid., 172.

99. Ibid.,172.

100. Ibid.,173.

101. The three projects are Mt. Vernon Village Center, The Calvert, and the Jackson Crossing project. Only the Jackson Crossing project is an affordable housing project.

Part Three: The Politics of Accountability

1   United States National Commission on Excellence in Education, *A Nation at Risk: The
Imperative for Educational Reform: A Report to the Nation and the Secretary of Education,
United States Department of Education* (Washington, DC: Superintendent of Documents, U.S.
Government Printing Office, 1983).

2   Donald T. Campbell, "Assessing the Impact of Planned Social Change," *Journal of
MultiDisciplinary Evaluation 7*, no. 15 (2011): 34.

3   Ibid., 35.

7 Local Activism and Accountability Politics

1. Alexandria City School Board, "Regular Meeting—Minutes," July 7, 1971.

2. Ibid., July 7, 1971.

3. Kathryn McDermott, *High Stakes Reform: The Politics of Educational Accountability.* Public
Management and Change (Washington, DC: Georgetown University Press, 2011), 3.

4. *High Stakes Reform: The Politics of Educational Accountability,* 62.

5   In some rural areas, local circuit court judges appointed the school board selection com-
mission, which then appointed school boards. For a full overview of the specifics of the
selection mechanisms, see *Irby v. Fitz-Hugh* 693 F. Supp. 424 (1988) at 426–427. See also
Subcommittee Studying School Board Selection, "Report of the Subcommittee Studying
School Board Selection (House Resolution 12) to the House Committee on Privileges and
Elections," ed. Virginia House of Delegates (Richmond, VA: State of Virginia, 1984).

6. R. J. Austin, "School Board Selection Methods and Fiscal Powers in the United States and
Virginia—Preliminary Staff Report," (Richmond, VA: House Privileges and Elections
Subcommittee Studying Selection of School Board Members, December 5, 1984), 6.

7. *Irby v. Fitz-Hugh* 693 F. Supp. 424 (1988).

8. The years and bill numbers of the reform effort are detailed in *Irby v. Fitz-Hugh* 693 F. Supp. 424
(1988) at 429,fn 1.

9. *Irby v. Fitz-Hugh* 693 F. Supp. 424 (1988) at 433.

10. Giving Virginia school boards autonomous taxation authority would require an amendment
to the Virginia Constitution. Subcommittee Studying School Board Selection, (see "Report
of the Subcommittee Studying School Board Selection (House Resolution 12) to the House
Committee on Privileges and Elections"). The perception was that this was a politically unvi-
able proposition.

11. John F. Harris, "Plan to Elect School Boards Advances to Virginia House," *Washington Post,*
January 17, 1991, D1.

12. Samuel Madden Homes was torn down in 2002, its one-hundred units replaced by Chatham
Square, a mixed-income development of fifty-two low-income units and one-hundred
market-rate condominiums. The remaining forty-eight low-income units were distributed
throughout the city Office of Planning and Zoning, "City of Alexandria Awarded for Mixed
Income Housing Redevelopment," City of Alexandria, Alexandriava.gov, 2005 http://alexan-
driava.gov/planning/info/default.aspx?id=9814. Accessed May 23, 2012.

13. Carol LaSasso, "Why We Took Our Kids out of George Mason," *Washington Post,* October 7
1990, D8.

14. Ibid.

15. Robert F. Howe and Pierre Thomas, "Alexandria Renames Three to School Board," ibid., June 27, G3.

16. Carol LaSasso, "Why We Took Our Kids out of George Mason," ibid., October 7.

17. Robert F. Howe, "Alexandria School Chief's Minority Effort Commended, Condemned," ibid., December 27, D1.

18. Lonnie Rich. in-person interview, December 10, 2011.

19. Ibid.

20. Patrick Welsh, "Fast-Track Trap: How 'Ability Grouping' Hurts Our Schools, Kids and Families," *Washington Post*, September 16 1990, B1.

21. Rich, interview.

22. Ibid.

23. Herb Berg, in-person interview, June 25, 2010.

24. Emmitt Carlton, "The School Board Must Not Be for Sale," *Washington Post*, August 26 1993, A27.

25. Ibid.

26. Evelyn Hsu, "Alexandria School Board Adds Four Kindergarten Classes in Approving Budget," *Washington Post*, March 20, 1992, C4.

27. Evelyn Hsu, "Alexandria Officials Spar on Kindergarten Expansion," *Washington Post*, June 20, 1992, D3.

28. Evelyn Hsu, "Alexandria Superintendent Proposes Plan to Reshape Schools," *Washington Post*, December 4, 1991, D6; "Alexandria School Board Approves Superintendent's Middle School Plan," *Washington Post*, December 18, 1991, C4.

29. Steve Bates, "For Ninth-Graders Only," ibid., September 2 1993, AVA1.

30. Patrick Welsh, "Board Silly: How Politics Are Wrecking Alexandria's Schools," ibid., June 20, C1.

31. Ibid.

32. Evelyn Hsu, "Alexandria Urged to Go Slow on School Changes," ibid., February 7, 1992, D3.

33. Vola Lawson, "Memorandum—Alexandria City Public Schools—Ninth-Grade Center Operating Costs," *City Council Docket*, October 23, 1992.

34. Steve Bates, "Budget Woes Threaten Alexandria School Plan," *Washington Post*, November 1, 1992, B3; Lawson, "Memorandum," October 23, 1992.

35. Steve Bates, "Urged to Cut Budget, Alexandria School Chief Seeks Increase," *Washington Post*, February 20, 1993, D3.

36. Steve Bates, "Top Alexandria Students Challenge Policy Change," *Washington Post*, December 18, 1992, C5.

37. Steve Bates, "Alexandria Votes to Offer Civilization Honors Courses," *Washington Post*, January 8, 1993, B6.

38. Steve Bates, "Academic Mixing Stirs Pot in Alexandria," *Washington Post*, January 31, 1993, B5.

39. Steve Bates, "More Parents Are Challenging School Quality," *Washington Post*, April 20, 1993, C1.

40. Bates, "Top Alexandria Students Challenge Policy Change."

41. Bates, "Academic Mixing Stirs Pot in Alexandria."

42. Ibid.

43. Ibid.

44. Ibid.

45. Steve Bates, "School Policy Riles Alexandria Parents," *Washington Post*, March 28, 1993, B3.

46. Ibid.

47. Ibid.

48. Ibid.

49. Welsh, "Staying on Tracks," ibid., March 7.

50. Ibid.

51. Ibid.

52. Ibid.

53. Welsh, "Board Silly: How Politics Are Wrecking Alexandria's Schools."

54. Herb Berg, in-person interview, June 25, 2010.

55. Ibid.

56. Welsh, "Board Silly: How Politics Are Wrecking Alexandria's Schools."

57. Ibid.

58. Office of Voter Registration and Elections, "Election Statistics," City of Alexandria, 2012. http://alexandriava.gov/elections/info/default.aspx?id=1668 Accessed May 24, 2012.

59. Steve Bates, "Alexandria Superintendent Is One of Two Seeking Similar Job in Ohio District," *Washington Post*, May 12, 1994, B6; "Controversy Is Part of Masem's Legacy to Alexandria's Schools," *Washington Post*, June 9, 1994, VA 2E.

60. Berg, in-person interview.

61. Ibid.

62. Ibid.

63. Ibid.

64. Daniel L. Duke and Brianne Reck, "The Evolution of Educational Accountability in the Old Dominion," in *Educational Leadership in an Age of Accountability: The Virginia Experience*, eds. Daniel L. Duke, et al. (Albany: State University of New York Press, 2003), 39.

65. Duke and Reck, "The Evolution of Educational Accountability in the Old Dominion," 40.

66. Alice Digilio and Peter Baker, "65 Pct. Pass Va. 6th-Grade Literacy Test," *Washington Post*, June 28, 1990, B1.

67. Alice Digilio, " 'Passport' to Reading," *Washington Post*, July 5, 1990, VA1.

68. Duke and Reck, "The Evolution of Educational Accountability in the Old Dominion," 42.

69. Frederick M Hess, "Reform, Resistance. . . Retreat? The Predictable Politics of Accountability in Virginia," *Brookings Papers on Educational Policy* 2002, no. 1 (2002): 82.

70. Duke and Reck, "The Evolution of Educational Accountability in the Old Dominion," 44.

71. Hess, "Reform, Resistance … Retreat? The Predictable Politics of Accountability in Virginia," 84–85.

72. Duke and Reck, "The Evolution of Educational Accountability in the Old Dominion," 45.

73. Hess, "Reform, Resistance … Retreat? The Predictable Politics of Accountability in Virginia," 85.

74. Lawrence H. Cross, "The Standards of Learning (SOL) Reform: Real Consequences Require Real Tests," *Virginia Issues and Answers* 7, no. 1 (2000). Available at: http://www.via.vt.edu/spring00/solreform.html. Accessed January 30, 2014.

75. Jay Mathews, "Alexandria to Count State Tests in High School Grades," *Washington Post*, January 7, 1999, V01.

76. Mathews, "Alexandria to Count State Tests in High School Grades."

77. Jay Mathews, "Bonuses Backed for Alexandria Principals; Incentive Plan Is Region's First," *Washington Post*, March 12, 1999, B1.

78. Mathews, "Bonuses Backed for Alexandria Principals; Incentive Plan Is Region's First."

79. Mathews, "In Alexandria, Boosting Test Scores," *Washington Post*, September 3, 1998, V10.

80. "Schools Block Plan for New SOL Survey; PTA Assessment Redundant, Officials Say," *Washington Post*, July 5, 2001, T03.

81. City of Alexandria, "Annual Report, 2001—City Schools," 2001.

82. Stephanie van Hover, et al., "From a Roar to a Murmur: Virginia's History and Social Science Standards, 1995–2009," *Theory & Research in Social Education* 38, no. 1 (2010): 80–113; Jay Mathews, "Virginia Schools Get Break on Crucial Test Scores," *Washington Post*, May 28, 1999, B01; Hess, "Reform, Resistance. . . Retreat? The Predictable Politics of Accountability in Virginia."

83. van Hover, et al., "From a Roar to a Murmur: Virginia's History and Social Science Standards, 1995–2009," 99.

84. Mike Allen, "Class Sizes Draw Some Attention; Other Issues Await New School Board," *Washington Post*, May 15, 1997, V01.

85. Ibid.
86. Rodger Digilio, in-person interview, 2011.
87. Berg, in-person interview.
88. Ibid.

8 The Titans Meet the State: Federal Accountability and School Transformation

1. Carla Branch, "Education Secretary Duncan, Redskin Legend Darrell Green Set Tone for New School Year," *Alexandria News*, September 2, 2010. http://www.alexandrianews. org/2010/schools/education-secretary-duncan-redskin-legend-darrell-greene-set-t one-for-new-school-year/18844/ Accessed January 30, 2014.

2. Michael Pope, "Education Secretary Responds to a Teacher,"WAMU 88.5, September 3, 2010. Available online at: http://wamu.org/news/10/09/03/education_secretary_responds_ to_a_teacher. Accessed January 30, 2014.

3. Full details of the calculation for "persistently low-achieving" schools in Virginia can be found at "Virginia School Improvement Grant Application," Commonwealth of Virgina: Department of Education, June 2, 2010. http://www2.ed.gov/programs/sif/summary/vaapp.pdf. Accessed January 18, 2014.

4. Michael Lee Pope, "T.C. In Crisis," *Alexandria Gazette Packet*, March 11, 2010. http://www. connectionnewspapers.com/article.asp?article=338587&paper=59&cat=104. Accessed December 22, 2011; Michael Alison Chandler, "Wake-Up Slap for T.C. Williams," *Washington Post*, June 18, 2010, B1.

5. Alexandria City Public Schools, "T.C. Williams High School Faculty Meeting," Department of Accountability, March 3, 2010, 10. Available at: http://www.acps.k12.va.us/mes/presentatio ns/20100303-tcw-faculty.pdf. Accessed January 30, 2014.

6. Alexandria City Public Schools, Department of Accountability, "T.C. Williams Transformation: Trend Data Report," June 6, 2011. http://www.acps.k12.va.us/ tcw-transformation/data-report-trend.pdf. Accessed January 30, 2014, p. 1.

7. Alexandria City Public Schools, March 3, 2010, 16.

8. Ibid.

9. "T.C. Williams High School—Transformation: 2010 Persistently Low Achieving (PLA) Designation," 2011. http://www.acps.k12.va.us/tcw-transformation/pla.php. Accessed December 17, 2011.

10. These figures are derived from the Virginia Department of Education's Virginia Assessment Results website, available at: http://bi.virginia.gov/BuildATab/rdPage.aspx. Accessed June 3, 2013.

11. Alexandria City Public Schools, "T.C. Williams High School—Transformation: 2010 Persistently Low Achieving (PLA) Designation."

12. This section draws primarily on Elizabeth H. Debray, *Politics, Ideology & Education: Federal Policy During the Clinton and Bush Administrations*. Foreword by Carl Kaestle (New York: Teachers College Press, 2006), and Paul Manna, *Collision Course: Federal Education Policy Meets State and Local Realities* (Washington, DC: CQ Press, 2011).

13. *Collision Course: Federal Education Policy Meets State and Local Realities*, p. 25.

14. David Tyack and Larry Cuban, *Tinkering toward Utopia* (Cambridge, MA: Harvard University Press, 1995).

15. Bryan Shelly, "Rebels and Their Causes: State Resistance to No Child Left Behind," *Publius: The Journal of Fedralism* 38, no. 3 (2008), 444–468. In 2005, Connecticut filed a lawsuit challenging NCLB's testing provisions as an impermissible unfunded mandate. In 2006 and 2008, the federal District Court ruled against the state of Connecticut. *Connecticut v. Spellings*, 453 F. Supp. 2d 459 (D. Conn. 2006) and *Connecticut v. Spellings*, 549 F. Supp. 2d 161 (D. Conn. 2008). The 2nd Circuit upheld the District court's opinion in *Connecticut v. Duncan* 612 F.3d 107 (2nd Cir. 2010) and the U.S. Supreme Court declined to hear the case.

16. Manna, *Collision Course: Federal Education Policy Meets State and Local Realities,* 17.

17. Virginia Department of Education, "Accreditation and Federal Reports—Adequate Yearly Progress (AYP) Reports: State Summary," Virginia Department of Education, 2013. http://www.doe.virginia.gov/statistics_reports/accreditation_federal_reports/ayp/. Accessed June 11, 2013.

18. "NCLB Waiver Approved by US Department of Education." Division of Policy and Communications (Richmond, VA: Virginia Department of Education, 2012).

19. Jay Mathews, "Principal Leaves Troubled School; Alexandria's Maury Elementary on Low Achievement List," *Washington Post,* April 21, 2004, B05.

20. *Alexandria Gazette Packet.* "Some Remain Concerned Over Principal Shift." Connection Newspapers, April 28 2004. Available from http://www.connectionnewspapers.com/news/2004/apr/28/some-remain-concerned-over-principal-shift/. Accessed June 13, 2013.

21. Alexandria City Public Schools, "Modified Open Enrollment, Charles Barrett PTA Q &A— Attachment B: ACPS Enrollment Trends by School," http://www.acps.k12.va.us/budgets/moe/cb-b-projections-no-moe.pdf. Accessed June 18, 2013.

22. S. Mitra Kalita and Jay Mathews, "Alexandria Schools Chief Faces DWI Charge; Perry Placed on Leave with Pay for a Week," *Washington Post,* April 24, 2004, B1.

23. *Alexandria Gazette Packet.* "Some Remain Concerned Over Principal Shift."

24. Kalita and Mathews, "Alexandria Schools Chief Faces DWI Charge; Perry Placed on Leave with Pay for a Week." According to a 2004 article in the *Washington Post,* Officer Weinstein was known in Alexandria as the "DWI King," averaging over one-hundred DWI arrests annually in the five years since he'd joined the Alexandria police force and accounting for a quarter to a third of all Alexandria DWI arrests in that time. (Sarah Park, "For DWI Enforcer, These Are Busy Nights," ibid., September 4, 2004, B1.).

25. S. Mitra Kalita and Jay Mathews, "Alexandria Schools Chief Faces DWI Charge; Perry Placed on Leave with Pay for a Week," ibid., April 24.

26. S. Mitra Kalita, "Alexandria's Superintendent Apologizes," ibid., April 28, B01.

27. Leef Smith and S. Mitra Kalita, "Schools Chief Is Fined for DWI in Alexandria," ibid., June 12, B01.

28. S. Mitra Kalita, "Alexandria Shortens Superintendent's Term; School Board Approves Raise for Perry Despite DWI Plea, Parents' Objections," ibid., June 16, B04.

29. Marc Fisher, "3 R's for Today: Rigid, Regressive and Unresponsive," ibid., May 6, 2004, B01.

30. S. Mitra Kalita, "Lewis Voted out as Board Vice Chair," ibid., July 8, 2004, T03.

31. Elaine Rivera, "Va. School Official's Son Charged in Vandalism," ibid., July 15, 2004, B1; S. Mitra Kalita, "2nd Teenager Charged in Alexandria Egging; Youth Is Son of City Council Member," ibid., July 17, 2004, B01.

32. S. Mitra Kalita, "Alexandria Squabble Reignites at Retreat," *Washington Post,* August 30, 2004, B1.

33. Tara Bahrampour, "Schools Chief on Alexandria Board Agenda; Vote on Renewing Perry's Contract May Follow Closed Session, Sources Say," ibid., November 16, 2004, B03.

34. Bahrampour, "Schools Chief on Alexandria Board Agenda."

35. The Board only compounded this perception of skewed priorities when it voted in December 2005 to double the pay for School Board members, from $7500 to $15,000 a year, with the Chairman earning $17,000. ("Alexandria School Board Will Have New Look, Priorities; Eight of Nine Current Members Are Not Seeking Re-Election," *Washington Post,* April 20, 2006, T03.)

36. Bahrampour, "Alexandria School Board Will Have New Look."

37. Mark O. Wilkoff, Arthur E. Schmalz, and Mark R. Eaton, "A Word of Advice: Humor and Humility Go a Long Way," ibid., March 30, 2006. p. T05.

38. Tara Bahrampour, "New School Board Aims for Firmness, No Rancor; Alexandria Officials Not Afraid to Challenge Superintendent, Past Decisions," ibid., October 31, 2006. p. B1.

39. Bahrampour, "New School Board Aims for Firmness."

40. *Alexandria Gazette Packet.* "How Transparent is the School Board; Secret meetings and lack of public input prompt criticism of the Backroom Five," Connection Newspapers, May 30 2007. Available from www.connectionnewspapers.com/news/2007/may/30/how-transparent-is-the-board/. Accessed June 17, 2013.

41. Tara Bahrampour, "Alexandria May Seek New Head of Schools," *Washington Post*, May 15, 2007.

42. Tara Bahrampour, "Schools Chief's Supporters Decry Decision," *Washington Post*, May 23, 2007. p. B1

43. *Alexandria Gazette Packet.* "School superintendent dumped". Connection Newspapers, May 24, 2007. Available from www.connectionnewspapers.com/news/2007/may/24/school-superintendent-dumped/. Accessed June 13, 2013.

44. Bahrampour, "Schools Chief's Supporters Decry Decision."

45. Tara Bahrampour, "Divided School Board Agrees To Work on Team-Building," *Washington Post*, May 31, 2007. Alexandria-Arlington Extra. Factiva Document ID: WP20070531AXNEWS31.

46. *Alexandria Gazette Packet.* "School superintendent dumped".

47. Bahrampour, "Schools Chief's Supporters Decry Decision."

48. Bahrampour, "Divided School Board Agrees To Work on Team-Building."

49. *Alexandria Gazette Packet.* "How Transparent is the School Board?"

50. Brigid Schulte, "Abrupt End to Tenure of Alexandria School Chief," *Washington Post*, January 19, 2008, B1; Carla Branch, "Rebecca Perry: What Really Happened—Actions and Reactions," *Alexandria News*, Archives 2008. http://alexandrianews.org/2008/top-stories/rebecca-perry-what-really-happened-actions-and-reactions/104/. Accessed January 18, 2014.

51. Schulte, "Abrupt End to Tenure of Alexandria School Chief."

52. Gene I. Maeroff, *School Boards in America: A Flawed Exercise in Democracy* (New York: Palgrave Macmillan, 2010); William G. Howell, *Besieged: School Boards and the Future of Education Politics* (Washington, DC: Brookings Institution Press, 2005).

53. MGT of America, "Alexandria City Public Schools School Division Efficiency Review," (Alexandria City Public Schools, 2007), i.

54. "Alexandria City Public Schools School Division Efficiency Review," 2–6 and 2–8.

55. "Alexandria City Public Schools School Division Efficiency Review," 2–8.

56. Porter's replacement, Mel Riddile, had been named the 2006 National High School Principal of the Year and was the 2005 Virginia High School Principal of the Year at J.E.B. Stuart High School in Fairfax. Riddile oversaw the opening of the new T.C. Williams building in the fall of 2007, but then abruptly quit in the spring of 2008, a few months after Perry left, to take a position with the National Association of Secondary Principals. His replacement, William Clendaniel, was hired on an interim basis in the summer of 2008, just as Superintendent Mort Sherman was coming on board, but eventually signed on to a three-year contract in the fall of 2008. (He was forced into retirement when T.C. Williams was named a persistently lowest-achieving school in March, 2010.) By many accounts Clendaniel was not a hands-on administrator and the disciplinary climate of the school grew worse during his tenure, with fights and student misbehavior increasingly common.

57. Alexandria City Public Schools, "T.C. Williams Faculty Meeting, April 4, 2010," (2010).

58. Morton Sherman, "An Open Letter to President Barack Obama and Arne Duncan, U.S. Secretary of Education," March 10, 2010. http://www.acps.k12.va.us/tcw-transformation/president-letter.pdf. Accessed March 4, 2012.

59. Alexandria City Public Schools, "T.C. Williams Faculty Meeting, April 4, 2010."

60. Suzanne Maxey, the principal hired to run T.C. Williams in the spring of 2010, came on board after the transformation plan was adopted. At the time of her hiring and shortly thereafter, she fully endorsed the plan as it was adopted. As we shall see, however, both Maxey and other ACPS leaders found that parts of the transformation plan needed further revision and refinement.

61. T.C. Williams Transformation Committee, *In the Matter of Transformation Meeting, November 8, 2010*, November 8, 2010, 291.

62. T.C. Williams Transformation Committee, *In the Matter of Transformation Meeting, December 8, 2010*, December 8, 2010, 226.

63. T.C. Williams Transformation Committee, *In the Matter of Transformation Meeting, April 28, 2011*, April 28, 2011, 19–20.

64. T.C. Williams Transformation Committee, *In the Matter Of: Transformation Meeting, October 8, 2010*, October 8, 2010, 64.

65. *In the Matter of Transformation Meeting, April 28, 2011*, 96.

66. Ibid., 110–11.

67. Ibid., 20–21.

68. Ibid., 29.

69. Ibid., 29.

70. Ibid., 39–40.

71. Ibid., 40.

72. Ibid., 40.

73. *In the Matter of Transformation Meeting, November 8, 2010*, 163–164.

74. Ibid., 46.

75. Patrick Welsh, in-person interview, August 15, 2013. To be fair, the U.S. Department of Education's transformation model required schools undergoing transformation to hire "lead external partners" to provide advice on how to undertake reforms. In T.C. Williams's case, Sherman drew on two consultants: Dr. Marty Brooks and Dr. BenaKallick. Kallick had worked with Sherman on multiple occasions throughout their careers. Brooks is head of the Tri-State Consortium, a group that provides advice to school districts in the New York-New Jersey-Connecticut region. At the end of Sherman's tenure, criticisms abounded of his use of expensive external consultants, as well as criticisms of his failure to provide sufficient oversight over the budgetary process and financial controls in the district. Vice Mayor Kerry Donley was particularly vocal, repeatedly calling for Sherman's resignation in the spring of 2012.

76. Patrick Welsh, "Four Decades of Failed School Reforms," *Washington Post*, September 27, 2013, C1.

77. *In the Matter of Transformation Meeting, November 8, 2010*, 173.

78. Ibid., 174.

79. *In the Matter of Transformation Meeting, December 8, 2010*, 210.

80. Ibid., 219.

81. *In the Matter of Transformation Meeting, April 28, 2011*, 327.

82. Ibid., 327.

83. Ibid., 328–29.

84. Ibid., 329.

85. Ibid., 329.

86. T.C. Williams Transformation Steering Committee, *In the Matter of Transformation Meeting, July 20, 2011*, 2011, 14.

87. T.C. Williams Transformation Steering Committee, *In the Matter of Transformation Meeting, April 29, 2011*, 2011, 72.

88. Ibid., 73.

89. *In the Matter Of: Transformation Meeting, October 8, 2010*, 68.

90. *In the Matter of Transformation Meeting, December 8, 2010*, 64.

91. Attention to the relationships between teachers and students at T.C. Williams was a significant part of the reform effort. Harvard Professor Ronald Ferguson, an external consultant brought in to survey students about their experiences at T.C. Williams, in earlier work has found that students performed much better academically when they had made a close personal connection with a teacher. His organization, The Tripod Project, surveyed T.C.Williams students, and the data (dubbed by Alexandria officials the "Tripod Survey") showed that many students at T.C. Williams mistrusted or did not respect their teachers. In an interview with Tammy Ignacio, she indicated that the release of this Tripod Data to teachers, reported on a classroom-level basis, proved to be a very sensitive issue. According to Ignacio, Ferguson's

data placed some teachers in a difficult position: "Ron's data was hard: Here is what the kids are saying about you." For some teachers, "it was one more piece of data we didn't want to see." (Tammy Ignacio, in-person interview, February 7, 2012.)

92. Only the math scores of students with disabilities failed to meet the federal benchmarks. All the English benchmarks were met. In 2012, Virginia changed its math standards and assessments, more closely aligning them with the Common Core. This produced a sharp drop in T.C. Williams's math scores, as it did in schools across the state. Nonetheless, the school met all its benchmarks in the spring of 2012 because its three-year average math scores met the proficiency criteria. (Hanover Research, "2011–12 T.C. Williams Transformation Process," (Washington, DC: Hanover Research, 2012)).

93. Morton Sherman, "Options for Jefferson-Houston Elementary School," July 3, 2103, p. 1. Available at http://eboard.acps.k12.va.us/attachments/550e4422-5f71-4 670-9bc4-69ffe59c5fe0.pdf. Accessed February 16, 2014.

94. Michael Lee Pope, "Alexandria Leaders Consider Lawsuit Challenging Takeover of Long-Troubled School," *Alexandria Gazette Packet*, July 10, 2013. Available at http://www.con-nectionnewspapers.com/news/2013/jul/10/alexandria-leaders-consider-lawsuit-takeover/. Accessed February 16, 2014.

9 Conclusion: Learning from the Education State

1. David K. Cohen and Susan L. Moffitt, *The Ordeal of Equality: Did Federal Regulation Fix the Schools?* (Cambridge, MA: Harvard University Press, 2009), p23.

2. Ibid.

3. James Scott coined the phrase "seeing like a state" in his book of the same title (James C. Scott, *Seeing Like a State: How Certain Schemes to Improve the Human Condition Have Failed* (Yale University Press, 1999) and Jal Mehta applies it to educational reform to good effect in his book *The Allure of Order* (Jal Mehta, *The Allure of Order: High Hopes, Dashed Expectations, and the Troubled Quest to Remake American Schooling* (New York: Oxford University Press, 2013)).

4. Adam Nelson's *The Elusive Ideal* reveals precisely this kind of simultaneity in his examination of federal educational policy implementation in Boston schools from the 1950s through the mid-1980s (Adam Nelson, *The Elusive Ideal: Equal Educational Opportunity and the Federal Role in Boston's Public Schools, 1950–1985* (Chicago: University of Chicago Press, 2005)).

5. Jeff Henig first identified this trend in his terrific book *The End of Exceptionalism in American Education: The Changing Politics of School Reform*. (Cambridge, MA: Harvard Education Press, 2013).

6. Gary Miron, et al., "Schools without Diversity: Education Management Organizations, Charter Schools and the Demographic Stratification of the American School System," (Boulder, CO and Tempe, AZ: Education and the Public Interest Center and the Education Policy Research Unit, 2010); Kevin Welner, 2013, "The Dirty Dozen: How Charter Schools Influence Student Enrollment," *Teachers College Record [online]* http://www.tcrecord.org. ID Number: 17104.

BIBLIOGRAPHY

Note on Sources: Unless otherwise noted, all archival material from Alexandria City Public Schools may be found at the Alexandria City Public Schools Record Center, in Alexandria, Virginia. The materials there are organized chronologically. Wherever possible, I have indicated the box number in which the item may be found.

Cases Cited

Adams v. Richardson, 51 Supp. 636 (1972)

Adams v. Richardson, 356 F. Supp. 92 (1973)

Almond v. Day, 89 S.E.2d 851 (1955)

Brown v. Board of Education of Topeka, Kansas 347 U.S. 483 (1954) (*Brown I*)

Brown v. Board of Education of Topeka, Kansas 349 U.S. 294 (1955) (*Brown II*)

City of Alexandria v. County of Fairfax, 212 Va. 437 (1971)

Connecticut v. Spellings, 453 F. Supp. 2d 459 (D. Conn. 2006)

Connecticut v. Spellings, 549 F. Supp. 2d 161 (D. Conn. 2008)

Connecticut v. Duncan 612 F.3d 107 (2nd Cir. 2010)

Evers v. Jackson Municipal Separate School District, 232 F. Supp. 241 (1964)

Evers v. Jackson Municipal Separate School District 357 F.2d 653 (5th Cir. 1966)

Green v. County School Board of New Kent County, 391 U.S. 430 (1968)

Griffin v. Board of Supervisors of Prince Edward County, 339 F.2d 486 (4th Cir. 1964)

Griffin v. State Board of Education, 239 F. Supp. 560 (1965)

Griffin v. State Board of Education, 296 F. Supp. 1178 (E.D. Va. 1969)

Irby v. Fitz-Hugh 693 F. Supp. 424 (1988)

Jones v. *School Board of City of Alexandria, Virginia*, unpublished. Reprinted at *Race Relations Law Reporter* 4, no. 1 (1959): 29–36

Lau v. Nichols, 414 U.S. 563 (1974)

Meyer v. Nebraska, 262 U.S. 390 (1923)

Mills v. District of Columbia 348 F. Supp. 866 (D DC 1972)

Pennsylvania Association for Retarded Children v. Commonwealth of Pennsylvania, 343 F. Supp. 279 (1972)

Sando v. Alexandria City School Board, 330 F. Supp. 773 (1971)

Swann v. Charlotte-Mecklenburg Board of Education, 402 U.S. 1 (1971)

School Board of City of Newport News v. Atkins, 246 F.2d 325 (4th Circ.) (1957)

Sources Cited

Abedi, Jamal. "The No Child Left Behind Act and English Language Learners: Assessment and Accountability Issues." *Educational Researcher* 33, no. 1 (2004): 4–14.

Advancement Project, Alexandria United Teens and Tony Roshan Samara. "Obstacles to Opportunity: Alexandria Virginia Students Speak Out." George Mason University, Alexandria, VA: Tenants and Workers United, October, 2007. http://virginia-organizing.org/sites/default/files/Obstacles2Opportunity-Final.pdf. Accessed February 16, 2014.

Albohm, John C. Integration: Constructive Steps Taken Since March 11, 1963. April 25, 1963. Folder "Leonard S. Brown Conference," April 25, 1963.

Albohm, John C. Letter to Eloise Severinson, Regional Civil Rights Director, HEW. July 8, 1971. School Board Minutes—July 7, 1971.

Albohm, John C. Letter to Eloise Severinson, Regional Civil Rights Director, HEW. July 30, 1971. School Board Minutes—August 4, 1971, Box 030114.

Albohm, John C. Letter to Harry R. Elmore, Assistant Superintendent of Public Instruction. January 29, 1965. Folder "Compliance—Rules, Regulations," Desegregation File Cabinet.

Albohm, John C. Letter to R. Worth Peters, Regional Representative, Office of Education, Region 3. April 2, 1965. Folder "Compliance—Rules, Regulations," Desegregation File Cabinet.

Albohm, John C. Letter to Walter H. Rogers, Jr. January 3, 1964. Folder "School Board Roundtable Meeting." January 3, 1964.

Albohm, John C. Memorandum Re: Alternate Plan for Pupil Distribution, Grades 7 Through 12. April 15, 1971. School Board Minutes, Box #030113.

Albohm, John C. Tuition Grant Study Committee. October 2, 1964. Work Session October 2, 1964.

Albohm, John C., and Raymond F. Sanger. "Disruption and Discipline." In *Internal: For the Teachers and Administrators of the Alexandria Public Schools*, 1–3: Alexandria City Public Schools, 1970. Copy available in *School Board Minutes*, December 12, 1970, Box #030113.

Alexandria Association for Retarded Children, Mrs. T. Edward Braswell, "Letter to T.C. Williams, June 28," School Board Minutes, Regular Meeting, July 21, 1961.

Alexandria Citizens Committee for Colored Voters. Letter to Alexandria City School Board. April 16, 1962. School Board Minutes, April 16, 1962.

Alexandria Citizens Committee for Colored Voters. Resolutions Adopted. November 21, 1962. School Board Minutes, November 21 1962.

Alexandria City Public Schools. Ad Hoc Committee on Learning Environment, Minutes of October 29, 1975 Meeting. Desegregation Cabinet, Ad Hoc Committee on the Learning Environment Folder.

Alexandria City Public Schools. Agenda for Work Session. September 12, 1963. Folder "Work Session."

Alexandria City Public Schools. Approved Applications for Tuition Grants. October 20, 1959. School Board Minutes, Executive Session, October 20, 1959.

Alexandria City Public Schools. Assurance of Compliance with Department of Health, Education and Welfare Regulation Under Title VI of the Civil Rights Act of 1964 (HEW Form 441). January 8, 1965. Folder "Compliance—Rules, Regulations," Desegregation File Cabinet,

Alexandria City Public Schools. Changes in List of Approved Scholarship Applications First Semester 1964–1965. December 16, 1964. School Board Minutes, December 16., 1964.

Alexandria City Public Schools. Checks Presented for Payment at School Board Meeting. June 16, 1960. School Board Minutes, June 16, 1960.

Alexandria City Public Schools. Enrollment, Membership, Racial Breakdown. September 29, 1972. School Board Minutes—October 18, 1972, Box 17-084.

Alexandria City Public Schools. List of Approved Scholarship Applications for First Semester 1961–1962. January 13, 1961. School Board Minutes, January 13, 1961.

Alexandria City Public Schools. List of Approved Scholarship Applications for First Semester 1962–1963. December 19, 1962. School Board Minutes, December 19, 1961.

Alexandria City Public Schools. List of Approved Scholarship Applications for First Semester 1963–1964. December 18, 1963. School Board Minutes, December 18, 1963.

Alexandria City Public Schools. List of Approved Scholarship Applications for Second Semester 1960–1961. May 10, 1961. School Board Minutes, May 10, 1961.

Alexandria City Public Schools. List of Approved Scholarship Applications for Second Semester 1961–1962. June 13, 1962. School Board Minutes, June 13, 1962.

Alexandria City Public Schools. List of Approved Scholarship Applications for Second Semester 1962–1963. May 15, 1963. School Board Minutes, May 15, 1963.

Alexandria City Public Schools. List of Approved Scholarship Applications for Second Semester 1963–1964. May 20, 1964. School Board Minutes, May 20, 1964.

Alexandria City Public Schools. Memorandum to High School Principals. November 23, 1963. Folder "Work Session,"

Alexandria City Public Schools. Memorandum to Members of the School Board, Re: Title III Proposal on Exploring Designs for Gifted Students, November 29, 1973. School Board Minutes, December 12, 1973.

Alexandria City Public Schools. "Modified Open Enrollment, Charles Barrett PTA Q & A—Attachment B: ACPS Enrollment Trends by School." 2010. http://www.acps.k12.va.us/budgets/moe/cb-b-projections-no-moe.pdf. Accessed June 18, 2013.

Alexandria City Public Schools. "Policy for Appraisal and Placement of Students in Special Education." December 19, 1973. School Board Minutes, December 19, 1973, Box 20-768.

Alexandria City Public Schools. Preliminary Report of the Special Education Advisory Committee, May 1973. School Board Minutes, June 6, 1973, Box 19-001.

Alexandria City Public Schools. Program for Irregular Classes or Underachievers. September 14, 1960. School Board Minutes, September 14, 1960.

Alexandria City Public Schools. A Proposal for an In-Service Training Program in the Alexandria City Public Schools under Title VI of the Civil Rights Act of 1964. July 18, 1966.

Alexandria City Public Schools. Racial Composition of Schools—Students and Faculty. July 19, 1966. Desegregation File Cabinet.

Alexandria City Public Schools. Receipts. December 16, 1964. School Board Minutes, December 16, 1964.

Alexandria City Public Schools. Report of the Alexandria School Board, Five-Year Plan for Special Education. June 6, 1973. School Board Minutes, June 6, 1973, Box 19-001.

Alexandria City Public Schools. Report of the Study Committee on the Underachiever in the City Schools of Alexandria, Virginia. 1960. School Board Minutes, Regular Meeting, May 12, 1960.

Alexandria City Public Schools. Scholarship Applications Ready for School Board Action, First Semester. January 14, 1960. School Board Minutes, January 14, 1960.

Alexandria City Public Schools. Scholarship Applications, First Semester 1959–1960. December 10, 1959. School Board Minutes, December 10, 1959.

Alexandria City Public Schools. Scholarship Applications, Second Semester 1959–1960. May 12, 1960. School Board Minutes, May 12, 1960.

Alexandria City Public Schools. School Zones 1959–60—1964–1965. 1959–1965. Desegregation cabinet, "Pre-Aiken Files." Copy also in author's possession.

Alexandria City Public Schools. T.C. Williams Faculty Meeting, April 4, 2010, video, 2010. http://acpsk12va.granicus.com/MediaPlayer.php?publish_id=52. Accessed March 8, 2012.

Alexandria City Public Schools. "T.C. Williams High School—Transformation: 2010 Persistently Low Achieving (PLA) Designation." 2011. http://www.acps.k12.va.us/tcw-transformation/pla.php. Accessed December 17, 2011.

Alexandria City Public Schools. T.C. Williams High School Faculty Meeting. March 3, 2010. Department of Accountability, http://www.acps.k12.va.us/mes/presentations/20100303-tcw-faculty.pdf. Accessed February 16, 2014].

Alexandria City Public Schools. Test Results of City Testing Program, May 1959 through Sept. 1959. November 16, 1960. School Board Minutes, November 16, 1960.

Alexandria City Public Schools. Total Number of Students Who Entered and Left the Public School System during the Summer of 1974, in Pre-Akin Files–Desegregation–Parent Survey, 1974. School Desegregation Cabinet.

Alexandria City Public Schools, Montoring and Evaluation Services. "English as a Second Language (ESL) Evaluation Report." Alexandria, VA: Alexandria City Public Schools, February, 1999. Available at: http://www.acps.k12.va.us/mes/reports/19990201_esl_full.pdf. Accessed May 30, 2013.

Alexandria City Public Schools, Office of the Superintendent. Minutes of Conference Held in Dr. Albohm's Office on July 20, 1971—2:15pm. July 20, 1971. Desegregation Cabinet.

Alexandria City Public Schools, Psychological Services. An Analysis of the Intellectual Strengths and Weaknesses of an Educationally Deprived 8th Grade Class. February 12, 1964. School Board Minutes, February 12, 1964.

Alexandria City Public Schools, Psychological Services. Description of a Project for Upgrading Education in One Section of the City of Alexandria, Virginia. July 8, 1964. Folder "Work Sessions,"

Alexandria City Public Schools, Psychological Services. An Inquiry into the Assimilation of Students Transferred to Nearby Schools in the City of Alexandria, 1963–1964. February 1, 1964. Folder "Work Session."

Alexandria City School Board. Agenda—Regular Meeting. March 1, 1972. School Board Minutes— March 1, 1972, Box 15-709.

Alexandria City School Board. Executive Session Minutes. February 4, 1959.

Alexandria City School Board. Exective Session Minutes. October 19, 1959.

Alexandria City School Board. Executive Session Minutes. September 8, 1960.

Alexandria City School Board. Executive Session Minutes. June 13, 1962.

Alexandria City School Board. George Washington High School—Incident of December 10, 1970. December 12, 1970. School Board Minutes, Box # 030113.

Alexandria City School Board. Items Carried Over from the Board Meeting of February 21, 1973. February 22, 1973. School Board Minutes—February 21, 1973, Box 17-2087.

Alexandria City School Board. Minutes—Regular Meeting. May 19, 1971. Box #030113.

Alexandria City School Board. Regular Meeting—April 18—Transcription. April 18, 1973. School Board Minutes, Box 18-1074.

Alexandria City School Board. Regular Meeting—Minutes. July 7, 1971.

Alexandria City School Board. Regular Meeting Minutes. September 2, 1959. School Board Minutes, September, 1959.

Alexandria City School Board, School Board Minutes—May 19, 1971, Box 030113, May 19, 1971.

Alexandria City School Board. School Board Minutes—Executive Session—Proceeedings. March 21, 1973. School Board Minutes—March 21, 1973, Box 18-674. Alexandria City School Board. School Board Minutes—February 23, 1972. Box 15-556. February 23, 1972.

Alexandria City School Board. School Board Minutes, Regular Meeting. August 9, 1960. School Board Minutes, August 9, 1960.

Alexandria City School Board. Superintendent's Report. December 19, 1962. School Board Minutes, December 19, 1962.

Alexandria City School Board. Transcript of February 20 Meeting. February 20, 1974. School Board Minutes, February 20, 1974, Box 20-1711.

Alexandria City School Board. Transcript of Regular Meeting. March 1, 1972. School Board Minutes, March 1, 1972. Box 15-709.

Alexandria City School Board. Transcript of Regular Meeting. November 15, 1972. School Board Minutes—November 15, 1972, Box 17-665.

Alexandria City School Board Public Hearing, March 14. June 6, 1973. School Board Minutes, March 14, Box 18-285.

Alexandria Council on Human Relations. Letter to Alexandria City School Board. July 18, 1962. School Board Minutes, July 18, 1962.

Alexandria Gazette. "School Cross Burning Incidents Under Investigation by Police." *Alexandria Gazette*, November 2, 1970.

Alexandria Gazette Packet. "How Transparent is the School Board; Secret meetings and lack of public input prompt criticism of the Backroom Five" Connection Newspapers, May 30 2007. Available from www.connectionnewspapers.com/news/2007/may/30/how-transparent-is-the-board/. Accessed June 17, 2013.

Alexandria Gazette Packet. "School Superintendent Dumped." *Alexandria Gazette Packet*, May 24, 2007. Available from www.connectionnewspapers.com/news/2007/may/24/school-superintendent-dumped/. Accessed June 13, 2013.

Alexandria Gazette Packet. "Some Remain Concerned Over Principal Shift." Connection Newspapers, April 28 2004. Available from http://www.connectionnewspapers.com/news/2004/apr/28/some-remain-concerned-over-principal-shift/. Accessed June 13, 2013.

Alexandria Nonviolent Action Group. Letter to Alexandria City School Board. April 16, 1962. Executive Session Minutes.

Allen, Mike. "Class Sizes Draw Some Attention; Other Issues Await New School Board." *Washington Post*, May 15, 1997.

Allen, Rick. "Alexandria Plans Push to Help Minority Students in Math, Reading." *Washington Post*, August 22, 1985.

Allen, Rick. "Program Set for Youngest Gifted." *Washington Post*, September 12, 1985.

Austin, R. J. "School Board Selection Methods and Fiscal Powers in the United States and Virginia—Preliminary Staff Report." Richmond, VA: House Privileges and Elections Subcommittee Studying Selection of School Board Members, December 5, 1984.

Bachinski, E. J. "Knife Planted in Killing, Alexandria Court Told." *Washington Post*, June 13, 1970.

Bachinski, E. J., and Michael Hodge. "Youth Slain, Disorder Hits Alexandria." *Washington Post*, May 30, 1970.

Bain, Chester W. *Annexation in Virginia: The Use of the Judicial Process for Readjusting City-County Boundaries.* Charlottesville: University Press of Virginia, 1966.

Bahrampour, Tara. "Alexandria May Seek New Head Of Schools." *Washington Post*, May 15, 2007.

Bahrampour, Tara. "Alexandria School Board Will Have New Look, Priorities; Eight of Nine Current Members are Not Seeking Re-Election." *Washington Post*, April 20, 2006.

Bahrampour, Tara. "Divided School Board Agrees to Work on Team-Building." *Washington Post*, May 31, 2007.

Bahrampour, Tara. "New School Board Aims for Firmness, No Rancor; Alexandria Officials Not Afraid to Challenge Superintendent, Past Decisions." *Washington Post*, October 31, 2006.

Bahrampour, Tara. "Schools Chief on Alexandria Board Agenda; Vote on Renewing Perry's Contract May Follow Closed Session, Sources Say." *Washington Post*, November 16, 2004.

Bahrampour, Tara. "Schools Chief's Supporters Decry Decision." *Washington Post*, May 23, 2007.

Baldwin, Donald. "Letters to the Editor: Busing and School Discipline." *Washington Post*, June 4, 1972.

Barnes, Bart. "Court Ruling Imperils Virginia Tuition Grants." *Washington Post*, December 6, 1964.

Bates, Steve. "Academic Mixing Stirs Pot in Alexandria." *Washington Post*, January 31, 1993.

Bates, Steve. "Alexandria Superintendent is One of Two Seeking Similar Job in Ohio District." *Washington Post*, May 12, 1994.

Bates, Steve. "Alexandria Votes to Offer Civilization Honors Courses." *Washington Post*, January 8, 1993.

Bates, Steve. "Budget Woes Threaten Alexandria School Plan." *Washington Post*, November 1, 1992.

Bates, Steve. "Controversy Is Part of Masem's Legacy to Alexandria's Schools." *Washington Post*, June 9, 1994.

Bates, Steve. "For Ninth-Graders Only." *Washington Post*, September 2, 1993.

Bates, Steve. "More Parents are Challenging School Quality." *Washington Post*, April 20, 1993.

Bates, Steve. "School Policy Riles Alexandria Parents." *Washington Post*, March 28, 1993.

Bates, Steve. "Top Alexandria Students Challenge Policy Change." *Washington Post*, December 18, 1992.

Bates, Steve. "Urged to Cut Budget, Alexandria School Chief Seeks Increase." *Washington Post,* February 20, 1993.

Berg, Herb. In-Person Interview, June 25, 2010.

Berkowitz, Edward D. "Politics of Mental Retardation During the Kennedy Administration." *Social Science Quarterly* 61, no. 1 (June 1980): 128–143.

Blair, William. "Implications of the Central High School Plan In Its Relationship of the Athletic Program in Alexandria." May 5, 1971. School Board Minutes—May 5.

Blanton, Carlos Kevin. *The Strange Career of Bilingual Education in Texas, 1836–1981.* College Station: Texas A&M University Press, 2004.

Branch, Carla. "Education Secretary Duncan, Redskin Legend Darrell Green Set Tone for New School Year." *Alexandria News,* September 2, 2010. Published electronically September 2. http://www.alexandrianews.org/2010/schools/education-secretary-duncan-redskin-legend-darrell-greene-set-tone-for-new-school-year/18844/. Accessed January 30, 2014.

Branch, Carla. "Rebecca Perry: What Really Happened—Actions and Reactions." Alexandria News, Archives 2008. http://alexandrianews.org/2008/top-stories/rebecca-perry-what-really-happened-actions-and-reactions/104/. Accessed January 18, 2014.

Braswell, T. Edward. Alexandria Association for Retarded Children. Letter to T.C. Williams, June 28. July 21, 1961. School Board Minutes, Regular Meeting, July 21, 1961.

Briffault, Richard. "The Local School District in American Law." In *Beseiged: School Boards and the Future of Education Politics,* edited by William G. Howell, 24–55. Washington, DC: Brookings Institution Press, 2005.

Burchard, Hank, and Carl W. Sims. "2 Police Firings Demanded." *Washington Post,* October 12, 1969.

Burgundy Farm Country Day School. "Audio History". http://www.burgundyfarm.org/gallery/Integration_at_Burgundy.mp3. Accessed January 29, 2014.

Burke, Harold, and J. Thomas Butler. Memo to Instructional Committee, Alexandria School Board, RE Special Education Status Report, September 11. September 11, 1973. School Board Minutes, October 3, 1973, Box 19-1665.

Campbell, Donald T. "Assessing the Impact of Planned Social Change." *Journal of MultiDisciplinary Evaluation* 7, no. 15 (February 2011): 3–43.

Carlton, Emmitt. "The School Board Must Not Be for Sale." *Washington Post,* August 26, 1993.

Center on Budget and Policy Priorities, "Policy Basics: Where Do Our Federal Tax Dolllars Go?" April 12, 2013. Available at http://www.cbpp.org/files/4-14-08tax.pdf. Accessed January 26, 2014.

Chandler, Michael Alison. "Wake-Up Slap for T.C. Williams." *Washington Post,* June 18, 2010.

"Changes in List of Approved Scholarship Applications First Semester 1964-1965," *School Board Minutes, December 16,* December 16, 1964

City of Alexandria. Annual Report, 2001—City Schools. 2001. http://alexandriava.gov/uploadedFiles/Homepage_Quicklinks/info/annual_report_2001/ar2001_city_schools.pdf. Accessed February 15, 2014.

City of Alexandria, Office of City Manager. *Annual Report,* 1971–1976.

City of Alexandria, Department of Planning. "City of Alexandria, Virginia." 1958. Map Reproduced from the Collections of The Library of Congress. LCCN permalink: http://lccn.loc.gov/89692601. Accessed February 13, 2014.

City of Alexandria, Office of Historic Alexandria. *Alexandria Legacies—City Employees Oral History Project,* "Interview with Vola Lawson, Retired City Manager." May 21, 2009. Available at: http://alexandriava.gov/uploadedFiles/historic/info/history/OHAOralHistoryLawson.pdf. Accessed February 15, 2014.

City of Alexandria, Office of Planning and Zoning. "City of Alexandria Awarded for Mixed Income Housing Redevelopment." City of Alexandria, Alexandriava.gov, 2005. http://alexandriava.gov/planning/info/default.aspx?id=9814. Accessed May 23, 2012.

Cohen, David K. and Susan L. Moffitt, *The Ordeal of Equality: Did Federal Regulation Fix the Schools?* (Cambridge, MA: Harvard University Press, 2009)

Cohen, Richard M., and Maurine McLaughlin. "Alexandria Turmoil Strains Old School Ties." *Washington Post*, March 2, 1969.

Collier, Virginia P. "How Long? A Synthesis of Research on Academic Achievement in a Second Language." *TESOL Quarterly* 23, no. 3 (Sept 1989): 509–531.

Committee for Education Funding, "Education Funding History," January 14, 2014. Available at: http://cef.org/wp-content/uploads/2011/04/ED-programs-funding-history-FY-14-omnibus.pdf. Accessed February 16, 2014.

"Council to Review Anti-Slum Plan." *Washington Post*, October 26, 1960, 20.

Coutin, Susan Bibler. *Nations of Emigrants*. Ithaca, NY: Cornell University Press, 2007.

Crawford, James. "The Bilingual Education Act, 1968–2002: An Obituary." In *Advocating for English Learners*, edited by James Crawford, 124–127, Clevedon, UK: Multilingual Matters, 2008.

Cross, Lawrence H. "The Standards of Learning (SOL) Reform: Real Consequences Require Real Tests." *Virginia Issues and Answers* 7, no. 1 (Spring 2000). Available at: http://www.via.vt.edu/spring00/solreform.html. Accessed January 30, 2014.

Crothers, A. Glenn. "The 1846 Retrocession of Alexandria: Protecting Slavery and the Slave Trade in the District of Columbia." In *In the Shadow of Freedom: The Politics of Slavery in the National Capital*, edited by Paul Finkelman and Donald R. Kennon, 141–168. Athens, OH: Ohio University Press, 2011.

Cue, Eduardo. "Alexandria School Chief John Bristol Has Become a Johnny-on-the-Spot." *Washington Post*, March 23, 1978.

Cue, Eduardo. "Alexandria Urged to Shut Two Schools." *Washington Post*, February 2, 1978.

Darling-Hammond, Linda. *The Flat World and Education*. New York: Teachers College Press, 2010.

Daughtery, Wayne F. "City Blocks Alexandria, Va." Washington, D.C., *U.S. Census of Housing: 1960*, HC(3)-395, 1961.

Davies, Gareth. *See Government Grow: Education Politics from Johnson to Reagan*. Lawrence: University Press of Kansas, 2007.

Debray, Elizabeth H. *Politics, Ideology and Education: Federal Policy during the Clinton and Bush Administrations*. Foreword by Carl Kaestle. New York: Teachers College Press, 2006.

Derthick, Martha. *The Influence of Federal Grants: Public Assistance in Massachusetts*. Cambridge: Harvard University Press, 1970.

Digilio, Alice. "'Passport' to Reading." *Washington Post*, July 5, 1990.

Digilio, Alice, and Peter Baker. "65 Pct. Pass Va. 6th-Grade Literacy Test." *Washington Post*, June 28, 1990.

Digilio, Rodger. In-Person Interview, 2011

Dilworth, Richardson, ed. *The City in American Political Development*. New York: Routledge, 2009.

Dougherty, Kerry. "Equal Education: Search for Answers." *Washington Post*, December 13, 1978.

DuFault, Dr. Nap C., "Request of the Northern Virginia Association for Retarded Children for Adequate Educational Provisions for the Mentally Retarded," Alexandria City School Board. School Board Minutes, Regular Meeting, February 20, 1963.

Duke, Daniel L., and Brianne Reck. "The Evolution of Educational Accountability in the Old Dominion." In *Educational Leadership in an Age of Accountability: The Virginia Experience*, edited by Daniel L. Duke, Margaret Grogan, Pamela D. Tucker and Walter F. Heinecke, 36–67. Albany: State University of New York Press, 2003.

Dunbar, Denise. "Monthly Chat: Interview with David Speck." *Alexandria Times*, November 1 2012. Available at http://alextimes.com/2012/11/monthly-chat-interview-with-david-speck/ Accessed January 29, 2014.

Edwards, Paul G. "Alexandria Blacks Criticize Schools." *Washington Post*, June 8, 1972.

Edwards, Paul G. "Alexandria School Talk Set Today." *Washington Post*, April 1, 1971.

Edwards, Paul G. "Busing Foe Named to School Board." *Washington Post*, October 11, 1972.

Edwards, Paul G. "Discipline Is Made Issue in Alexandria." *Washington Post*, November 26, 1970, M1.

Edwards, Paul G. "Discipline Urged in Schools." *Washington Post*, November 5, 1970, A36.

Edwards, Paul G. "Eleven Black Students Suspended After Protest." *Washington Post*, March 28, 1971.

Edwards, Paul G. "Fires Set at Alexandria's GW High as Black Students List Demands." *Washington Post*, March 26, 1971.

Edwards, Paul G. "GW Principal Hit in New Racial Unrest." *Washington Post*, March 31 1971.

Edwards, Paul G. "Jury Splits 11 to 1, Ends Hanna Trial." *Washington Post*, November 29, 1970.

Edwards, Paul G. "Lobbying a Key to Victory for Alexandria Busing Foe." *Washington Post*, October 16, 1972.

Edwards, Paul G. "Melee Disrupts School." *Washington Post*, September 9, 1971.

Edwards, Paul G. "School Proposal Attacked." *Washington Post*, January 25, 1973.

Edwards, Paul G. "Schools Drop Grouping in Alexandria." *Washington Post*, August 3, 1972.

Edwards, Paul G. "Two Top Alexandria Officials Back Putting Black on Board." *Washington Post*, January 11, 1973.

Edwards, Paul G. "Youths Express Outrage in Memorial to Gibson." *Washington Post*, January 22, 1971.

Ely, James W. *The Crisis of Conservative Virginia*. Knoxville: University of Tennessee Press, 1976.

Engelhardt and Engelhardt, Inc. Public Elementary School Needs—City of Alexandria, Virginia. January, 1973. School Board Minutes—January 17, 1973, Box 17-1410.

Feinberg, Lawrence. "Alexandria Desegregation: Problems Persist." *Washington Post*, January 22, 1979.

Feinberg, Lawrence. "Alexandria Makes Little Progress Toward School Balance." *Washington Post*, March 5, 1972.

Filson, Susan. "Integated Schools Want 'The Best.'" *Washington Post*, April 17, 1966.

Fisher, Marc. "3 R's for Today: Rigid, Regressive and Unresponsive." *Washington Post*, May 6, 2004.

Foley, Neil. *The White Scourge: Mexicans, Blacks, and Poor Whites in Texas Cotton Culture*. Berkeley: University of California Press, 1997.

Freeman, Rebecca. "Reviewing the Research on Language Education Programs." In *Bilingual Education: An Introductory Reader*, edited by Ofelia García and Colin Baker, 3–18. Bilingual Education and Bilingualism. Clevedon, UK: Multilingual Matters, 2007.

Fuller, Bruce, Joseph Wright, Kathryn Gesicki, and Erin Kang. "Gauging Growth: How to Judge No Child Left Behind?" *Educational Researcher* 36, no. 5 (June–July 2007): 268–278.

Gándara, Patricia, and Megan Hopkins, eds. *Forbidden Language: English-Learners and Restrictive Language Policies*. New York: Teachers College Press, 2010.

García, Ofelia, and Jo Anne Kleifgen. *Educating Emergent Bilinguals*. New York: Teachers College Press, 2010.

Gates, Robbins L. *The Making of Massive Resistance*. Chapel Hill: University of North Carolina Press, 1962.

Goldenberg, Claude. "Teaching English Language Learners." *American Educator* 32, no. 2 (Summer 2008): 8–44.

Graham, Hugh Davis. *The Uncertain Triumph*. Chapel Hill: University of North Carolina Press, 1984.

Gray Commission. "Report of the Commission on Public Education to the Governor of Virginia." Senate Document No. 1, November 11, 1955.

Munsey, Everard. "Slum Residents Suffer with Cold, Filth, Vermin," *Washington Post*, October 24, 1960

Munsey, Everard. "Slum Dwellers Face Choice: Risk Fire or Freeze," *Washington Post*, December 16, 1960.

Hakuta, Kenji. *Mirror of Language: The Debate on Bilingualism*. New York: Basic Books, 1986.

Hanover Research. "2011–12 TC Williams Transformation Process." Washington, DC: Hanover Research, November, 2012. http://eboard.acps.k12.va.us/attachments/3b83a2fc-e663-4cc4-8c95-cfac84f62763.pdf. Accessed January 18, 2014.

Harris, John F. "Plan to Elect School Boards Advances to Virginia House." *Washington Post*, January 17, 1991.

Henig, Jeffrey R. *The End of Exceptionalism in American Education: The Changing Politics of School Reform*. Cambridge, MA: Harvard Education Press, 2013.

Hess, Frederick M. "Reform, Resistance. . . Retreat? The Predictable Politics of Accountability in Virginia." *Brookings Papers on Educational Policy* 2002, no. 1 (2002): 69–122.

Higham, John. *Strangers in the Land: Patterns of American Nativism, 1860–1925,* 2nd ed. New Brunswick, NJ: Rutgers University Press, 2002,

Hoffman, Maurine. "Albohm Views School Busing as Real Issue." *Washington Post,* May 12, 1966.

Hoffman, Maurine. "Alexandria School Plans Under Fire." *Washington Post,* May 1, 1966.

Holmes, Peter E. Letter to John C. Albohm, June 13. 1973. School Board Minutes, June 20, 1973, Box 19-636.

Hong, Peter Y. "High School to Hire Counselor for Latinos." *Washington Post,* December 30, 1993.

Howard, Mark. "An Historical Study of the Desegregation of the Alexandria, Virginia, City Public School." PhD diss., George Washington University, 1976.

Howe, Robert F. "Alexandria School Chief's Minority Effort Commended, Condemned." *Washington Post,* December 27, 1990.

Howe, Robert F., and Pierre Thomas. "Alexandria Renames Three to School Board." *Washington Post,* June 27, 1990.

Howell, William G. *Besieged: School Boards and the Future of Education Politics.* Washington, DC.: Brookings Institution Press, 2005.

Hsu, Evelyn. "Alexandria Officials Spar on Kindergarten Expansion." *Washington Post,* June 20, 1992.

Hsu, Evelyn. "Alexandria School Board Adds Four Kindergarten Classes in Approving Budget." *Washington Post,* March 20, 1992.

Hsu, Evelyn. "Alexandria School Board Approves Superintendent's Middle School Plan." *Washington Post,* December 18, 1991.

Hsu, Evelyn. "Alexandria Superintendent Proposes Plan to Reshape Schools." *Washington Post,* December 4, 1991.

Hsu, Evelyn. "Alexandria Urged to Go Slow on School Changes." *Washington Post,* February 7, 1992.

Ignacio, Tammy. In-Person Interview, February 7, 2012.

"In the Region of Babel: Public Bilingual Schooling in the Midwest, 1840s–1880s," pp. 270–71.

Jeffrey, Julie Roy. *Education for Children of the Poor: A Study of the Origins and Implementation of the Elementary and Secondary Education Act of 1965.* Columbus, OH: Ohio State University Press, 1978.

Johansen, O.U. Letter to William C. Pace, February 12, 1971. School Board Minutes, February 17, 1971, Box 030113.

Jordan, Mary. "Black Leaders Allege Alexandria Schools Focus on Whites' Needs." *Washington Post,* August 27, 1985.

Kaestle, Carl. *Pillars of the Republic: Common Schools and American Society, 1780–1860.* New York: Hill and Wang, 1983.

Kalita, S. Mitra. "2nd Teenager Charged in Alexandria Egging; Youth is Son of City Council Member." *Washington Post,* July 17, 2004.

Kalita, S. Mitra. "Alexandria Shortens Superintendent's Term; School Board Approves Raise for Perry Despite DWI Plea, Parents' Objections." *Washington Post,* June 16, 2004.

Kalita, S. Mitra. "Alexandria Squabble Reignites at Retreat." *Washington Post,* August 30, 2004.

Kalita, S. Mitra. "Alexandria's Superintendent Apologizes." *Washington Post,* April 28, 2004.

Kalita, S. Mitra. "Lewis Voted Out as Board Vice Chair." *Washington Post,* July 8, 2004, T03.

Kalita, S. Mitra, and Jay Mathews. "Alexandria Schools Chief Faces DWI Charge; Perry Placed on Leave With Pay for a Week." *Washington Post,* April 24, 2004.

Kantor, Harvey. "Education, Social Reform, and the State: ESEA and Federal Education Policy in the 1960s." *American Journal of Education* 100, no. 1 (1991): 47–83.

Karen Orren and Stephen Skowronek, *The Search for American Political Development* (Cambridge, MA: Cambridge University Press, 2004), 22.

Kelly, D., Xie, H., Nord, C.W., Jenkins, F., Chan, J.Y., and Kastberg, D. (2013). *Performance of U.S. 15-Year-Old Students in Mathematics, Science, and Reading Literacy in an International Context: First Look at PISA 2012* (NCES 2014-024). U.S. Department of Education.

Washington, DC: National Center for Education Statistics. http://nces.ed.gov/pubs2014/2014024.pdf. Accessed February 13, 2014.

Kennedy, Pres. John. "Letter to Gorman Ridgely." July 12, 1963. Folder "Work Sessions." School Board Minutes, July 12, 1963.

King, Desmond, and Marc Stears. "How the U.S. State Works: A Theory of Standardization." *Perspectives on Politics* 9, no. 3 (2011): 505–518.

Klose, Kevin. "Alexandria Secretly Drafts Plan to Meet Most of Negro Demands." *Washington Post*, October 19, 1969.

Kluger, Richard. *Simple Justice*. New York: Vintage Books, 1975.

Koncius, Jura. "Alexandria Studies Increased Class Size." *Washington Post*, October 29, 1981.

Kruse, Kevin. *White Flight: Atlanta and the Making of Modern Conservativism*. Princeton, NJ: Princeton University Press, 2005.

LaSasso, Carol. "Why We Took Our Kids Out of George Mason." *Washington Post*, October 7, 1990.

Lawson, John. "Parent Advised State Deals With All Placements." *Washington Post*, August 16, 1958.

Lawson, Vola. Memorandum—Alexandria City Public Schools—Ninth-Grade Center Operating Costs. October 23, 1992. City Council Docket, http://dockets.alexandriava.gov/icons/FY93/110992sm/dit8a.tif. Accessed January 30, 2014.

Lee, Jaekyung, and Todd Reeves. "Revisiting the Impact of NCLB High-Stakes School Accountability, Capacity and Resources." *Educational Evaluation and Policy Analysis* 34, no. 2 (2012): 209–231.

Levin, Betsy. "An Analysis of the Federal Attempt to Regulate Bilingual Education: Protecting Civil Rights or Controlling Curriculum." *Journal of Law & Education* 12, no. 1 (1983): 29–60.

Liss, Jon. In-Person Interview. October 11, 2013.

Lyons, James J. "The Past and Future Directions of Federal Bilingual Education Policy." *Annals of the American Academy of Political and Social Science* 508, no. 1 (March 1990): 66–80.

Maeroff, Gene I. *School Boards in America: A Flawed Exercise in Democracy*. New York: Palgrave Macmillan, 2010.

Mann, Jim. "Municipal Candidates Cite Disorder." *Washington Post*, June 2, 1970.

Manna, Paul. *Collision Course: Federal Education Policy Meets State and Local Realities*. Washington, DC: CQ Press, 2011.

Mathews, Jay. "Aide Says U.S. Won't Push Alexandria School Mixing." *Washington Post*, August 13, 1971.

Mathews, Jay. "Alexandria to Count State Tests in High School Grades." *Washington Post*, January 7, 1999.

Mathews, Jay. "Bonuses Backed for Alexandria Principals; Incentive Plan is Region's First." *Washington Post*, March 12, 1999.

Mathews, Jay. "In Alexandria, Boosting Test Scores." *Washington Post*, September 3, 1998.

Mathews, Jay. "Principal Leaves Troubled School; Alexandria's Maury Elementary on Low Achievement List." *Washington Post*, April 21, 2004.

Mathews, Jay. "Schools Block Plan for New SOL Survey; PTA Assessment Redundant, Officials Say." *Washington Post*, July 5, 2001.

Mathews, Jay. "Virginia Schools Get Break on Crucial Test Scores." *Washington Post*, May 28, 1999.

McBee, Susanna. "Bogle Gets Moeller's School Post." *Washington Post*, June 24, 1959.

McBee, Susanna. "Negro Alexandria Cook Fired After She Joined Bias Suit Is Rehired." *Washington Post*, October 3 1958.

McBee, Susanna. "Schools Post, Politics Linked." *Washington Post*, June 12, 1959.

McBee, Susanna. "U.S. to Aid Alexandria Slum Fight." *Washington Post*, September 28, 1957.

McDermott, Kathryn. *High Stakes Reform: The Politics of Educational Accountability*. Public Management and Change. Washington, DC: Georgetown University Press, 2011.

McDonnell, Lorraine M., and Paul T. Hill. *Newcomers in American Schools: Meeting the Educational Needs of Immigrant Youth*. Santa Monica, CA: Rand, 1993.

McGuinn, Patrick, *No Child Left Behind and the Transformation of Federal Education Policy, 1965–2005*. Lawrence, KS: University Press of Kansas, 2006.

McLaughlin, Maurine. "Alexandria Acts on Race Tension." *Washington Post*, October 21, 1969.

McLaughlin, Maurine. "Alexandria Has 6th Night of Disorder." *Washington Post*, June 4, 1970.

McLaughlin, Maurine. "Alexandria Lifts 'Emergency' Bans." *Washington Post*, June 7, 1970.

McLaughlin, Maurine. "Alexandria to Improve Urban Grade Schools." *Washington Post*, June 25, 1966.

McLaughlin, Maurine. "Alexandria Vote Puts Negro on City Council." *Washington Post*, June 10, 1970.

McLaughlin, Maurine. "Arlandia's Dilemma: Floods, Buck-Passing." *Washington Post*, August 21, 1969.

McLaughlin, Maurine. "Broad Vote Base Elected Kennahan." *Washington Post*, November 6, 1969.

McLaughlin, Maurine. "Controversial Policeman: 'I'm Paid to Defend Citizens.'" *Washington Post*, October 10, 1969.

McLaughlin, Maurine. "Grade School Licks Desegregation Fears." *Washington Post*, October 10, 1966.

McLaughlin, Maurine. "Pvt. Callahan is Honored in Alexandria." *Washington Post*, October 30, 1969.

Meador, Daniel J. "The Consitution and Assignment of Pupils to Public Schools." *Virginia Law Review* 45, no. 4 (1959): 517–571.

Mehta, Jal. *The Allure of Order: High Hopes, Dashed Expectations, and the Troubled Quest to Remake American Schooling*. New York: Oxford University Press, 2013.

Melnick, R. Shep. *Between the Lines: Interpreting Welfare Rights*. Washington, DC: The Brookings Institution, 1994.

Menken, Kate. "No Child Left Behind and Its Effects on Language Policy." *Annual Review of Applied Linguistics* 29, no. 1 (2009): 103–117.

Menken, Kate, and Cristian Solorza. "No Child Left Bilingual: Accountability and the Elimination of Bilingual Education Programs in New York City Schools." *Educational Policy*, vol. 28, no. 1 (January 2014): 96–125.

Mettler, Suzanne. *From Soldiers to Citizens: The G.I. Bill and the Making of the Greatest Generation*. New York: Oxford University Press, 2005.

Meyers, Robert. "Alexandria School Superintendent Moving to Illinois." *Washington Post*, January 26, 1980.

MGT of America. "Alexandria City Public Schools School Division Efficiency Review." Alexandria City Public Schools, June 15, 2007. http://www.acps.k12.va.us/superintendent/efficiency_review.pdf. Accessed February 16, 2014.

Mirel, Jeffrey E. *Patriotic Pluralism: Americanization Education and European Immigrants*. Cambridge, MA: Harvard University Press, 2010.

Miron, Gary, Jessica L. Urschel, William J. Mathis, and Elana Tornquist. "Schools Without Diversity: Education Management Organizations, Charter Schools and the Demographic Stratification of the American School System." Boulder, CO and Tempe, AZ: Education and the Public Interest Center and the Education Policy Research Unit, 2010. http//epicpolicy.org/publications/schools-without-diversity. Accessed January 18, 2014.

Moore, Hullihen W. "In Aid of Public Education: An Analysis of the Education Article of the Virginia Constitution of 1971." *University of Richmond Law Review* 5, no. 2 (Spring 1971): 263–318.

Moore, Mechlin. "Smoot-Thomson Race Turns Into Debate Over School Integration Issue." *Washington Post*, April 13, 1957.

Moran, Rachel F. "The Politics of Discretion: Federal Intervention in Bilingual Education." *California Law Review* 76, no. 6 (December 1988): 1249–1352.

Morra, Frank Jr. "Design Exploration for Talented Elementary Students, Evaluation 1975–76." (Microform) Alexandria Public Schools Program for the Gifted and Talented, Alexandria, Virginia (Washington, DC: ERIC Clearinghouse, 1976)

Morra, Frank Jr. "Design Exploration for Talented Elementary Students, Evaluation 1976–77." Microform Alexandria Public Schools Program for the Gifted and Talented, Alexandria, Virginia (Washington, DC: ERIC Clearinghouse, 1977)

Munger, Frank J., and Richard F. Fenno, Jr. *National Politics and Federal Aid to Education.* Syracuse, NY: Syracuse University Press, 1962.

Munsey, Everard. "Slum Dwellers Face Choice: Risk Fire or Freeze." *Washington Post*, December 16, 1960.

Munsey, Everard. "Slum Residents Suffer With Cold, Filth, Vermin." *Washington Post*, October 24, 1960.

National Center for Education Statistics. "Digest of Education Statistics." (Washington, DC: U.S. Department of Education, 2011).

National Center for Educational Statistics. "The Nation's Report Card: Mathematics, 2011." (Washington, DC: Institute of Education Sciences, NCES 2012-458, November, 2011). http://nces.ed.gov/nationsreportcard/pdf/main2011/2012458.pdf. Accessed February 16, 2014.

National Center for Educational Statistics. "The Nation's Report Card: Reading 2011." (Washington, DC: Institute of Education Sciences, NCES 2012-457, November, 2011). http://nces.ed.gov/nationsreportcard/pdf/main2011/2012457.pdf. Accessed February 16, 2014.

Nelson, Adam. *The Elusive Ideal: Equal Educational Opportunity and the Federal Role in Boston's Public Schools, 1950–1985.* Chicago: University of Chicago Press, 2005.

NeSmith, Samuel E. "Statement on Education and Secondary Reorganization in Alexandria." May 19, 1971. School Board Minutes—May 19, 1971, Box 030113.

Nicholls, Walter. "Where Do Salvadorans Go for Authentic Tortillas, Tamales and Pupusas? A Neighborhood in Alexandria." *Washington Post*, March 24, 2004.

Office of Voter Registration and Elections. "Election Statistics." City of Alexandria, 2012. http://alexandriava.gov/elections/info/default.aspx?id=1668. Accessed May 24, 2012.

Omang, Joanne. "Action on Seat Was in Doubt." *Washington Post*, June 30, 1973.

Omang, Joanne. "Alexandria Race is a Drag; 16 Candidates Complain of Scanty Audiences." *Washington Post*, April 19, 1973.

Omang, Joanne. "Alexandria School Mix Plans Scored." *Washington Post*, May 3, 1973.

Omang, Joanne. "Alexandria Schools Get HEW Deadline." *Washington Post*, March 30, 1973.

Omang, Joanne. "Board Official Removes Children from Schools." *Washington Post*, June 14, 1973.

Omang, Joanne. "Grade School Race Balance Plan Ordered." *Washington Post*, March 22, 1973.

Omang, Joanne. " 'Moral Issue' Decides Busing Plan." *Washington Post*, May 16, 1973.

Omang, Joanne. "White Pupils Leaving Alexandria Schools." *Washington Post*, May 26, 1974.

Orfield, Gary. *The Reconstruction of Southern Education: The Schools and the 1964 Civil Rights Act.* New York: Wiley-Interscience, 1968.

Orfield, Gary, Susan E. Eaton, and Harvard Project on School Desegregation. *Dismantling Desegregation.* New York: New Press, 1996.

Orren, Karen, and Stephen Skowronek. *The Search For American Political Development.* Cambridge, MA: Cambridge University Press, 2004.

Pan, Philip P. "At Home in Chirilagua, Va." *Washington Post*, December 6, 1999.

Park, Sarah. "For DWI Enforcer, These are Busy Nights." *Washington Post*, September 4, 2004.

Parker, Julie. "Lin Robinson Is Elected GW Senior Class President." *Alexandria Gazette*, October 31, 1970.

Parker, Julie. "Parents Complain About GW Scuffle." *Alexandria Gazette*, October 22, 1970,.

Patterson, James. *Brown v. Board of Education: A Civil Rights Milestone and its Troubled Legacy.* New York: Oxford University Press, 2001.

Petrilli, Michael. *The Diverse Schools Dilemma: A Parent's Guide to Socioeconomically Mixed Public Schools.* Washington, DC: Thomas B. Fordham Institute, 2012.

Petrozziello, Allison. "Feminised Financial Flows: How Gender Affects Remittances in Honduran-US Transnational Families." *Gender and Development* 19, no. 1 (March 2011): 53–67.

Pierce, Marion C. "Alexandria School Budget Focuses on Special Education." *Washington Post*, February 20, 1986.

Pierson, Paul. "Increasing Returns, Path Dependency and the Study of Politics." *American Political Science Review* 94, no. 2 (2000): 251–267.

Pollard, Harold G. Letter to Chairman William Hurd and School Board Members. October 16, 1973. School Board Minutes—October 17, 1973, Box 19-1854.

Pope, Michael. "How Transparent Is the School Board; Secret Meetings and Lack of Public Input Prompt Criticism of the Backroom Five." *Alexandria Gazette Packet*, May 30, 2007.

Pope, Michael, "Education Secretary Responds to a Teacher." WAMU 88.5, September 3, 2010. http://wamu.org/news/10/09/03/education_secretary_responds_to_a_teacher. Accessed January 30, 2014.

Pope, Michael Lee. "Alexandria Leaders Consider Lawsuit Challenging Takeover of Long-Troubled School," *Alexandria Gazette Packet*, July 10, 2013. Available at http://www.connectionnews-papers.com/news/2013/jul/10/alexandria-leaders-consider-lawsuit-takeover/. Accessed February 16, 2014.

Pope, Michael Lee. *Hidden History of Alexandria, DC*. Charleston, SC: The History Press, 2011.

Pope, Michael Lee. "T.C. in Crisis." *Alexandria Gazette Packet*, March 11, 2010.

Poretz, Doug. "School Officials, Students Meet on School Discipline." *Alexandria Gazette*, November 30, 1970.

Poretz, Doug. "Student Violence Increases." *Alexandria Gazette*, October 28, 1970.

Pottinger, J. Stanley. Letter to John C. Albohm. February 28, 1972. School Board Minutes, March 1, Box 15-209.

Pottinger, J. Stanley. Letter to John C. Albohm. February 3, 1972. School Board Minutes—February 23, 1973, Box 15-556.

Pratt, Robert. *The Color of Their Skin: Education and Race in Richmond, Virginia, 1954–1989*. Charlottesville, VA: University of Virginia Press, 1992.

Ramsey, Paul J. "In the Region of Babel: Public Bilingual Schooling in the Midwest, 1840s–1880s." *History of Education Quarterly* 49, no. 3 (August 2009): 267–290.

Ramsey, Paul J. "A Polyglot Boardinghouse: A History of Bilingual Schooling in the United States." Phd diss., Indiana University, 2008.

Reed, Douglas S. *On Equal Terms: The Constitutional Politics of Educational Opportunity*. Princeton, NJ: Princeton University Press, 2001.

"Report of the Child Study Committee on the Underacheiver in the City Schools of Alexandria Virginia," p. 6. School Board Minutes, Regular Meeting, May 12, 1960.

Rhodes, Jesse. *An Education in Politics: The Origins and Evolution of No Child Left Behind*. Ithaca: Cornell University Press, 2012.

Rich, Lonnie. In-Person Interview. December 10, 2011.

Ridgely, Gorman. "Letter to President John Kennedy." July 12, 1963. Folder "Work Sessions." School Board Minutes, July 12, 1963.

Ringle, Ken. "Fire Alexandria Superintendent, Alexandria Councilman Asks." *Washington Post*, April 26, 1971, C1.

Ringle, Ken. "Teachers Get Right to Expel in Alexandria." *Washington Post*, January 22, 1971, A1.

Rivera, Elaine. "Va School Official's Son Charged in Vandalism." *Washington Post*, July 15, 2004.

Sabin, Archie R. Statement by Archie R. Sabin. March 1, 1972. School Board Minutes, March 1, 1972, Box 15-709.

Samson, Susan. "Proposed Plan for Central City High School." May 5, 1971. Alexandria City School Board Minutes, May 5, 1971, Box 030113.

San Miguel, Guadalupe, Jr. *Contested Policy: The Rise and Fall of Bilingual Education in the United States, 1960–2001*. Denton, TX: University of North Texas Press, 2004.

Sánchez Molina, Raúl. "Modes of Incorporation, Social Exclusion, and Transnationalism: Salvadoran's Adaptation to the Washington, DC Metropolitan Area." *Human Organization* 67, no. 3 (Fall 2008): 269–280.

Scannell, Nancy. "U.S. Prods Alexandria on Schools." *Washington Post*, February 24, 1972.

Schneider, Susan Gilbert. *Revolution, Reaction or Reform: The 1974 Bilingual Education Act*. New York: Las Americas, 1976.

Schulte, Brigid. "Abrupt End to Tenure of Alexandria School Chief." *Washington Post*, January 19, 2008.

Schulte, Brigid. "Year-Round School? My Kids Love It. Yours Will, Too,." *Washington Post*, June 7, 2009.

Schumaier, C. Peter. Letter to Gorman Ridgely. July 17, 1963. School Board Minutes, July 17, 1963.

Scott, James. *Seeing Like a State: How Certain Schemes to Improve the Human Condition Have Failed* (Yale University Press, 1999)

Selden, Ina Lee. "Handling Crises in the Schools: Bristol's Job." *Washington Post*, March 8, 1979.

Severinson, Eloise, Regional Civil Rights Director, HEW. "Letter to Dr. John C. Albohm." January 19, 1971. School Board Minutes April 7, 1971, Box # 030113.

Severinson, Eloise, Regional Civil Rights Director, HEW. Letter to Dr. John C. Albohm, June 24, 1971. July 7, 1971. School Board Minutes—July 7, 1971 Box # 030114.

Shapiro, Leonard. "Williams' Success is Seen in Black and White." *Washington Post*, October 24, 1971.

Shelly, Bryan. "Rebels and Their Causes: State Resistance to No Child Left Behind." *Publius: The Journal of Fedralism* 38, no. 3 (2008), 444–468

Sherman, Morton. An Open Letter to President Barack Obama and Arne Duncan, U.S. Secretary of Education. March 10, 2010. http://www.acps.k12.va.us/tcw-transformation/president-letter. pdf. Accessed February 16, 2014.

Sherman, Morton. "Options for Jefferson-Houston Elementary School," July 3, 2103, Available at http://eboard.acps.k12.va.us/attachments/550e4422-5f71-4670-9bc4-69ffe59c5fe0.pdf. Accessed February 16, 2014.

Singer, Audrey. *At Home in the Nation's Capital: Immigrant Trends in Metropolitian Washington*. Washington, DC: Brookings Institution Center on Urban and Metropolitan Policy, 2003. http://www.brookings.edu/~/media/research/files/reports/2003/6/washington singer/ immigration.pdf. Accessed February 16, 2014.

Skowronek, Stephen. *Building a New American State: The Expansion of National Administrative Capacities, 1877–1920*. New York: Cambridge University Press, 1982.

Smith, Douglas J. " 'When Reason Collides With Prejudice': Armistead Lloyd Boothe and the Politics of Moderation." In *The Moderates' Dilemma: Massive Resistance to School Desegregation in Virginia*, edited by M.D. Lassiter and A.B. Lewis. Charlottesville: University Press of Virginia, 1998, pp. 22–50.

Smith, Leef, and S. Mitra Kalita. "Schools Chief is Fined for DWI in Alexandria." *Washington Post*, June 12, 2004.

Solórzano, Ronald W. "High Stakes Testing: Issues, Implications and Remedies for English Language Learners." *Review of Educational Research* 78, no. 2 (June 2008): 260–329.

Some Remain Concerned Over Principal Shift. *Alexandria Gazette Packet*, April 28, 2004. http://www.connectionnewspapers.com/news/2004/apr/28/some-remain-concerned-o ver-principal-shift/. Accessed June 13, 2013.

Special Staff Meeting—Agenda for December 16, 1963. February 12, 1964. Folder "Work Session,".

Specter, Michael. "Alexandria Targets Pupil Gap." *Washington Post*, November 21, 1985.

Staib, Lisa. Phone Interview. September 9, 2013.

"Statement of Policies for School Desegregation Plans Under Title VI of the Civil Rights Act of 1964," 45 Code of Federal Regulations Sec. 181.54. (1967 Supp), 407.

Stone, Clarence. "Introduction: Urban Education in Political Context." In *Changing Urban Education*, edited by Clarence Stone, 1–20. Lawrence: University Press of Kansas, 1998.

Stone, Clarence. *Regime Politics: Governing Atlanta: 1946–1988*. Lawrence: University Press of Kansas, 1989.

Stone, Clarence. "Systemic Power in Community Decision-Making: A Restatement of Stratification Theory." *American Political Science Review* 74, no. 4 (1980): 978–990.

Stubbings, John R. "Reorganization of the Secondary Schools in Alexandria." May 5, 1971. School Board Minutes, Box 030113.

Suárez-Orozco, Carola, Marcelo Suárez-Orozco, and Irina Todorova. *Learning a New Land: Immigrant Students in American Society*. Cambridge, MA: Belknap Press of Harvard University Press, 2008.

Subcommittee Studying School Board Selection. "Report of the Subcommittee Studying School Board Selection (House Resolution 12) to the House Committee on Privileges and Elections." edited by Virginia House of Delegates. Richmond, VA: State of Virginia, 1984.

Sun, Lena H. "Alexandria Schools Climbing a Language Barrier to Parents." *Washington Post*, June 21, 1984.

Superintendent's Report. November 18, 1964. School Board Minutes, November 18, 1964.

Test Results of City Testing Program, May 1959 through Sept. 1959," *School Board Minutes*, November 16, 1960.

Thomas, Jim. Statement of Jim Thomas, George Mason School PTA. March 1, 1972. School Board Minutes, March 1, 1972, Box 15-709.

Thurmond, Arnold J. "Justification and How Students Benefit From the Resource Center," Addendum for Report on Resource Centers Submitted to Alexandria School Board on June 4. June 4, 1975. Desegregation Cabinet, Ad Hoc Committee on the Learning Environment Folder.

Titus, Jill. *Brown's Battleground: Students, Segregationists and the Struggle for Justice in Prince Edward County, Virginia*. Chapel Hill, NC: University of North Carolina Press, 2011.

T.C. Williams Transformation Committee. Transformation Meeting Transcript, October 8, 2010. *In the Matter of Transformation Meeting*, Available at http://www.acps.k12.va.us/tcw-transformation/meeting-transcript-20101008.pdf. Accessed February 16, 2014.

T.C. Williams Transformation Committee. Transformation Meeting Transcript, November 8, 2010. *In the Matter of Transformation Meeting*, Available at: http://www.acps.k12.va.us/tcw-transformation/meeting-transcript-20101108.pdf Accessed February 16, 2014.

T.C. Williams Transformation Committee, Transformation Meeting Transcript, December 8, 2010. *In the Matter of Transformation Meeting*, Available at: http://www.acps.k12.va.us/tcw-transformation/meeting-transcript-20101208.pdf Accessed February 16, 2014.

T.C. Williams Transformation Committee. Transformation Meeting Transcript. April 28, 2011. In the Matter of Transformation Meeting. Available at: http://www.acps.k12.va.us/tcw-transformation/meeting-transcript-20110428.pdf. Accessed February 16, 2014.

T.C. Williams Transformation Committee. Transformation Meeting Transcript. July 20, 2011. *In the Matter of Transformation Meeting V*, Available at: http://www.acps.k12.va.us/tcw-transformation/meeting-transcript-20110720.pdf. Accessed February 16, 2014.

T.C. Williams Transformation: Trend Data Report," June 6, 2011. http://www.acps.k12.va.us/tcw-transformation/data-report-trend.pdf. Accessed January 30, 2014, p. 1.

T.C. Williams Transformation Committee. Transformation Meeting Transcript, *In the Matter of Transformation Meeting*, http://www.acps.k12.va.us/tcw-transformation/meeting-transcript-20110428.pdf. Accessed April 28, 2011.

"T.C. Williams High School—Transformation: 2010 Persistently Low Achieving (PLA) Designation," 2011. http://www.acps.k12.va.us/tcw-transformation/pla.php. Accessed December 17, 2011.

"Transcript, Alexandria City School Board -- Regular Meeting, August 8, 1972." School Board Minutes, August 8, 1972, Box 16-1461.

Turque, Bill. "New WTU Pres Nathan Saunders: 'It's Been All Teacher Blood' on the Floor." In *D.C. Schools Insider*. Washington Post On-Line, December 2, 2010, Available at http://voices.washingtonpost.com/dcschools/2010/12/saunders_its_been_all_teacher.html. Accessed January 27, 2014.

Tyack, David, and Larry Cuban. *Tinkering toward Utopia*. Cambridge, MA: Harvard University Press, 1995.

U.S. Bureau of the Census, *U.S. Census of Population and Housing, 1970*: "General Population Characteristics. Table 16. Summary of General Characteristics: 1970, Virginia (pt. 48-43)

U.S. Bureau of the Census, *U.S. Census of Population and Housing, 1970*: "General Population Characteristics. Table 23: Race by Sex, for Areas and Places: 1970, Virginia," pt. 48-61.

U.S. Bureau of the Census, *U.S. Census of Population and Housing, 1970*: "General Population Characteristics. Table 16: Summary of General Characteristics: 1970, Virginia (pt48-43).

U.S. Bureau of the Census, *U.S. Census of Population and Housing, 1980*: "General Population Characteristics. Table 14: Summary of General Characteristics: 1980, Virginia (pt48-8).

U.S. Bureau of the Census, *U.S. Census of Population and Housing, 1980*: "General Population Characteristics. Table 26: Persons by Age for Areas and Places: 1980 and 1970, Virginia (pt.48-64).

U.S. Bureau of the Census, *U.S. Census of Population and Housing, 1980*: "General Population Characteristics. Table 15: Persons by Race: 1980, Virginia" pt. 48–13.

U.S. Bureau of the Census. *U.S. Census of Population and Housing: 1970 and 1980*. Vol. I, Characteristics of the Population. Part XX, Virginia. (Washington, DC: U.S. Government Printing Office).

U.S. Department of Education. *Digest of Education Statistics*, "Table 29: Expenditures of Educational Institutions, by level and control of institution." Available at http://nces.ed.gov/programs/digest/d12/tables/dt12_029.asp [access date January 26, 2014].

U.S. Department of Education, *Digest of Education Statistics*, Table 235.10: Revenues for public elementary and secondary schools, by source of funds. Available at http://nces.ed.gov/programs/digest/d13/tables/dt13_235.10.asp. [access date January 27, 2014

U.S. Department of Education. *Digest of Education Statistics*, "Table 47: Number and percentage of public school students participating in programs for English language learners, by state" Available at: http://nces.ed.gov/programs/digest/d12/tables/dt12_047.asp. Accessed February 16, 2014.

U.S. Department of Education, Office of Planning, Evaluation and Policy Development. "National Evaluation of Title III Implementation—Report on State and Local Implementation." Washington, DC, May, 2012. http://www2.ed.gov/about/offices/list/opepd/ppss/reports.html—titleiii. Accessed October 14, 2013.

U.S. Department of Education, Office of the Assistant Secretary for Civil Rights. The Office for Civil Rights' Title VI Language Minority Compliance Procedures. December 3, 1985. http://www.stanford.edu/~hakuta/www/archives/syllabi/Education388/OCRComplianceProcedures.htm. Accessed October 14, 2013.

United States. National Commission on Excellence in Education. *A Nation at Risk: The Imperative for Educational Reform: A Report to the Nation and the Secretary of Education, United States Department of Education*. Washington, D.C.: The Commission: Superintendent of Documents, U.S. Government Printing Office, 1983.

Urrutia, Evelin. In-Person Interview, October 11 2013.

U.S. English Foundation. "Many Languages, One America." Washington, DC: US English Foundation, Inc., 2005. http://usefoundation.org/view/29. Accessed September 27, 2013.

van Hover, Stephanie, David Hicks, Jeremy Stoddard, and Melissa Lisanti. "From a Roar to a Murmur: Virginia's History & Social Science Standards, 1995–2009." *Theory & Research in Social Education* 38, no. 1 (2010): 80–113.

Virginia Advisory Legislative Council. "Needs of the Handicapped," Virginia General Assembly, 1972, Senate Document [no.] 4. Richmond, VA: Commonwealth of Virginia, 1971.

Virginia Department of Education. "Accreditation and Federal Reports—Adequate Yearly Progress (AYP) Reports: State Summary." Virginia Department of Education, 2013. http://www.doe.virginia.gov/statistics_reports/accreditation_federal_reports/ayp/. Accessed June 11, 2013.

Virginia Department of Education. "NCLB Waiver Approved by US Department of Education." Division of Policy and Communications. Richmond, VA: Virginia Department of Education, 2012. http://www.doe.virginia.gov/news/news_releases/2012/jun29.shtml. Accessed January 18, 2014.

Virginia High School League. "Alexandria Warned by VHSL." February 18, 1971. School Board Minutes, February 17, 1971, Box 030113.

Walsh, Elsa L. "Bilingual Plan Opposed."*Washington Post*, October 23, 1980.

Warden, Dick. Statement of Dick Warden. n.d., 1973. School Board Minutes, April 18, 1973, Box 18-1074.

Washington Post. "Alexandria Blacks Protest." *Washington Post*, October 15, 1969

Washington Post. "Cross Burned at Virginia School." *Washington Post*, November 3, 1970.

Washington Post. "Hanna Judge Ousts Confederate Flag." *Washington Post*, January 20, 1971.

Washington Post. "Melee Shakes Alexandria." *Washington Post*, October 10, 1969.

Washington Post. "Nazis Picket at Home of School Head." *Washington Post*, November 9, 1970.

Washington Post. "Nixon Aide Flemming Resigns From Alexandria City Council." *Washington Post*, January 15, 1969.

Washington Post. "School Board Won't Reinstate Cook Fired for Role in Desegregation." *Washington Post*, September 11, 1958.

Washington Post, "Va. Attorney Won't Serve School Unit," *Washington Post*, July 30, 1971, D3.

Washington Post. "Youths Scatter as Cross Burns." *Washington Post*, October 25. 1970.

Welner, Kevin, 2013, "The Dirty Dozen: How Charter Schools Influence Student Enrollment," *Teachers College Record [online]* http://www.tcrecord.org. ID Number: 17104.

Welsh, Patrick. "Board Silly: How Politics are Wrecking Alexandria's Schools." *Washington Post*, June 20, 1993.

Welsh, Patrick. "Fast-Track Trap: How 'Ability Grouping' Hurts Our Schools, Kids and Families." *Washington Post*, September 16, 1990.

Welsh, Patrick. "Four Decades of Failed School Reforms." *Washington Post*, September 27, 2013.

Welsh, Patrick. "Our Classroom Barrios: For Hispanic Students, American Schools Can Be a Nightmare." *Washington Post*, September 8, 1991.

Welsh, Patrick. "Staying on Tracks." *Washington Post*, March 7, 1993.

Welsh, Patrick. In-Person Interview. August 15, 2013.

Whitaker, Joseph D. "Black Youth Tells of Chase: 'Then He Took Out His Gun.'" *Washington Post*, October 10, 1969.

Whitaker, Joseph D. "Mayor, Blacks Give Views on City's Unrest." *Washington Post*, June 2 1970.

Wilkoff, Mark O., Arthur E. Schmalz, and Mark R. Eaton. "A Word of Advice: Humor and Humility Go a Long Way." *Washington Post*, March 30, 2006.

"Williams Elected Schools' Director." *Washington Post*, April 13, 1933.

Williams, T.C. Superintendent's Report, April, 1960. School Board Minutes, April 20, 1960.

Williams, T.C. Superintendent's Report, February, 1960. School Board Minutes, Regular Meeting February 10, 1960.

Williams, T.C. Superintendent's Report, May, 1960. School Board Minutes, Regular Meeting, May 12, 1960.

Williams, T.C, "Superintendent's Report", September 1961. School Board Minutes, Regular Meeting, September 13, 1961

Williams, T.C. "Superintendent's Report, October 1961", School Board Minutes, Regular Meeting, October 11, 1961.

INDEX

in Alexandria, 21, 125, 129, 159, 161, 171–173, 177–183, 185–186, 200, 217–218
bilingual education advocacy among, 167
at T.C. Williams High School, 177–180, 182–183, 185–186, 218
Lau v. Nichols, 99, 165–167, 175, 259n21
Lawson, Vola, 127–128, 206
Lewis, Gwendolyn H., 225
Lewis, Oren, 83, 269n77
Lincolnia (Alexandria neighborhood), 108
Liss, Jon, 177, 180–181
Little, Gerald, 92
López, Lulu, 181
Loudon County (Virginia), 22
Luby, Melissa, 224–225
Lyles-Crouch Elementary School (Alexandria)
busing and, 102, 121
desegregation and, 43, 54, 72, 90, 93, 102, 268n53
Jackson as principal of, 223–225, 228
Lyles-Crouch Parents Committee and, 54
"model school" proposal and, 54–55
Parent-Teacher Association at, 223–224
segregation and, 27, 54

Mann, Frank, 54
Manna, Paul, 221
Masem, Paul
achievement gaps and, 26, 197, 202, 204, 207
departure from Alexandria of, 205
education budget shortfalls and, 201
English-language learners and, 179
junior high school structural and curricular changes and, 200
opposition to, 202, 204
tracking and, 202
white flight and, 197
Massachusetts, 20
Massive Resistance
in Alexandria, 28–29, 33, 38, 55–56, 59–60, 67, 91–92, 94, 99
diminution of, 49
moderates' opposition to, 43, 92
political logic of, 32
private school vouchers and, 34–36, 99, 101, 103, 105, 107
in Virginia, xi, 32–36, 38–39, 45, 102, 138
Maury Elementary School (Alexandria)
cross burning at, 67
desegregation and, 72, 109
Jackson as principal of, 223, 225, 228
No Child Left Behind Act (NCLB) and, 223
Maxey, Suzanne
English-language learners and, 183–185
Individual Academic Plans (IAPs) and, 236–237
Professional Learning Plans (PLPs) and, 240

school transformation campaign at T.C. Williams and, 232, 236–237, 240–242
McCauley, Carlas L., 246
McConchie, H. Winfield, 271n115
McDonnell, Robert, 245
McGough, T.F., 137
McGuinn, Patrick, 19
Mettler, Suzanne, 20
Mexican immigrants, 129, 159, 164
Mexico, 2, 174
Meyer v. Nebraska, 163
Miller, Melvin, 77, 93, 153
Mills v. Board of Education of the District of Columbia, 139–140
Milwaukee (Wisconsin), 162
Minnesota, 162
Minnie Howard Elementary School (Alexandria), 102, 109, 274n13
Minnie Howard Middle School (Alexandria), 56, 201, 265n74
Mississippi, 52
Missouri, 162–163
Mitchell, Wiley, 62, 125
Mize, Sidney, 267n32
Moeller, Herman G., 38
Moffitt, Susan L., 247, 259n21
Montgomery County (Maryland), 21
Moran, Jim, 197, 216
Moran, Patricia, 204
Morrison, Jim, 21
Mount Vernon (George Washington ancestral home), 33
Mount Vernon Community School (Alexandria), 181
Mount Vernon Elementary School (Alexandria), 72, 109
Mudtown (Alexandria neighborhood), 102, 108
Mulligan, Hugh, 271n115
Murphy, James, 196

National Assessment of Educational Progress (NAEP), 1–2
National Association for the Advancement of Colored People (NAACP)
Alexandria chapter of, 152, 205, 213
Alexandria desegregation lawsuits and, 27, 90, 152
Alexandria desegregation proposal by, 90, 93
Alexandria School Board elections and, 205
English-language learners and, 185
Perry and, 227
Virginia State Convention (1970) of, 67
National Council Against Forced Busing, 87
National Defense Education Act of 1958, 9
National Socialist White People's Party, 67
Nation at Risk report, 189
Nebraska, 163